BASICS OF THE U.S. HEALTH CARE SYSTEM

NANCY J. NILES, PHD, MS, MBA, MPH

Associate Professor
Lander University
Greenwood, South Carolina

JONES & BARTLETT
LEARNING

World Headquarters
Jones & Bartlett Learning
5 Wall Street
Burlington, MA 01803
978-443-5000
info@jblearning.com
www.jblearning.com

Jones & Bartlett Learning books and products are available through most bookstores and online booksellers. To contact
Jones & Bartlett Learning directly, call 800-832-0034, fax 978-443-8000, or visit our website, www.jblearning.com.

Production Credits
Executive Publisher: William Brottmiller
Publisher: Michael Brown
Associate Editor: Chloe Falivene
Editorial Assistant: Nicholas Alakel
Production Manager: Carolyn Rogers Pershouse
Senior Marketing Manager: Sophie Fleck Teague
Manufacturing and Inventory Control Supervisor: Amy Bacus
Composition: Cenveo Publisher Services
Cover Design: Scott Moden
Director of Photo Research and Permissions: Amy Wrynn
Cover Image: © avian/ShutterStock, Inc.
Printing and Binding: Edwards Brothers Malloy
Cover Printing: Edwards Brothers Malloy

To order this product, use ISBN: 978-1-284-04376-1

Library of Congress Cataloging-in-Publication Data
Niles, Nancy J., author.
 Basics of the U.S. health care system / Nancy J. Niles. — Second edition.
   p. ; cm.
 Includes bibliographical references and index.
 ISBN 978-1-284-03441-7 (pbk.)
 I. Title.
 [DNLM: 1. Delivery of Health Care—United States. 2. Insurance, Health—United States. 3. Government Programs—
United States. 4. National Health Programs—United States. W 84 AA1]
 RA445
 362.1--dc23
                        2013035792

6048

Printed in the United States of America
18 17 16 15 14   10 9 8 7 6 5 4

Contents

Contents

Contents

Contents

About the Author

Nancy J. Niles, PhD, MS, MBA, MPH, is in her 11th year of full-time undergraduate teaching. She is in her 7th year of teaching undergraduate business and healthcare management classes in the AACSB-accredited School of Management at Lander University in Greenwood, South Carolina, having spent 4 years teaching in the Department of Business Administration at Concord University in Athens, West Virginia. She became very interested in health issues as a result of spending two tours with the U.S. Peace Corps in Senegal, West Africa. She focused on community assessment and development, obtaining funding for business- and health-related projects. Her professional experience also includes directing the New York State lead poisoning prevention program and managing a small business development center in Myrtle Beach, South Carolina.

Her graduate education has focused on health policy and management. She received a master of public health from the Tulane School of Public Health in New Orleans, Louisiana, a master of management with a healthcare administration emphasis, and a master of business administration from the University of Maryland University College, and a doctorate from the University of Illinois at Urbana, Champaign in health policy.

Acknowledgments

My mother, Joyce Robinson, continues to amaze me with her energy and love of life and her devotion to her volunteer work at AGAPE hospice. They are lucky to have her. I am so happy that she finally found a wonderful man, Fred Volpe, who treats her like a queen. I would like to thank my husband, Donnie Niles, the love of my life, for his continued love and support. I would also like to thank Mike Brown at Jones & Bartlett Learning, who provided me with this opportunity to write my first textbook and now the second edition to my first effort. Chloe Falivene, Nick Alakel, and Carolyn Pershouse have been wonderful to work with and I appreciate their input into my projects. I would also like to give a special thanks to my two fall semester Introduction to Healthcare Management classes at Lander University. As students who use my textbook, they provided me with help as I revised the content.

Preface

I am very pleased to be updating this textbook because of the monumental change in the U.S. healthcare system: the passage of the Affordable Care Act (ACA) in 2010. The complicated act has nearly 50 mandates that impact many different components of the system; however, there have already been some delays in the timeline of the implementation of some of the mandates.

The ACA continues to be very controversial. There have been several lawsuits and constant discussions in Congress about repealing several different mandates. As of this writing, there are many mandates that have already been implemented that will impact healthcare consumers, which are discussed in the textbook. Because of the ACA impact, each chapter has been updated as it relates to ACA changes and as the healthcare industry has evolved over the past few years.

I also placed the ACA chapter, which was originally an add-on to the first edition, as the second chapter of this edition. That way, the student can become familiar with the mandates in the early learning process of the course and the textbook. The OECD data, discussed in Chapter 2 of the first edition, has also been updated from 2000–2005 to 2005–2010 data. Although the data reflected are still 3 years old, they are the most current data available.

Recognizing how education delivery has changed, I have modified the crossword puzzles so they can be done online or on-ground. I have also included three additional case studies for each chapter that can be done on-ground or online. I have developed a glossary that will allow students to review vocabulary and take additional quizzes. I also included discussion boards for each chapter that can be used for both online and on-ground classes. I also wrote each chapter as a standalone chapter that can be included in other courses. I truly hope this textbook will provide a foundation for additional learning about the U.S. healthcare system. I also hope it encourages students to have careers in health care. The healthcare system's growth will continue due to the aging of the U.S. population and the increased focus of providing quality health care to healthcare consumers.

The following is a summary of each chapter:

CHAPTER 1

It is important as a healthcare consumer to understand the history of the U.S. healthcare delivery system, how it operates today, who participates in the system, what legal and ethical issues arise as a result of the system, and what problems continue to plague the healthcare system. We are all consumers of health care. Yet, in many instances, we are ignorant of what we are actually purchasing. If we were going to spend $1,000 on an appliance or a flat screen television, many of us would research the product to determine if what we are purchasing is the best product for us. This same concept should be applied to purchasing healthcare services.

Increasing healthcare consumer awareness will protect you in both the personal and professional aspects of your life. You may decide to pursue a career in health care either as a provider or as an administrator. You may also decide to manage a business where you will have the responsibility of providing health care to your employees. And lastly, from a personal standpoint, you should have the knowledge from a consumer point of view so you can make informed decisions about what matters most—your health. The federal government agrees with this philosophy. Recently, the Centers for Medicare and Medicaid Services used its claims data to publish the hospital costs of the 100 most common treatments nationwide. The purpose of this effort is to provide data to consumers regarding healthcare costs because the costs vary considerable across the United States. This effort may also encourage pricing competition of healthcare services.

As the U.S. population's life expectancy continues to increase, the United States will be confronted with more chronic health issues because, as we age, more chronic health conditions develop. The U.S. healthcare system is one of the most expensive systems in the world. According to 2010 statistics, the United States spent $2.6 trillion on healthcare expenditures or 17.6% of its gross domestic product. The gross domestic product is the total finished products or services that are produced in a country within a year. These statistics mean that nearly 18% of all of the products made within the borders of the United States within a year are healthcare related. Estimates indicate that healthcare spending will be $4.6 trillion by 2020, which represents nearly 20% of the gross domestic product. In 2011, there were 48.6 million uninsured U.S. citizens, a decrease from 50 million in 2010. The Institute of Medicine's (IOM) 1999 report indicated that nearly 100,000 citizens die each year as a result of medical errors. Although there have been quality improvement initiatives in the healthcare industry such as the Patient Safety and Quality Improvement Act of 2005, recent research indicates that medical errors in hospitals remain high. Employers are offering less healthcare benefits. In 2002, 72% offered health insurance benefits, which has dropped to 67.5% in 2010. This is typical of smaller businesses that have a small number of employees who need benefits.

These rates are some of the highest in the world but, unlike most developed countries, the United States does not offer healthcare coverage as a right of citizenship. Most developed countries have a universal healthcare program, which means access to all citizens. Many of these systems are typically run by the federal government, have centralized health policy agencies, are financed through different forms of taxation, and payment of healthcare services are by a single payer—the government. France and the United Kingdom have been discussed as possible models for the United States to follow to improve access to health care, but these programs have problems and may not be the ultimate solution for the United States. However, because the United States does not offer any type of universal healthcare coverage, many citizens who are not eligible for government-sponsored programs are expected to provide the service for themselves through the purchase of health insurance or the purchase of actual services. Many citizens cannot afford these options resulting in their not receiving routine medical care. The passage of the 2010 Patient Protection and Affordable Care Act has attempted to increase access to affordable health care. A mandate of the Affordable Care Act will require employees with 50 or more employees to offer affordable healthcare insurance. There is also a mandate that individuals who do not have healthcare insurance purchase health insurance if they can afford it. States will be establishing health insurance marketplaces for affordable health insurance for both individuals and businesses. Both of these mandates should decrease the number of uninsured in the United States. These programs will be closely evaluated to assess whether their goals will be achieved.

CHAPTER 2

The Patient Protection and Affordable Care Act (PPACA) or, as it is commonly called, the Affordable Care Act (ACA) and its amendment, the Healthcare and Education Affordability Reconciliation Act of 2010, was signed into law on March 23, 2010 by President Barack Obama. The goal of the Act is to improve the accessibility and quality of the U.S. healthcare system. There are nearly 50 healthcare reform initiatives that are being implemented during 2010–2017 and beyond. The passage of this complex landmark legislation has been very controversial and continues to be contentious today.

There were national public protests and a huge division among the political parties regarding the components of the legislation. People, in general, agreed that the healthcare system needed some type of reform but it was difficult to develop common recommendations that had majority support. Criticism, in part, focused on the increased role of government in implementing and monitoring the healthcare system. Proponents of healthcare reform reminded people that Medicare is a federal government entitlement program because when individuals reach 65 years of age, they can receive their healthcare insurance from this program. Millions of individuals are enrolled in Medicare. Medicaid, which is a public welfare insurance program based on income, is a state-based government program for millions of individuals including children that provides health care for their enrollees. So the government already plays a huge role in providing healthcare coverage.

However, regardless of these two programs, many critics felt that the federal government was forcing people to purchase health insurance. In fact, the ACA does require most individuals to obtain health insurance only if they can afford it. But with the healthcare system expenditures comprising 17.6% of the U.S. gross domestic product and with millions of Americans not having the accessibility of health care resulting in poor health indicators, the current Administration's priority was to create mandated healthcare reform. The Congressional Budget Office estimates that the act will enable an additional 32 million Americans or a total of 94% of Americans to have access to healthcare insurance.

CHAPTER 3

The one commonality with all of the world's healthcare systems is that they all have consumers or users of their systems. Systems were developed to provide a service to their citizens. The U.S. healthcare system, unlike other systems in the world, does not provide healthcare access to all of its citizens. It is a very complex system that is comprised of many public and private components. Healthcare expenditures comprise approximately 17.6% of the gross domestic product (GDP). Healthcare costs are very expensive and most citizens cannot afford it if they had to pay for it themselves. Individuals rely on health insurance to pay a large portion of their healthcare costs. Healthcare insurance is predominantly offered by employers. According to a 2011 CDC survey, there were nearly 48.2 million uninsured in the United States with approximately 29 million who are underinsured, which means their health insurance does not adequately cover their medical expenses. (It will be interesting to assess the impact of the Affordable Care Act on this statistic because a major focus is individual insurance coverage nationwide.) The ACA projects there will be a decrease of nearly 70% in these statistics when the ACA is fully implemented.

In the United States, in order to provide healthcare services, there are several stakeholders or interested entities that participate in the industry. There are providers, of course, that consist of trained professionals such as physicians, nurses, dentists, and chiropractors. There are also inpatient and outpatient facilities, the payers such as the insurance companies, the government, and self-pay individuals, and the suppliers of products such as pharmaceutical companies, medical equipment companies, and the research and educational facilities. Each component plays an integral role in the healthcare industry. These different components further emphasize the complexity of the U.S. system. The current operations of the delivery system and utilization statistics will be discussed in depth in this chapter. An international comparison of the U.S. healthcare system and select country systems will also be discussed in this chapter, which provides another aspect of analyzing the U.S. healthcare system.

CHAPTER 4

During the Depression and World War II, the United States had no funds to start a universal healthcare program—an issue that had been discussed for years. As a result, a private sector system was developed that did not provide healthcare services to all citizens. However, the government's role of providing healthcare coverage evolved as a regulatory body to ensure that the elderly and poor were able to receive health care. The passage of the Social Security Act of 1935 and the establishment of the Medicaid and Medicare programs in 1965 mandated government's increased role in providing healthcare coverage. Also, the State Children's Health Insurance Program (SCHIP), now the Children's Health Insurance Program, established in 1997 and reauthorized by the Affordable Care Act through 2019 with extended funding through 2015, continues to expand government's role in children's health care. In addition to the reauthorization of the SCHIP program, the Affordable Care Act has increased government interaction with the healthcare system by developing several government initiatives that focus on increasing the ability of individuals to make informed decisions about their health care.

In these instances, the government increased accessibility to health care as well as provided financing for health care to certain targeted populations. This chapter will focus on the different roles the federal, state, and local governments play in the U.S. healthcare system. This chapter will also highlight different government programs and regulations that focus on monitoring how health care is provided.

CHAPTER 5

There are two important definitions of public health. In 1920, public health was defined by Charles Winslow as the science and art of preventing disease, prolonging life, and promoting physical health and efficiency through organized community efforts for the sanitation of the environment, control of community infections, and education of individuals regarding hygiene to ensure a standard of living for health maintenance. Sixty years later, the Institute of Medicine (IOM), in its 1988 *Future of Public Health* report, defined public health as an organized community effort to address public health by applying scientific and technical knowledge to promote health. Both definitions point to broad community efforts to promote health activities to protect the population's health status. The Affordable Care Act is also emphasizing the importance of prevention and wellness. The establishment of the Prevention and Public Health Fund has supported several community-based public health programs.

The development of public health is important to note as part of the basics of the U.S. healthcare system because its development was separate from the development of private medicine practices. Public health specialists view health from a collectivist and preventative care viewpoint: to protect as many citizens as possible from health issues and to provide strategies to prevent health issues from occurring. The definitions cited in the previous paragraph emphasize this viewpoint. Public health concepts were in stark contrast to traditional medicine, which focused on the sole relationship between a provider and patient. Private practitioners held an individualistic viewpoint—citizens more often would be paying for their services from their health insurance or from their own pockets. Physicians would be providing their patients guidance on how to cure their diseases, not preventing disease. This chapter will discuss the concept of health and healthcare delivery and the role of public health in delivering health care. The concepts of primary, secondary, and tertiary prevention and the role of public health in those delivery activities will be highlighted. Discussion will also focus on the origins of public health, the major role epidemiology plays in public health, the role of public health in disasters, core public health activities, the collaboration of public health and private medicine, and the importance of public health consumers.

CHAPTER 6

Inpatient services are services that involve an overnight stay of a patient. Historically, the U.S. healthcare industry was based on the provision of inpatient services provided by hospitals and outpatient services provided by physicians. As our healthcare system evolved, hospitals became the mainstay of the healthcare system offering primarily inpatient services with limited outpatient services. Over the past 2 centuries, hospitals have evolved from serving the poor and homeless to providing the latest medical technology to serve the seriously ill and injured (Shi & Singh, 2008). Although their original focus was inpatient services, as a result of cost containment and consumer preferences, more outpatient services are now being offered by hospitals.

Hospitals have evolved into medical centers that provide the most advanced service. Hospitals can be classified by who owns them, length of stay, and the type of services they provide. Inpatient services typically focus on acute care, which includes secondary and tertiary care levels that most likely require inpatient care. Inpatient care is very expensive and, throughout the years, has been targeted for cost containment measures. Hospitals began offering more outpatient services that do not require an overnight stay and were less financially taxing on the healthcare system. As U.S. healthcare expenditures have increased as part of the gross domestic product, more cost containment measures have evolved. Outpatient services have become more popular because they are less expensive and they are preferred by consumers. This chapter will discuss the evolution of outpatient and inpatient healthcare services in the United States.

CHAPTER 7

The healthcare industry is the fastest growing industry in the U.S. economy, employing a workforce of 18 million healthcare workers. Considering the aging of the U.S. population and the impact of the Affordable Care Act, it is expected that the healthcare industry will continue to experience strong job growth. When we think of healthcare providers, we automatically think of physicians and nurses. However, the healthcare industry is comprised of many different health services professionals. The healthcare industry includes dentists, optometrists, psychologists, chiropractors, podiatrists, nonphysician practitioners (NPPs), administrators, and allied health professionals. It is important to identify allied health professionals because they provide a range of essential healthcare services that complement the services provided by physicians and nurses. This category of health professionals is an integral component of providing quality health care.

Health care can occur in varied settings. Physicians have traditionally operated in their own practices but they also work in hospitals, mental health facilities, managed care organizations, or community health centers. They may also hold government positions or teach at a university. They could be employed by an insurance company. Health professionals, in general, may work at many different organizations, both for profit and nonprofit. Although the healthcare industry is one of the largest employers in the United States, there continues to be shortages of physicians in geographic areas of the country. Rural areas continue to suffer physician shortages, which limits consumer access to health care. There have been different incentive programs to encourage physicians to relocate to rural areas, but shortages still exist. In most states, only physicians, dentists, and a few other practitioners may serve patients directly without the authorization of another licensed independent health professional. Those categories authorized include chiropractic, optometry, psychotherapy, and podiatry. Some states authorize midwifery and physical therapy. There also continues to be a shortage of registered nurses nationwide. The American Association of Colleges of Nursing (AACN) is publicizing this issue with policy makers.

With the passage of the Affordable Care Act, it is anticipated there will continue to be a shortage of physicians in certain areas. The Association of American Medical Colleges estimates that by 2015 there will be a shortage of over 60,000 physicians. The number will double by 2025 because of the aging of the population as well as the impact of the Affordable Care Act. Medicare officials predict that Medicare enrollment will increase by nearly 45% by 2025, which will further place strain on physician shortages. This chapter will provide a description of the different types of healthcare professionals and their role in providing care in the U.S. system.

CHAPTER 8

The percentage of the U.S. gross domestic product (GDP) devoted to healthcare expenditures has increased over the past several decades. In 2010, the United States spent $2.6 trillion on healthcare spending or 17.6% of the gross domestic product, which is the highest in the world. In 2011, U.S. Census data indicates there were 48.6 million uninsured U.S. citizens, which is a decrease from 50 million in 2010. The Centers for Medicare and Medicaid Services (CMS) predicts annual healthcare costs will be $4.64 trillion by 2020, which represents nearly 20% of the U.S. gross domestic product. The increase in healthcare spending can be attributed to three causes: (1) When prices increase in an economy overall, the cost of medical care will increase and, even when prices are adjusted for inflation, medical prices have increased; (2) as life expectancy increases in the United States, more individuals will require more medical care for chronic diseases, which means there will be more healthcare expenses; and (3) as healthcare technology and research provide for more sophisticated and more expensive procedures, there will be an increase in healthcare expenses.

There are four areas that account for a large percentage of national healthcare expenditures: hospital care, physician and clinical services, prescription drugs, and nursing and home healthcare expenditures. Unlike countries that have universal healthcare systems, payment of healthcare services in the United States is derived from (1) out-of-pocket payments from patients who pay entirely or partially for services rendered; (2) health insurance plans, such as indemnity plans or managed care organizations; (3) public/government funding such as Medicare, Medicaid, and other government programs; and (4) health savings accounts (HSAs). Much of the burden of healthcare expenditures has been borne by private sources—employers and their health insurance programs have borne much of the cost. Employers are offering less healthcare benefits. In 2002, 72% offered health insurance benefits, which has dropped to 67.5% in 2010. When people are downsized, individuals may continue to pay their health insurance premiums through the Consolidated Omnibus Budget Reconciliation Act (COBRA) once they are unemployed but most individuals cannot afford to pay the expensive premiums. As a result of the passage of the Affordable Care Act of 2010, the government is playing a proactive role in developing a healthcare system that is consumer oriented. The act is requiring more employers to offer health insurance benefits and individuals to purchase healthcare insurance if they can afford it so these statistics may increase.

To understand the complexity of the U.S. healthcare system, this chapter will provide a breakdown of U.S. healthcare spending by source of funds, state, and the major private and public sources of funding for these expenditures. It is important to reemphasize that there are three parties involved in providing health care: the provider, the patient, and the fiscal intermediary such as a health insurance company or the government. Therefore, included in the chapter is also a description of how healthcare providers are reimbursed for their services and how reimbursement rates were developed for both private and public funds.

CHAPTER 9

Managed care refers to the cost management of healthcare services by controlling who the consumer sees and how much the services cost. Managed care organizations (MCOs) were introduced 40 years ago, but became more entrenched in the healthcare system when the Health Maintenance Organization Act of 1973 was signed into law by President Nixon. Healthcare costs were spiraling out of control during that period. Encouraging the increase in the development of HMOs, the first widely used managed care model, would help to control the healthcare costs. MCOs' integration of the financial industry with the medical service industry resulted in controlling the reimbursement rate of services, which allowed them more control over the health insurance portion of health care. Physicians were initially resistant to managed care models because they were threatened by loss of income. As the number of managed care models increased, physicians realized they had to accept this new form of healthcare delivery and, if they participated in a managed care organization, it was guaranteed income. Managed care health plans have become a standard option for consumers. Medicare Part C or Medicare Advantage offers managed care options to their enrollees. Many employers offer managed care plans to their employees. This chapter will discuss the history of the evolution of managed care and why it developed, the different types of managed care, the MCO assessment measures used for cost control, the issues regarding managed care, and how managed care has impacted the delivery of healthcare services.

CHAPTER 10

The general term of **informatics** refers to the science of computer application to data in different industries. **Health informatics**, or **medical informatics**, is the science of computer application that supports clinical and research data in different areas of health care. It is a methodology of how the healthcare industry thinks about patients and how their treatments are defined and evolved. For example, **imaging informatics** applies computer technology to organs and tissue. **Health information systems** are systems that store, transmit, collect, and retrieve these data. **Health information technology's (HIT's)** goal is to manage the health data that can be used by patients/consumers, insurance companies, healthcare providers, healthcare administrators, and any stakeholder that has an interest in health care.

HIT impacts every aspect of the healthcare industry. All of the stakeholders in the healthcare industry use HIT. Information technology (IT) has had a tremendous impact on the healthcare industry because it allows documentation of every transaction to be more quickly documented. When an industry focuses on saving lives, it is important that all activity has a written document that describes the activity. Computerization of documentation has increased the management efficiency of healthcare data. The main focus of HIT is the national implementation of an electronic patient record. Both Presidents Bush and Obama have supported this initiative. This is the foundation of many IT systems because it will enable different systems to share the patient information, which will increase the quality and efficiency of health care. This chapter will discuss the history of IT, different applications of IT to health care, and discuss the evolution of the electronic medical records/electronic health records and the barriers for implementation.

CHAPTER 11

To be an effective healthcare manager, it is important to understand basic legal and ethical principles that influence the work environment, including the legal relationship between the organization and the consumer—the healthcare provider and the patient. The basic concepts of law, both civil and criminal healthcare law, tort reform, employment-related legislation, safety in the workplace, and the legal relationship between the provider and the patient will be discussed in this chapter.

CHAPTER 12

Legal standards are the minimal standard of action established for individuals in a society. Ethical standards are considered one level above a legal action because individuals make a choice based on what is the "right thing to do," not what is required by law. There are many interpretations of the concept of ethics. Ethics has been interpreted as the moral foundation for standards of conduct. The concept of ethical standards applies to actions that are hoped for and expected by individuals. Actions may be considered legal but not ethical. There are many definitions of ethics but, basically, ethics is concerned with what are right and wrong choices as perceived by society and its individuals.

The concept of ethics is tightly woven throughout the healthcare industry. It dates back to Hippocrates, the father of Western medicine, in the 4th century BCE, and evolved into the Hippocratic Oath, which is the foundation for the ethical guidelines for patient treatment by physicians. In 1847, the American Medical Association (AMA) published a *Code of Medical Ethics* that provided guidelines for the physician–provider relationship, emphasizing the duty to treat a patient. To this day, physicians' actions have followed codes of ethics that demand the "duty to treat."

Applying the concept of ethics to the healthcare industry has created two areas of ethics: medical ethics and bioethics. Medical ethics focuses on the decisions healthcare providers make on the patient's medical treatment. Euthanasia or physician-assisted suicide would be an example of a medical ethic. Advance directives are orders that patients give to providers to ensure that, if they are terminally ill and incompetent to make a decision, certain measures will not be taken to prolong that patient's life. If advance directives are not provided, the ethical decision of when to withdraw treatment may be placed on the family and provider. These issues are legally defined, although there are ethical ramifications surrounding these decisions.

This chapter will focus primarily on **bioethics**, which emerged as a field in World War II when Nazis in Germany used prisoners in war camps as medical experiments, illustrating the rights of human subjects in medical research. This field of study is concerned with the ethical implications of certain biologic and medical procedures and technologies, such as cloning; alternative reproductive methods, such as in vitro fertilization; organ transplants; genetic engineering; and care of the terminally ill, which will be discussed in this chapter. Additionally, the rapid advances in medicine in these areas raised questions about the influence of technology on the field of medicine.

It is important to understand the impact of ethics in different aspects of providing health care. Ethical dilemmas in health care are situations that test a provider's belief and what the provider should do professionally. Ethical dilemmas are often a conflict between personal and professional ethics. A healthcare ethical dilemma is a problem, situation, or opportunity that requires an individual, such as a healthcare provider, or an organization, such as a managed care practice, to choose an action that could be unethical. A decision making model is presented that can help resolve ethical dilemmas in the healthcare field. This chapter will discuss ethical theories, codes of healthcare conduct, informed consent, confidentiality, special populations, research ethics, ethics in public health, end-of-life decisions, genetic testing and profiling, and biomedical ethics, which focuses on technology use and health care.

CHAPTER 13

According to the World Health Organization, mental wellness or mental health is an integral and essential component of health. It is a state of well-being in which an individual can cope with normal stressors, can work productively, and is able to make a contribution to his or her community. Mental health behavioral disorders can be caused by biological, psychological, and personality factors. By 2020, behavioral health disorders will surpass all physiological diseases as a major cause of disability worldwide. Mental disorders are the leading cause of disability in the United States. Mental illnesses can impact individuals of any age, race, religion or income. In 2011, an estimated 10 million adults ages 18 and older had a serious mental illness. Two million youths ages 12–17 had a major depressive episode during a year. Although mental health is a disease that requires medical care, its characteristics set it apart from traditional medical care.

U.S. Surgeon General David Satcher released a landmark report in 1999 on mental health illness, *Mental Health: A Report of the Surgeon General*. The Surgeon General's report on mental health defines **mental disorders** as conditions that alter thinking processes, moods, or behavior that results in dysfunction or stress. It can be psychological or biological in nature. The most common conditions include **phobias**, which are excessive fear of objects or activities; substance abuse; and affective disorders, which are emotional states such as depression. Serious mental illness would include schizophrenia, major depression, and psychosis. Obsessive–compulsive disorders (OCD), mental retardation, Alzheimer's disease, and dementia are also considered mentally disabling conditions. According to the report, mental health ranks second to heart disease as a limitation on health and productivity. People who have mental disorders often exhibit feelings of anxiety, or may have hallucinations or feelings of sadness or fear that can limit normal functioning in their daily life. Because the cause or etiology of mental health disorders are less defined and less understood compared to traditional medical problems, interventions are less developed than other areas of medicine. This chapter will provide a discussion on the following topics: the history of the U.S. mental healthcare system, a background of healthcare professionals, mental healthcare law, insurance coverage for mental health, barriers to mental health care, the populations at risk for mental disorders, the types of mental health disorders as classified by the American Psychiatric Association's *Diagnostic and Statistical Manual of Mental Disorders (DSM)*, liability issues associated with mental health care, an analysis of the mental healthcare system, and guidelines and recommendations to improve U.S. mental health care.

CHAPTER 14

The U.S. healthcare system has long been recognized as providing state-of-the-art health care. It has also been recognized as the most expensive healthcare system in the world and the price tag is expected to increase. Despite offering two large public programs—Medicare and Medicaid for the elderly, indigent, and disabled—current statistics indicate that over 48 million individuals are uninsured.

This chapter will provide an international comparison between the U.S. healthcare system and the healthcare systems of other countries and discuss whether universal healthcare coverage should be implemented in the United States. This chapter will also discuss U.S. healthcare trends that may positively impact the healthcare system, including the increased use of technology in prescribing medicine and providing health care, complementary and alternative medicine use, a nursing home model, accountable care organizations, and a discussion of the universal healthcare coverage programs in Massachusetts and San Francisco, California. The Affordable Care Act will also be discussed because of its major impact on the U.S. healthcare system.

Chapter 1

History of the U.S. Healthcare System

LEARNING OBJECTIVES

The student will be able to:

- Identify five milestones of medicine and medical education and their importance to health care.

- Identify five milestones of the hospital system and their importance to health care.

- Identify five milestones of public health and their importance to health care.

- Identify five milestones of health insurance and their importance to health care.

- Explain the difference between primary, secondary, and tertiary prevention.

- Explain the concept of the iron triangle as it applies to health care.

DID YOU KNOW THAT?

- When the practice of medicine first began, tradesmen such as barbers practiced medicine. They often used the same razor to cut hair as to perform surgery.

- In 2010, the United States spent $2.6 trillion on healthcare spending or 17.6% of the gross domestic product, which is the highest in the world.

- In 2011, U.S. Census data indicate there were 48.6 million uninsured U.S. citizens, which is a decrease from 50 million in 2010.

- The Centers for Medicare and Medicaid Services (CMS) predicts annual healthcare costs will be $4.64 trillion by 2020, which represents nearly 20% of the U.S. gross domestic product.

- The United States is one of only a few developed countries that does not have universal healthcare coverage.

- In 2002, the Joint Commission issued hospital standards requiring them to inform their patients if their results were not consistent with typical care results.

INTRODUCTION

It is important as a healthcare consumer to understand the history of the U.S. healthcare delivery system, how it operates today, who participates in the system, what legal and ethical issues arise as a result of the system, and what problems continue to plague the healthcare system. We are all consumers of health care. Yet, in many instances, we are ignorant of what we are actually purchasing. If we were going to spend $1,000 on an appliance or a flat screen television, many of us would research the product to determine if what we are purchasing is the best product for us. This same concept should be applied to purchasing healthcare services.

Increasing healthcare consumer awareness will protect you in both the personal and professional aspects of your life. You may decide to pursue a career in health care either as a provider or as an administrator. You may also decide to manage a business where you will have the responsibility of providing health care to your employees. And lastly, from a personal standpoint, you should have the knowledge from a consumer point of view so you can make informed decisions about what matters most—your health. The federal government agrees with this philosophy. Recently, the Centers for Medicare and Medicaid Services (CMS) used its claim data to publish the hospital costs of the 100 most common treatments nationwide. The purpose of this effort is to provide data to consumers regarding healthcare costs because the costs vary considerably across the United States. This effort may also encourage pricing competition of healthcare services (Godert, 2013).

As the U.S. population's life expectancy continues to increase—increasing the **"graying" of the population**—the United States will be confronted with more chronic health issues because, as we age, more chronic health conditions develop. The U.S. healthcare system is one of the most expensive systems in the world. According to 2010 statistics, the United States spent $2.6 trillion on healthcare expenditures or 17.6% of its gross domestic product (CMS, 2013a). The **gross domestic product (GDP)** is the total finished products or services that are produced in a country within a year. These statistics mean that nearly 18% of all of the products made within the borders of the United States within a year are healthcare related. Estimates indicate that healthcare spending will be $4.6 trillion by 2020, which represents nearly 20% of the gross domestic product. In 2011, there were 48.6 million uninsured U.S. citizens, a decrease from 50 million in 2010 (Kaiser Family Foundation [KFF], 2013). The Institute of Medicine's (IOM) 1999 report indicated that nearly 100,000 citizens die each year as a result of medical errors. Although there have been quality improvement initiatives in the healthcare industry such as the Patient Safety and Quality Improvement Act of 2005, recent research indicates that medical errors in hospitals remain high (Classen et al., 2011).

Employers are offering less healthcare benefits. In 2002, 72% offered health insurance benefits, which has dropped to 67.5% in 2010. This is typical of smaller businesses that have a small number of employees who need benefits (Kliff, 2012).

These rates are some of the highest in the world but, unlike most developed countries, the United States does not offer healthcare coverage as a right of citizenship. Most developed countries have a **universal healthcare program**, which means access to all citizens. Many of these systems are typically run by the federal government, have centralized health policy agencies, are financed through different forms of taxation, and payment of healthcare services are by a single payer—the government (Shi & Singh, 2008). France and the United Kingdom have been discussed as possible models for the United States to follow to improve access to health care, but these programs have problems and may not be the ultimate solution for the United States. However, because the United States does not offer any type of universal healthcare coverage, many citizens who are not eligible for government-sponsored programs are expected to provide the service for themselves through the purchase of health insurance or the purchase of actual services. Many citizens cannot afford these options, resulting in their not receiving routine medical care. The passage of the **Patient Protection and Affordable Care Act of 2010 (PPACA, or ACA)** has attempted to increase access to affordable healthcare. One of the mandates of the Act is the establishment of state-run health insurance marketplaces, which provide opportunities for consumers to search for affordable health insurance plans. There is also a mandate that individuals who do not have health insurance purchase health insurance if they can afford it or pay a fine. Both of these mandates should decrease the number of uninsured in the United States. These programs will be closely evaluated to assess whether their goals will be achieved.

CONSUMER PERSPECTIVE ON HEALTH CARE

Basic Concepts of Health

Prior to discussing this complex system, it is important to identify three major concepts of healthcare delivery: primary, secondary, and tertiary prevention. These concepts are vital to understanding the U.S. healthcare system because different components of the healthcare system focus on these different areas of health, which often results in lack of coordination between the different components.

Primary, Secondary, and Tertiary Prevention

According to the *American Heritage Dictionary* (2001), prevention is defined as "slowing down or stopping the course of an event." **Primary prevention** avoids the development of a disease. Promotion activities such as health education are primary prevention. Other examples include smoking cessation programs, immunization programs, and educational programs for pregnancy and employee safety. State health departments often develop targeted, large education campaigns regarding a specific health issue in their area. **Secondary prevention** activities are focused on early disease detection, which prevents progression of the disease. Screening programs, such as high blood pressure testing, are examples of secondary prevention activities. Colonoscopies and mammograms are also examples of secondary prevention activities. Many local health departments implement secondary prevention activities. **Tertiary prevention** reduces the impact of an already established disease by minimizing disease-related complications. Tertiary prevention focuses on rehabilitation and monitoring of diseased individuals. A person with high blood pressure who is taking blood pressure medication is an example of tertiary prevention. A physician who writes a prescription for that blood pressure medication to control high blood pressure is an example of tertiary prevention. Traditional medicine focuses on tertiary prevention, although more primary care providers are encouraging and educating their patients on healthy behaviors (Centers for Disease Control and Pretention [CDC], 2007).

We, as healthcare consumers, would like to receive primary prevention to prevent disease. We would like to participate in secondary prevention activities such as screening for cholesterol or blood pressure because it helps us manage any health problems we may be experiencing and reduces the potential impact of a disease. And, we would like to also visit our physicians for tertiary measures so, if we do have a disease, it can be managed by taking a prescribed drug or some other type of treatment. From our perspective, these three areas of health should be better coordinated for the healthcare consumer so the United States will have a healthier population.

In order to understand the current healthcare delivery system and its issues, it is important to learn the history of the development of the U.S. healthcare system. There are four major sectors of our healthcare system that will be discussed in this chapter that have impacted our current system of operations: (1) the history of practicing medicine and the development of medical education, (2) the development of the hospital system, (3) the history of public health, and (4) the history of health insurance. In **Tables 1-1 to 1-4**, several important milestones are listed by date and illustrate historic highlights of each system component. The list is by no means exhaustive, but provides an introduction to how each sector has evolved as part of the U.S. healthcare system.

MILESTONES OF MEDICINE AND MEDICAL EDUCATION

The early practice of medicine did not require a major course of study, training, board exams, and licensing, as is required today. During this period, anyone who had the inclination to set up a physician practice could do so; oftentimes, clergy were also medical providers, as well as tradesmen such as barbers. The red and white striped poles outside barber shops represented blood and bandages because the barbers were often also surgeons. They used the same blades to cut hair and to perform surgery (Starr, 1982). Because there were no restrictions, competition was very intense. In most cases, physicians did not possess any technical expertise; they relied mainly on common sense to make diagnoses (Stevens, 1971). During this period, there was no health insurance, so consumers decided when they would visit a physician and paid for their visits out of their own pockets. Often, physicians treated their patients in the patients' homes. During the late 1800s, the medical profession became more cohesive as more technically advanced services were delivered to patients. The establishment of the **American Medical Association (AMA)** in 1847 as a professional membership organization for physicians was a driving force for the concept of private practice in medicine. The AMA was also responsible for standardizing medical education (AMA, 2013a; Goodman & Musgrave, 1992).

In the early history of medical education, physicians gradually established large numbers of medical schools because they were inexpensive to operate, increased their prestige, and enhanced their income. Medical schools only required four or more physicians, a classroom, some discussion rooms, and legal authority to confer degrees. Physicians received the students' tuitions directly and operated the school from this influx of money. Many physicians would affiliate with established colleges to confer degrees. Because there were no entry restrictions, as more students entered into medical schools, the existing

TABLE 1-1   Milestones of Medicine and Medical Education 1700–2013

- 1700s: Training and apprenticeship under one physician was common until hospitals were founded in the mid-1700s. In 1765, the first medical school was established at the University of Pennsylvania.

- 1800s: Medical training was provided through internships with existing physicians who often were poorly trained themselves. There were only four medical schools in the United States that graduated only a handful of students. There was no formal tuition with no mandatory testing.

- 1847: The AMA was established as a membership organization for physicians to protect the interests of its providers. It did not become powerful until the 1900s when it organized its physician members by county and state medical societies. The AMA wanted to ensure they were protecting their financial well-being. It also began to focus on standardizing medical education.

- 1900s to 1930s: The medical profession was represented by general or family practitioners who operated in solitary practices. A small percentage of physicians were women. Total expenditures for medical care were less than 4% of the gross domestic product.

- 1904: The AMA created the Council on Medical Education to establish standards for medical education.

- 1928: Formal medical education was attributed to Abraham Flexner, who wrote an evaluation of medical schools in the United States and Canada indicating many schools were substandard. He made recommendations to close several schools, enact admission requirements, and set a standard curriculum. The Flexner Report led to standardized admissions testing for students called the Medical College Admission Test (MCAT), which is still used as part of the admissions process today.

- 1930s: The healthcare industry was dominated by male physicians and hospitals. Relationships between patient and physicians were sacred. Payments for physician care were personal.

- 1940s to 1960s: When group health insurance was offered, the relationship between patient and physician changed because of third-party payers (insurance). In the 1950s, federal grants supported medical school operations and teaching hospitals. In the 1960s, the Regional Medical Programs provided research grants and emphasized service innovation and provider networking.

- 2008: There is increased racial diversity in the number of medical school graduates. Although whites continue to represent the largest number of medical school graduates, there continues to be a decline in white graduates. Asians represent the largest ethnicity of medical school graduates. Women medical graduates continue to enter the workforce in great numbers, but men still outnumber women physicians.

- 2001–2012: In 2011, the ACA established the Center for Medicare & Medicaid Innovation that will examine ways to deliver care to patients. In 2012, the ACA provided incentives for physicians to establish accountable care organizations.

- 2012: In 2012–2013, the average annual cost for a public medical school for an in-state resident was $30,000. The annual cost for a private medical school was $50,000. Approximately 47% of the students were females.

internship program with physicians was dissolved and the Doctor of Medicine (MD) became the standard (Vault Career Intelligence, 2013). Although there were major issues with the quality of education provided because of the lack of educational requirements, medical school education became the gold standard for practicing medicine (Sultz & Young, 2006). The publication of the **Flexner Report** in 1910, which evaluated medical schools in Canada and the United States, was responsible for forcing medical schools to develop curriculums and admission testing. Curriculums and admission testing are still in existence today.

In 2008, there was increased racial diversity in the number of medical school graduates. Although whites continue to represent the largest number of medical school graduates, their numbers are declining. Asians represent the largest ethnic group of medical school graduates. Women medical graduates continue to enter the workforce in great numbers but men still outnumber women physicians. In 2012–2013, the average annual cost for a public medical school for an in-state resident was $30,000. The annual cost for a private medical school was $50,000 (Association of American Medical Colleges [AAMC], 2013).

MILESTONES OF THE HOSPITAL SYSTEM

In the early 19th century, **almshouses** or **poorhouses** were established to serve the indigent. They provided shelter while treating illness. Government-operated **pesthouses** segregated those who could spread their disease. The framework of these institutions set up the conception of the hospital. Initially, wealthy people did not want to go to hospitals because the conditions were deplorable and the providers were not skilled, so hospitals, which were first built in urban areas, were used by the poor. During this period, many of the hospitals were owned by the physicians who practiced in them (Rosen, 1983).

In the early 20th century, with the establishment of a more standardized medical education, hospitals became more accepted across socioeconomic classes and became the symbol of medicine. With the establishment of the AMA, who protected the interests of providers, the reputation of providers became more prestigious. During the 1930s and 1940s, the ownership of the hospitals changed from physician-owned to church-related and government-operated (Starr, 1982).

In 1973, the first **Patient Bill of Rights** was established to protect healthcare consumers in the hospitals. In 1974, a federal law was passed that required all states to have **Certificate of Need (CON)** laws to ensure the state approved any capital expenditures associated with hospital/medical facilities' construction and expansion. The Act was repealed in 1987, but as of 2011, 36 states still have some type of CON mechanism (National Conference of State Legislatures [NCSL], 2013). The concept of CON was important because it encouraged

state planning to ensure their medical system was based on need. In 1985, the **Emergency Medical Treatment and Active Labor Act (EMTALA)** was enacted to ensure that consumers were not refused treatment for an emergency. During this period, inpatient hospital use was typical; however, by the 1980s, many hospitals were offering outpatient or ambulatory surgery that continues into the 21st century. The Balanced Budget Act of 1997 authorized outpatient Medicare reimbursement to support these cost-saving measures (CDC, 2001). **Hospitalists**, created in 1996, are providers that focus specifically on the care of patients when they are hospitalized. This new type of provider recognized the need of providing quality hospital care (American Hospital Association [AHA], 2013; Sultz & Young, 2006). In 2002, the Joint Commission on the Accreditation of Healthcare Organizations (now **The Joint Commission**) issued standards to increase consumer awareness by requiring hospitals to inform patients if their results were not consistent with typical results (AHA, 2013).

Hospitals are the foundation of our healthcare system. As our health insurance system evolved, the first type of health insurance was hospital insurance. As society's health needs increased, expansion of different medical facilities increased. There was more of a focus on ambulatory or outpatient services because we, as consumers, prefer outpatient services and, secondly, it is more cost effective. In 1980, the AHA estimated that 87% of hospitals offered outpatient surgery. Although hospitals are still an integral part of our healthcare delivery system, the method of their delivery has changed. More hospitals have recognized the trend of outpatient services and have integrated those types of services in their delivery.

MILESTONES OF PUBLIC HEALTH

The development of public health is important to note because its development was separate from the development of private medical practices. Physicians were worried that government health departments could regulate how they practiced medicine, which could limit their income. Public health specialists also approached health from a collectivistic and preventive care viewpoint—to protect as many citizens as possible from health issues and to provide strategies to prevent health issues from occurring. Private practitioners held an individualistic

TABLE 1-2   Milestones of the Hospital and Healthcare Systems 1820–2013

- 1820s: Almshouses or poorhouses, the precursor of hospitals, were developed to serve the poor primarily. They provided food and shelter to the poor and consequently treated the ill. Pesthouses, operated by local governments, were used to quarantine people who had contagious diseases such as cholera. The first hospitals were built around urban areas in New York City, Philadelphia, and Boston and were used often as a refuge for the poor. Dispensaries or pharmacies were established to provide free care to those who could not afford to pay and to dispense drugs to ambulatory patients.

- 1850s: A hospital system was finally developed but their conditions were deplorable because there were unskilled providers. Hospitals were owned primarily by the physicians who practiced in them.

- 1890s: Patients went to hospitals because they had no choice. There became more cohesiveness among providers because they had to rely on each other for referrals and access to hospitals, which gave them more professional power.

- 1920s: The development of medical technological advances increased the quality of medical training and specialization and the economic development of the United States. The establishment of hospitals became the symbol of the institutionalization of health care. In 1929, President Coolidge signed the Narcotic Control Act, which provided funding for hospital construction for drug addicts.

- 1930s to 1940s: Once physician-owned hospitals were now owned by church groups, larger facilities, and government at all levels.

- 1970 to 1980: The first Patient Bill of Rights was introduced to protect healthcare consumer representation in hospital care. In 1974, the National Health Planning and Resources Development Act required states to have CON laws to qualify for federal funding.

- 1980 to 1990: According to the AHA, 87% of hospitals were offering ambulatory surgery. In 1985, the EMTALA was enacted, which required hospitals to provide screening and stabilize treatment regardless of the ability to pay by the consumer.

- 1990 to 2000s: As a result of the Balanced Budget Act cuts of 1997, the federal government authorized an outpatient Medicare reimbursement system.

- 1996: Hospitalists are clinicians that provide care once a patient is hospitalized.

- 2002: The Joint Commission on the Accreditation of Healthcare Organizations (now The Joint Commission) issued standards to increase consumer awareness by requiring hospitals to inform patients if their results were not consistent with typical results.

- 2011: In 1974, a federal law was passed that required all states to have certificate of need (CON) laws to ensure the state approved any capital expenditures associated with hospital/medical facilities' construction and expansion. The act was repealed in 1987 but as of 2011, 36 states still have some type of CON mechanism.

- 2013: The Center of Medicare & Medicaid Services developed a Bundled Payments for Care Improvement initiative. Acute care hospitals and other providers will enter into payment arrangements that include financial and performance accountability for episodes of care for each patient.

viewpoint—citizens more often would be paying for physician services from their health insurance or from their own pockets and physicians would be providing them guidance on how to cure their diseases, not prevent them. The two contrasting viewpoints still exist today, but there have been efforts to coordinate and collaborate more of the traditional and public health activities.

During the 1700s into the 1800s, the concept of public health was born. In their reports, Edwin Chadwick,

TABLE 1-3	Milestones in Public Health 1700–2013

- 1700 to 1800: The United States was experiencing strong industrial growth. Long work hours in unsanitary conditions resulted in massive disease outbreaks. U.S. public health practices targeted reducing **epidemics**, or large patterns of disease in a population, that impacted the population. Some of the first public health departments were established in urban areas as a result of these epidemics.

- 1800 to 1900: Three very important events occurred. In 1842, Britain's Edwin Chadwick produced the *General Report on the Sanitary Condition of the Labouring Population of Great Britain*, which is considered one of the most important documents of public health. This report stimulated a similar U.S. survey. In 1854, Britain's John Snow performed an analysis that determined contaminated water in London was the cause of the cholera epidemic in London. This discovery established a link between the environment and disease. In 1850, Lemuel Shattuck, based on Chadwick's report and Snow's activities, developed a state public health law that became the foundation for public health activities.

- By 1900 to 1950: In 1920, Charles Winslow defined **public health** as a focus of preventing disease, prolonging life, and promoting physical health and efficiency through organized community efforts.
- During this period, most states had public health departments that focused on sanitary inspections, disease control, and health education. Throughout the years, **public health functions** included child immunization programs, health screenings in schools, community health services, substance abuse programs, and sexually transmitted disease control.
- In 1923, a vaccine for diphtheria and whooping cough was developed. In 1928, Alexander Fleming discovered penicillin. In 1933, the polio vaccine was developed. In 1946, the **National Mental Health Act (NMHA)** provided funding for research, prevention, and treatment of mental illness.

- 1950 to 1980: In 1950, cigarette smoke is identified as a cause of lung cancer.
- In 1952, Dr. Jonas Salk developed the polio vaccine.
- The **Poison Prevention Packaging Act of 1970** was enacted to prevent children from accidentally ingesting substances. Childproof caps were developed for use on all drugs. In 1980, the eradication of smallpox was announced.

- 1980 to 1990: The first recognized cases of AIDS occurred in the United States in the early 1980s.
- 1988: The *Institute of Medicine Report* defined public health as organized community efforts to address the public interest in health by applying scientific and technical knowledge and promote health. The first *Healthy People Report* (1987) was published that recommended a national prevention strategy.

- 1990 to 2000: In 1997, Oregon voters approved a referendum that allowed physicians to assist terminally ill, mentally competent patients to commit suicide. From 1998 to 2006, 292 patients exercised their rights under the law.

- 2000s: The second *Healthy People Report* was published in 2000. The terrorist attack on the United States on September 11, 2001, impacted and expanded the role of public health. The **Public Health Security and Bioterrorism Preparedness and Response Act of 2002** provided grants to hospitals and public health organizations to prepare for bioterrorism as a result of September 11, 2001.

- 2010: The ACA was passed. Its major goal is to improve the nation's public health level. The third *Healthy People Report* was published.

- 2013: The ACA provided funding to state Medicaid programs to increase preventive services at little or no cost.

Dr. John Snow, and Lemuel Shattuck demonstrated a relationship between the environment and disease (Chadwick, 1842; Turnock, 1997). As a result of their work, public health law was enacted and, by the 1900s, public health departments were focused on the environment and its relationship to disease outbreaks.

Disease control and health education were also integral components of public health departments. In 1916, The Johns Hopkins University, one of the most prestigious universities in the world, established the first public health school (Duke University Library, 2013). Winslow's definition of public health focuses on the prevention of disease, while the IOM defines public health as the organized community effort to protect the public by applying scientific knowledge (IOM, 1988; Winslow, 1920). These definitions are exemplified by the development of several vaccines for whooping cough, polio, smallpox, diphtheria, and the discovery of penicillin. All of these efforts focus on the protection of the public from disease.

The three most important public health achievements are (1) the recognition by the Surgeon General that tobacco use is a health hazard; (2) the number of vaccines that have been developed that have eradicated some diseases and controlled the number of childhood diseases that exist; and (3) early detection programs for blood pressure and heart attacks and smoking cessation programs, which have dramatically reduced the number of deaths in this country (Novick, Morrow, & Mays, 2008).

Assessment, policy development, and assurance, core functions of public health, were developed based on the 1988 report, *The Future of Public Health*, which indicated there was an attrition of public health activities in protecting the community (IOM, 1988). There was poor collaboration between public health and private medicine, no strong mission statement and weak leadership, and politicized decision making. **Assessment** was recommended because it focused on the systematic continuous data collection of health issues, which would ensure that public health agencies were vigilant in protecting the public (IOM, 1988; Turnock, 1997). **Policy development** should also include planning at all health levels, not just federally. Federal agencies should support local health planning (IOM, 1988). **Assurance** focuses on evaluating any processes that have been put in place to assure that the programs are being implemented appropriately. These core functions will ensure that public health remains focused on the community, has programs in place that are effective, and has an evaluation process in place to ensure that the programs do work (Turnock, 1997).

The *Healthy People 2000* report, which started in 1987, was created to implement a new national prevention strategy with three goals: increase life expectancy, reduce health disparities, and increase access to preventive services. Also, three categories of health promotion, health prevention, and preventive services were identified and surveillance activities were emphasized. *Healthy People* provided a vision to reduce preventable disabilities and death. Target objectives were set throughout the years to measure progress (CDC, 2013a).

The *Healthy People 2010* report was released in 2000. The report contained a health promotion and disease prevention focus to identify preventable threats to public health and to set goals to reduce the threats. Nearly 500 objectives were developed according to 28 focus areas. Focus areas ranged from access to care, food safety, education, environmental health, to tobacco and substance abuse. An important component of *Healthy People 2010* is the development of an infrastructure to ensure public health services are provided. Infrastructure includes skilled labor, information technology, organizations, and research. In 2010, *Healthy People 2020* was released. It contains 1,200 objectives that focus on 42 topic areas. According to the **Centers for Disease Control and Prevention (CDC)**, a smaller set of *Healthy People 2020* objectives, called Leading Health Indicators (LHIs), have been targeted to communicate high-priority health issues. (CDC, 2013a). The goals for all of these reports are consistent with the definitions of public health in both Winslow's and the IOM's reports.

It is important to mention the impact the terrorist attack on the United States on September 11, 2001, the anthrax attacks, the outbreak of global diseases such as severe acute respiratory syndrome (SARS), and the U.S. natural disaster of Hurricane Katrina had on the scope of public health responsibilities. As a result of these major events, public health has expanded its area of responsibility. The terms "bioterrorism" and "disaster preparedness" have more frequently appeared in public health literature and have become part of strategic planning. The Public Health Security and Bioterrorism Preparedness and Response Act of 2002 provided grants to hospitals and public health organizations to prepare for bioterrorism as a result of September 11, 2001 (CDC, 2009).

Public health is challenged by its very success because the public now takes public health measures for granted: There are several successful vaccines that targeted almost all childhood diseases, tobacco use has decreased significantly, accident prevention has increased, there are safer workplaces because of the Occupational Safety and Health Administration (OSHA), fluoride is added to the public water supply,

TABLE 1-4	Milestones of the U.S. Health Insurance System 1800–2014

- 1800 to 1900: Insurance was purchased by individuals like one would purchase car insurance. In 1847, the Massachusetts Health Insurance Co. of Boston was the first insurer to issue "sickness insurance." In 1853, a French mutual aid society established a prepaid hospital care plan in San Francisco, California. This plan resembles the modern Health Maintenance Organization (HMO).

- 1900 to 1920: In 1913, the International Ladies Garment Workers began the first union-provided medical services. The National Convention of Insurance Commissioners drafted the first model for regulation of the health insurance industry.

- 1920s: The blueprint for health insurance was established in 1929 when J. F. Kimball began a hospital insurance plan for school teachers at the Baylor University Hospital in Texas. This initiative became the model for Blue Cross plans nationally. The Blue Cross plans were nonprofit and covered only hospital charges so as not to infringe on private physicians' income.

- 1930s: There were discussions regarding the development of a national health insurance program. However, the AMA opposed the move (Raffel & Raffel, 1994). With the Depression and U.S. participation in World War II, the funding required for this type of program was not available. In 1935, President Roosevelt signed the **Social Security Act (SSA)**, which created "old age insurance" to help those of retirement age. In 1936, Vassar College, in New York, was the first college to establish a medical insurance group policy for students.

- 1940s to 1950s: The War Labor Board froze wages, forcing employers to offer health insurance to attract potential employees. In 1947, the Blue Cross Commission was established to create a national doctors network. By 1950, 57% of the population had hospital insurance.

- 1965: President Johnson signed Medicare and Medicaid programs into law.

- 1970s to 1980s: President Nixon signed the HMO Act, which was the predecessor of managed care. In 1982, Medicare proposed paying for hospice or end-of-life care. In 1982, diagnosis related groups (DRGs) and prospective payment guidelines were developed to control insurance reimbursement costs. In 1985, the **Consolidated Omnibus Budget Reconciliation Act (COBRA)** required employers to offer partially subsidized health coverage to terminated employees.

- 1990 to 2000: President Clinton's Health Security Act proposed a universal healthcare coverage plan, which was never passed. In 1993, the **Family Medical Leave Act (FMLA)** was enacted, which allowed employees up to 12 weeks of unpaid leave because of family illness. In 1996, the **Health Insurance Portability and Accountability Act (HIPAA)** was enacted, making it easier to carry health insurance when changing employment. It also increased the confidentiality of patient information. In 1997, the Balanced Budget Act (BBA) was enacted to control the growth of Medicare spending. It also established the State Children's Health Insurance Program (SCHIP).

- 2000: The SCHIP, now known as the Children's Health Insurance Program (CHIP), was implemented.

- 2000: The Medicare, Medicaid, and SCHIP Benefits Improvement and Protection Act provided some relief from the BBA by providing across-the-board program increases.

- 2003: The **Medicare Prescription Drug, Improvement, and Modernization Act** was passed, which created Medicare Part D, prescription plans for the elderly.

- 2006: Massachusetts mandated all residents have health insurance by 2009.

- In 2009, President Obama signed the **American Recovery and Reinvestment Act (ARRA)**, which protected health coverage for the unemployed by providing a 65% subsidy for COBRA coverage to make the premiums more affordable.

(continues)

TABLE 1-4 **Milestones of the U.S. Health Insurance System 1800–2014** *(continued)*

- 2010: The ACA was signed into law, making it illegal for insurance companies to rescind insurance on their sick beneficiaries. Consumers can also appeal coverage claim denials by the insurance companies. Insurance companies are unable to impose lifetime limits on essential benefits.

- 2013: As of October 1, individuals can buy qualified health benefits plans from the Health Insurance Marketplaces. If an employer does not offer insurance, effective 2015, consumer can purchase it from the federal Health Insurance Marketplace.

- 2014: The ACA requires all individuals to purchase health insurance if they can afford it.

or there is decreased mortality because of heart attacks (Turnock, 1997). When some major event occurs like anthrax poisoning or a SARS outbreak, people immediately think that public health will automatically control these problems. The public may not realize how much effort, dedication, and research takes place to protect them.

MILESTONES OF THE HEALTH INSURANCE SYSTEM

There are two key concepts in **group insurance**: "risk is transferred from the individual to the group and the group shares the cost of any covered losses incurred by its member" (Buchbinder & Shanks, 2007). Like life insurance or homeowner's insurance, **health insurance** was developed to provide protection should a covered individual experience an event that requires health care. In 1847, a Boston insurance company offered sickness insurance to consumers (Starr, 1982).

During the 19th century, large employers such as coal mining and railroad companies offered medical services to their employees by providing company doctors. Fees were taken from their pay to cover the service. In 1913, a union-provided health insurance was provided by the International Ladies Garment Workers where health insurance was negotiated as part of their contract (Duke University Library, 2013). During this period, there were several proposals for a national health insurance program but the efforts failed. The AMA was worried that any national health insurance would impact the financial security of their providers. The AMA persuaded the federal government to support private insurance efforts (Raffel & Raffel, 1994).

In 1929, a group hospital insurance plan was offered to teachers at a hospital in Texas. This became the foundation of the nonprofit Blue Cross plans. In order to placate the AMA, Blue Cross initially offered only hospital insurance in order to avoid infringement of physicians' incomes (Blue Cross Blue Shield Association [BCBS], 2007; Starr, 1982). In 1935, the Social Security Act was created and was considered "old age" insurance. During this period, there was continued discussion of a national health insurance program. But, with the impact of World War II and the Depression, there was no funding for this program. The government felt that the Social Security Act was a sufficient program to protect consumers. These events were a catalyst for the development of a health insurance program that included private participation. Although a universal health coverage program was proposed during President Clinton's administration in the 1990s, it was never passed. In 2009, there has been a major public outcry at regional town hall meetings opposing any type of government universal healthcare coverage. In 2006, Massachusetts proposed mandatory health coverage for all citizens, so it may be that universal health coverage would be a state-level initiative (KFF, 2013).

By the 1950s, nearly 60% of the population had hospital insurance (AHA, 2007). Disability insurance was attached to Social Security. In the 1960s, President Johnson signed **Medicare** and **Medicaid** into law, which protects the elderly, disabled, and indigent. President Nixon established the Health Maintenance Organization (HMO), which focused on effective cost measures for health delivery. Also, in the 1980s, diagnostic related groups (DRGs) and prospective payment guidelines were established to provide guidelines for treatment. These DRGs were attached to appropriate insurance reimbursement categories for treatment. The Consolidated Omnibus Budget

Reconciliation Act (COBRA) was passed to provide health insurance protection if an individual changes jobs. In 1993, the Family Medical Leave Act (FMLA) was passed to protect an employee if there is a family illness. An employee can receive up to 12 weeks of unpaid leave and maintain his or her health insurance coverage during this period. In 1994, the **Uniformed Services Employment and Reemployment Rights Act (USERRA)** entitles individuals who leave for military service to return to their job. Also, in 1996, the Health Insurance Portability and Accountability Act (HIPAA) was passed to provide stricter confidentiality regarding the health information of individuals. In 1997, the Balanced Budget Act (BBA) was passed that required massive program reductions for Medicare and authorized Medicare reimbursement for outpatient services (CMS, 2013b).

At the start of the 21st century, cost, access, and quality continue to be issues for U.S. health care. Employers continue to play an integral role in health insurance coverage. In 2009, nearly 57% of the population was covered by employer insurance (AMA, 2013b). The largest public coverage program is Medicare—14% of the population. The State Children's Health Insurance Program (SCHIP); renamed CHIP was implemented to ensure that children, who are not Medicaid eligible, receive health care. The Medicare, Medicaid, and SCHIP Benefits Improvement and Protection Act provided some relief from the BBA of 1997 by restoring some funding to these consumer programs. In 2003, a consumer law, the **Medicare Prescription Drug, Improvement, and Modernization Act**, created a major overhaul of the Medicare system (CMS, 2013b). The Act created Medicare Part D, a prescription plan that became effective in 2006 that provided different prescription programs to the elderly, based on their prescription needs. It has been criticized because it is so complex. The elderly had a difficult time understanding which plan to select. It also has not been cost effective; the cost of the program has been estimated at $550 billion. The 10-year estimated cost of this program is $1.2 trillion (Brownlee, 2007). In 2008, the National Defense Authorization Act expanded the FMLA to include families of military service members to take a leave of absence if the spouse, parent, or child was called to active military service. The 2010 ACA requires individuals to purchase health insurance by 2014. Despite these efforts, health insurance coverage continues to be an issue for the United States.

CURRENT SYSTEM OPERATIONS

Government's Participation in Health Care

The U.S. government plays an important role in healthcare delivery. The United States has three governmental levels participating in the healthcare system: federal, state, and local. The federal government provides a range of regulatory and funding mechanisms including Medicare and Medicaid, established in 1965 as federally funded programs to provide health access to the elderly (65 years or older) and the poor, respectively. Over the years, these programs have expanded to include the disabled. They also have developed programs for military personnel, veterans, and their dependents.

Federal law does ensure access to emergency services regardless of ability to pay as a result of EMTALA (Regenstein, Mead, & Lara, 2007). The federal government determines a national healthcare budget, sets reimbursement rates, and also formulates standards for providers for eligible Medicare and Medicaid patients (Barton, 2003). The state level is responsible for regulatory and funding mechanisms but also provides healthcare programs as dictated by the federal government. The local or county level of government is responsible for implementing programs dictated by both the federal and state level.

The U.S. healthcare system is not a true system because of its fragmentation and lack of centralized decision making (Shi & Singh, 2008). The United States has several federal health regulatory agencies including the CDC for public health, the **Food and Drug Administration (FDA)** for pharmaceutical controls, and **Centers for Medicare & Medicaid Services (CMS)** for the indigent, disabled, and the elderly. There is also The Joint Commission, a private organization that focuses on healthcare organizations' oversight and the **Agency for Healthcare Research and Quality (AHRQ)** is the primary federal source for quality delivery of health services. The **Center for Mental Health Services (CMHS)**, in partnership with state health departments, leads national efforts to assess mental health delivery services. Although the federal government is to be commended because of the many agencies that focus on major healthcare issues, with multiple organizations there is often duplication of effort and miscommunication that results in inefficiencies (KFF, 2013). However, there are several regulations in place that protect patient rights. One of the first pieces of legislation is the **Sherman**

Antitrust Act of 1890 and ensuing legislation, which ensures fair competition in the marketplace for patients by prohibiting monopolies (Niles, 2013). Regulations such as HIPAA protects patient information; COBRA gives workers and families the right to continue healthcare coverage if they lose their job; the **Newborns' and Mothers' Health Protection Act (NMHPA)** of 1996 prevents health insurance companies from discharging a mother and child too early from the hospital; the **Women's Health and Cancer Rights Act (WHCRA)** of 1998 prevents discrimination of women who have cancer; the **Mental Health Parity Act (MHPA)** of 1996 and its 2008 amendment requires health insurance companies to provide fair coverage for mental health conditions; the **Genetic Information Nondiscrimination Act of 2008** prohibits U.S. insurance companies and employers from discriminating based on genetic test results; the **Lilly Ledbetter Fair Pay Act of 2009** provides protection for unlawful employment practices related to compensation discrimination; and finally, the **ACA** of 2010 focuses on increasing access to healthcare, improving the quality of healthcare delivery, and increasing the number of those individuals who have health insurance. All of these regulations are considered **social regulations** because they were enacted to protect the healthcare consumer.

Private Participation in Health Care

The private sector focuses on the financial and delivery aspects of the system. Healthcare costs are paid by a health insurance plan, private, or government, and the enrollee of the plan. Approximately 34% of the 2009 healthcare expenditures were paid from private health insurance, insurance offered by a private insurance company such as Blue Cross; private **out-of-pocket expenses or payments**, funds paid by the individual, were 14%; and federal, state, and local governments paid 40%. Out-of-pocket payments are considered the individual's **cost share** of his or her healthcare costs. Approximately 57% of private healthcare financing is through **employer health insurance**, a type of **voluntary health insurance** set up by an individual's employer. The delivery of the services provided is through legal entities such as hospitals, clinics, physicians, and other medical providers (National Center for Health Statistics [NCHS], 2011). The different providers are an integral part of the medical care system and need to coordinate their care with the layers of the U.S. government. In order to ensure access to health care, communication is vital between public and private components of healthcare delivery.

Figure 1-1 The Iron Triangle of Health Care
Source: Reproduced from Kissick, William, MD, DR, PH, *Medicine's Dilemmas*, p. 3. New Haven, CT: Yale University Press, 1994. Reprinted by permission.

ASSESSING YOUR HEALTHCARE SYSTEM USING THE IRON TRIANGLE

Many healthcare systems are evaluated using the **Iron Triangle of Health Care**—a concept that focuses on the balance of three factors: quality, cost, and accessibility to health care (see **Figure 1-1**). This concept was created in 1994 by Dr. William Kissick (Kissick, 1994). If one factor is emphasized, such as cost reduction, it may create an inequality of quality and access because costs are being cut. Because lack of access is a problem in the United States, healthcare systems may focus on increasing access, which could increase costs. In order to assess the success of a healthcare delivery, it is vital that consumers assess their health care by analyzing the balance between cost, access, and quality. Are you receiving quality care from your provider? Do you have easy access to your healthcare system? Is it costly to receive health care? Although the Iron Triangle is used by many experts in analyzing large healthcare delivery systems, as a healthcare consumer, you can also evaluate your healthcare delivery system by using the Iron Triangle. An effective healthcare system should have a balance between the three components.

CONCLUSION

Despite U.S. healthcare expenditures, the U.S. disease rates remain higher than many developed countries because the United States has an expensive system that is available to only those who can afford it (Regenstein, Mead, & Lara, 2007). Findings from the 11th MetLife annual survey indicate that healthcare costs are worrying employees and their employers. Over 60% of employees are worried they will not be able to pay out-of-pocket expenses not covered by insurance. Employers are increasing the cost sharing of their employees for healthcare benefits because of the cost increases (Business Wire, 2013). Because the United States does not have universal health coverage, there are more health disparities across the nation. Persons living in poverty are more likely to be in poor health and less likely to use the healthcare system compared to those with incomes above the poverty line. If the United States offered universal health coverage, the per capita expenditures would be more evenly distributed and likely more effective. The major problem for the United States is that healthcare insurance is a major determinant of access to health care. With nearly 49 million uninsured in the United States with limited access to routine health care, disease rates and mortality rates will not improve. Based on the fragmented development of U.S. health care, the system is based on individualism and self-determination and focusing on the individual rather than collectivistic needs of the population. In a recent 2013 report, the CDC indicates there was a decline in U.S. infant mortality rates between 2005 and 2011 because of declines in certain geographic areas. However, despite this positive result, the United States is still ranked worldwide much lower than other developed countries due to the continued preterm birth rates. This is an important statistic because it is often used to compare the health status of nations worldwide. Although our healthcare expenditures are very high, our infant mortality rates rank higher than many countries. Racial disparities in disease and death rates continue to be a concern (CDC, 2013b). Both private and public participants in the U.S. health delivery system need to increase their collaboration to reduce these disease rates. Leaders need to continue to assess our healthcare system using the Iron Triangle to ensure there is a balance between access, cost, and quality.

VOCABULARY

Agency for Healthcare Research and Quality (AHRQ)

Almshouses

American Medical Association (AMA)

American Recovery and Reinvestment Act (ARRA)

Assessment

Assurance

Center for Mental Health Services (CMHS)

Centers for Disease Control and Prevention (CDC)

Centers for Medicare and Medicaid Services (CMS)

Certificate of Need (CON)

Consolidated Omnibus Budget Reconciliation Act (COBRA)

Cost sharing

Emergency Medical Treatment and Active Labor Act (EMTALA)

Employer health insurance

Epidemics

Family Medical Leave Act (FMLA)

Flexner Report

Food and Drug Administration (FDA)

Genetic Information Nondiscrimination Act of 2008

Graying of the population

Gross domestic product (GDP)

Group insurance

Health insurance

Health Insurance Portability and Accountability Act (HIPAA)

Healthy People reports (2000, 2010, 2020)

Hospitalists

Iron Triangle of Health Care

Joint Commission

Lilly Ledbetter Fair Pay Act of 2009

Medicaid

Medicare

Medicare Prescription Drug, Improvement, and Modernization Act

Mental Health Parity Act (MHPA)

National Defense Authorization Act

National Mental Health Act (NMHA)

Newborns' and Mothers' Health Protection Act (NMHPA)

Out-of-pocket payments or expenses

Patient Bill of Rights

Patient Protection and Affordable Care Act of 2010 (PPACA, or ACA)

Pesthouses

Poison Prevention Packaging Act of 1970

Policy development

Poorhouses

Primary prevention

Public health

Public health functions

Public Health Security and Bioterrorism Preparedness and Response Act of 2002

Secondary prevention

Sherman Antitrust Act of 1890

Social regulations

Social Security Act (SSA)

Tertiary prevention

Uniformed Services Employment and Reemployment Rights Act (USERRA)

Universal healthcare program

Voluntary health insurance

Women's Health and Cancer Rights Act (WHCRA)

REFERENCES

American Heritage Dictionary. (4th ed.). (2001). New York: Bantam Dell.

American Hospital Association. (2007). Community accountability and transparency: Helping hospitals better serve their communities. Retrieved from http://www.aha.org/aha/content/2007/pdf/07accountability.pdf

American Medical Association. (2013a). Our history. Retrieved from http://www.ama-assn.org/ama/pub/about-ama/our-history.shtml

American Medical Association. (2013b). Reports of council on medical service. Retrieved from http://www.ama-assn.org/ama1/pub/upload/mm/38/i05cmspdf.pdf

Association of American Medical Colleges. (2013). Tuition and student fees, first-year medical school students 2012–2013. Retrieved from https://services.aamc.org/tsfreports/report_median.cfm?year_of_study=2013

Barton, P. (2003). *Understanding the U.S. health services system*. Chicago: Health Administration Press.

Blue Cross Blue Shield Association. (2007). Blue beginnings. Retrieved from http://www.bcbs.com/about/history/blue-beginnings.html

Buchbinder, S., & Shanks, N. (2007). *Introduction to health care management*. Sudbury, MA: Jones and Bartlett.

Business Wire. (2013). MetLife study finds six out of ten employees are concerned about out-of-pocket medical costs. Retrieved from http://finance.yahoo.com/news/metlife-study-finds-six-ten-130000050.html

Centers for Disease Control and Prevention. (2001). Trends in hospital emergency department utilization: United States, 1992–1999. *Vital and Health Statistics*, 13(150 revised). Retrieved from http://www.cdc.gov/nchs/data/series/sr_13/sr13_150.pdf

Centers for Disease Control and Prevention. (2007). Skin cancer module: Practice exercises. Retrieved from http://www.cdc.gov/excite/skincancer/mod13.htm

Centers for Disease Control and Prevention. (2009). Selected Federal Legal Authorities Pertinent to Public Health Emergencies. Retrieved from http://www.cdc.gov/phlp/docs/ph-emergencies.pdf

Centers for Disease Control and Prevention. (2013a). *Healthy People 2020: Tobacco use*. Retrieved from http://www.cdc.gov/tobacco/basic_information/healthy_people

Centers for Disease Control and Prevention. (2013b). NCHS Data Brief: Recent Declines in Infant Mortality in the United States, 2005–2011. Retrieved from http://www.cdc.gov/nchs/data/databriefs/db120.htm

Centers for Medicare and Medicaid Services (2013a). National health expenditure projections 2010–2020. Retrieved from http://www.cms.gov/Research-Statistics-Data-and-Systems/Statistics-Trends-and-Reports/NationalHealth ExpendData/downloads/proj2010.pdf

Centers for Medicare and Medicaid Services. (2013b). HIPAA: General information. Retrieved from http://www .cms.hhs.gov/HIPAAGenInfo/01_Overview.asp

Chadwick, E. (1842). *The sanitary conditions of the labouring class*. London: W. Clowes.

Classen, D., Resar, R., Griffin, F., Federico, F., Frankel, T., Kimmel, N., . . . James, B. (2011). Global Trigger Tool shows that adverse events in hospitals may be ten times greater than previously measured. *Health Affairs, 30*(4), 109.

Duke University Library. (2013). Medicine and Madison Avenue. Timeline. Retrieved from http://library.duke .edu/digitalcollections/mma/timeline.html

Godert, J. (2013). CMS releases hospital price ranges of 100 most common treatments. Retrieved from http://www .healthdatamanagement.com/news/medicare-hospital-price-transparency-claims-data-released-46120-1 .html?zkPrintable=true

Goodman, J. C., & Musgrave, G. L. (1992). *Patient power: Solving America's health care crisis*. Washington, DC: CATO Institute.

Institute of Medicine. (1988). *The future of public health* (pp. 1–5). Washington, DC: National Academies Press.

Kaiser Family Foundation. (2013). Making sense of the Census uninsured numbers. Retrieved from http://www .kff.org/insurance/snapshot/chcm010307oth.cfm

Kissick, W. (1994). *Medicine's dilemmas*. New Haven and New London, CT: Yale University Press.

Kliff, S. (2012). Study: Fewer employers are offering health insurance. Retrieved from http://www.washingtonpost .com/blogs/wonkblog/post/study-fewer-employers-are-offering-health-insurance/2012/04/24/gIQAfGH6eT _print.html

National Center for Health Statistics (2011). Health, United States, 2011. With special feature on socioeconomic status and health. Washington, DC: U.S. Government Printing Office.

National Conference of State Legislatures. (2013). *Certificate of need: State health laws and programs*. Retrieved from http://www.ncsl.org/issues-research/health/con-certificate-of-need-state-laws.aspx

Niles, N. (2013). Basic concepts of health care human resource management (pp. 37–50). Sudbury, MA: Jones and Bartlett.

Novick, L., Morrow, C., & Mays, G. (2008). *Public health administration* (2nd ed., pp. 1–68). Sudbury, MA: Jones and Bartlett.

Raffel, M. W., & Raffel, N. K. (1994). *The U.S. health system: Origins and functions* (4th ed.). Albany, NY: Delmar Publishers.

Regenstein, M., Mead, M., & Lara, A. (2007). The heart of the matter: The relationship between communities, cardiovascular services and racial and ethnic gaps in care. *Managed Care Interface, 20*, 22–28.

Rosen, G. (1983). *The structure of American medical practice 1875–1941*. Philadelphia: University of Pennsylvania Press.

Shi, L., & Singh, D. (2008). *Delivering health care in America*. Sudbury, MA: Jones and Bartlett.

Starr, P. (1982). *The social transformation of American medicine*. Cambridge, MA: Basic Books.

Stevens, R. (1971). *American medicine and the public interest*. New Haven, CT: Yale University Press.

Sultz, H., & Young, K. (2006). *Health care USA: Understanding its organization and delivery* (5th ed.). Sudbury, MA: Jones and Bartlett.

Turnock, J. (1997). *Public health and how it works*. Gaithersburg, MD: Aspen Publishers, Inc.

Vault Career Intelligence. (2013). Home page. Retrieved from http://www.vault.com/wps/portal/usa

Winslow, C. E. A. (1920). *The untilled fields of public health* (pp. 30–35). New York: Health Service, New York Chapter of the American Red Cross.

NOTES

IN YOUR OWN WORDS

Based on this chapter, please provide a definition of the following vocabulary words in your own words. DO NOT RECITE the text definition.

Group insurance: _____

_____

_____

Gross domestic product (GDP): _____

_____

_____

Pesthouses: _____

_____

_____

Voluntary health insurance: _____

_____

_____

Public health functions: _____

_____

_____

Primary prevention: _____

_____

_____

Secondary prevention: _____

_____

_____

Tertiary prevention: _____

_____

_____

Universal healthcare program: _____

_____

_____

Epidemics: _____

_____

_____

STUDENT ACTIVITY 1-2

Complete the following case scenarios based on the information provided in the chapter. Your answer must be **IN YOUR OWN WORDS.**

REAL-LIFE APPLICATIONS: CASE SCENARIO ONE

Your mother knows that you are taking classes for your healthcare management degree. She just returned from a physician checkup and she was confused by the terminology they were using at the office. They mentioned several activities related to primary, secondary, and tertiary prevention.

ACTIVITY

Define each of the terms and provide examples of these types of prevention.

RESPONSES

_____

_____

_____

_____

_____

_____

_____

_____

_____

_____

_____

_____

_____

CASE SCENARIO TWO

You recently were promoted to assistant to the Chief Executive Officer of the Niles Hospital system.

The CEO is interested in building a hospital to expand their healthcare system. She has asked you to investigate the Certificate of Need (CON) process for this proposal.

ACTIVITY

Perform Internet research on the CON process and provide a report on the necessary steps to achieve this CON.

RESPONSES

_____

_____

_____

_____

_____

_____

_____

_____

_____

_____

_____

_____

_____

CASE SCENARIO THREE

One of your friends had a very serious medical emergency and had to go to the hospital for treatment. She was very upset because upon her arrival, she was asked for her insurance card, which she did not have, and was transferred to another hospital quickly. You had learned there was a law that was passed that made this type of treatment by a hospital illegal. However, before telling your friend your opinion, you wanted to find out more about this law and whether it applied to her situation.

ACTIVITY

Perform Internet research on public health regulations and write up a report on whether you think the Emergency Medical Treatment and Active Labor Act (EMTALA) was applicable in this situation.

RESPONSES

_____

_____

_____

_____

_____

_____

_____

_____

_____

_____

_____

_____

_____

CASE SCENARIO FOUR

As a public health student, you are interested in different public health initiatives the CDC has put forth over the years and whether they have been successful. You continue to hear the term "*Healthy People* reports." You are interested in the results of these reports.

ACTIVITY

Visit the CDC website and write a report on the *Healthy People* initiatives and whether or not you think they are successful initiatives.

RESPONSES

_____

_____

_____

_____

_____

_____

_____

_____

_____

_____

_____

_____

_____

STUDENT ACTIVITY 1-3

INTERNET EXERCISES

Write your answers in the space provided.

- Visit each of the websites listed here.
- Name the organization.
- Locate their mission statement or statement of purpose on their website.
- Provide a brief overview of the activities of the organization.
- How do these organizations participate in the U.S. healthcare system?

Websites

http://www.ama-assn.org

Organization Name: _____

Mission Statement:

_____

_____

_____

Overview of Activities: _____

_____

_____

Importance of organization to U.S. health care:

_____

_____

_____

http://www.cdc.gov

Organization Name: _____

Mission Statement:

_____

_____

_____

Overview of Activities: _____

_____

_____

Importance of organization to U.S. health care:

_____

_____

_____

Organization Name: _____

Mission Statement:

_____

_____

_____

Overview of Activities: _____

_____

_____

Importance of organization to U.S. health care:

_____

_____

_____

http://www.hhs.gov

Organization Name: _____

Mission Statement:

_____

_____

_____

Overview of Activities: _____

_____

_____

Importance of organization to U.S. health care:

_____

_____

_____

http://www.jointcommission.org

Organization Name: _____

Mission Statement:

_____

_____

_____

Overview of Activities: _____

_____

_____

Importance of organization to U.S. health care:

_____

_____

_____

http://www.ahrq.gov

Organization Name: _____

Mission Statement:

_____

_____

_____

Overview of Activities: _____

_____

_____

Importance of organization to U.S. health care:

_____

_____

_____

DISCUSSION QUESTIONS

The following are suggested discussion questions for this chapter.

(1) What is the *Flexner Report*? How did it impact health care in the United States?

_____

_____

_____

_____

_____

(2) What are the *Healthy People* report initiatives? Describe three current initiatives to your classmates.

_____

_____

_____

_____

_____

(3) Why was health insurance developed? What was Kaiser's role in this?

_____

_____

_____

_____

_____

(4) Describe how the Iron Triangle can be used to assess health care. Give specific examples.

_____

_____

_____

_____

(5) What is the Patient Bill of Rights? Why was it developed? Have you ever seen the Patient Bill of Rights posted anywhere?

_____

_____

_____

_____

_____

The Navigate Companion Website for this text is a great source for additional information on the U.S. healthcare system. You can gain a new perspective on many of the topics presented in this chapter by visiting http://go .jblearning.com/Niles2e. You'll find additional student activities, further reading, and interactive study tools that explore:

• Basic concepts of health
• Milestones of U.S. healthcare systems development
• Current U.S. healthcare system operations
• And much more.

Chapter 2

Impact of the Affordable Care Act on Healthcare Services

LEARNING OBJECTIVES

The student will be able to:

- List and summarize the 10 major provisions of the Patient Protection and Affordable Care Act of 2010.
- Evaluate the impact of the ACA on accessibility of healthcare plans to individuals and small businesses.
- Discuss the impact of the ACA on the health insurance industry.
- Describe the impact of the ACA on public health programs.
- Define and discuss the Health Insurance Marketplace.
- Define community choice and its impact on healthcare services.

DID YOU KNOW THAT?

- The ACA requires most U.S. citizens and legal residents to purchase health insurance if they can afford it or pay a penalty.
- The ACA mandates that every state create a consumer-oriented marketplace where individuals are provided information and can purchase healthcare insurance.
- The ACA bans health plans from establishing lifetime dollar limits on healthcare insurance reimbursement.
- The new Independence at Home program provides an opportunity for the chronically ill to be treated at home.
- The ACA established the Medicare and Medicaid Innovation Center, which provides opportunities for innovative healthcare research.
- The Elder Justice Act, passed as part of the Affordable Care Act, targets abuse, neglect, and exploitation of the elderly.

INTRODUCTION

The **Patient Protection and Affordable Care Act (PPACA)** or as it is commonly called, the **Affordable Care Act (ACA),** and its amendment, the **Healthcare and Education Affordability Reconciliation Act of 2010 ,** was signed into law on March 23, 2010 by President Barack Obama. The goal of the act is to improve the accessibility and quality of the U.S. healthcare system. There are nearly 50 healthcare reform initiatives that are being implemented during 2010–2017 and beyond. The passage of this complex landmark legislation has been very controversial and continues to be contentious today.

There were national public protests and a huge division among the political parties regarding the components of the legislation. People, in general, agreed that the healthcare system needed some type of reform, but it was difficult to develop common recommendations that had majority support. Criticism, in part, focused on the increased role of government in implementing and monitoring the healthcare system. Proponents of healthcare reform reminded people that Medicare is a federal government entitlement program because when individuals reach 65 years of age, they can receive their health insurance from this program. Millions of individuals are enrolled in Medicare. Medicaid is a state-established government public welfare insurance program based on income for millions of individuals, including children, that provides health care for its enrollees.

However, regardless of these two programs, many critics felt that the federal government was forcing people to purchase health insurance. In fact, the ACA does require most individuals to obtain health insurance only if they can afford it. But with the healthcare system expenditures comprising 17.6% of the U.S. gross domestic product and with millions of Americans not having the accessibility of health care, resulting in poor health indicators, the current administration's priority was to create mandated healthcare reform. The Congressional Budget Office estimates that the act will enable an additional 32 million Americans or a total of 94% of Americans to have access to health insurance (ProCon.org, 2013b).

The goal of the act is to improve the accessibility and quality of the U.S. healthcare system. There are nearly 50 healthcare reform initiatives that are being implemented over several years. As discussed earlier, the main bone of contention is the requirement of the act that U.S. citizens and legal residents must purchase health insurance or pay an annual fine for inaction. As a result of this mandate, there were over 20 states that filed lawsuits, primarily questioning the constitutionality of this mandate. The second major contentious issue is whether Medicaid expansion requirements were constitutional because the federal government could withhold federal Medicaid funding to states that refuse to expand their Medicaid programs. On June 28, 2012, the U.S. Supreme Court upheld the constitutionality of the ACA in a 5–4 ruling in the *Florida v. Sebelius* lawsuit regarding individual health insurance

mandates and the *National Federation of Independent Businesses v. Sebelius* lawsuits filed regarding Medicaid expansion (ProCon.org, 2013a). However, the federal government could not withhold federal funding to states that refuse the Medicaid expansion because it could be considered coercion. As a result of this decision, the federal government is required to develop state incentives to accept the Medicaid expansion and to restrict the type of funding limitations to states who refuse the Medicaid expansions (Svendiman & Baumrucker, 2012).

MAJOR PROVISIONS OF THE AFFORDABLE CARE ACT

Table 2-1 provides a summary of the 46 major action items of the ACA (Centers for Medicare & Medicaid Services, 2013c). The key features of the law include: rights and protection of healthcare consumers, insurance choice and insurance costs, benefits for those 65 and older, and employer requirements of providing healthcare benefits. The law itself is divided into 10 titles or areas of healthcare reform. This chapter will provide a summary of each title and an update on the implementation of these areas of healthcare reform.

Title 1—Affordability and Accessibility of Healthcare

The following are some of the major reforms that were implemented in 2010:

- Create small business tax credits for employers who provide health insurance.
- Eliminate lifetime and unreasonable annual caps or limits on healthcare reimbursement with annual limitations prohibited by 2014.
- Provide assistance for the uninsured with pre-existing conditions and prohibit denial of insurance coverage for pre-existing conditions for children.
- Develop a temporary national high-risk pool for health insurance for individuals with pre-existing conditions who have no insurance.
- Extend dependent coverage up to age 26.
- Establish www.healthcare.gov for consumers to access information about healthcare insurance.
- Create a reinsurance program for retirees who are not yet eligible for Medicare.

TABLE 2-1	Timeline for Affordable Care Act Regulations
2010	Affordable Care Act Signed into Law
	Small Business Health Insurance Tax Credits (deferred until 2015)
	States to Increase Medicaid coverage
	One-Time $250 rebate for Medicare Part D Donut Hole
	Target Healthcare Fraud
	Early Retiree Reinsurance Program (ERRP)
	Insurance for Pre-Existing Conditions
	Online Information for Healthcare Consumers at http://www.healthcare.gov
	Extend Age for Young Adults Coverage to 26
	Free Preventive Care
	Prohibit Insurance from Dropping Coverage
	Appeal of Insurance Coverage Denials
	Eliminate Lifetime Limits on Insurance Coverage
	Regulate Annual Limits on Insurance Coverage
	Ban of Coverage Denial of Children with Pre existing Conditions
	Accountability of Insurance for High Rate Hikes
	Focus on Primary Health Workforce
	Establish State Consumer Assistance Programs
	Prevent Disease and Illness Initiatives
	Strengthen Community Health Centers
	Increased Payments for Rural Health
2011	Prescription Drug Discounts
	Free Preventive Care for Seniors
	Reduce Healthcare Premiums
	Strengthen Medicare Advantage
	Improve Quality and Efficiency of Health Care
	Improve Senior Care Post Discharge from Hospital
	Innovation to Reduce Costs
	Increase Home and Community Health Services
2012	Encourage Integrated Healthcare Systems

(continues)

TABLE 2-1	Timeline for Affordable Care Act Regulations *(continued)*
2012	Decrease Health Disparities
	Reduce Administrative Costs
	Link Payment to Quality Care
2013	Increase Preventive Care Coverage
	Increase Medicaid Payments to Primary MDs
	Expanding Bundled Payments
	Open Enrollment in Health Insurance Marketplace
2014	Establish Health Insurance Marketplace
	Promote Individual Responsibility
	Increase Access to Medicaid
	Make Care More Affordable
	Coverage for Participants in Clinical Trials
	Eliminate Annual Limits of Insurance Coverage
	Anti-Discrimination of Pre-Existing Conditions or Gender
	Increase of Small Business Health Insurance Tax Credit
2015	Payment to Physicians Based on Quality Care

Source: Data from Centers for Medicare & Medicaid Services. Timeline of the health care law. Retrieved from https://www.healthcare.gov /timeline-of-the-health-care-law/#part=1

Discussion

The ACA establishes tax credits for small businesses to assist them with providing employee insurance benefits. This is a multi-phase program. The first phase provides a credit up to 35% of the employer's contribution to the employee's health insurance. Although there are up to 4 million small businesses eligible for these credits, according to a U.S. General Accountability Office (GAO) 2012 report, less than 200,000 small businesses have claimed the tax credit because it was not large enough to incentivize small businesses to offer health insurance. There are also complicated administrative procedures that limited claims. The government is reviewing the procedures to streamline the application process. *Due to business input, this mandate has been deferred to 2015.* (U.S. General Accountability Office , 2012).

In the past, health insurance companies would establish an annual or lifetime cap on reimbursement of consumers' healthcare insurance claims. This practice would be eliminated. Unlike the past, health insurance companies would also be prohibited from dropping individuals and children with certain conditions or not providing insurance to those individuals with pre-existing conditions This Pre-Existing Condition Insurance Plan (PCIP) provides new healthcare coverage options to individuals who have a pre-existing condition and have had no insurance for the last 6 months. This serves as a bridge to 2014, when all discrimination against pre-existing conditions will be prohibited.

Prior to the ACA, dependent coverage stopped at age 25. The act requires insurance companies to cover young adults on their parents' insurance until age 26, even if they are not living with their parents, are not declared dependents on their parents' taxes, or are no longer students. However, this would not apply to individuals who have employer-based coverage (U.S. Department of Labor, 2010).

In July 2010, the federal government established a Web portal, www.healthcare.gov, to increase consumer awareness about their eligibility for specific healthcare insurance company information and about government programs. The Web portal will be developed in phases. Also, a government temporary **reinsurance program** for employers who provide coverage to retirees over age 55 who are not yet eligible for Medicare will reimburse the employer 80% of the retiree claims of $50,000–$90,000. The act created a $5 billion program to provide needed financial assistance for employment-based plans to supply this coverage. This program will be effective through January 2014, when the state-based Health Insurance Marketplaces will be in place and retirees not yet eligible for Medicare can buy their own insurance (U.S. General Accountability Office, 2012).

The following are selected major reforms that must be implemented by 2014:

- Insurance companies will be prohibited from setting insurance rates based on health status, medical condition, genetic information, or other related factors.

- Private health insurance coverage offered in the Marketplaces must offer the same **essential health benefits (EHBs).**

- By October 1, 2013, states must establish the **Health Insurance Marketplaces,** which are marketplaces where consumers can obtain information and buy health insurance. Open enrollment for health insurance also begins on October 1 for health insurance that will become effective January 1, 2014. Most individuals who are uninsured must enroll in an insurance plan by January 1, 2014 that has minimum essential healthcare coverage or pay an annual fee.

- In the past, there were issues with health insurance companies denying coverage based on health status or other conditions. Premiums now will be based on family type, geography, tobacco use, and age. In 2014–2016, only individuals and small group employers are eligible to participate in the Marketplaces. In 2017, states may permit large group employers to participate. States may also organize regional exchanges. On May 8, 2013, the Department of Labor (DOL) issued guidance for employers regarding the requirement to notify employees of coverage options available through the exchanges. (United Health Care, 2013). The ACA also established a **Summary of Benefits and Coverage (SBC)** which offers consumers

the opportunity to easily compare health insurance plans.

- There will also be **Consumer Operated and Oriented Plans (CO-OPs),** which are member-run health organizations in all 50 states and must be consumer focused with profits targeted to lowering premiums and improving benefits.

- There is enrollment assistance for the Health Insurance Marketplaces. The **Centers for Consumer Information and Insurance Oversight** awarded nearly $70 million in co-operative agreements to 105 organizations to provide assistance to insurance marketplaces.

- The **Small Business Health Options Program (SHOP)** is available to small businesses with up to 100 employers to purchase health coverage. These programs are required to maintain a call center for customer service. Employers who have 50 or more employers must automatically enroll new full-time employees in healthcare coverage. Employers would pay a fee of $3,000 if they did not offer affordable insurance. Employers will also receive tax credits depending on the size of the company. *Based on input from business groups, this mandate has been delayed until 2015.*

Health insurance plans in the Marketplaces must offer at a minimum the following essential health benefits:

- Ambulatory patient services (outpatient care you get without being admitted to a hospital)

- Emergency services

- Hospitalization (such as surgery)

- Maternity and newborn care (care before and after your baby is born)

- Mental health and substance use disorder services, including behavioral health treatment (this includes counseling and psychotherapy)

- Prescription drugs

- Rehabilitative and habilitative services and devices (services and devices to help people with injuries, disabilities, or chronic conditions gain or recover mental and physical skills)

- Laboratory services

- Preventive and wellness services and chronic disease management

- Pediatric services (Centers for Medicare & Medicaid Services, 2013d)

Health Insurance Marketplaces, run by state or federal government, are central locations for healthcare consumers to purchase health insurance coverage. They provide standardized information on the different types of health insurance coverage to suit consumer needs. Consumers complete an application to determine what types of coverage are available to them, based on their need. Health insurance coverage is provided by private health insurance companies. Open enrollment for 2014 started on October 1, 2013.

If individuals do not apply for health insurance coverage by March 31, 2014, which is when open enrollment ends, they will be required to pay a fee and cannot obtain coverage until the next annual open enrollment. However, if there is a **life qualifying event** such as job change or geographic change, they could be eligible to enroll. The 2014 fee is 1% of the individual's yearly income or $95 per person, whichever is higher. The fee for an uninsured child is $47.50. The maximum amount a family would pay is $285. The fee does increase every year. In 2016, it is 2.5% of income or $695, whichever is higher. Individuals who have very low income, participate in a religious sect that does not believe in health insurance, or are part of a federally recognized Indian tribe, will not be charged a fee (Centers for Medicare & Medicaid Services, 2013e).

The SBC was developed as a result of the ACA. This summary allows the consumer to compare the different types of benefits offered by health insurance companies. A consumer can compare price, benefits, and other features. This is required for all health insurance companies.

Recognizing that in some states only a small number of insurance companies offer coverage for individuals and small businesses, the Centers for Medicare and Medicaid Services has awarded nearly $2 billion in loans to help create 24 new CO-OPs in 24 states. The CO-OP sponsors—consumer-run groups, membership associations, and other nonprofit organizations—are now moving forward to offer health coverage in competition with established commercial and nonprofit insurance companies. As of June 2013, the CO-OPs were hiring staff and obtaining licensure. The success of these CO-OPs may be dependent on the state Marketplaces. (Health Affairs, 2013; Office of Inspector General, 2013).

The Health and Human Services Administration's Centers for Consumer Information and Insurance Oversight is responsible for the oversight of the health insurance provisions of the ACA. They will work with state governments to ensure the Marketplaces are being implemented properly. They will also help states with reviews of any unreasonable rate increases by insurance companies and other social regulations (Centers for Medicare & Medicaid Services, 2013b). The Health Resources and Services Administration also awarded $150 million to 1,200 community health centers to enroll uninsured individuals.

A **Public Plan Option** was also authorized to create a government-run health insurance agency that would compete with other health insurance companies. This would provide health insurance for those who could not afford private health insurance premiums. *This program has not been implemented.* However, in 2013, this type of program has been reintroduced by the Senate as an amendment to the ACA. The purpose of these programs is to increase the number of consumers who have access to affordable health care.

Title II—The Role of Public Programs: Medicaid, CHIP, Medicare

- Medicaid eligibility has been expanded to cover lower incomes. The baseline is all individuals under 133% of the federal poverty level. States will receive matching funds to expand their Medicaid services, increasing accessibility to more consumers. As of September 2013, 24 states have opted to expand their Medicaid programs. More states are expected to adopt the expansion because the federal government is willing to pay 100% of the state's costs through 2016 for the expansion.

- Children's Health Insurance Program (CHIP) will be required to maintain income level eligibility through 2019.

- A new Medicaid benefit, **Community First Choice**, has been created to offer community services.

- In 2010, a onetime $250 rebate was given to Medicare Part D beneficiaries who enter the coverage gap or **donut hole** in 2010. There are approximately 4 million seniors impacted by this financing gap.

- Medicare beneficiaries will receive an annual wellness visit with no cost sharing.

Discussion

Medicaid will expand to increase coverage for consumers who are not Medicare eligible. As discussed earlier, this mandate was contentious because states felt that the federal government was forcing them to expand their programs by withholding federal aid if states refused to expand. The federal government has limited the withholding mandate to certain newly eligible populations. From 2014 to 2016, the federal government will assist the states with payment of the newly eligible individuals. The CHIP program will maintain its existing coverage for children through 2015. It also simplifies enrollment for both individuals and families. The federal government will increase its payments to the states through 2019. Individuals will be able to enroll in these programs through the exchange and state websites. Community First Choice is an optional Medicaid benefit that focuses on community health services to Medicaid enrollees with disabilities. This will enable consumers to receive care at home or at community health centers rather than going to a hospital or their facility. This option became available on October 1, 2011 and provides a 6% increase in federal matching payments to states for expenditures related to this option (Medicaid.gov, 2013). These mandates will enable lower income consumers and children to have access to healthcare at an affordable cost.

There is an issue with the Medicare Part D coverage gap, more commonly known as the "donut hole" for Medicare Part D beneficiaries that this act should remedy. A typical beneficiary for Part D pays 25% of drug costs, including the deductible during the first part of the drug coverage phase. Once you reach the threshold of $2,830, the donut hole is activated, which means the beneficiary pays 100% of the drug costs until both the plan and beneficiary costs reach the maximum of $6,440. This maximum changes annually. Once this threshold is reached, which is called the catastrophic threshold limit, Medicare Part D will cover the costs of the drugs (approximately 95%), with the beneficiary paying $2.40 for generic drugs and $6.00 for brand drugs for the remainder of the year (Allsup, 2010). However, this donut hole restarts every year. This increase in beneficiary payout was very expensive for those enrolled and often resulted in individuals not obtaining necessary medication because of cost. In 2010, those beneficiaries that fall into the donut hole received a $250 rebate check from Medicare (Bihari, 2010). Since the passage of the ACA, 6.6 million Medicare enrollees who were impacted by the donut hole have saved over $7 billion on prescription drugs, which averages $1,061 per beneficiary. In addition to the $250 rebate check, those impacted received discounts and increased

coverage. They will continue to receive these benefits until the coverage gap is closed in 2020 (Centers for Medicare & Medicaid Services, 2013a).

Title III–Improving the Quality and Efficiency of Health Care

- The **Independent Payment Advisory Board** was established to develop quality improvement proposals
- Establishment of a **Patient-Centered Outcomes Research Institute**
- Creation of an **Independence at Home program**

Discussion

Medicare payments will be linked to the quality of care. Long-term care hospitals, rehabilitation services, cancer hospitals, and hospice providers will participate in quality performance measures. A federal interagency **Working Group on Healthcare Quality** was established to develop national initiatives on quality performance. They collaborate with other federal agencies to implement the National Quality Strategy developed by the U.S. Department of Health and Human Services. They convened in March and October 2011 to discuss the collaboration of federal agencies in the implementation of the national healthcare strategy (Agency for Healthcare Research and Quality, 2012). Also, a new **Center for Medicare and Medicaid Innovation** will research different payment and delivery systems. Effective 2012, hospital reimbursements will be based on the hospital's percentage of preventable Medicare readmissions of patients. **The Center for Medicare and Medicaid Innovation's** goal is to support the development and testing of innovative healthcare payment and service delivery models. They currently have 41 demonstration projects for payment and care models, including accountable care organizations, value-based purchasing, and coordinated and prevention care.

The 15-member Independent Payment Advisory Board will present to Congress proposals for cost savings and quality performance measures. This 15-member board, appointed by the President and confirmed by the Senate, will have the authority in 2014 to make recommendations to reduce Medicare spending, which will be implemented by the U.S. Department of Health and Human Services. This is the first time Congress has established a mechanism to set a cap on future Medicare spending (Moffitt, 2011).

The community health teams will increase access to community-based coordinated health care. Local healthcare providers will be encouraged to develop medication management services to assist with chronic disease management. These measures increase the efficiency and effectiveness of Medicare. Also, there is a continued focus on community health activities that reduce the cost of healthcare services.

The Patient-Centered Outcomes Research Institute (PCORI) will compare the outcomes of disease treatments. A nonprofit private organization established in 2010, the PCORI, is responsible for providing assistance to physicians, patients, and policy makers in improving health outcomes. They will perform research that targets quality and efficiency of care. A trust fund has been established to pay for the administration and research of the PCORI (Sullivan, 2012).

The Independence at Home program will provide Medicare beneficiaries with at-home primary care and allocate any cost savings of this type of care to the healthcare professionals if they reduce hospital admissions and improve health outcomes (American Association of Nurse Practitioners, 2010). This 3-year demonstration program, starting in January 2012, assesses home health care for Medicare beneficiaries who are chronically ill. Medical care is administered by a team of providers and is available 7 days a week around the clock. The goal of the program is to compare the cost of this type of care to hospital care of those Medicare beneficiaries who are chronically ill (Home Caregiver Services, 2012).

Title IV—Prevention of Chronic Disease and Improving Public Health

- The **National Prevention, Health Promotion, and Public Health Council** (National Prevention Council) is established to develop a national health prevention strategy.

- To waive copayments or cost sharing for most preventive services, Medicare will cover 100% of the total cost.

- Require Medicaid coverage for counseling and drug therapy for pregnant women for tobacco cessation and incentives for enrollees who participate in healthy lifestyles.

Discussion

The National Health Prevention, Health Promotion, and Public Health Council, commonly called the National Prevention Policy, published a report in 2011 that focused on six health priorities to improve the health of the United States. The National Prevention Council is an interagency council of 17 federal organizations chaired by the U.S. Surgeon General to promote health policies and assess infrastructures. The health priorities include: tobacco-free living, drug and alcohol prevention programs, injury and violence-free living, active lifestyle for all ages, mental and sexual health, and healthy eating. **The Prevention and Public Health Fund** was established to provide funding for public health programs. As of 2013, there is approximately $616 million to fund activities. Research indicates that these types of funding programs have the potential to improve health outcomes and reduce healthcare costs (American Public Health Association, 2013).

In addition, there will be no copayment for Medicare annual wellness visits and the development of a patient prevention program (discussed in Title II). Medicaid will also expand its coverage for prevention activities such as drug or tobacco cessation programs. There will be additional federal funding to Medicaid programs if they provide free immunizations or other clinical preventive services.

Title V—Healthcare Workforce

- Establish a **National Health Care Workforce Commission** to review healthcare workforce and projected needs.

- Develop programs to increase the supply of healthcare workers by training and education incentives.

- Develop a **Primary Care Extension Program (PCEP)** to educate and provide assistance to primary care providers about preventive medicine.

Discussion

A **National Health Care Workforce Commission** was developed to review workforce needs and make recommendations to the federal government to ensure that national policies are in alignment with consumer needs. As of January 2013, Congress had allocated funding for the commission, which is approximately $3 million.

As part of educational incentives to increase the workforce supply, the Nursing Student Loan Program will be expanded. Special loan programs will be implemented to providers who will be working in underserved areas. Workforce training will be provided to rural physicians, dentists, nurse practitioners in community health centers, and long-term care workers.

The Primary Care Extension Program (PCEP) will be established to provide technical assistance to primary care providers about health promotion, chronic disease management, mental health, and preventive medicine. These initiatives are focused on the emphasis of prevention and health promotion. However, as of 2013, there has been no funding allocated to this program. Family medicine groups have recommended annual funding of $120 million to administer the program. The PCEP would establish patient-centered medical homes by creating community-based Health Extension Agents. Their role would be to collaborate with local health agencies to identify community health priorities and determine the workforce needs for local areas (The Clinical Advisor, 2013).

Title VI–Transparency and Program Integrity

- The Department of Health and Human Services will publish standardized information on long-term care options for consumers so they can compare facilities.
- Establish a national system for direct patient access to employee background checks.
- Creation of a screening process for Medicare and Medicaid providers.
- **Elder Justice Act** was established to prevent and eliminate elder patient abuse.

Discussion

As the U.S. population is graying, many individuals may spend part of their lives in nursing homes. There will be continued enrollment in both Medicare and Medicaid. These mandates focus on the importance of providing information about long-term facilities to consumers so they can select the appropriate facility for their relative. This title also focuses on providing additional information about the quality of the care given at long-term facilities. There is also a screening mechanism to ensure that the providers of these services are providing quality care.

The Elder Justice bill was introduced in the Senate in 2003 and contained landmark initiatives in the development of a national policy to prevent elder abuse and neglect. The Elder Justice Act was finally passed as part of the ACA. It targets abuse, neglect, and exploitation of the elderly. There will also be incentives for employees who want to work at such facilities (Biancato, 2010). Funding was allocated to provide grants to study elder abuse. However, Congress did not award funding until 2012 for the activities associated with the act. In 2012, nearly $6 million in funding was awarded to implement Elder Justice Act activities in tribal organizations and programs in Texas, New York, Alaska, and California (Biancata, 2013).

Title VII–Improving Access to Innovative Medical Therapies

- The existing section 340B of the Public Health Service Act of 1992 will be expanded so there will be more affordable drugs for children and underserved community residents.

Discussion

The 340B section expansion will increase the allowance of more drug discounts for inpatient use at children's hospitals, cancer hospitals, critical care hospitals, and rural centers. This mandate increases the affordability for these patients who may need long-term care. Drug companies who participate in the Medicaid drug rebate program must sign pricing agreements for discounts on outpatient drugs purchased by qualified public health facilities. As of this writing, there are 14,500 facilities and 800 drug companies. The ACA will expand the participation to 5,000 additional facilities (Wakefield, 2010).

Title VIII–Community Living Assistance Services and Supports

- The establishment of the **CLASS Independence Benefit Plan**, which is a self-funded long term care insurance program for individuals with limited financial assistance.

Discussion

The CLASS Plan, effective January 1, 2011, enables consumers to purchase community living assistance.

Although supported by many community organizations, the Obama administration indicated it was not a viable program and the act was repealed on January 1, 2013 (The Arc, 2012).

Title IX–Revenue Provisions

- Requires employers to report on the employee's annual W-2 form the value of the health insurance benefit coverage provided by the employer. An excise tax will be levied on expensive employer health insurance plans.

- An annual flat fee is imposed on the branded prescription pharmaceutical companies and exporters, medical device manufacturing industry, and the health insurance providers, according to market share. Also, there is an excise tax on indoor tanning services.

- Establishment of a **cafeteria plan** for healthcare benefits to employees, which enables them to select different benefits based on current lifestyle.

Discussion

The requirement for employers to inform their employees about the cost of the health insurance benefit as well as report the cost on W-2 forms emphasizes transparency. The employer must report it accurately because it will be reported on a federal form. In addition, a 40% excise tax will be placed on expensive employer-sponsored health plans.

Annual pharmaceutical fees of approximately $2.5 billion will be applied to the drug manufacturing sector and are based on the market share of the U.S. drug market. This is allocated across the industry sector with some exclusions. The fees began in 2011. The fee component, for example, was $2.5 billion in 2011 and $2.8 billion in 2012. The fee will steadily rise to $4.1 billion in 2018 and will be $2.9 billion a year thereafter. These fees will cost the industry approximately $85 billion over a decade (Silverman, 2012). The same type of fee is applied to the health insurance industry in 2014. The fee will be $8 billion and will increase in years thereafter. It is important to note that these fees are nondeductible. A tax will be imposed on medical devices equal to 2.3% of the sales price and it is deductible. The fees and taxes will contribute to the operation of the healthcare reform mandates. Effective July 1, 2010, a 10% excise tax is imposed on indoor tanning services.

A cafeteria plan is a type of employer-sponsored benefit plan that allows employees to select the type of benefits appropriate for their lifestyle. This plan could benefit both employers and employees because not all employees need the same type of benefits. Although cafeteria plans can be difficult to administer, they can be more cost effective because employees have different healthcare needs and may require less healthcare insurance coverage in some instances.

Title X–Strengthening Quality Affordable Care

- Development of a **Physician Compare website**.

- Development of a **Nursing Home Compare website**.

- Development of a **Cures Acceleration Network**.

- Permanent legal authority for the **Indian Health Care Improvement Act (IHCIA)**, which provides health care to American Indians and Alaska Natives.

Discussion

Located on the Centers for Medicare and Medicaid Services (CMS) website, the Physician Compare website is established to help consumers with research about physicians who accept Medicare. It provides basic information about their address and contact information, education, languages spoken, gender, hospital affiliation, Medicare acceptance, and specialty (Medicare.gov, 2013a). Also located on the CMS website, a Nursing Home Compare website was developed as a tool for consumers to research all nursing homes in the United States that are Medicare and Medicaid certified. A consumer can review the inspection findings from the past 3 years of these facilities. There are also Hospital, Home Health, and Dialysis Compare software tools. (Medicare.gov, 2013b).

Also, the National Institute of Health is establishing the Cures Acceleration Network, which is a grants center to encourage research in the cure and treatment of diseases. All of these initiatives are targeting primary prevention, increasing consumer awareness of their health care and providing incentives for disease research. The National Institute of Health may award grants annually up to $15 million to research these priority areas. In fiscal year 2013, the priority area of research is improving drug safety and expanding drug usage for different diseases.

The Indian Healthcare Improvement Act, originally passed in 1979 and had no appropriations since 2000, was made permanent by the ACA. The improved act will authorize the establishment of comprehensive health services for American Indians and Alaskan Natives. The major goal of the act is to improve access and quality of care, including mental health services and alcohol and substance abuse programs to these targeted populations (U.S. Department of Health and Human Services, 2010).

CONCLUSION

The Patient Protection and Affordable Care Act of 2010, or Affordable Care Act, and its amendment have focused on primary care as the foundation for the U.S. healthcare system (Goodson, 2010). The legislation has focused on 10 areas to improve the U.S. healthcare system, including quality, affordable and efficient healthcare, public health and primary prevention of disease, healthcare workforce increases, community health, and increasing revenue provisions to pay for the reform. However, once the bill was signed, several states filed lawsuits. Several of these lawsuits argue that the act violates the Constitution because of the mandate of individual healthcare insurance coverage as well as infringes on state rights with the expansion of Medicaid (Arts, 2010). The 2012 U.S. Supreme Court Decision that supported the constitutionality of the individual mandates should decrease the number of lawsuits. Despite these lawsuits, this legislation has clearly provided opportunities to increase consumer empowerment of the healthcare system by establishing the state American Health Benefit Exchanges, providing insurance to those individuals with pre-existing conditions, eliminating lifetime and annual caps on health insurance payouts, improving the healthcare workforce, and providing databases so consumers can check the quality of their health care. The 10 titles of this comprehensive legislation are also focused on increasing the role of public health and primary care in the U.S. healthcare system and increasing accessibility to the system by providing affordable healthcare opportunities.

Although this legislation continues to be controversial, a system-wide effort needed to be implemented to curb rising healthcare costs. There are five areas of health care that account for a large percentage of healthcare costs: hospital care, physician and clinician services, prescription drugs, nursing, and home healthcare expenditures (Longest & Darr, 2008). The legislation targets these areas by increasing quality assurance and providing a system of reimbursement tied to quality performance, providing accessibility to consumers regarding the quality of their health care and increasing access to community health services. Also, the Affordable Care Act has focused on improving the U.S. public health system by increasing the accessibility to primary prevention services such as screenings and wellness visits at no cost. The ACA has mandated with no cost sharing to the healthcare consumer 15 preventive services for adults, 22 preventive services for women, 25 preventive services for children, and 23 preventive services for Medicare enrollee (Youdelman, 2013). There are revenue provisions in place to offset some of the costs of this legislation. However, there are still components of the Act, although authorized, that have not yet been funded. During a recent House of Representatives vote, a bill was passed that defunded the ACA. The Senate has indicated it will not pass the bill and President Obama will veto the bill. With continued controversy, it will be difficult to assess quickly how cost effective and how impactful this health reform will be on improving the health care of U.S. citizens.

VOCABULARY

Affordable Care Act (ACA)

Cafeteria plan

Centers for Consumer Information and Insurance Oversight

Center for Medicare and Medicaid Innovation

CLASS Independence Benefit Plan

Community First Choice

Consumer Operated and Oriented Plans (CO-OPs)

Cures Acceleration Network

Donut hole

Elder Justice Act

Essential Health Benefits (EHBs)

Health Insurance Marketplace

Healthcare and Education Affordability Reconciliation Act of 2010

Independence at Home program

Independent Payment Advisory Board

Indian Health Care Improvement Act (IHCIA)

Life qualifying event

National Health Care Workforce Commission

National Prevention, Health Promotion, and Public
Health Council

Nursing Home Compare website

Patient-Centered Outcomes Research Institute

Patient Protection and Affordable Care Act (PPACA)

Physician Compare website

Prevention and Public Health Fund

Primary Care Extension Program (PCEP)

Public Plan Option

Reinsurance Program

Small Business Health Options Program (SHOP)

Summary of Benefits and Coverage (SBC)

Working Group on Healthcare Quality

REFERENCES

Agency for Healthcare Research and Quality. (2012). National Strategy for Quality Improvement in Health Care: 2012 Annual Progress Report. Retrieved from http://www.ahrq.gov/workingforquality/nqs/nqs2012annlrpt.pdf

Allsup. (2010). Making the most of your Medicare coverage. Retrieved from http://www.allsup.com

American Association of Nurse Practitioners. (2010). Summary of new health reform law. Retrieved from http://www.aanp.org/NR

American Public Health Association. (2013, May). Get the facts: Prevention and Public Health Fund. Retrieved from http://www.apha.org/NR/rdonlyres/3060CA48-35E3-4F57-B1A5-CA1C1102090C/0/APHA_PPHF_factsheet_May2013.pdf

The Arc. (2012). Keeping the financing of long term services and supports a priority. Retrieved from http://insider.thearc.org/tag/community-living-assistance-services-and-supports-class

Arts, K. (2010). Legal challenges to health reform: An alliance for health reform toolkit. Retrieved from http://www.allhealth.org/publications/Uninsured/Legal_Challenges_to_New_Health_Reform_Law_97.pdf

Bihari, M. (2010). Understanding the Medicare Part D donut hole. Retrieved from http://healthinsurance.about.com/od/medicare/a/understanding_part_d.htm?p=1

Blancato, R. (2010). Elder Justice: A Congressional approach to a national problem. Retrieved from http://www.elderjusticecoalition.com/docs/Bob_Sept_speech.doc

Blancato, R. (2013). Health policy and promoting awareness: The Elder Justice Act. Power Point presentation, April 18, 2013, at Institute of Medicine. Retrieved from http://www.iom.edu/~/media/Files/Activity%20Files/Global/ViolenceForum/2013-APR-17/Presentations/02-14-Blancato.pdf

Centers for Medicare & Medicaid Services. (2013a). Details for title: On eve of Medicare anniversary, over 6.6 million seniors save over $7 billion on drugs. Retrieved from http://cms.gov/Newsroom/MediaReleaseDatabase/Press-Releases/2013-Press-Releases-Items/2013-07-29.html

Centers for Medicare & Medicaid Services. (2013b). Ensuring the Affordable Care Act serves the American people. Retrieved from http://www.cms.gov/cciio/index.html

Centers for Medicare & Medicaid Services. (2013c). Timeline of the health care law. Retrieved from http://www.healthcare.gov/timeline-of-the-health-care-law

Centers for Medicare & Medicaid Services. (2013d). What does marketplace health insurance cover? Retrieved from https://www.healthcare.gov/what-does-marketplace-health-insurance-cover

Centers for Medicare & Medicaid Services. (2013e). What if someone doesn't have health insurance coverage? Retrieved from https://www.healthcare.gov/what-if-someone-doesnt-have-health-coverage-in-2014

The Clinical Advisor. (2013). Family medicine group recommends funding Primary Care Extension Program.

Goodson, J. (2010). Patient Protection and Affordable Care Act: Promise and peril for primary care. Retrieved from http://www.annals.org/content/early/2010/04/15/0003-4819-152-11-201006010-00249.full

Health Affairs. (2013). Health policy briefs: The co-op health insurance program. Retrieved from http://www .healthaffairs.org/healthpolicybriefs/brief.php?brief_id=87

Home Caregiver Services. (2012). Doctors making house calls coming back. Retrieved from http://www.homecare giverservices.com/doctors-making-house-calls-coming-back

Longest, Jr., B., & Darr, K. (2008). *Managing health services organizations and systems*. Baltimore: Health Professions Press.

Medicaid.gov. (2013). Community first choice. Retrieved from http://www.medicaid.gov/Medicaid-CHIP-Program -Information/By-Topics/Long-Term-Services-and-Support/Home-and-Community-Based-Services/Community -First-Choice-1915-k.html

Medicare.gov. (2013a). About physician compare. Retrieved from http://www.medicare.gov/find-a-doctor/static pages/about/Physician-Compare-Information.aspx

Medicare.gov. (2013b). Nursing home compare, Retrieved from http://www.medicare.gov/nursinghomecompare

Moffitt, R. (2011). Obamacare and the Independent Payment Advisory Board: Falling short of real Medicare reform. Retrieved from http://www.heritage.org/research/reports/2011/01/obamacare-and-the-independent-payment -advisory-board-falling-short-of-real-medicare-reform

Office of Inspector General. (2013). Early implementation of the consumer operated and oriented plan loan program Retrieved from https://oig.hhs.gov/oei/reports/oei-01-12-00290.asp

ProCon.org. (2013a). Constitutional challenges to Obamacare: Patient Protection and Affordable Care Act (PPACA) in the courts. Retrieved from http://healthcarereform.procon.org/view.resource.php?resourceID=004134

ProCon.org. (2013b). Did you know? Retrieved from http://healthcarereform.procon.org/view.resource.php? resourceID=003726

Retrieved from http://www.clinicaladvisor.com/family-medicine-group-recommends-funding-primary-care -extension-program/article/286469

Silverman, E. (2012). What the Supreme Court ruling means to big pharma. Retrieved from http://www.forbes.com /sites/edsilverman/2012/06/28/what-the-supreme-court-ruling-means-for-pharma

Sullivan, S. (2012). First PCORI fees due July 31, 2013 for most health plans. Retrieved from http://www.erisa exchangeblog.com/2013/03/18/first-pcori-fees-due-july-31-2013-for-most-health-plans

Swendiman, K., & Baumrucker, E. (2012). Congressional Research Service Memorandum. Selected issues related to the effect of *NFIB vs. Sebelius* on the Medicaid expansion requirements in Section 201 of the Affordable Care Act. Retrieved from http://www.ncsl.org/documents/health/aca_medicaid_expansion_memo_1.pdf

U.S. Department of Health and Human Services. (2010). Indian Healthcare Improvement Act made permanent (IHCIA). Retrieved from http://www.hhs.gov/news/press/2010pres/03/20100326a.html

U.S. Department of Labor. (2010). Young adults and the Affordable Care Act: Protecting young adults and eliminating burdens on families and businesses. Retrieved from http://www.dol.gov/ebsa/newsroom/fsdependentcoverage .html

U.S. General Accountability Office (GAO). (2012a). Small employer health tax credit: Factors contributing to low use and complexity. Retrieved from http://www.gao.gov/products/GAO-12-549

United Health Care. (2013). Health benefit exchanges. Retrieved from http://www.uhc.com/united_for_reform _resource_center/health_reform_provisions/health_benefit_exchanges.htm

Wakefield, M. (2010). Remarks to the 35th National Primary Care Nurse Practitioner Symposium. Retrieved from http://www.hrsa.gov/about/news/speeches/2010/071610npsymposium.html

Youdelman, M. (2013). Health Advocate: Countdown to open enrollment 2013. Retrieved from http://healthlaw .org/images/stories/2013_09_Vol_17_Health_Advocate.pdf

NOTES

STUDENT ACTIVITY 2-1

IN YOUR OWN WORDS

Based on this chapter, please provide an explanation of the following concepts in your own words. DO NOT RECITE the text.

American Health Benefit Exchanges: _____

_____

_____

Community First Choice: _____

_____

_____

Consumer Operated and Oriented Plan: _____

_____

_____

Elder Justice Act: _____

_____

_____

Independent Payment Advisory Board: _____

_____

_____

National Health Care Workforce Commission: _____

_____

_____

Nursing Home Compare website: _____

_____

_____

Physician Compare website: _____

_____

_____

Primary Care Extension Program: _____

_____

_____

Reinsurance Program: _____

_____

_____

STUDENT ACTIVITY 2-2

Complete the following case scenarios based on the information provided in the chapter. Your answer must be IN YOUR OWN WORDS.

REAL LIFE APPLICATIONS: CASE SCENARIO ONE

Your mother has a chronic healthcare condition that requires many visits to her healthcare provider. She recently changed jobs, which will require your family to move to a new state. She is also afraid that she will not receive healthcare insurance from her new company and is worried about finding a new provider to take care of her.

ACTIVITY

Explain to her about the new healthcare reform bill and how that will impact her situation.

RESPONSES

_____

_____

_____

_____

_____

_____

_____

_____

_____

_____

_____

_____

_____

_____

CASE SCENARIO TWO

You have two elderly relatives who you think are not being treated well by their nursing home. You are not sure what to do. You speak to your parents about it and they suggest you research the www.healthcare.gov website about this issue. They know there are some mandates in the ACA regarding elderly care.

ACTIVITY

Visit the www.healthcare.gov website and perform research regarding the Elder Justice Act to determine if there are any solutions to this problem.

RESPONSES

_____

_____

_____

_____

_____

_____

_____

_____

_____

_____

_____

_____

_____

_____

CASE SCENARIO THREE

Your mother is turning 55 and is being downsized from her job. She has yet to find another job. She has COBRA benefits for a certain period of time but is not sure what to do after. She is too young for Medicare.

ACTIVITY

Visit the www.healthcare.gov website to determine if there are any options for her to purchase health insurance.

RESPONSES

_____

_____

_____

_____

_____

_____

_____

_____

_____

_____

_____

_____

_____

CASE SCENARIO FOUR

You work for a healthcare facility that would like to apply for a grant to develop new ways to improve the quality of its health care.

ACTIVITY

Visit the Innovation Center on the www.cms.gov website. Develop a report on possible grants available for your healthcare facility.

RESPONSES

_____

_____

_____

_____

_____

_____

_____

_____

_____

_____

_____

_____

_____

_____

_____

_____

STUDENT ACTIVITY 2-3

INTERNET EXERCISES

Write your answers in the space provided.

- Visit each of the websites listed here.
- Name the organization.
- Locate their mission statement on their website.
- Provide a brief overview of the activities of the organization.
- How do these organizations participate in the U.S. healthcare system?

Websites

http://www.healthcare.gov

Organization Name: _____

Mission Statement:

_____

_____

_____

Overview of Activities: _____

_____

_____

Importance of organization to U.S. health care:

_____

_____

_____

_____

http://www.allhealth.org

Organization Name: _____

Mission Statement:

_____

_____

_____

Overview of Activities: _____

_____

_____

Importance of organization to U.S. health care:

_____

_____

_____

http://www.pnhp.org

Organization Name: _____

Mission Statement:

_____

_____

_____

Overview of Activities: _____

_____

_____

Importance of organization to U.S. health care:

_____

_____

_____

http://www.ahip.org

Organization Name: _____

Mission Statement:

_____

_____

_____

Overview of Activities: _____

_____

_____

Importance of organization to U.S. health care:

_____

_____

_____

http://www.hfma.org

Organization Name: _____

Mission Statement:

_____

_____

_____

Overview of Activities: _____

_____

_____

Importance of organization to U.S. health care:

_____

_____

_____

http://www.acep.org

Organization Name: _____

Mission Statement:

_____

_____

_____

Overview of Activities: _____

_____

_____

Importance of organization to U.S. health care:

_____

_____

_____

STUDENT ACTIVITY 2-4

DISCUSSION QUESTIONS

The following are suggested discussion questions for this chapter.

(1) Select three initiatives of the Affordable Care Act in any of the ten title areas that you feel are important to improving our healthcare system. Defend your answer.

_____

_____

_____

_____

(2) Do you feel that the mandate for individual health insurance coverage is constitutional? Defend your answer.

_____

_____

_____

_____

(3) What do you think of the Nursing Home Compare and Physician Compare websites? Do you think they provide valuable information for consumers to support these important healthcare decisions?

_____

_____

_____

_____

(4) Go to the website http://www.heatlhcare.gov and locate the new Patient Bill of Rights. Discuss five rights that are of interest to you and why.

_____

_____

_____

_____

(5) What is a cafeteria plan? Do you think this is an effective way to provide health insurance benefits to employees? Perform an Internet search and locate a company that provides a cafeteria plan and report back to the discussion board on what they offer.

_____

_____

_____

_____

The Navigate Companion Website for this text is a great source for additional information on the U.S. healthcare system. You can gain a new perspective on many of the topics presented in this chapter by visiting http://go.jblearning.com/Niles2e. You'll find additional student activities, further reading, and interactive study tools that explore:

• Major Affordable Care Act initiatives
• Implementation of individual health insurance coverage mandate
• Role of Medicare and Medicaid in Affordable Care Act implementation
• And much more.

Chapter 3

Current Operations of the Healthcare System

LEARNING OBJECTIVES

The student will be able to:

- Identify the stakeholders of the U.S. healthcare system and their relationships with each other.
- Discuss the importance of healthcare statistics.
- Compare the United States to five other countries using different health statistics.
- List at least five current statistics regarding the U.S. healthcare system.
- Discuss complementary and alternative medicine and its role in health care.
- Define OECD and its importance to international health care.

DID YOU KNOW THAT?

- The healthcare industry employs approximately 18 million individuals with a projected 3.2 million new jobs by 2018.
- Most healthcare workers have jobs that do not require a 4-year college degree but health diagnostic and treatment providers are the most educated workers in the United States.
- Healthcare employment is found predominantly in large states such as California, New York, Texas, and Florida.

- Working full-time increases the likelihood of having health insurance, although one in seven full-time workers are uninsured.
- The healthcare industry and social assistance industry reported more work-related injuries than any other private industry.
- Life expectancy rates are an indication of the health of a population.

INTRODUCTION

The one commonality with all of the world's healthcare systems is that they all have consumers or users of their systems. Systems were developed to provide a service to their citizens. However, the U.S. healthcare system, unlike other systems in the world, does not provide healthcare access to all of its citizens. It is a very complex system that is comprised of many public and private components. Healthcare expenditures comprise approximately 17.6% of the **gross domestic product (GDP)**. Healthcare costs are very expensive and most citizens do not have the money to pay for health care themselves. Individuals rely on health insurance to pay a large portion of their healthcare costs. Health insurance is predominantly offered by employers. According to a 2011 Centers for Disease Control and Prevention (CDC) survey, there were nearly 48.2 million uninsured people in the United States, as well as approximately 29 million who were underinsured, which means their health insurance did not adequately cover their medical expenses. It will be interesting to assess the impact of the Affordable Care Act (ACA) on this statistic because a major focus is individual insurance coverage nationwide. The ACA projects there will be a decrease of nearly 70% in these statistics when the ACA is fully implemented (Science Daily, 2013). In the United States, in order to provide healthcare services, there are several **stakeholders** or interested entities that participate in the industry. There are providers, of course, that consist of trained professionals such as physicians, nurses, dentists, and chiropractors. There are also inpatient and outpatient facilities; the payers such as the insurance companies, the government, and self-pay individuals; and the suppliers of products such as pharmaceutical companies, medical equipment companies, and the research and educational facilities (Sultz & Young, 2006). Each component plays an integral role in the healthcare industry. These different components further emphasize the complexity of the U.S. system. The current operations of the delivery system and utilization statistics will be discussed in depth in this chapter. An international comparison of the U.S. healthcare system and select country systems will also be discussed in this chapter, which provides another aspect of analyzing the U.S. healthcare system.

OVERVIEW OF THE CURRENT SYSTEM

As of 2011, the healthcare industry provided over 14 million jobs and is expected to generate over 3 million wage and salary jobs by 2018 (Bureau of Labor Statistics [BLS], 2013a). The United States spends the highest proportion of its GDP on healthcare expenditures. The system is a combination of private and public resources. Since World War II, the United States has had a private fee-for-service system that has produced generous incomes for physicians and has been profitable for many participants in the healthcare industry (Jonas, 2003). The healthcare industry operates like traditional business industries. For those organizations designated as for-profit, they need to make money in order to operate. For those entities that are designated not-for-profit, their main goal is based on a particular social goal, but they also have to make money in order to continue their operations.

There are several major stakeholders that participate or have an interest in the industry. The stakeholders identified as participants in the healthcare industry include: consumers, employers, healthcare and non healthcare employers, healthcare providers, healthcare facilities, government (federal, state, local), insurance companies, educational and training institutions, professional associations that represent the different stakeholders, pharmaceutical companies, and research institutions. It is also important to mention the increasing prominence of alternative therapy medicine. Each role will be discussed briefly.

MAJOR STAKEHOLDERS IN THE HEALTHCARE INDUSTRY

Consumers

The main group of consumers is patients who need healthcare services either from a physician, hospital, or outpatient facility. From an organizational perspective, the consumer is the most important stakeholder for an organization. The healthcare industry operates like a business. If a consumer has the means to pay out-of-pocket, from government sources, or from health insurance, the services will be provided. If an individual does not have the means to pay from any of these sources of funding, a service may not be provided. There is a principle of the U.S. healthcare system, **duty to treat**, which means that any person deserves basic care (Pointer et al., 2007). In some instances, healthcare providers will give care to someone who has no funding source and designate the care provided as a **charitable care or bad debt**, which means the provider either does not expect payment after the person's inability to pay has been determined or efforts to secure the payment have failed (Smith, 2008). Businesses also take the same action. Many of them provide a community service or donate funds to a charitable cause, yet both traditional businesses and healthcare organizations need to charge for their services in order to continue their operations.

There are also other consumer relationships in the healthcare industry. Consumers purchase drugs either from their provider or over the counter from pharmacies. The pharmaceutical companies market their products to physicians who in turn prescribe their products to their patients. The pharmaceutical companies also market their products to hospitals and outpatient facilities to encourage the use of their drugs in these facilities. Medical equipment companies also sell their products to facilities and individual providers.

Employers

Employers consist of both private and public employers. The healthcare industry is the largest U.S. employer. According to the **Bureau of Labor Statistics (BLS)**, there are several segments of the healthcare industry, including ambulatory healthcare services, hospitals, and nursing and residential care facilities. Ambulatory healthcare services are comprised of physicians, dentists, other health practitioners, outpatient care centers, medical and diagnostic laboratories, home healthcare services, and other ambulatory care The hospital segment provides inpatient services primarily with outpatient as a secondary source. It provides general and surgical care, psychiatric substance abuse hospitals, and other specialty hospitals. Residential care facilities include nursing care, mental health, substance abuse and mental disabilities, community care for the elderly, and other residential care facilities (BLS, 2013a). Healthcare employment opportunities can be more easily found in large states such as California, New York, Texas, and Florida (BLS, 2013a). Employers outside the healthcare industry are also stakeholders because they provide a large percentage of health insurance coverage to individuals nationwide.

Hospitals

There are approximately 11,000 hospitals across the United States. Hospitals provide total medical care that ranges from diagnostic services to surgery and continuous nursing care. They traditionally provide inpatient care, although more hospital systems are also providing outpatient care. Some hospitals specialize in treatments for cancer, children's health, and mental health. It is important to note that hospitals are an integral component of the healthcare system. Many of the uninsured and underinsured present themselves at emergency departments (EDs) across the country and use EDs as their primary care provider. In 2011, more than 118 million individuals presented themselves to the emergency department as their entry into health care. During times of public health crises, hospitals are the backbone of providing care. In 2011, hospitals provided $41.1 billion in uncompensated care; an increase of $1.8 billion from 2010 (American Hospital Association, 2013).

Nursing and Residential Care Facilities

These types of facilities provide nursing, rehabilitation, and health-related personal care to those who need ongoing care. There are 73,000 facilities nationwide.

Nursing aides provide the majority of care. **Residential care facilities** provide around-the-clock social and personal care to the elderly, children, and others who cannot take care of themselves. Examples of residential care facilities are drug rehabilitation centers, group homes, and assisted living facilities (BLS, 2013b).

Physicians and Other Healthcare Practitioners

In 2010, there were nearly 700,000 U.S. physicians. Physicians traditionally practice solo, but more often physicians are practicing in a group practice to reduce administrative costs. In 2010, there were 156,000 dentists. Job outlook for both physicians and dentists is very positive due to the aging of the U.S. population. Other healthcare practitioners include chiropractors, optometrists, psychologists, therapists, and alternative medicine practitioners (BLS, 2013c).

Alternative health or **complementary and alternative medicine (CAM)** practitioners who practice unconventional health therapies such as yoga, vitamin therapy, and spiritual healing are being sought out by consumers who have to pay out-of-pocket for these services because they are currently not covered by health insurance companies. However, chiropractors and acupuncturists who are also considered alternative medicine practitioners are more likely to be covered by health insurance companies. Recognizing consumer interest in this type of medicine, in 1998, as part of the National Institute of Health, the **National Center for Complementary and Alternative Medicine (NCCAM)** was established. Its purpose was to explore these types of practices in the context of rigorous science, train complementary and alternative researchers, and disseminate information. More medical schools are now offering some courses in alternative medicine. In the United States, nearly 40% of adults (about 4 in 10) and over 10% of children (about 1 in 9) are using some form of CAM. Adults are most likely to use CAM for musculoskeletal problems such as back, neck, or joint pain (National Center for Health Statistics, 2013).

Home Healthcare Services

Home healthcare services, which offer medical care in the home, are provided primarily to the elderly, chronically ill, and mentally impaired. Mobile medical technology allows for more home health care for medical problems. Home health care is one of the fastest growing components of the industry as a form of employment because of consumer preference and the cost effectiveness of home medical care (BLS, 2013d).

Outpatient Care Centers and Ambulatory Healthcare Services

Outpatient care centers include kidney dialysis centers, mental health and substance abuse clinics, and surgical and emergency centers. Ambulatory healthcare services include transport services, blood and organ banks, and smoking cessation programs (BLS, 2013e).

Laboratories

Medical and diagnostic laboratories provide support services to the medical profession. Workers may take blood, take scans or X-rays, or perform other medical tests. This segment provides the fewest number of jobs in the industry (BLS, 2013f).

Government

As a result of the Medicare and Medicaid government programs, the federal and state governments are the largest stakeholders in the U.S. healthcare system. The government at both levels is responsible for financing health care through these programs as well as playing the public provider role through state and local health departments. Veterans' Affairs medical facilities also provide services to those in the armed forces (Sultz & Young, 2006).

Insurance Companies

The insurance industry is also a major stakeholder in the healthcare industry. It is often blamed for the problems with the healthcare system because of the millions that are underinsured and uninsured. There have been many news reports highlighting the number of medical procedures that have been disproved for insurance coverage, the cost of health insurance coverage, etc. There are traditional indemnity plans such as **Blue Cross and Blue Shield,** but managed care, which is also considered an insurance plan, has become more popular for cost control. The Affordable Care Act has placed restrictions on what health insurance companies can do regarding reimbursement restrictions.

Educational and Training Organizations

Educational and training facilities such as medical schools, nursing schools, public health schools, and allied health programs play an important role in the U.S. healthcare industry because they are responsible for the education and training of healthcare employees. These institutions help formulate behaviors of the healthcare workforce.

Research Organizations

Government research organizations such as the National Institutes of Health (NIH) and the CDC not only provide regulatory guidance but also perform research activities to improve health care. However, there are also private research organizations such as the **Robert Wood Johnson Foundation**, the **Pew Charitable Trusts**, and the **Commonwealth Fund** that support research efforts through grants.

Professional Associations

Professional associations play an important role in healthcare policy. There are associations that represent physicians, nurses, hospitals, long-term care facilities, etc. Most healthcare stakeholders are represented by a professional organization that guides them regarding their role in the healthcare industry. They also play a large role in government regulations because they often lobby at all government levels to protect their constituents. The following are examples of professional associations that represent some of the major stakeholder organizations in this industry.

- **American Hospital Association (AHA):** The AHA is the most prominent association for all types of hospitals and healthcare networks. Founded in 1898, the AHA, which is a membership organization, provides education and lobbies for hospital representation in the political process at all governmental levels (AHA, 2013).

- **American Health Care Association (AHCA):** Founded in 1949, the AHCA is a membership organization that represents not-for-profit and for-profit nursing, assisted living, developmentally disabled, and subacute providers. Their focus is to monitor and improve standards of nursing home facilities (AHCA, 2013).

- **American Association of Homes and Services for the Aging (AAHSA):** The AAHSA, which is a membership organization, represents not-for-profit adult day care services, home healthcare services, community services, senior housing, assisted living facilities, continuous care retirement communities, and nursing homes. It lobbies all government levels regarding legislation that can impact their industry and provides technical assistance for these organizations (AAHSA, 2013).

Pharmaceutical Companies

A functioning healthcare system needs medicine that is prescribed by a provider or is purchased as an over-the-counter medicine from a pharmacy. The pharmaceutical industry is integral to the success of a healthcare system. Innovative drugs have improved people's quality of life. There has been an internal division within the pharmaceutical industry between the manufacturing of **brand name drugs** and generic or 'me too' drugs. A **generic drug**, which does not have name recognition, is a less costly alternative to a brand name drug. The generic drug manufacturer must provide the same active ingredients as the brand name drugs, however, the approval process is less costly to manufacture. A generic drug has no patent protection and is sold at discounted prices (Zhong, 2012).

Brand name drugs such as Lipitor and Viagra are typically more expensive than generic drugs because it costs a pharma company over $1 billion over several years to develop. In 2012, pharmaceutical companies spent $48.5 billion in researching new brand name drugs. The Food and Drug Administration, which is responsible for approving the drug for human use, has a very strict and lengthy approval process. Once approved, a pharma company has up to 14 years of patent protection of the name. Once that protection has ended, there are more opportunities for generic drug companies to control the market (Zhong, 2012).

Like health insurance companies, the pharmaceutical industry is often vilified because of the cost of some prescribed medicines that often preclude any consumers from purchasing these medications themselves without health insurance assistance. The industry's response is that it takes millions of dollars and years of research to develop an effective medicine and that is a major reason why some medicines cost so much. The pharmaceutical industry is represented by the **Pharmaceutical Research and Manufacturers of America (PhRMA)** (PhRMA, 2013).

STAKEHOLDERS' ENVIRONMENT

Working Conditions

Healthcare workers have many varied opportunities for workplace settings. Hospitals are a typical work environment, as are physician offices. As outpatient services have become more popular, healthcare professionals can work from their homes. Healthcare professionals can work in outpatient facilities, schools, laboratories, corporations, and other unconventional settings. They are exposed to serious health hazards, including contaminated blood, chemicals, drugs, and X-ray hazards. Depending on the job, there may be ergonomic issues due to heavy lifting of patients and equipment. This industry has one of the highest injury and illness rates. In 2010, the healthcare and social assistance industry reported more injury and illness cases than any other private industry sector—653,900 cases, which is 152,000 more cases than the next industry sector, manufacturing. In 2010, the incidence rate for work-related injuries and illness in health care was 139.9; the incidence rate for injury and illness in all private industry was 107.7.

Nursing aides, orderlies, and attendants had the highest rates of physiological disorders of all occupations in 2010. The incidence rate of work-related physiological disorders for these occupations was 249 per 10,000 workers. This compares to the average rate for all workers in 2010 of 34 (U.S. Department of Labor, 2013).

Projected Outlook for Employment

The healthcare industry's employment outlook is positive. It is anticipated that there will be over 3 million new wage and salary jobs generated by 2018, which is more than any other industry (BLS, 2013a). Growth will most likely be outside the inpatient hospital centers because cost containment is the major priority for health care. Health care will continue to grow for three major reasons: the aging of the U.S. population, advances in medical technology, and the increased focus on outpatient care.

HEALTHCARE STATISTICS

U.S. Healthcare Utilization Statistics

The **National Center for Health Statistics (NCHS)**, which is part of the CDC, produces an annual report on the health status of the United States. This publication, *Health, United States, 2012*, provides an overview of healthcare utilization, resources, and expenditures. This publication examines all different aspects of the U.S. healthcare delivery system as well as assessing the health status of U.S. citizens. The following information was summarized from this publication.

U.S. Demographics and Healthcare

Life expectancy rates are an indication of the health of a designated population. From 1980 to 2008, the life expectancy at birth increased from 70 to 76 years for males and 77 to 81 years for females. Racial disparities exist for life expectancy at birth for both genders but have narrowed since 1990. In 2008, Hispanic males and females had a longer life expectancy than non-Hispanic white or non-Hispanic black females and males (CDC, 2012a).

Access to Health Care

Health insurance is a major reason for healthcare access. In 2010, 42.5 million adults (18–64 years of age) had no health insurance coverage. Among adults 18–44 years old, the percentage with private health insurance decreased from 71% in 2000 to 61% in 2010. The percentage of that age group that was uninsured increased from 22% to 27%. Adults 45–64 years of age also experienced a decline in private insurance coverage from 79% to 71%. (CDC, 2012b)

The percentage of those that were uninsured increased from 13% to 16%. In 2009–2010, data indicate that as income level increased, routinely going for needed medical care increased. For example, Hispanic data indicate that 8% of those individuals living at 400% above the poverty level did not go for health care. White data indicates that 7% with the same income level as the Hispanic data did not go: black was 9% and Asian was 4%. As the income level dropped, there was a huge increase in the percentage that did not go to the doctor because of cost. Below 100% of the poverty level, the percentage was 21% for Hispanics, 27% for whites, 24% for blacks and 16% for Asians. Due to the impact of the ACA, the percentage of uninsured for both age groups should decrease due to the health insurance mandates (CDC, 2012c).

Access to healthcare services varies across the country. In 2009, there was an average of 25 physicians per 10,000 population. The New England states, Mid-Atlantic states, Washington, D.C., Hawaii, and Minnesota had the highest ratio. The southern part of the United States, and mountain states including Iowa and Indiana, has the lowest ratio. Massachusetts has the highest ratio and Mississippi has the lowest ratio (CDC, 2012d).

Healthcare Resources

The United States spends more on health **per capita** or per person than any other country worldwide. In 2009, the total expenditure on health per capita was approximately $8,000. In 2009, national healthcare expenditures totaled $2.5 trillion—an increase of 4%. In 2010, hospital spending accounted for nearly 36% of personal

healthcare expenditures, prescription drugs accounted for 12%, 24% on physician care, and 7% on nursing care and continuing care communities. In 2010, private health insurance paid 46.4% of total personal health care, the federal government 34%, state and local governments 11%, and out-of-pocket payments were 15% (CDC, 2012d).

U.S. and International Comparison of Health Statistics

Established in 1961, the **Organisation for Economic Cooperation and Development (OECD)** is a membership organization that provides comparable statistics of economic and social data worldwide and monitors trends of economic development. There are currently 34 countries, including the United States, that are members of this organization. Their budget is derived from the member countries, of which the United States contributes 25% of the budget. The OECD produces, on a continual basis, a health data set of the 34 member countries (OECD, 2013). The following are highlights from the 2005–2010 U.S. health data.

Health indicators such as infant mortality rates, average life expectancy, and health risk behaviors are used to evaluate the health status of a population. Because the United States spends the highest per capita on health care in the world, it is expected that United States health indicators would rank superior to all other countries' healthcare indicators.

2005–2010 Health Expenditures as a Percentage of the Gross Domestic Product (Table 3-1, pages 59–60)

In 2010, the United States spent 17.6% of its GDP on health care, which is the highest of the 30 OECD members. The U.S. percentage has increased from 15.8% in 2005. The Netherlands, Germany, and France were the next three highest percentages with 12%, 11.6%, and 11.6%, respectively. Turkey, Mexico, and Estonia spent the least amount of their GDP of the 30 countries. The percentages in 2010 were 6.1%, 6.2%, and 6.3% respectively. All of these countries experienced an increase during the 6-year period.

2005–2010 Total Expenditures on Health/ Per Capita (Table 3-2, pages 60–61)

The United States also spends per capita the most in relation to their member countries. In 2005, the United States spent $6,728 with an increase to $8,233

TABLE 3-1	2005–2010 Health Expenditures as a Percentage of the Gross Domestic Product					
	2005	**2006**	**2007**	**2008**	**2009**	**2010**
Australia	8.4	8.5	8.5	8.7	9.1	8.9
Austria	10.4	10.2	10.3	10.5	11.2	11.0
Belgium[1]	10.1	9.6	9.6	10.0	10.7	10.5
Canada	9.8	10.0	10.0	10.3	11.4	11.4
Chile	6.9	6.6	6.9	7.5	8.4	8.0
Czech Republic	6.9	6.7	6.5	6.8	8.0	7.5
Denmark	9.8	9.9	10.0	10.2	11.5	11.1
Estonia	5.0	5.0	5.2	6.0	7.0	6.3
Finland	8.4	8.3	8.0	8.3	9.2	8.9
France	11.2	11.1	11.1	11.0	11.7	11.6
Germany	10.8	10.6	10.5	10.7	11.7	11.6
Greece	9.7	9.7	9.8	10.1	10.6	10.2
Hungary	8.4	8.3	7.7	7.5	7.7	7.8
Iceland	9.4	9.1	9.1	9.1	9.6	9.3
Ireland	7.6	7.6	7.8	8.9	9.9	9.2
Israel	7.8	7.5	7.5	7.6	7.5	7.5
Italy	8.9	9.0	8.6	8.9	9.3	9.3
Japan	8.2	8.2	8.2	8.6	9.5	9.5
Korea	5.7	6.0	6.3	6.5	6.9	7.1
Luxembourg	7.9	7.7	7.1	6.8	7.9	7.9
Mexico	5.9	5.7	5.8	5.8	6.4	6.2
Netherlands	9.8	9.7	10.8	11.0	11.9	12.0
New Zealand	8.4	8.8	8.5	9.3	10.0	10.1
Norway	9.0	8.6	8.7	8.6	9.8	9.4
Poland	6.2	6.2	6.3	6.9	7.2	7.0
Portugal	10.4	10.0	10.0	10.2	10.8	10.7
Slovak Republic	7.0	7.3	7.8	8.0	9.2	9.0
Slovenia	8.3	8.3	7.8	8.3	9.3	9.0
Spain	8.3	8.4	8.5	8.9	9.6	9.6
Sweden	9.1	8.9	8.9	9.2	9.9	9.6

(continues)

TABLE 3-1	2005–2010 Health Expenditures as a Percentage of the Gross Domestic Product (*continued*)

	2005	2006	2007	2008	2009	2010
Switzerland	11.2	10.8	10.6	10.7	11.4	11.4
Turkey	5.4	5.8	6.0	6.1	6.1	6.1
United Kingdom	8.2	8.5	8.5	8.8	9.8	9.6
United States	15.8	15.9	16.2	16.6	17.7	17.6
OECD AVERAGE						

[1] Excluding investments

Source: Data taken from OECD Health Data 2012: http://stats.oecd.org/Index.aspx?DataSetCode=SHA

TABLE 3-2	2005–2010 Total Expenditures on Health Per Capita

	2005	2006	2007	2008	2009	2010
Australia	2979.6	3163.7	3350.8	3451.9	3670.2	3670
Austria	3503.4	3737.9	3907	4173.1	4346.3	4394.8
Belgium[1]	3246.8	3277.6	3423.3	3698.4	3911.4	3968.8
Canada	3448.1	3674	3849.8	4002.4	4316.9	4444.9
Chile	842.6	863.2	958.1	1093.8	1209.7	1202.2
Czech Republic	1474.5	1557.1	1658.7	1765	2048.3	1883.5
Denmark	3243	3577.4	3766.5	4055.9	4384.9	4463.9
Estonia	831.3	961.5	1114.4	1336.8	1385.4	1293.8
Finland	2588.5	2765.5	2908.9	3161.8	3270.5	3250.9
France	3294	3483.9	3667.3	3749.6	3930.2	3974
Germany	3362.1	3566.5	3722.3	3967.2	4225.1	4338.4
Greece	2352.5	2609.6	2723.2	2997.9	3106.4	2913.7
Hungary	1433.6	1511.2	1452.9	1524.7	1559.3	1600.5
Iceland	3304.2	3271.1	3379.4	3606	3538.7	3309.3
Ireland	2955.7	3217.1	3532.9	3805.6	3944.1	3718.2
Israel	1829.3	1873.4	1994.4	2100.2	2071.1	2071
Italy	2516.1	2727	2769	2967.3	3004.7	2963.7

TABLE 3-2	2005–2010 Total Expenditures on Health/Per Capita (continued)					
	2005	**2006**	**2007**	**2008**	**2009**	**2010**
Japan	2490.8	2606.9	2746.2	2877.6	3034.6	3035
Korea	1290.6	1466.3	1644.9	1723.5	1863.9	2035.4
Luxembourg	4151.9	4605.6	4492.7	4444.9	4786	4786
Mexico	730.8	780.1	836.1	891.8	923	915.7
Netherlands²	3450.3	3701.9	4410.2	4728.5	4886.2	5056.2
New Zealand	2124.4	2388	2447.1	2697.3	2922.7	3022.1
Norway	4300.8	4611.6	4883.5	5245.5	5348.4	5387.6
Poland	856.5	934.7	1061.2	1240.9	1365.1	1388.7
Portugal	2212.4	2304.2	2418.7	2548.5	2696.8	2727.7
Slovak Republic	1139.5	1350.6	1618.8	1861.7	2066.3	2095.5
Slovenia	1960.1	2106.3	2142	2416	2524.1	2428.5
Spain	2274.1	2552.5	2738.6	2965.5	3096.7	3055.7
Sweden	2963.4	3194.8	3431.2	3655.8	3711	3757.7
Switzerland	4015.3	4252.3	4569.8	4933.1	5135.1	5269.6
Turkey	590.7	731.6	840.2	913	913	913
United Kingdom	2699.8	2961.3	3029.7	3143	3379.1	3433.2
United States	6727.7	7107.2	7482.5	7760.5	7989.9	8232.9
OECD AVERAGE						

1. Excluding investments
2. Current expenditure

Source: Data taken from OECD Health Data 2012: http://stats.oecd.org/Index.aspx?DataSetCode=SHA

per capita in 2010. In 2010, the next three highest per capita on health expenditures were Norway with $5,388, Switzerland with $5,269, and the Netherlands with $5,056. In 2010, those countries who spent the least amount per capita were Turkey, Mexico, and Chile, at $913, $915, and $1,202, respectively. These data are important because they should reflect the health status of a country. For example, U.S. health indicators should be at the top of the rankings because of their spending, and Turkey, Mexico, and Chile would have less healthy indicators because they spend less money.

2005–2010 Public Expenditures on Health (Table 3-3, pages 62–63)

The public sector is the main source of healthcare funding in all of the OECD countries except for the United States and Mexico, which is logical because they all have some form of universal health coverage. The United States spent only 48%, Mexico spent

| TABLE 3-3 | 2005–2010 Public Expenditures on Health |

	2005	2006	2007	2008	2009	2010
Australia	66.9	66.6	67.5	67.9	68.5	68.5
Austria	75.3	75.7	75.8	76.3	76.4	76.2
Belgium[1]	75.8	73.6	73.2	74.7	76.1	75.6
Canada	70.2	69.8	70.2	70.5	70.9	71.1
Chile	40.0	42.1	43.2	44.1	47.7	48.2
Czech Republic	87.3	86.7	85.2	82.5	84.0	83.8
Denmark	84.5	84.6	84.4	84.7	85.0	85.1
Estonia	76.7	73.3	75.6	77.8	75.3	78.9
Finland	75.4	74.8	74.4	74.5	75.2	74.5
France	78.8	78.7	78.3	76.7	76.9	77.0
Germany	76.6	76.5	76.4	76.6	76.9	76.8
Greece	60.1	62.0	60.3	59.9	61.7	59.4
Hungary	70.0	69.8	67.3	67.1	65.7	64.8
Iceland	81.4	82.0	82.5	82.6	82.0	80.4
Ireland	75.9	75.1	75.5	75.1	72.0	69.5
Israel	59.3	59.8	59.0	59.5	60.5	60.5
Italy	76.2	76.6	76.6	78.9	79.6	79.6
Japan	81.6	79.4	80.4	80.8	80.5	80.5
Korea	52.9	55.3	55.8	55.9	58.2	58.2
Luxembourg	84.9	85.1	84.1	84.1	84.0	84.0
Mexico	45.0	45.2	45.4	46.9	48.3	47.3
Netherlands[2]	65.8	82.4	84.1	84.8	85.4	85.7
New Zealand	79.7	80.1	82.4	82.8	83.0	83.2
Norway	83.5	83.8	84.1	84.4	84.6	85.5
Poland	69.3	69.9	70.4	71.8	71.6	71.7
Portugal	68.0	67.0	66.7	65.3	66.5	65.8
Slovak Republic	74.4	68.3	66.8	67.8	65.7	64.5
Slovenia	72.7	72.3	71.8	73.9	73.2	72.8
Spain	71.0	71.6	71.9	73.2	74.7	74.2

TABLE 3-3	2005–2010 Public Expenditures on Health (*continued*)					
	2005	**2006**	**2007**	**2008**	**2009**	**2010**
Sweden	81.2	81.1	81.4	81.5	81.5	81.0
Switzerland	59.5	59.1	59.1	65.2	65.5	65.2
Turkey	67.8	68.3	67.8	73.0	73.0	73.0
United Kingdom	81.7	81.3	81.2	82.5	83.4	83.2
United States	44.2	45.0	45.2	46.0	47.3	48.2
OECD AVERAGE						

1. Excluding investments
2. Current expenditure

Source: Data taken from OECD Health Data 2012: http://stats.oecd.org/Index.aspx?DataSetCode=SHA

47%, and Chile spent 48%.. In 2012, Mexico achieved universal healthcare coverage, which is not reflected in this 2010 data. Mexico's public health expenditure percentages should increase. Chile has a private and public insurance system, which is why their percentage is low. In 2010, the Netherlands, Norway, and Denmark were first with 85.7%, 85.5% and 85.1% respectively. In 2010, there were 10 countries that had over 80% of their health expenditures derived from public funding. These percentages represent the fact that all of these countries have a form of a national healthcare system. The U.S. public expenditures are due in part to Medicaid and Medicare expenditures.

2005–2010 Pharmaceutical Expenditures (Tables 3-4 pages 64–65)

In 2005, the United States spent 12.2% of total health expenditures on pharmaceuticals. In 2010, the percentage decreased slightly to 11.9%. In 2010, Hungary, Mexico, and the Slovak Republic spent the most with 33.6%, 27.1%, and 26.4%, respectively. During this period, there was a minimal increase of pharmaceutical spending in the United States. The U.S. statistics reflect the culture of U.S. traditional medicine that provides drugs to resolve medical issues as well as the increasing use of generic drugs, which are much less costly than brand name drugs.

2005–2010 Healthcare Resources: Physician Resources and Nurses Resources (Tables 3-5 and 3-6, pages 65–68)

Physician Resources

In the United States, there are fewer physicians per capita than in most other OECD countries. In 2005, the United States had 2.4 practicing physicians per 1,000, which remained static through 2010. This statistic, coupled with the fact that there are not enough primary care physicians in the United States and there is a shortage of physicians in rural areas, continues to present issues for the healthcare system. In 2005, Turkey, Mexico, and Korea had the fewest physicians per 1,000 at 1.3, 1.8, and 1.6, respectively. In 2010, the rates were 1.7, 2.0, and 2.0, respectively, which were all small increases. The highest number of physicians per 1,000 in 2010 were Austria at 4.8 and Norway at 4.1. There were several countries tied at 3.8, including Sweden and Switzerland.

Nurses Resources

In 2005, the U.S. rate of nurses per 1,000 population was 10.4 which increased to 11 in 2010. In 2005, Denmark, Switzerland, and Iceland had 14.4, 14.1, and 14 nurses per 1,000 population, respectively. In 2010, Denmark's rate increased to 15.4, Switzerland's increased to 16, and Iceland slightly increased to 14.5. The U.S. data reflects the continued nursing shortage in this country.

TABLE 3-4	2005–2010 Pharmaceutical Expenditures					
	2005	**2006**	**2007**	**2008**	**2009**	**2010**
Australia	14.3	14.3	14.3	14.6	14.7	14.7
Austria	12.8	12.9	13.1	13.1	12.1	12.0
Belgium	16.6	16.6	16.5	16.4	16.0	15.8
Canada	17.2	17.4	17.2	17.0	17.0	16.7
Chile	13.9	13.0	12.2	12.2	11.1	11.1
Czech Republic	24.8	22.8	21.5	20.4	19.4	19.9
Denmark	8.2	8.3	8.5	8.0	7.3	7.4
Estonia	23.9	23.5	21.4	20.7	23.5	21.8
Finland	16.0	14.7	14.8	14.8	14.2	13.9
France	16.7	16.3	16.4	16.4	16.1	16.0
Germany	15.0	14.7	15.0	15.0	14.9	14.8
Greece	21.5	22.7	24.8	24.8	24.8	24.8
Hungary	30.3	31.0	30.6	31.1	32.5	33.6
Iceland	14.4	14.2	13.5	14.6	15.7	15.8
Ireland	16.2	17.1	17.2	17.2	16.8	18.5
Israel	..	..	..	..	..	..
Italy	20.2	19.8	19.3	18.1	17.6	17.2
Japan	19.7	19.5	19.9	19.4	20.8	..
Korea	24.9	24.5	23.4	23.2	22.5	21.6
Luxembourg	9.2	8.8	9.1	9.1	9.1	9.1
Mexico	25.4	26.3	28.2	28.3	27.1	27.1
Netherlands	..	..	10.4	9.9	9.7	9.5
New Zealand	10.7	11.3	10.4	9.7	9.5	9.4
Norway	9.1	8.7	8.0	7.5	7.3	7.3
Poland	28.0	27.2	24.8	23.0	22.9	22.7
Portugal	20.7	21.2	21.0	20.3	19.4	18.6
Slovak Republic	31.9	29.7	27.9	27.6	26.6	26.4
Slovenia	20.8	20.4	19.7	18.5	18.6	19.4
Spain	20.1	19.1	18.6	18.2	18.3	18.4
Sweden	13.4	13.4	13.1	12.9	12.7	12.6

TABLE 3-4	2005–2010 Pharmaceutical Expenditures *(continued)*					
	2005	**2006**	**2007**	**2008**	**2009**	**2010**
Switzerland	10.6	10.4	10.3	10.1	10.1	9.7
Turkey	..	..	..	..	..	..
United Kingdom	12.8	12.3	12.1	11.8	11.8	11.8
United States	12.2	12.4	12.3	12.1	12.2	11.9
OECD AVERAGE						

Source: Data taken from OECD Health Data 2012: http://stats.oecd.org/Index.aspx?DataSetCode=SHA

TABLE 3-5	2005–2010 Healthcare Resources: Physician Resources					
	2005	**2006**	**2007**	**2008**	**2009**	**2010**
Australia[1]	2.8	2.8	3.0	3.0	3.1	3.1
Austria[1]	4.3	4.5	4.5	4.6	4.7	4.8
Belgium[1]	2.9	2.9	2.9	2.9	2.9	2.9
Canada[2]	2.2	2.2	2.2	2.3	2.3	2.4
Chile[3]	..	..	..	..	..	1.4
Czech Republic[1]	3.6	3.6	3.6	3.5	3.6	3.6
Denmark[1]	3.3	3.4	3.4	3.4	3.5	3.5
Estonia[1]	3.2	3.2	3.3	3.3	3.3	3.2
Finland[2]	3.0	3.0	3.0	3.1	3.1	3.3
France[2]	3.3	3.3	3.3	3.3	3.3	3.3
Germany[1]	3.4	3.5	3.5	3.6	3.6	3.7
Greece[2]	5.0	5.4	5.6	6.0	6.1	6.1
Hungary[1]	2.8	3.0	2.8	3.1	3.0	2.9
Iceland[1]	3.6	3.6	3.6	3.6	3.7	3.6
Ireland[2]	..	2.7	2.8	2.9	3.1	3.1
Israel[1]	3.3	3.0	3.4	3.4	3.5	3.5
Italy[1]	..	..	..	..	3.7	..
Japan[1]	..	2.1	..	2.2	..	2.2

(continues)

TABLE 3-5 **2005–2010 Healthcare Resources: Physician Resources** (*continued*)

	2005	2006	2007	2008	2009	2010
Korea[1]	1.6	1.7	1.7	1.9	1.9	2.0
Luxembourg[1]	2.6	2.6	2.7	2.7	2.7	2.8
Mexico[1]	1.8	1.9	2.0	2.0	2.1	2.0
Netherlands[2]	2.7	2.8	2.8	2.9	2.9	2.9
New Zealand[1]	2.1	2.3	2.3	2.5	2.6	2.6
Norway[1]	3.6	3.8	3.9	4.0	4.0	4.1
Poland[1]	2.1	2.2	2.2	2.2	2.2	2.2
Portugal[3]	3.4	3.4	3.5	3.6	3.7	3.8
Slovak Republic[2]	3.0	3.2	3.2	3.4	3.3	3.3
Slovenia[1]	2.4	2.4	2.4	2.4	2.4	2.4
Spain[1]	3.8	3.6	3.7	3.5	3.5	3.8
Sweden[1]	3.5	3.6	3.7	3.7	3.8	3.8
Switzerland[1]	..	..	..	3.8	3.8	3.8
Turkey[2]	1.3	1.5	1.6	1.6	1.7	1.7
United Kingdom[1]	2.4	2.5	2.5	2.6	2.7	2.7
United States[1]	2.4	2.4	2.4	2.4	2.4	2.4
OECD AVERAGE						

1. Data refer to practising physicians. Practising physicians are defined as those providing care directly to patients.
2. Data refer to professionally active physicians. They include practising physicians plus other physicians working in the health sector as managers, educators, researchers, etc. (adding another 5–10% of doctors).
3. Data refer to all physicians who are licensed to practice.

Source: Data taken from OECD Health Data 2012: http://stats.oecd.org/Index.aspx?DataSetCode=HEALTH_REAC

2005–2010 Medical Graduates (Table 3-7, pages 68–69)

From 2005 to 2010 there was a slight increase in medical graduates from 6.3 to 6.6 per 100,000 population in the United States. The United States has one of the lowest graduate rates compared to the rest of the OECD countries. In 2005, Austria had the highest medical graduate rate of 20.6, followed by Iceland at 14.9, and Ireland at 14.3. In 2010, Austria's rates increased to 22.8, Iceland's decreased to 13.8, and Ireland's rate increased to 17.5.

This lower rate of U.S. medical graduates could be reflective of the difficult curriculum as well as the exorbitant cost of U.S. medical schools.

2005–2010 Hospital Beds (Table 3-8, pages 70–71)

In 2005, Japan had the highest number of beds—14.1 per 1,000 population. The rate was nearly double than the rest of the OECD countries. In 2010, Japan's rate dropped slightly to 13.6. In 2005, the United States had

TABLE 3-6	2005–2010 Healthcare Resources: Nurses Resources					
	2005	**2006**	**2007**	**2008**	**2009**	**2010**
Australia[1]	9.7	..	10.1	10.2	10.1	10.1
Austria[1]	7.2	7.3	7.4	7.5	7.6	7.7
Belgium[3]	..	..	..	..	14.8	15.1
Canada[1]	8.7	8.8	9.0	9.1	9.3	9.3
Chile[3]	..	..	..	..	..	..
Czech Republic[1]	8.1	8.1	8.0	7.9	8.1	8.1
Denmark[1]	14.4	14.5	14.3	14.7	15.4	15.4
Estonia[1]	6.3	6.3	6.4	6.4	6.1	6.1
Finland[1]	9.1	9.3	9.4	9.6	9.6	9.6
France[2]	7.6	7.8	7.6	7.9	8.2	8.5
Germany[1]	10.2	10.4	10.5	10.7	11.0	11.3
Greece[2]	3.3	3.2	3.2	3.2	3.3	3.3
Hungary[1]	6.0	6.1	6.1	6.2	6.2	6.2
Iceland[1]	14.0	13.7	14.0	14.8	15.3	14.5
Ireland[2]	12.2	12.6	12.8	12.8	12.7	13.1
Israel[1]	5.3	5.2	5.2	5.0	4.5	4.8
Italy[3]	5.8	6.1	6.1	6.2	6.3	6.3
Japan[1]	..	9.1	..	9.5	..	10.1
Korea[1]	3.9	4.0	4.2	4.3	4.5	4.6
Luxembourg[1]	11.0	10.9	..	..	..	11.1
Mexico[1]	2.3	2.3	2.4	2.4	2.5	2.5
Netherlands[1]	8.2	8.2	8.3	8.4	8.4	8.4
New Zealand[1]	9.0	8.8	9.2	9.7	9.7	10.0
Norway[1]	13.6	13.9	13.9	14.0	14.2	14.4
Poland[1]	5.1	5.1	5.2	5.2	5.3	5.3
Portugal[2]	4.4	4.7	4.9	5.2	5.4	5.7
Slovak Republic[2]	6.0	6.0	6.3	6.3	6.0	6.0
Slovenia[1]	7.5	7.6	7.8	7.9	8.0	8.2
Spain[1]	4.2	4.1	4.4	4.6	4.9	4.9

(continues)

| TABLE 3-6 | 2005–2010 Healthcare Resources: Nurses Resources (*continued*) |

	2005	2006	2007	2008	2009	2010
Sweden[1]	10.7	10.9	11.0	11.0	11.0	11.0
Switzerland[1]	14.1	14.5	14.7	14.9	15.2	16.0
Turkey[2]	1.2	1.2	1.4	1.4	1.5	1.6
United Kingdom[1]	..	..	9.6	9.7	9.8	9.6
United States[2]	10.4	10.5	10.6	10.8	10.8	11.0
OECD AVERAGE						

1. Data refer to practising nurses. Practising nurses are defined as those providing care directly to patients.
2. Data refer to professionally active nurses. They include practising nurses plus other nurses working in the health sector as managers, educators, researchers, etc. (adding another 5–10% of nurses).
3. Data refer to all nurses who are licensed to practice.

Source: Data taken from OECD Health Data 2012: http://stats.oecd.org/Index.aspx?DataSetCode=HEALTH_REAC

| TABLE 3-7 | 2005–2010 Medical Graduates |

	2005	2006	2007	2008	2009	2010
Australia	8.8	9.1	10.1	11.1	10.8	12.0
Austria	20.6	19.4	23.8	23.6	22.8	22.8
Belgium	7.3	6.5	6.9	7.1	7.9	9.0
Canada	5.8	6.0	6.2	6.4	6.9	7.2
Chile	4.6	4.6	4.0	4.9	6.5	5.5
Czech Republic	10.4	10.1	10.7	11.2	12.6	13.9
Denmark	15.1	15.8	16.0	14.7	15.2	16.4
Estonia	9.2	9.5	7.9	8.4	9.0	11.1
Finland	6.4	7.5	6.9	10.3	9.4	10.6
France	5.5	5.3	6.0	6.0	6.0	6.0
Germany	10.7	10.6	11.6	12.1	12.5	12.3
Greece	13.3	14.7	14.3	14.3	14.3	14.3
Hungary	11.4	10.6	10.0	9.6	9.2	10.4
Iceland	14.9	13.1	11.6	15.3	11.6	13.8
Ireland	14.3	15.1	16.7	15.2	16.2	17.5

TABLE 3-7	2005–2010 Medical Graduates *(continued)*					
	2005	**2006**	**2007**	**2008**	**2009**	**2010**
Israel	4.5	4.4	4.1	4.5	4.0	4.1
Italy	11.0	10.4	11.5	11.4	11.1	11.1
Japan	5.8	6.0	6.0	5.8	5.9	6.0
Korea	9.1	8.2	9.0	9.1	8.8	7.1
Luxembourg	..	..	..	..	..	..
Mexico	11.0	10.0	11.2	12.1	11.8	11.6
Netherlands	9.5	9.3	10.2	10.4	9.5	8.2
New Zealand	7.2	6.9	6.7	7.2	7.8	7.3
Norway	10.1	9.9	10.6	10.4	10.7	11.3
Poland	6.2	6.1	6.7	7.2	7.3	8.1
Portugal	7.0	7.7	9.7	10.4	10.6	11.9
Slovak Republic	10.3	9.4	9.9	9.0	8.5	8.5
Slovenia	8.1	6.4	6.4	8.6	7.9	11.2
Spain	9.4	9.0	8.6	8.6	8.5	8.4
Sweden	8.9	10.0	10.2	10.3	10.7	10.7
Switzerland	8.4	7.9	8.1	8.7	9.4	10.4
Turkey	6.2	6.4	7.0	6.7	7.1	7.0
United Kingdom	8.6	9.2	10.2	9.1	9.2	9.3
United States	6.3	6.2	6.4	6.4	6.5	6.6
OECD AVERAGE						

Source: Data taken from OECD Health Data 2012: http://stats.oecd.org/Index.aspx?DataSetCode=HEALTH_REAC

one of the lower hospital bed rates of 3.2, Mexico was lowest at 1.8, Turkey at 2.2, and Chile at 2.3. In 2009, the U.S. rate was 3.1, Mexico's rate dropped slightly to 1.6, Chile to 2.0, and Turkey's rate increased to 2.5. These rates may address that fact that the United States has increased its outpatient services, as have other countries.

2005–2010 Total Life Expectancy at Birth (Table 3-9, pages 71–72)

Life expectancy rates calculate the average life span of a country. In 2005, the United States' life expectancy at birth was 77.4 years, which increased to 78.7 in 2010.

Japan continues to lead the life expectancy at birth with 82 in 2005, which increased to 83.0 in 2010. Switzerland was second in 2005 with 81.3 and Iceland was third with 81.2. In 2010, Switzerland increased to 82.6 but Iceland was replaced by Spain, who jumped from 80.3 to 82.2 in 2010. Iceland's rate was 81.5, only a 0.2 increase from 2005. In 2005 the lowest life expectancy rates of the OECD countries were Estonia at 72.7 and Hungary at 72.8. In 2010, the lowest rates were Estonia at 70.6 and Hungary at 70.5. These statistics are a reflection of the gender life expectancy statistics, and are often used as a comparison of countries worldwide to assess their health status.

TABLE 3-8	2005–2010 Hospital Beds					
	2005	**2006**	**2007**	**2008**	**2009**	**2010**
Australia	3.9	3.9	..	3.8	3.7	3.7
Austria	7.7	7.7	7.8	7.7	7.7	7.6
Belgium	7.4	6.7	6.6	6.6	6.5	6.4
Canada	3.4	3.4	3.3	3.2	3.2	3.2
Chile	2.3	2.3	2.3	2.3	2.3	2.0
Czech Republic	7.6	7.4	7.3	7.2	7.1	7.0
Denmark	3.9	3.8	3.7	3.6	3.5	3.5
Estonia	5.5	5.7	5.6	5.7	5.4	5.3
Finland	7.1	7.0	6.7	6.6	6.2	5.9
France	7.2	7.1	7.1	6.9	6.7	6.4
Germany	8.5	8.3	8.2	8.2	8.2	8.3
Greece	4.7	4.8	4.8	4.8	4.9	4.9
Hungary	7.9	7.9	7.2	7.1	7.1	7.2
Iceland	..	..	5.8	..	..	..
Ireland	5.5	5.3	5.2	4.9	3.3	3.1
Israel	3.9	3.6	3.5	3.5	3.4	3.3
Italy	4.0	3.9	3.8	3.7	3.6	3.5
Japan	14.1	14.0	13.9	13.8	13.7	13.6
Korea	5.9	6.5	7.3	7.7	8.2	8.8
Luxembourg	5.8	5.7	5.7	5.6	5.5	5.4
Mexico	1.8	1.7	1.7	1.7	1.7	1.6
Netherlands	4.5	4.8	4.7	4.7	4.7	4.7
New Zealand	..	..	..	..	2.4	2.7
Norway	4.0	4.0	3.8	3.5	3.4	3.3
Poland	6.5	6.5	6.4	6.6	6.7	6.6
Portugal	3.5	3.5	3.4	3.4	3.4	3.4
Slovak Republic	6.8	6.7	6.8	6.6	6.5	6.4
Slovenia	4.8	4.8	4.7	4.7	4.6	4.6
Spain	3.4	3.3	3.3	3.2	3.2	3.2
Sweden	2.9	2.9	2.9	2.8	2.8	2.7

TABLE 3-8	2005–2010 Hospital Beds (continued)					
	2005	**2006**	**2007**	**2008**	**2009**	**2010**
Switzerland	5.5	5.4	5.4	5.2	5.1	5.0
Turkey	2.2	2.4	2.4	2.4	2.5	2.5
United Kingdom	3.7	3.6	3.4	3.4	3.3	3.0
United States	3.2	3.2	3.1	3.1	3.1	..
OECD AVERAGE						

Source: Data taken from OECD Health Data 2012: http://stats.oecd.org/Index.aspx?DataSetCode=HEALTH_REAC

TABLE 3-9	2005–2010 Total Life Expectancy at Birth					
	2005	**2006**	**2007**	**2008**	**2009**	**2010**
Australia	80.9	81.1	81.3	81.5	81.6	81.8
Austria	79.4	79.9	80.2	80.5	80.4	80.7
Belgium	79.0	79.5	79.8	79.8	80.0	80.3
Canada	80.1	80.4	80.7	80.8	80.8	80.8
Chile	77.9	78.4	77.8	77.8	78.8	79.0
Czech Republic	76.0	76.7	77.0	77.3	77.3	77.7
Denmark	78.2	78.4	78.4	78.8	79.0	79.3
Estonia	72.7	72.9	72.9	73.9	75.0	75.6
Finland	79.1	79.5	79.6	79.9	80.0	80.2
France	80.3	80.7	80.9	81.0	81.1	81.3
Germany	79.4	79.8	80.0	80.2	80.3	80.5
Greece	79.2	79.5	79.5	80.0	80.3	80.6
Hungary	72.8	73.2	73.3	73.8	74.0	74.3
Iceland	81.2	81.2	81.2	81.3	81.5	81.5
Ireland	79.4	79.7	79.8	80.1	80.0	81.0
Israel	80.2	80.6	80.5	81.0	81.5	81.7
Italy	80.8	81.3	81.5	81.8	82.0	82.0
Japan	82.0	82.4	82.6	82.7	83.0	83.0

(continues)

TABLE 3-9   **2005–2010 Total Life Expectancy at Birth** *(continued)*

	2005	2006	2007	2008	2009	2010
Korea	78.5	79.0	79.4	79.9	80.4	80.7
Luxembourg	79.5	79.3	79.5	80.6	80.7	80.7
Mexico	74.6	74.8	75.0	75.1	75.3	75.5
Netherlands	79.4	79.8	80.2	80.3	80.6	80.8
New Zealand	79.8	80.1	80.2	80.4	80.8	81.0
Norway	80.3	80.5	80.6	80.8	81.0	81.2
Poland	75.1	75.3	75.3	75.6	75.8	76.3
Portugal	78.1	78.9	79.0	79.3	79.5	79.8
Slovak Republic	74.0	74.3	74.3	74.8	75.0	75.2
Slovenia	77.7	78.4	78.2	78.8	79.0	79.5
Spain	80.3	81.1	81.0	81.3	81.8	82.2
Sweden	80.6	80.8	81.0	81.2	81.4	81.5
Switzerland	81.3	81.7	82.0	82.2	82.3	82.6
Turkey	73.0	73.2	73.3	73.6	73.8	74.3
United Kingdom	79.2	79.5	79.7	79.8	80.4	80.6
United States	77.4	77.7	77.9	78.1	78.5	78.7
OECD AVERAGE						

Source: Data taken from OECD Health Data 2012: http://stats.oecd.org/Index.aspx?DataSetCode=HEALTH_STAT

2005–2010 Female and Male Life Expectancy at Birth (Tables 3-10 and 3-11, pages 73–75)

Female Life Expectancy

Life expectancy rates can be calculated for the general population, by gender, and how long a life span is after 65 years of age. In 2005 in the United States, the female life expectancy at birth was 79.9 years of age, which increased to 81.1 in 2010. In 2005, the highest ranking was Japan at 85.5 years of age. By 2010, it had increased to 86.4, which is nearly another year of life. In 2005, the second country was Switzerland at 84, which increased to 84.9 by 2010. In 2005, third place was Spain at 83.7, which in 2010 took over second place at 85.3. Last place in 2005 was Turkey at 75, which increased to 76.8 in 2010. These are interesting statistics for the United States because it spends so

much of its GDP on healthcare expenditures but it is not at the top of the rankings. The U.S. statistics could also reflect the sedentary lifestyle and poor diet in the United States and unequal access to healthcare.

Male Life Expectancy

The United States' rate in 2005 was 74.9 and 76.2 in 2010. In 2005, Iceland had the highest rate at 79.2, which increased to 79.5 in 2010. However, although in 2005 Japan, had a rate of 78.6, it but passed Iceland in 2010 with a rate of 79.6. In 2005, Switzerland was in second place with 78.7, edging out Japan at 78.6. However, in 2010, Switzerland was first with 80.3. Despite high healthcare expenditures, the U.S. statistics could reflect the sedentary lifestyle and poor eating habits.

TABLE 3-10	2005–2010 Female Life Expectancy at Birth					
	2005	**2006**	**2007**	**2008**	**2009**	**2010**
Australia	83.3	83.5	83.7	83.7	83.9	84.0
Austria	82.2	82.8	83.1	83.3	83.2	83.5
Belgium	81.9	82.3	82.6	82.6	82.8	83.0
Canada	82.5	82.8	83.0	83.1	..	..
Chile	80.9	81.4	80.7	80.6	81.9	82.0[e]
Czech Republic	79.2	79.9	80.2	80.5	80.5	80.9
Denmark	80.5	80.7	80.6	81.0	81.1	81.4
Estonia	78.1	78.5	78.7	79.2	80.1	80.5
Finland	82.5	83.1	83.1	83.3	83.5	83.5
France	83.8	84.2	84.4	84.3	84.5[e]	84.7[e]
Germany	82.0	82.4	82.7	82.7	82.8	83.0
Greece	81.6	81.9	81.8	82.3	82.7	82.8
Hungary	76.9	77.4	77.3	77.8	77.9	78.1
Iceland	83.1	83.0	82.9	83.0	83.3	83.5
Ireland	81.6	82.1	82.1	82.4	82.5	83.2
Israel[1]	82.2	82.5	82.4	83.0	83.3[b]	83.6
Italy	83.6	84.2	84.2	84.5	84.6	..
Japan	85.5	85.8	86.0	86.1	86.4	86.4
Korea	81.9	82.4	82.7	83.3	83.8	84.1
Luxembourg	82.3	81.9	82.2	83.1	83.3	83.5
Mexico	77.0	77.2	77.4	77.5	77.6	77.8
Netherlands	81.6	81.9	82.3	82.3	82.7	82.7
New Zealand	82.0	82.2	82.2	82.4	82.7	82.8
Norway	82.7	82.9	82.9	83.2	83.2	83.3
Poland	79.4	79.6	79.7	80.0	80.1	80.6
Portugal	81.3	82.3	82.2	82.4	82.6	82.8
Slovak Republic	77.9	78.2	78.1	78.7	78.7	78.8
Slovenia	81.3	81.9	81.8	82.3	82.3	82.7
Spain	83.7	84.4	84.3	84.5	84.9	85.3

(continues)

TABLE 3-10	2005–2010 Female Life Expectancy at Birth *(continued)*

	2005	2006	2007	2008	2009	2010
Sweden	82.8	82.9	83.0	83.2	83.4	83.5
Switzerland	84.0	84.2	84.4	84.6	84.6	84.9
Turkey	75.0	75.3	75.6	75.8	76.1	76.8
United Kingdom	81.3	81.7	81.8	81.9	82.5	82.6
United States	79.9	80.2	80.4	80.6	80.9	81.1[e]

.. Not available

1. The statistical data for Israel are supplied by and under the responsibility of the relevant Israeli authorities. The use of such data by the OECD is without prejudice to the status of the Golan Heights, East Jerusalem, and Israeli settlements in the West Bank under the terms of international law.

b. Break in series

e. Estimate

Source: Data taken from OECD Health Data 2012: http://stats.oecd.org/Index.aspx?DataSetCode=HEALTH_STAT

TABLE 3-11	2005–2010 Male Life Expectancy at Birth

	2005	2006	2007	2008	2009	2010
Australia	78.5	78.7	79.0	79.2	79.3	79.5
Austria	76.6	77.1	77.4	77.8	77.6	77.9
Belgium	76.2	76.6	77.1	76.9	77.3	77.6
Canada	77.7	78.0	78.3	78.5	78.5	78.5
Chile	74.9	75.5	75.0	75.1	75.8	75.9
Czech Republic	72.9	73.5	73.8	74.1	74.2	74.5
Denmark	76.0	76.1	76.2	76.5	76.9	77.2
Estonia	67.3	67.4	67.1	68.6	69.8	70.6
Finland	75.6	75.9	76.0	76.5	76.6	76.9
France	76.7	77.1	77.4	77.6	77.7	78.0
Germany	76.7	77.2	77.4	77.6	77.8	78.0
Greece	76.8	77.2	77.1	77.7	77.8	78.4
Hungary	68.6	69.0	69.2	69.8	70.0	70.5
Iceland	79.2	79.4	79.4	79.6	79.7	79.5
Ireland	77.2	77.3	77.4	77.8	77.4	78.7

TABLE 3-11	2005–2010 Male Life Expectancy at Birth *(continued)*					
	2005	**2006**	**2007**	**2008**	**2009**	**2010**
Israel	78.2	78.7	78.7	79.0	79.6	79.7
Italy	78.0	78.5	78.7	79.1	79.4	79.4
Japan	78.6	79.0	79.2	79.3	79.6	79.6
Korea	75.1	75.7	76.1	76.5	77.0	77.2
Luxembourg	76.7	76.8	76.7	78.1	78.1	77.9
Mexico	72.2	72.4	72.6	72.7	72.9	73.1
Netherlands	77.2	77.6	78.0	78.3	78.5	78.8
New Zealand	77.7	78.0	78.2	78.4	78.8	79.1
Norway	77.8	78.2	78.3	78.4	78.7	79.0
Poland	70.8	70.9	71.0	71.3	71.5	72.1
Portugal	74.9	75.5	75.9	76.2	76.5	76.7
Slovak Republic	70.1	70.4	70.5	70.9	71.3	71.6
Slovenia	74.1	74.8	74.6	75.4	75.8	76.3
Spain	77.0	77.7	77.8	78.2	78.7	79.1
Sweden	78.4	78.7	78.9	79.1	79.4	79.5
Switzerland	78.7	79.2	79.5	79.8	79.9	80.3
Turkey	70.9	71.1	71.1	71.4	71.5	71.8
United Kingdom	77.1	77.3	77.6	77.8	78.3	78.6
United States	74.9	75.1	75.4	75.6	76.0	76.2
OECD AVERAGE						

Source: Data taken from OECD Health Data 2012: http://stats.oecd.org/Index.aspx?DataSetCode=HEALTH_STAT

2005–2010 Life Expectancy of Females and Males at Age 65 (Tables 3-12 and 3-13, pages 76–78)

Life Expectancy of Females at Age 65

These statistics address the quality of health care for the elderly. This statistic focuses on life expectancy after age 65 or what is the average life span after 65 years of age. In 2005, The United States' life expectancy for females was 19.5, which did increase to 20.3 in 2010. In 2005, Japan was the top country at 23.2 years of life expectancy for females age 65, which increased to 23.9 years in 2010. France was second with 22 years and

Switzerland was third with 21.7 additional years. In 2010, however, Spain edged out France for second with 22.7 versus 22.6. The bottom country was Turkey with an expectancy rate of 15.6 in 2005, which did marginally increase to 16.1 years in 2010.

Life Expectancy of Males at Age 65

In 2005, the United States' male expectancy after age 65 was 16.8 years, which increased to 17.7 years by 2010. In 2005, Japan, Switzerland, and Australia were the lead countries for male life expectancy at age 65 with

TABLE 3-12	2005–2010 Life Expectancy of Females at Age 65					
	2005	**2006**	**2007**	**2008**	**2009**	**2010**
Australia	21.4	21.5	21.6	21.6	21.8	21.8
Austria	20.3	20.7	21.0	21.1	21.2	21.4
Belgium	20.2	20.6	21.0	20.9	21.1	21.3
Canada	20.9	21.1	21.3	21.5	21.5	21.5
Chile	19.7	20.2	19.5	20.4	20.6	20.8
Czech Republic	17.7	18.3	18.5	18.8	18.8	19.0
Denmark	19.1	19.2	19.2	19.5	19.5	19.7
Estonia	18.1	18.2	18.5	18.6	18.3	18.8
Finland	20.9	21.2	21.2	21.3	21.5	21.5
France	22.0	22.4	22.5	22.5	22.6	22.6
Germany	20.1	20.5	20.7	20.7	20.8	20.9
Greece	19.2	19.4	19.4	19.8	20.2	20.4
Hungary	16.9	17.2	17.3	17.5	17.6	17.6
Iceland	20.7	20.6	20.6	20.5	20.6	20.8
Ireland	19.8	20.2	20.1	20.3	20.6	21.1
Israel	20.2	20.4	20.2	20.7	21.0	21.1
Italy	21.3	21.8	21.8	22.0	22.1	22.1
Japan	23.2	23.4	23.6	23.6	24.0	23.9
Korea	19.9	20.1	20.5	21.0	21.5	21.6
Luxembourg	20.4	20.3	20.3	21.0	21.4	21.6
Mexico	18.2	18.2	18.2	18.3	18.3	18.3
Netherlands	20.0	20.1	20.5	20.5	20.8	21.2
New Zealand	20.5	20.6	20.7	20.8	21.1	21.2
Norway	20.9	20.8	20.8	21.0	21.1	21.2
Poland	18.6	18.8	18.9	19.0	19.1	19.4
Portugal	19.4	20.2	20.2	20.3	20.5	20.6
Slovak Republic	16.9	17.1	17.1	17.5	17.6	17.5
Slovenia	19.9	20.1	19.9	20.2	20.1	20.5
Spain	21.3	22.0	21.9	22.1	22.4	22.7
Switzerland	21.7	22.1	22.2	22.3	22.2	22.5

| TABLE 3-12 | 2005–2010 Life Expectancy of Females at Age 65   (*continued*) | | | | | |

	2005	2006	2007	2008	2009	2010
Switzerland	21.7	22.1	22.2	22.3	22.2	22.5
Turkey	15.6	15.7	15.8	15.8	15.9	16.1
United Kingdom	19.7	20.1	20.2	20.3	20.8	20.9
United States	19.5	19.7	19.9	20.0	20.3	20.3
OECD AVERAGE						

Source: Data taken from OECD Health Data 2012: http://stats.oecd.org/Index.aspx?DataSetCode=HEALTH_STAT

| TABLE 3-13 | 2005–2010 Life Expectancy of Males at Age 65 | | | | | |

	2005	2006	2007	2008	2009	2010
Australia	18.1	18.3	18.5	18.6	18.7	18.9
Austria	17.0	17.3	17.5	17.7	17.7	17.9
Belgium	16.6	17.0	17.3	17.3	17.5	17.6
Canada	17.6	17.9	18.1	18.3	18.3	18.3
Chile	16.2	16.7	16.2	17.0	17.1	17.1
Czech Republic	14.4	14.8	15.1	15.3	15.2	15.5
Denmark	16.1	16.2	16.5	16.6	16.8	17.0
Estonia	13.1	13.2	13.2	13.6	14.4	14.6
Finland	16.8	16.9	17.0	17.5	17.3	17.5
France	17.7	18.0	18.1	18.2	18.4	18.4
Germany	16.9	17.2	17.4	17.5	17.6	17.8
Greece	17.1	17.5	17.4	17.8	18.1	18.5
Hungary	13.1	13.4	13.4	13.6	13.7	13.8
Iceland	18.0	18.3	18.3	18.2	18.3	18.2
Ireland	16.7	16.7	17.1	16.8	17.2	18.1
Israel	18.0	18.3	18.1	18.5	18.7	18.9
Italy	17.4	17.9	18.0	18.2	18.3	18.3
Japan	18.1	18.4	18.6	18.6	18.9	18.9

(continues)

| TABLE 3-13 | 2005–2010 Life Expectancy of Males at Age 65   (continued) |

	2005	2006	2007	2008	2009	2010
Korea	15.8	16.1	16.3	16.6	17.1	17.2
Luxembourg	16.7	17.0	16.4	17.4	17.6	17.3
Mexico	16.8	16.8	16.8	16.8	16.8	16.8
Netherlands	16.4	16.7	17.0	17.3	17.4	17.9
New Zealand	17.7	18.0	18.1	18.3	18.6	18.8
Norway	17.2	17.7	17.4	17.6	18.0	18.0
Poland	14.4	14.5	14.6	14.7	14.7	15.1
Portugal	16.1	16.6	16.8	16.9	17.1	17.1
Slovak Republic	13.2	13.3	13.4	13.8	13.9	13.9
Slovenia	15.5	16.1	15.8	16.3	16.3	16.6
Spain	17.3	17.9	17.8	18.1	18.3	18.6
Sweden	17.4	17.6	17.8	17.9	18.2	18.2
Switzerland	18.1	18.5	18.6	18.9	19.0	19.0
Turkey	13.9	13.9	13.9	14.0	14.0	14.1
United Kingdom	17.0	17.4	17.6	17.7	18.1	18.3
United States	16.8	17.0	17.2	17.3	17.7	17.7
OECD AVERAGE						

Source: Data taken from OECD Health Data 2012: http://stats.oecd.org/Index.aspx?DataSetCode=HEALTH_STAT

18.1 years. By 2010, Switzerland increased the age to 19 years with Japan and Australia tied at 18.9. In 2005, the lowest ranked countries were Estonia and Hungary, which both had 13.1. The Slovak Republic reported 13.2 years for males. In 2010, Estonia had the largest increase to 14.6. The Slovak Republic increased to 13.9 and Hungary to 13.8. These statistics support the general international statistics that females have a higher life expectancy than males do. These statistics further support the quality of care provided to the elderly.

2005–2010 Infant Mortality Rates per 1,000 Births (Table 3-14, pages 79–80)

Infant mortality rates are calculated as a comparison measure of country health status. According to the OECD, **the infant mortality rate** is the number of deaths per 1,000 live births occurring among the population of a designated area during the same calendar year. The United States ranks near the bottom of the 30 countries. In 2005, the infant mortality rate was 6.9, which decreased to 6.1 in 2010. In 2005, Turkey reported a rate of 18.4, and Mexico reported a rate of 16.8. They were the only two countries that reported double digit infant mortality rates. By 2010, Turkey had dramatically dropped its rate to 10.1 with Mexico dropping its rate to 14.1. The lowest infant mortality rates were in Iceland, Sweden, and Finland. Their rates in 2005 were 2.3, 2.4, and 3.0, respectively. By 2010, the rates for Finland and Iceland dropped to 2.3 and 2.2, respectively, while Sweden's rate increased slightly to 2.5, 2.8, and 2.3, which points to the quality of prenatal care in their healthcare system. One of the criticisms of the U.S. delivery system is the poor

TABLE 3-14	2005–2010 Infant Mortality Rates per 1,000 Births					
	2005	**2006**	**2007**	**2008**	**2009**	**2010**
Australia	5.0	4.7	4.2	4.1	4.3	4.1
Austria	4.2	3.6	3.7	3.7	3.8	3.9
Belgium	3.7	4.0	3.9	3.7	3.4	3.5
Canada	5.4	5.0	5.1	5.1	5.1	5.1
Chile	7.9	7.6	8.3	7.8	7.9	7.9
Czech Republic	3.4	3.3	3.1	2.8	2.9	2.7
Denmark	4.4	3.5	4.0	4.0	3.1	3.4
Estonia	5.4	4.4	5.0	5.0	3.6	3.3
Finland	3.0	2.8	2.7	2.6	2.6	2.3
France	3.8	3.8	3.8	3.8	3.9	3.6
Germany	3.9	3.8	3.9	3.5	3.5	3.4
Greece	3.8	3.7	3.5	2.7	3.1	3.8
Hungary	6.2	5.7	5.9	5.6	5.1	5.3
Iceland	2.3	1.4	2.0	2.5	1.8	2.2
Ireland	4.0	3.6	3.1	3.8	3.2	3.8
Israel	4.4	4.0	3.9	3.8	3.8	3.7
Italy	3.8	3.6	3.5	3.3	3.9	3.4
Japan	2.8	2.6	2.6	2.6	2.4	2.3
Korea	4.7	4.1	3.6	3.5	3.2	3.2
Luxembourg	2.6	2.5	1.8	1.8	2.5	3.4
Mexico	16.8	16.2	15.7	15.2	14.7	14.1
Netherlands	4.9	4.4	4.1	3.8	3.8	3.8
New Zealand	5.0	5.1	4.8	5.0	5.2	5.2
Norway	3.1	3.2	3.1	2.7	3.1	2.8
Poland	6.4	6.0	6.0	5.6	5.6	5.0
Portugal	3.5	3.3	3.4	3.3	3.6	2.5
Slovak Republic	7.2	6.6	6.1	5.9	5.7	5.7
Slovenia	4.1	3.4	2.8	2.4	2.4	2.5
Spain	3.7	3.5	3.4	3.3	3.2	3.2

(*continues*)

TABLE 3-14	2005–2010 Infant Mortality Rates per 1,000 Births *(continued)*					
	2005	**2006**	**2007**	**2008**	**2009**	**2010**
Sweden	2.4	2.8	2.5	2.5	2.5	2.5
Switzerland	4.2	4.4	3.9	4.0	4.3	3.8
Turkey	18.4	16.9	15.9	14.9	13.1	10.1
United Kingdom	5.1	5.0	4.8	4.7	4.6	4.2
United States	6.9	6.7	6.8	6.6	6.4	6.1
OECD AVERAGE						

Source: Data taken from OECD Health Data 2012: http://stats.oecd.org/Index.aspx?DataSetCode=HEALTH_STAT

prenatal care received by different ethnic groups, particularly because the United States spends more per capita on health expenditures. It is important to note that the U.S. infant mortality rates vary by state, which impact the overall country rate.

2005–2010 Obese Percentage of Female and Male Population (Tables 3-15 and 3-16, pages 81–83)

Obesity has become an issue in the United States. It is a contributing factor to **diabetes mellitus**, which is a disease in which the body does not produce enough insulin, a hormone needed to convert starches and sugar needed for the body (American Diabetes Association, 2013). The country reporting of obesity rates for males was low. Only 14 of the 34 countries reported rates during different years. Japan, Luxembourg, and Korea were the only countries that reported all years. However, it is important to discuss this health issue because obesity is correlated with increased disease and death rates (CDC, 2012d). An individual is considered obese with a body mass index 30 kh/m^2. In 2005–2006, of the 9 countries reporting, the United States, Canada, and Mexico had highest reported obesity rates of 33.3% (2006), 25.2% (2005), and 23.7.% (2005) respectively of their total population. In 2010, the U.S. rate increased to 35.5%. Mexico only reported rates in 2006, which was an increase to 24.2%. In 2008, Canada reported the same rate of 25.2%.

All of the countries reported double-digit rates with the exception of Japan and Korea, which had very low rates of 3.4–4.3% from 2005 to 2010. Japan's rate increased to 4.8% in 2009 but decreased to 3.8% in 2010.

Korea's increased from 3.6% in 2005 to 4% in 2008, but decreased to 3.5% in 2010.

The rates for obese females in the United States were higher than the male rates. In 2005, the rate was 35.3% (2006), which increased to 36.3% in 2010. These rates were only 1.5% higher than male rates. Mexico's only reported rates in 2005 and 2006 for females were 34.7% and 34.5% for each year. These figures are 10% higher than the male rates. The female rates for both Japan and Korea were low. Rates ranged from 4.3% and 3.3% respectively (2005) to 3.2% and 4.7% (2010). Japan's rate for females decreased while Korea's rates for females increased.

Despite the underreporting of this statistic, these rates indicate a serious problem not only in the U.S. population but it is becoming a global health problem in many countries. People are more sedentary than in previous decades. There are also more options for unhealthy eating. Franchises such as McDonalds and Burger King have expanded worldwide and are very popular.

2005–2010 Tobacco Consumption (15 Years and Older Who Are Daily Smokers) (Table 3-17, pages 83–84)

The Affordable Care Act selected both smoking and alcohol consumption as two health behaviors that can be detrimental to one's health. There are programs established as a result of the Act to reduce the prevalence rates of these risk behaviors. As a result of the Act's focus, these global data were included in the analysis. Tobacco consumption is responsible for 1

TABLE 3-15	2005–2010 Obese Percentage of Females					
	2005	**2006**	**2007**	**2008**	**2009**	**2010**
Australia	..	..	23.6	..	..	..
Austria	..	..	..	..	..	..
Belgium	..	..	..	..	..	..
Canada	22.1	..	..	23.3	..	..
Chile	..	..	..	..	30.7	..
Czech Republic	17.0	..	..	21.0	..	21.0
Denmark	..	..	..	..	..	..
Estonia	..	..	..	..	..	..
Finland	..	..	21.1	..	..	..
France	..	..	..	..	..	..
Germany	..	..	..	..	..	..
Greece	..	..	..	..	..	..
Hungary	..	..	..	..	30.4	..
Iceland	..	..	..	..	..	..
Ireland	..	..	24.0	..	..	..
Israel	..	..	..	..	..	..
Italy	..	..	..	..	..	..
Japan	4.3	3.3	3.3	3.4	3.5	3.2
Korea	3.3	..	3.9	3.4	4.1	4.7
Luxembourg	18.5	19.4	18.8	18.9	19.0	21.0
Mexico	34.7	34.5	..	..	..	..
Netherlands	..	..	..	..	..	..
New Zealand	..	..	27.0	..	27.8	..
Norway	..	..	..	..	..	..
Poland	..	..	..	..	..	..
Portugal	..	..	..	..	..	..
Slovak Republic	17.9	..	..	16.7	..	..
Slovenia	..	..	..	..	..	..
Spain	..	..	..	..	..	..

(*continues*)

TABLE 3-15   2005–2010 Obese Percentage of Females   (*continued*)

	2005	2006	2007	2008	2009	2010
Sweden	..	..	..	..	..	..
Switzerland	..	..	..	..	..	..
Turkey	..	..	..	..	..	..
United Kingdom	24.2	24.2	24.4	24.9	23.9	26.1
United States	..	35.3	..	35.5	..	36.3
OECD AVERAGE						

Source: Data taken from OECD Health Data 2012: http://stats.oecd.org/Index.aspx?DataSetCode=HEALTH_LVNG

TABLE 3-16   2005–2010 Obese Percentage of Males

	2005	2006	2007	2008	2009	2010
Australia	..	..	25.5	..	..	..
Austria	..	..	..	..	..	..
Belgium	..	..	..	..	..	..
Canada	25.2	..	..	25.2	..	..
Chile	..	..	..	..	19.2	..
Czech Republic	18.0	..	..	23.0	..	21.0
Denmark	..	..	..	..	..	..
Estonia	..	..	..	..	..	..
Finland	..	..	19.3	..	..	..
France	..	..	..	..	..	..
Germany	..	..	..	..	..	..
Greece	..	..	..	..	..	..
Hungary	..	..	..	..	26.3	..
Iceland	..	..	..	..	..	..
Ireland	..	..	22.0	..	..	..
Israel	..	..	..	..	..	..
Italy	..	..	..	..	..	..

TABLE 3-16	2005–2010 Obese Percentage of Males *(continued)*					
	2005	**2006**	**2007**	**2008**	**2009**	**2010**
Japan	3.4	3.4	3.4	3.4	4.3	3.8
Korea	3.6	..	3.9	4.0	3.6	3.5
Luxembourg	18.8	21.1	20.9	21.3	24.5	23.6
Mexico	23.7	24.2	..	..	..	..
Netherlands	..	..	..	..	..	..
New Zealand	..	..	26.0	..	27.7	..
Norway	..	..	..	..	..	..
Poland	..	..	..	..	..	..
Portugal	..	..	..	..	..	..
Slovak Republic	16.8	..	..	17.1	..	..
Slovenia	..	..	..	..	..	..
Spain	..	..	..	..	..	..
Sweden	..	..	..	..	..	..
Switzerland	..	..	..	..	..	..
Turkey	..	..	..	..	..	..
United Kingdom	22.1	23.7	23.6	24.1	22.1	26.2
United States	..	33.3	..	32.2	..	35.5
OECD AVERAGE						

Source: Data taken from OECD Health Data 2012: http://stats.oecd.org/Index.aspx?DataSetCode=HEALTH_LVNG

in 10 adult deaths worldwide or 6 million deaths per year (OECD, 2011a).

All countries reported at least 1 year of tobacco consumption rates. The highest reported rates were Greece and Turkey, which reported 40% and 33.4% respectively in 2006 and which dropped to 31.9% and 25.4% by 2009 and 2010, respectively. In 2005, of the 15 countries reporting, Denmark had the highest rate of 26% who consumed tobacco—Korea was second with 25.9%. The third highest percentage was Norway and the Netherlands at 25% and 25.2%, respectively. The United States and Canada had the lowest reported rates in 2005,

at 16.9% and 17.3%, respectively. All rates decreased in 2010. Denmark's rate dropped to 25%, Korea's to 22.9%, and Norway and the Netherlands decreased to 19% and 22.9%, respectively. The United States and Canadian rates decreased to 15.1% and 16.3%, respectively.

2005–2010 Alcohol Consumption (Liter per Capita, 15 Years and Older) (Table 3-18, pages 85–86)

(1 gallon = 3.785 liters)

According to OECD, high alcohol intake is associated with increased risk of heart disease, stroke risk, and certain cancers. Alcohol is also associated with

TABLE 3-17	2005–2010 Tobacco Consumption (15 Years and Older Who Are Daily Smokers)

	2005	2006	2007	2008	2009	2010
Australia	..	..	16.6	..	..	15.1
Austria	..	23.2	..	..	..	..
Belgium	..	..	..	20.5	..	..
Canada	17.3	..	18.2	17.5	16.2	16.3
Chile	..	..	..	..	29.8	..
Czech Republic	..	..	..	24.6	..	..
Denmark	26.0	25.0	24.0	23.0	19.0	20.0
Estonia	..	27.8	..	26.2	..	26.2
Finland	21.8	21.4	20.6	20.4	18.6	19.0
France	..	25.9	..	26.2	..	23.3
Germany	23.2	..	..	..	21.9	..
Greece	..	40.0	..	39.7	31.9[b]	..
Hungary	..	..	..	..	26.5	..
Iceland	19.5	19.3	19.4	17.8	15.8	14.3
Ireland	..	..	29.0	..	..	..
Israel[1]	..	19.5	..	18.7	20.3	18.6[e]
Italy	22.3	23.0	22.4	22.4	23.3	23.1
Japan	24.2	23.8	24.1	21.8	23.4	19.5
Korea	25.9	..	24.0	26.3	25.6	22.9
Luxembourg	23.0	21.0	21.0	20.0	19.0	18.0
Mexico	..	13.3	..	..	..	..
Netherlands	25.2	25.2	23.1	23.3	22.6	20.9
New Zealand	22.5	20.7[b,e]	18.1	..	..	..
Norway	25.0	24.0	22.0	21.0	21.0	19.0
Poland	..	..	..	..	23.8	..
Portugal	..	18.6	..	..	..	..
Slovak Republic	..	..	..	..	19.5	..

| TABLE 3-17 | 2005–2010 Tobacco Consumption (15 Years and Older Who Are Daily Smokers)   *(continued)* |

	2005	2006	2007	2008	2009	2010
Slovenia	..	..	18.9	..	..	..
Spain	..	26.4	..	..	26.2[b]	..
Sweden	15.9	14.5	14.0	15.0	14.3	14.0
Switzerland	..	..	20.4	..	..	..
Turkey	..	33.4	..	27.4	..	25.4
United Kingdom	24.0	22.0	21.0	22.0	21.5	..
United States	16.9	16.7	15.4	16.5	16.1	15.1

1. The statistical data for Israel are supplied by and under the responsibility of the relevant Israeli authorities. The use of such data by the OECD is without prejudice to the status of the Golan Heights, East Jerusalem and Israeli settlements in the West Bank under the terms of international law.

b. Break in series

e. Estimate

Source: Reprinted by permission from OECD (2012), "Tobacco Consumption," Health: Key Tables from OECD, No. 21. http://dx.doi .org/10.1787/tobacco-table-2012-2-en

| TABLE 3-18 | 2005–2010 Alcohol Consumption (Liter per Capita, 15 Years and Older) |

	2005	2006	2007	2008	2009	2010
Australia	10.3	10.6	10.6	10.4	10.3	..
Austria	12.6	12.9	12.9	12.4	12.2	..
Belgium	9.7	9.7	11.2	10.8	..	..
Canada	7.8	8.0	8.1	8.2	8.2	8.2
Chile	7.2	..	..	..	8.6[b]	..
Czech Republic	12.0	11.9	12.1	12.1	12.1	11.4
Denmark	12.7	12.2	12.1	10.9	10.1	10.3
Estonia	13.1	13.4	14.8	14.2	11.9	11.4
Finland	10.0	10.1	10.4	10.3	10.0	9.7

(continues)

TABLE 3-18	2005-2010 Alcohol Consumption (Liter per Capita, 15 Years and Older) (*continued*)

	2005	2006	2007	2008	2009	2010
France	12.7	12.9	12.7	12.3	12.3	12.0
Germany	12.2	12.4	12.1	12.0	11.7	..
Greece	9.2	8.8	9.0	9.3	8.2	..
Hungary	13.0	13.2	12.6	11.8	11.5	..
Iceland	7.1	7.2	7.5	7.3	..	..
Ireland	13.4	13.4	13.4	12.4	11.3	11.9
Israel[1]	2.4	2.3	2.4	..	..	..
Italy	8.0	7.8	7.8	7.4	6.9	..
Japan	8.5	7.9	7.7	7.5	7.4	7.3
Korea	9.0	9.2	9.3	9.5	8.9	9.0
Luxembourg	17.7	16.3	16.2	16.5	15.3	..
Mexico	5.1	5.3	5.5	5.9[b]	..	..
Netherlands	9.6	9.6	9.6	9.7	9.4	..
New Zealand	9.3	9.3	9.2	9.5	9.3	9.6
Norway	6.4	6.5	6.6	6.8	6.7	6.6
Poland	9.1	9.9	10.3	10.8	10.2	10.1
Portugal	12.2	11.9	11.4	..	..	..
Slovak Republic	11.0	10.6	10.7	11.2	10.7	..
Slovenia	10.3	12.2	11.0	10.9	10.5	10.3
Spain	10.0	10.0	12.2	12.0	11.4	
Sweden	6.6	6.9	6.9	6.9	7.3	7.3
Switzerland	10.1	10.2	10.4	10.2	10.1	10.0
Turkey	1.3	1.2	1.3	1.5	1.5	1.5
United Kingdom	11.4	11.0	11.2	10.8	10.2	10.2
United States	8.4	8.6	8.7	8.8	8.7	..

1. The statistical data for Israel are supplied by and under the responsibility of the relevant Israeli authorities. The use of such data by the OECD is without prejudice to the status of the Golan Heights, East Jerusalem, and Israeli settlements in the West Bank under the terms of international law.

b. Break in series

Source: Reprinted by permission from OECD (2012), "Alcohol Consumption," Health: Key Tables from OECD, No. 24. http://dx.doi .org/10.1787/alcoholcons-table-2012-2-en

fatalities through accidents, assault, violence, homicide, and suicide (OECD, 2011b). In 2005, the highest rate was reported by Luxembourg at 17.7 liters. Ireland reported 13.4%, respectively. Estonia and Hungary reported at 13.1% and 13%. In 2005, the United States reported at 8.4% which increased to 8.9% in 2010. The lowest reported rate was Turkey at 1.3%. In 2009, Luxembourg's rate dropped to 15.3% and Ireland's dropped to 11.9%. Estonia had dropped to 11.4% and Hungary reported 11.5%. It is important to note that alcohol rates can have varied ranges because alcohol consumption is often influenced by culture and religion.

CONCLUSION

The U.S. healthcare system is a complicated system that is comprised of both public and private resources. Health care is available to those who have health insurance or who are entitled to health care through a public program. One can think of the healthcare system as several concentric circles that surround the most important stakeholders in the center circle: the healthcare consumers and providers. Immediately

surrounding this relationship are health insurance companies and government programs, healthcare facilities, pharmaceutical companies, and laboratories, all of which provide services to consumers to ensure they receive quality health care, as well as and support providers to ensure they provide quality health care. The next circle consists of peripheral stakeholders that do not have an immediate impact on the main relationship but are still important to the industry. These consist of the professional associations, the research organizations, and the medical and training facilities.

It is important to assess the system from an international perspective. Comparing different statistics from the OECD is valuable to assess the health of the United States.

Despite the cost of the healthcare system, many of the U.S. healthcare statistics ranked lower than other countries that spend less on their healthcare system. These statistics may point to the fact that other countries' healthcare systems are more effective than the U.S. system or that their citizens have healthier lifestyles, although obesity rates are increasing globally.

VOCABULARY

American Association of Homes and Services for the Aging (AAHSA)

American Health Care Association (AHCA)

American Hospital Association (AHA)

Blue Cross and Blue Shield

Brand name drugs

Bureau of Labor Statistics (BLS)

Charitable care or bad debt

Commonwealth Fund

Complementary and alternative medicine (CAM)

Diabetes mellitus

Duty to treat

Generic drugs

Gross domestic product (GDP)

Home healthcare services

Infant mortality rates

Life expectancy rates

National Center for Complementary and Alternative Medicine (NCCAM)

National Center for Health Statistics (NCHS)

Organisation for Economic Cooperation and Development (OECD)

Per capita

Pew Charitable Trusts

Pharmaceutical Research and Manufacturers of America (PhRMA)

Professional associations

Residential care facilities

Robert Wood Johnson Foundation

Stakeholder

REFERENCES

American Association of Homes and Services for the Aging. (2013). Retrieved from http://www.aahsa.org/about.aspx

American Diabetes Association. (2013). Diabetes basics. Retrieved from http://www.diabetes.org/diabetes-basics/

American Hospital Association. (2013). Financial Fact Sheets. Retrieved from http://www.aha.org/research/policy/finfactsheets.shtml

American Health Care Association. (2013). Retrieved from http://www.ahcancal.org/about_ahca/who_we_are/Pages/default.aspx

American Hospital Association. (2013). Retrieved from http://www.aha.org

Bureau of Labor Statistics. (2013a). Industries at a glance: Healthcare and social assistance sector. Retrieved from http://www.bls.gov/iag/tgs/iag62.htm

Bureau of Labor Statistics. (2013b). Industries at a glance: Nursing and residential care facilities. Retrieved from http://www.bls.gov/iag/tgs/iag623.htm

Bureau of Labor Statistics. (2013c). Occupational outlook handbook: Healthcare occupations. Retrieved from http://www.bls.gov/ooh/healthcare/

Bureau of Labor Statistics. (2013d). Occupational outlook handbook: Home health and personal care aides. Retrieved from http://www.bls.gov/ooh/healthcare/home-health-and-personal-care-aides.htm#tab-2

Bureau of Labor Statistics. (2013e). Industries at a glance: Ambulatory health care services: NAICS 621. Retrieved from http://www.bls.gov/iag/tgs/iag621.htm

Bureau of Labor Statistics. (2013f). Occupational outlook handbook. Medical and clinical laboratory technologists and technicians. Retrieved from http://www.bls.gov/ooh/healthcare/medical-and-clinical-laboratory-technologists-and-technicians.htm

Centers for Disease Control and Prevention. (2012a). Chartbook on trends in the health of Americans (Figure 1). Retrieved from http://www.cdc.gov/nchs/hus/contents2012.htm#fig1

Centers for Disease Control and Prevention. (2012b). Chartbook on trends in the health of Americans (Figure 14). Retrieved from http://www.cdc.gov/nchs/hus/contents2012.htm#fig14

Centers for Disease Control and Prevention. (2012c). Chartbook on trends in the health of Americans (Figure 40). Retrieved from http://www.cdc.gov/nchs/hus/contents2012.htm#fig40

Centers for Disease Control and Prevention. (2012d). Chartbook on trends in the health of Americans (Figure 19). Retrieved from http://www.cdc.gov/nchs/hus/contents2012.htm#fig19

Jonas, S. (2003). *An introduction to the U.S. health care system* (pp. 17–45). New York: Springer Publishing.

National Center for Health Statistics. (2013). The use of complementary and alternative medicine in the United States. Retrieved from http://nccam.nih.gov/news/camstats/208

OECD. (2011a). Tobacco consumption among adults. Retrieved from http://dx.doi.org/10.1787/health_glance-2011-16-en

OECD. (2011b). Alcohol consumption among adults. Retrieved from http://dx.doi.org/10.1787/health_glance-2011-17-3n

OECD. (2013). Health at a glance. Retrieved from http://www.oecd-ilibrary.org/social-issues-migration-health/health-at-a-glance_19991312

Pharmaceutical Research and Manufacturers of America. (2013). Retrieved from http://www.phrma.org/about_phrma/

Pointer, D., Williams, S., Isaacs, S., & Knickman, J. (2007). *Introduction to U.S. health care*. Hoboken, NJ: Wiley Publishing.

Science Daily. (2013). Insured and still at risk: Number of underinsured in U.S. increased 80 percent between 2003–2010. Retrieved from http://www.sciencedaily.com/releases/2011/09/110908081303.htm

Smith, D. (2008). The uninsured in the U.S. health care system. *Journal of Health Care Management, 53*, 2, 79–81.

Sultz, H., & Young, K. (2006). *Health care USA: Understanding its organization and delivery* (5th ed.). Sudbury, MA: Jones and Bartlett.

U.S. Department of Labor. (2013). Occupational safety and health administration. Retrieved from http://www.osha.gov/SLTC/healthcarefacilities/

Zhong, H. (2012). Primer: The pharmaceutical industry. Retrieved from http://americanactionforum.org/topic/primer-pharmaceutical-industry

NOTES

IN YOUR OWN WORDS

Based on this chapter, please provide a definition of the following vocabulary words in your own words. DO NOT RECITE the text definition.

Duty to treat: _____

_____

_____

Infant mortality rate: _____

_____

_____

Life expectancy rates: _____

_____

_____

Charitable care or bad debt: _____

_____

_____

Complementary and alternative medicine: _____

_____

_____

Outpatient care centers: _____

_____

_____

Professional associations: _____

_____

_____

Residential care facilities: _____

_____

_____

STUDENT ACTIVITY 3-2

REAL LIFE APPLICATIONS: CASE SCENARIO ONE

You have decided to become a health education teacher for a high school. One of your first class lessons will be on explaining the complexity of the U.S. healthcare system to your students.

ACTIVITY

You want to be creative so you have your students role play the stakeholders in the healthcare system. You also want them to understand how the United States compares to other countries. You develop a lesson plan that is outlined below. Your lesson plan outlines the major stakeholders in the system and how they interact with each other.

RESPONSES

_____

_____

_____

_____

_____

_____

_____

_____

_____

_____

_____

_____

_____

_____

CASE SCENARIO TWO

Your grandmother will be moving to a continuous care retirement community and is unsure of how to evaluate them. She asked you for assistance.

ACTIVITY

Visit the American Association of Homes and Services for the Aging (AAHSA) to find out what information is available for continuing care communities. Give that information to your grandmother to help her make a decision.

RESPONSES

_____

_____

_____

_____

_____

_____

_____

_____

_____

_____

_____

_____

_____

_____

_____

CASE SCENARIO THREE

You eventually would like to work for a pharmaceutical company. You decided to perform research on pharmaceutical companies such as Pfizer and Glaxco Smith Kline. You actually did not realize that there are brand name drugs and generic drugs.

ACTIVITY

Perform an Internet search on the difference between generic and brand name drugs. Discuss the difference between the two products.

RESPONSES

_____

_____

_____

_____

_____

_____

_____

_____

_____

_____

_____

_____

_____

CASE SCENARIO FOUR

You have heard the phrase "graying of our population" frequently but are not sure what it means. All of your coworkers are young so you are not sure if it is valid.

ACTIVITY

Define the concept and find four statistics that support or refute this concept.

RESPONSES

_____

_____

_____

_____

_____

_____

_____

_____

_____

_____

_____

_____

_____

_____

_____

_____

STUDENT ACTIVITY 3-3

INTERNET EXERCISES

Write your answers in the space provided.

- Visit each of the websites listed here.
- Name the organization.
- Locate their mission statement on their website.
- Provide a brief overview of the activities of the organization.
- How do these organizations participate in the U.S. healthcare system?

Websites

http://www.rwjf.org

Organization Name: _____

Mission Statement:

_____

_____

_____

Overview of Activities: _____

_____

_____

Importance of organization to U.S. health care:

_____

_____

_____

http://www.commonwealthfund.org

Organization Name: _____

Mission Statement:

_____

_____

_____

Overview of Activities: _____

_____

_____

Importance of organization to U.S. health care:

_____

_____

_____

Organization Name: _____

Mission Statement:

_____

_____

_____

Overview of Activities: _____

_____

_____

Importance of organization to U.S. health care:

_____

_____

_____

Organization Name: _____

Mission Statement:

_____

_____

_____

Overview of Activities: _____

_____

_____

Importance of organization to U.S. health care:

_____

_____

_____

Organization Name: _____

Mission Statement:

_____

_____

_____

Overview of Activities: _____

_____

_____

Importance of organization to U.S. health care:

_____

_____

_____

http://www.ahcancal.org

Organization Name: _____

Mission Statement:

_____

_____

Overview of Activities: _____

_____

_____

_____

Importance of organization to U.S. health care:

_____

_____

_____

DISCUSSION QUESTIONS

The following are suggested discussion questions for this chapter.

(1) Which of the OECD statistics surprised you about the United States?

_____

_____

_____

_____

_____

(2) Identify three stakeholders and their role in the healthcare industry.

_____

_____

_____

_____

_____

(3) Do you feel the United States should have a universal healthcare system? Defend your answer.

_____

_____

_____

_____

_____

(4) Select one of the OECD countries and discuss three of its statistics. You cannot pick the United States.

_____

_____

_____

_____

(5) Review the alcohol and tobacco statistics for the United States and comment on their ranking among the other countries.

_____

_____

_____

_____

The Navigate Companion Website for this text is a great source for additional information on the U.S. health care system. You can gain a new perspective on many of the topics presented in this chapter by visiting http://go.jblearning.com/Niles2e. You'll find additional student activities, further reading, and interactive study tools that explore:

- Basic concepts of health
- Milestones of U.S. healthcare systems development
- Current U.S. healthcare system operations
- And much more.

Chapter 4

Government's Role in U.S. Health Care

LEARNING OBJECTIVES

The student will be able to:

- Describe five government organizations and their roles in health care.
- Explain the importance of the National Association of County and City Health Officials in health care.
- Analyze the integration of the collaboration of the Department of Homeland Security and the Federal Emergency Management Agency and its importance to disaster management.
- Describe the role of the National Institutes of Health in healthcare research.
- Discuss the U.S. Food and Drug Administration's regulatory responsibility in health care.
- Evaluate the role of the Centers for Medicare and Medicaid Services in health care.

DID YOU KNOW THAT?

- Social regulation focuses on actions such as those in the healthcare industry that impact an individual's safety or well-being.
- The U.S. Surgeon General is the chief health educator in the United States.

- The Food and Drug Administration is responsible for accrediting and inspecting mammography facilities.
  - Over the last several years, there has been a trend to regionalize local health departments in order to maximize population services.
- The Department of Homeland Security is responsible for ensuring that all government levels have an emergency preparedness plan for catastrophic events.

INTRODUCTION

During the Depression and World War II the United States had no funds to start a universal healthcare program—an issue that had been discussed for years. As a result, a private sector system was developed that did not provide healthcare services to all citizens. However, the government's role of providing healthcare coverage evolved as a regulatory body to ensure that the elderly and poor were able to receive health care. The passage of the **Social Security Act of 1935** and the establishment of the Medicaid and Medicare programs in 1965 mandated the government's increased role in providing healthcare coverage. Also, the State Children's Health Insurance Program (SCHIP), now the Children's Health Insurance Program, established in 1997 and reauthorized by the Affordable Care Act (ACA) through 2019 with extended funding through 2015, continues to expand the government's role in children's health care (CHIP, 2013). In addition to the reauthorization of the SCHIP program, the ACA has increased government interaction with the healthcare system by developing several of the government initiatives that focus on increasing the ability of individuals to make informed decisions about their health care.

In these instances, the government increased accessibility to health care as well as provided financing for health care to certain targeted populations. This chapter will focus on the different roles the federal, state, and local governments play in the U.S. healthcare system. This chapter will also highlight different government programs and regulations that focus on monitoring how health care is provided.

HISTORY OF THE ROLE OF GOVERNMENT IN HEALTH CARE

Social regulation focuses on organizations' actions, such as those in the healthcare industry, that impact an individual's safety. Social regulations focus on protecting individuals as employees and consumers (Carroll & Buchholtz, 2009). These types of regulations are common in the U.S. healthcare system. The healthcare industry claims it is the most regulated industry in the world. It is important to mention that government regulations aside, there are nongovernmental regulations of U.S. health care by accrediting bodies such as the Joint Commission, which began over 80 years ago and accredits over 20,000 healthcare organizations (The Joint Commission, 2013). However, regulatory oversight is mainly handled at the federal, state, and local government levels.

U.S. GOVERNMENT AGENCIES

Regulatory healthcare power is shared among federal and state governments. State governments have a dominant role of regulating constituents in their jurisdiction. To assure success in this regulatory process, state governments also developed local government levels to provide direct services to constituents and regulate their geographic region. Their legal authority is derived from legislatures that establish the legal framework for their authority (Jonas, 2003).

Important Federal Government Agencies

Many federal agencies are responsible for a sector of healthcare. The **U.S. Department of Health and Human Services (HHS)** is the most important federal agency. HHS collaborates with state and local governments because many HHS services are provided at those levels. There are 11 operating divisions: the **Centers for Disease Control and Prevention (CDC)**, **Administration for Community Living (ACL)**, **National Institutes of Health (NIH)**, **Agency for Toxic Substances and Disease Registry (ATSDR)**, **Indian Health Service (IHS)**, the **Health Resources and Services Administration (HRSA)**, the **Agency for Healthcare Research and Quality (AHRQ)**, the **Substance Abuse and Mental Health Services Administration (SAMHSA)**, the **U.S. Food and Drug Administration (FDA)**, **Administration for Children and Families (ACF)**, and the **Centers for Medicare and Medicaid Services (CMS)**. Each of these agencies will be discussed individually (HHS, 2013).

Centers for Disease Control and Prevention (CDC)

Established in 1946 and headquartered in Atlanta, Georgia, the CDC's mission is to protect health and promote quality of life through the prevention and control of disease, injury, and disability. The CDC has created four health goals that focus on (1) healthy people in healthy places, (2) preparing people for emerging health threats, (3) positive international health, and (4) healthy people at all stages of their life. To achieve these goals, the CDC focuses on six areas: health impact, customer focus, public health research, leadership, globalization, and accountability. On the CDC website, they provide information on disease, healthy living, emergency preparedness, injury prevention, environmental health, workplace safety, data and statistics, and global health. They also provide specific information for traveler, infant and children, pregnancies, and state and tribal associations (CDC, 2013).

Administration for Community Living (ACL)

All Americans—including people with disabilities and older adults—should be able to live at home with the supports they need, participating in communities that value their contributions. To help meet these needs, the HHS created a new organization, the ACL.

Established in 2012, the ACL brings together the efforts and achievements of the Administration on Aging, the Administration on Intellectual and Developmental Disabilities, and the HHS Office on Disability to serve as the federal agency responsible for increasing access to community supports, while focusing attention and resources on the unique needs of older Americans and people with disabilities across the lifespan.

The ACL mission is to maximize the independence, well being, and health of older adults, people with disabilities across the lifespan, and their families and caregivers (ACL, 2013).

Agency for Toxic Substances and Disease Registry (ATSDR)

Established in 1985, headquartered in Atlanta, Georgia, and authorized by the Comprehensive Environmental Response, Compensation, and Liability Act of 1980 (CERCLA; more commonly known as the Superfund law), ATSDR is responsible for finding and cleaning the most dangerous hazardous waste sites in the country. ATSDR's mission is to protect the public against harmful exposures and disease-related exposures to toxic substances. ATSDR is the lead federal public health agency responsible for determining human health effects associated with toxic exposures, preventing continued exposures, and mitigating associated human health risks. ATSDR is administered organizationally with the CDC. The ATSDR has 10 regional offices within the Environmental Protection Agency (EPA) across the country (ATSDR, 2013).

National Institutes of Health (NIH)

Established in 1930 and headquartered in Bethesda, Maryland, this agency is the primary federal agency for research toward preventing and curing disease worldwide. Its mission is the pursuit of knowledge about the nature and behavior of living systems and the application of that knowledge to extend healthy life and reduce the burdens of illness and disability. They have 27 institutes and centers that focus on different diseases and conditions including cancer, ophthalmology, heart and lung and blood, genes, aging, alcoholism and drug abuse, infectious diseases, chronic diseases, children's diseases, and mental health. Although they have sponsored external research, they also have a large internal research program (NIH, 2013).

The Health Resources and Services Administration (HRSA)

Created in 1982 and headquartered in Rockville, Maryland, the HRSA is the primary federal agency for improving access to healthcare services for people in every state who are uninsured, isolated, or medically vulnerable. They have six bureaus: primary health care, health professions, healthcare systems, maternal and child, the HIV/AIDS bureau, and the Bureau of Clinician Recruitment and Service. HRSA provides funding to grantees that provide health care to those vulnerable populations. They also oversee organ, bone marrow, and cord blood donation; support programs against bioterrorism; and maintain databases that protect against healthcare malpractice and healthcare waste, fraud, and abuse. Tens of millions of Americans get affordable health care and other help through HRSA's 100-plus programs and more than 3,000 grantees (HRSA, 2013).

The Agency for Healthcare Research and Quality (AHRQ)

Created in 1989 and headquartered in Rockville, Maryland, the agency's mission is to improve the quality, safety, efficiency, and effectiveness of health care for all U.S. citizens. AHRQ's cutting edge research helps people make more informed decisions and improve the quality of healthcare services. AHRQ focuses on the following areas of research: healthcare costs and utilization, information technology, disaster preparedness, medication safety, healthcare consumerism, prevention of illness, and special needs populations (AHRQ, 2013). There is a **Coalition for Health Services Research (CHSR)**, an organization of volunteers who advocate for the AHRQ. It is comprised of more than 250 nonprofit organizations that support the AHRQ. They send letters to Congress encouraging more funds for research (CHSR, 2013).

Indian Health Service (IHS)

Established in 1921 and headquartered in Rockville, Maryland, the mission of IHS is to raise the physical, mental, social, and spiritual health of American Indians and Alaska Natives to the highest level. It is also their mission to assure that comprehensive, culturally acceptable personal and public health services are available and accessible to American Indian and Alaska Native people. They are also responsible to promote their communities and cultures and to honor and protect the inherent sovereign rights of these people. The IHS provides a comprehensive health service delivery system for approximately 1.9 million American Indians and Alaska Natives who belong to 566 federally recognized tribes (IHS, 2013).

The Substance Abuse and Mental Health Services Administration (SAMHSA)

Established in 1992, the SAMHSA is the main federal agency for improving access to quality substance abuse and mental health services in the United States by working with state, community, and private organizations. SAMHSA is the umbrella agency for mental health and substance abuse services, which includes the **Center for Mental Health Services (CMHS)**, the **Center for Substance Abuse Prevention (CSAP)**, and the **Center for Substance Abuse Treatment (CSAT)**. The **Center for Behavioral Health Statistics and Quality (CBHSQ)** is responsible for data collection, analysis, and dissemination of critical health data to assist policymakers, providers, and the public for the use in making informed decisions regarding the prevention and treatment of mental and substance use disorders (SAMHSA, 2013).

U.S. Food and Drug Administration (FDA)

Established in 1906 as a result of the **Federal Food, Drug, and Cosmetic Act**, the FDA is responsible for ensuring that the following products are safe: food, human and veterinary products, biologic products, medical devices, cosmetics, and electronic products. The FDA is also responsible for ensuring that product information is accurate. The following is a summary of FDA responsibility for each category:

1. Food: The FDA ensures that labeling of food has accurate information. Also, they regulate the safety of all food except poultry and meat. They also oversee bottled water.

2. Veterinary products: The FDA has oversight of the production of livestock feed, pet food, and veterinary drugs and devices.

3. Human drugs: The FDA has regulatory oversight of both prescription and over-the-counter (OTC) drug development and labeling, which includes the manufacturing standards for these drug products.

4. Medical devices: The FDA has the authority for premarket approval for any new devices as well as developing standards for their manufacturing and performance. They also must track reports of any malfunction of these devices.

5. Cosmetics: The FDA oversees both the safety and labeling of cosmetic products.

6. Electronic products: The FDA must develop and regulate standards for microwaves, television receivers, and diagnostic equipment such as X-ray equipment, laser products, ultrasonic therapy equipment, and sunlamps. They also must accredit and inspect any mammography facilities.

The FDA is also responsible for advancing public health by speeding up innovations to make medicine and food more effective, safer, and more affordable. They are also responsible for ensuring that the public receives accurate information to be able to make informed decisions about using medicine and food products (USFDA, 2013).

The Administration for Children and Families (ACF)

The ACF, which has 10 regional offices, is responsible for federal programs that promote the economic and social well-being of families, children, individuals, and communities. Their mission is to empower people to increase their own economic well-being, support communities that have a positive impact on the quality of life of its residents, partner with other organizations to support Native American tribes, improve needed access to services, and work with those who are special needs populations (ACF, 2013).

Centers for Medicare and Medicaid Services (CMS)

CMS was established when the Medicare and Medicaid programs were signed into law in 1965 by President Lyndon B. Johnson as a result of the Social Security Act. At that time, only half of those 65 years or older had health insurance. Medicaid was established for low-income children, the elderly, the blind, and the disabled and was linked with the Supplemental Security Income program (SSI). In 1972, Medicare was extended to cover people under the age of 65 with permanent disabilities. CMS also has oversight of SCHIP,

Title XXI of the Social Security Act, which is financed by both federal and state funding and is administered at the state level.

Headquartered in Baltimore, Maryland, the CMS has over 20 offices that oversee different aspects of their programs. Their primary responsibility is to provide policy, funding, and oversight to the elderly and poor healthcare programs. For years, their organizational oversight was a geographically based structure with 10 field offices. In 2007, CMS was reorganized to a consortia structure based on the priorities of Medicare health plans and financial management, Medicare fee for service, Medicaid and children's health, surveys and certification, and quality assurance and improvement. The consortia are responsible for oversight of the 10 regional offices for each priority. In 2010, the Center for Program Integrity was formed as part of the CMS that focuses on best practices for program implementation (CMS, 2013a). As part of the Affordable Care Act, the Innovation Center was established. Congress created the Innovation Center for the purpose of testing "innovative payment and service delivery models to reduce program expenditures while preserving or enhancing the quality of care" for those individuals who receive Medicare, Medicaid, or Children's Health Insurance Program (CHIP) benefits (CMS, 2013b).

Occupational Safety and Health Administration (OSHA)

Established on December 29, 1970, and part of the U.S. Department of Labor, the **Occupational Safety and Health Administration (OSHA)** was established to govern workplace environments to ensure that employees have a safe and healthy environment (OSHA, 2013). The **Hazard Communication Standard (HCS)** ensures that all hazardous chemicals are properly labeled and that companies are informed of these risks (Hazard Communication, 2013). The **Medical Waste Tracking Act** requires companies to have medical waste disposal procedures so that there is no risk to employees and the environment (Environmental Protection Agency, 2013). The **Occupational Exposure to Blood-borne Pathogen Standard** developed behavioral standards for employees who deal with blood products such as wearing gloves and other equipment, disposal of blood collection materials (OSHA Quicktakes, 2013).

Surgeon General/U.S. Public Health Service

The **Surgeon General** is the U.S. chief health educator who provides information on how to improve the health of the U.S. population. The Surgeon General, who is appointed by the President of the United States, and the Office of the Surgeon General oversee the operations of the commissioned **U.S. Public Health Service Corps**, who provide support to the Surgeon General. The U.S. Public Health Service Commissioned Corps consists of 6,500 public health professionals who are stationed within federal agencies and programs. These commissioned employees include various professionals such as dentists, nurses, physicians, mental health specialists, environmental health specialists, veterinarians, and therapists. The Surgeon General serves a 4-year term and reports to the Secretary of Health and Human Services. The Surgeon General focuses on certain health priorities for the United States and publishes reports on these issues (Office of the Surgeon General, 2013).

Department of Homeland Security (DHS)

The **Department of Homeland Security (DHS)** was established in 2002 as a result of the 2001 terrorist attack on the United States. It combined 22 different federal departments to form the DHS. The **Federal Emergency Management Agency (FEMA)**, which is responsible for managing catastrophic events, was integrated into DHS in 2003. Together, they are responsible for coordinating efforts at all government levels to ensure emergency preparedness for any catastrophic events such as bioterrorism; chemical and radiation emergencies; mass casualties as a result of explosions, natural disasters, and severe weather; and disease outbreaks. They coordinate with the CDC to ensure there are plans in place to quickly resolve these events. DHS has also developed a **National Incident Management System (NIMS)** that provides a systematic, proactive approach to all levels of government and private sector agencies to collaborate and ensure there is a seamless plan to manage any major incidents. The **National Integration Center (NIC)** requires the development of preparedness-related doctrine, policy, and guidance to reflect the collective expertise and experience of the whole community. The NIC has primary responsibility for the maintenance and management of national preparedness doctrine. The NIC develops strategies, doctrine, policies, guidance, and best practices in collaboration with practitioners and subject matter experts from the whole community. The second edition of the **National Response Framework**, updated in 2013, provides context for how the whole community works together and how response efforts relate to other parts of national preparedness (DHS, 2013).

Office of the Assistant Secretary for Preparedness and Response (ASPR)

The **Office of the Assistant Secretary for Preparedness and Response (ASPR)** was created under the Pandemic and All Hazards Preparedness Act in the wake of Hurricane Katrina to prevent, prepare, and respond to the adverse health effects of public health emergencies and disasters. ASPR focuses on preparedness planning and response; building federal emergency medical operational capabilities; countermeasures research, advance development, and procurement; and grants to strengthen the capabilities of hospitals and healthcare systems in public health emergencies and medical disasters. The office provides federal support, including medical professionals through ASPR's **National Disaster Medical System**, to augment state and local capabilities during an emergency or disaster. The Secretary of HHS delegates to ASPR the leadership role for all health and medical services support function in a health emergency or public health event (ASPR, 2013).

State Health Departments' Role in Health Care

The U.S. constitution gives state governments the primary role in providing health care for their citizens. Most states have several different agencies that are responsible for specific public health services. There is usually a lead state agency with approximately 20 agencies that target health issues like aging, living, and working environments, as well as alcoholism and substance abuse. Many state agencies are responsible for implementing several different federal acts such as the Clean Water Act; Clean Air Act; Food, Drug, and Cosmetic Act; and Safe Drinking Water Act (Turnock, 2007). **State health departments** monitor communities to identify health problems. Additionally, they diagnose and investigate health problems and provide education about health issues. They also develop policies to support community health. They must enforce laws and regulations to promote health and safety. Most state agencies are responsible for or share responsibility for federal programs related to maternal and infant health services and cancer prevention. They are responsible

for providing population-based services for the CDC's health priorities, which include: motor vehicle injuries, HIV, obesity, food safety, tobacco use, teen pregnancy, and nutrition. Vital statistics collected include deaths, births, marriages, and health and disease statuses of the population. These statistics are important to collect because they serve as a basis for funding. The **Council of State and Territorial Epidemiologists (CSTE)** decides which diseases should be considered reportable to the CDC, which are then produced in a weekly report, **Morbidity and Mortality Weekly Report (MMWR)**. The *MMWR* is an estimate of the prevalence of disease throughout the country (Association of State and Territorial Health Officials, 2013).

State health departments also license health professionals such as physicians, dentists, chiropractors, nurses, pharmacists, optometrists, and veterinarians who practice within the state. Further, they inspect and license healthcare facilities such as hospitals and nursing homes. Most state agencies provide technical assistance to their local health departments in the following areas: (1) quality improvement, (2) data management, (3) public health law, (4) human resource management, and (5) policy development. It is important to emphasize that the state health department provides oversight to their local health departments who are directly responsible for providing public health activities for their community (Mays, 2008). State agencies are funded primarily by federal sources, state resources, and Medicaid/Medicare, with the remaining sources supplied by fines and fees, indirect federal funding, and other minor sources. (Association of State and Territorial Health Officials Profile, 2013).

Local Health Departments' Role in Health Care

Local health departments are the government organizations that provide the most direct services to the population. There are 2,700 local health departments across the United States. Although their organizational structures may differ across the United States, their basic role is to provide direct public health services to their designated areas. It is difficult to generalize what types of services are offered by local health departments because they do vary according to geographic location, but most are involved in communicable disease control. According to a recent **National Association for County and City Health Officials (NACCHO)** survey, the following are highlights of what types of direct services are offered by local health departments:

- Over 90% of local health departments provide adult and children immunizations.
- Over 90% offer communicable/infectious disease surveillance.
- Over 80% offer tuberculosis screening and 75% offer tuberculosis treatment.
- Over 75% offer environmental surveillance.
- Approximately 70% offer population nutrition services.
- Nearly 75% provide school/day care center inspection.
- Approximately 75% provide food safety education (NACCHO, 2010).

Local health departments receive funding from their state government, the federal government, direct funding such as from the CDC, reimbursement for services from Medicaid and Medicare, private health insurance, and fees for services. Because of population size and coverage, local health department funding varies from state to state. Local sources are the greatest contributor to funding local health departments, followed by state allocations, Medicare and Medicaid, fees, and other federal funding (NACCHO, 2010). However, the ACA has strengthened the position of the local health departments by increasing funding for educating the public health workforce and increasing the focus on preventive services that are traditionally performed by the local health departments. (Historic Health Reform Legislation, 2013).

Regionalization of Local Health Departments

Over the last 10 years, there has been a trend to **regionalize** local health departments in order to maximize the service provided to their populations. Counties that normally provide health services separately have formed regional health departments, which means that smaller local health departments unite as one operation to provide services within a geographic area. This type of organizational restructure reduced redundancy in services. Usually, one larger county health department will serve as the leader of the region. The regionalization in many states has been voluntary. Individual counties still have autonomy for funding and regulatory issues but have become more efficient in providing services regionally (Functional Regionalization, 2013). For example, when bioterrorism grants were distributed, those regional areas received more funds than counties that were not regionalized.

Public Health Accreditation and Emergency Preparedness

In May 2007, the **Public Health Accreditation Board** was established to set standards for voluntary national accreditation for both state and local health departments. This accreditation assures that the health departments deliver the core functions of public health and essential public health services. In 2011, public health department accreditation became mandatory. Based on population served, there is a fee for this accreditation. As of March 2013, nine local and two state health departments have received this accreditation (NAACHO, 2013). Both state and local health departments are also expected to have an **emergency preparedness** planning protocol in place to ensure there is coordination of public health activities during large-scale events that impact public health (Turnock, 2007).

CONCLUSION

The government plays an important role in the quality of the U.S. healthcare system. The federal government provides funding for state and local government programs. Federal healthcare regulations are implemented and enforced at the state and local levels. Funding is primarily distributed from the federal government to the state government, which consequently allocates funding to their local health departments. Local health departments provide the majority of services for their constituents. More local health departments are working with local organizations such as schools and physicians to increase their ability to provide education and prevention services.

DHS and FEMA now play an integral role in the management and oversight of any catastrophic events such as natural disasters, earthquakes, floods, pandemic diseases, and bioterrorism. DHS and FEMA collaborate closely with the CDC to ensure that both the state and local health departments have a crisis management plan in place for these events. These attacks are often horrific and frightening with a tremendous loss of life, and as a result, the state and local health departments need to be more prepared to deal with catastrophic events. They are required to develop plans and be trained to deal effectively with many of these catastrophic issues. Finally, the Affordable Care Act has increased government involvement in the healthcare industry to promote access to a quality healthcare system.

VOCABULARY

Administration for Children and Families (ACF)

Administration for Community Living (ACL)

Agency for Healthcare Research and Quality (AHRQ)

Agency for Toxic Substances and Disease Registry (ATSDR)

Center for Behavioral Health Statistics and Quality (CBHSQ)

Center for Mental Health Services (CMHS)

Center for Substance Abuse Prevention (CSAP)

Center for Substance Abuse Treatment (CSAT)

Centers for Disease Control and Prevention (CDC)

Centers for Medicare and Medicaid Services (CMS)

Coalition for Health Services Research (CHSR)

Council of State and Territorial Epidemiologists (CSTE)

Department of Homeland Security (DHS)

Emergency preparedness

Federal Emergency Management Agency (FEMA)

Federal Food, Drug, and Cosmetic Act (FDCA)

Hazard Communication Standard (HCS)

Health Resources and Services Administration (HRSA)

Indian Health Service (IHS)

Local health departments

Medical Waste Tracking Act

Morbidity and Mortality Weekly Report (*MMWR*)

National Association for County and City Health Officials (NACCHO)

National Disaster Medical System

National Incident Management System (NIMS)

National Institutes of Health (NIH)

National Integration Center (NIC)

National Response Framework (NRF)

Occupational Exposure to Blood-borne Pathogen Standard

Occupational Safety and Health Administration (OSHA)

Office of the Assistant Secretary for Preparedness and Response (ASPR)

Public Health Accreditation Board

Regionalization

Social regulation

Social Security Act of 1935

State health departments

Substance Abuse and Mental Health Services Administration (SAMHSA)

Surgeon General

U.S. Department of Health and Human Services (HHS)

U.S. Food and Drug Administration (FDA)

U.S. Public Health Service Corps

REFERENCES

Administration for Children and Families (ACF). (2013). What we do. Retrieved from http://www.acf.hhs.gov/about/what-we-do

Administration for Community Living (ACL). (2013). Retrieved from http://www.acl.gov/About_ACL/Index.aspx

Agency for Healthcare Research and Quality (AHRQ). (2013). Retrieved from http://www.ahrq.gov/about/mission/glance/index.html

Agency for Toxic Substances and Disease Registry (ATSDR). (2013). Retrieved from http://www.atsdr.cdc.gov/about/index.html

ASPR. (2013). Office of the Assistant Secretary for preparedness and response. Retrieved from http://www.phe.gov/about/aspr/Pages/default.aspx

Association of State and Territorial Health Officials (ASTHO). (2013). Profile. Retrieved from http://www.astho.org/about/.org/about/

Carroll, A., & Buchholtz, A. (2009). *Business and society: Ethics and stakeholder management*. Mason, OH: Cengage.

Centers for Disease Control and Prevention (CDC). (2013). Retrieved from http://www.cdc.gov/about/

Centers for Medicare and Medicaid Services (CMS). (2013a). About CMS. Retrieved from http://www.cms.gov/About-CMS/About-CMS.html

Centers for Medicare and Medicaid Services (CMS). (2013b). Innovation Center. Retrieved from http://innovation.cms.gov/

Children's Health Insurance Program (CHIP). (2013). Retrieved from http://www.medicaid.gov/medicaid-chip-program-information/by-topics/childrens-health-insurance-program-chip/childrens-health-insurance-program-chip.html

Coalition for Health Services Research (CHSR). (2013). Retrieved from http://www.chsr.org/about.htm

Council of State and Territorial Epidemiologists (CSTE). (2013). Retrieved from http://www.cste.org/dnn/AboutCSTE/AboutCSTE/tabid/56/Default.aspx

Department of Homeland Security (DHS). (2013). Retrieved from http://www.dhs.gov/xabout/index.shtm

Environmental Protection Agency (EPA). (2013). Medical Waste Tracking Act of 1988. Retrieved from http://www.epa.gov/osw/nonhaz/industrial/medical/tracking.htm

Functional Regionalization Project. (2013). Retrieved from http://www.kalhd.org/en/cms/?1109

Hazard Communication (2013). Retrieved from http://www.osha.gov/dsg/hazcom/index.html

Health and Human Services (HHS). (2013). Retrieved from http://www.hhs.gov/about/

Health Resources and Services Administration (HRSA). (2013). Retrieved from http://www.hrsa.gov/about/index.html

Historic health reform legislation (2013). Retrieved from NACCHO LHU Profile, 2013.

Indian Health Service (IHS). (2013). Retrieved from http://www.ihs.gov/PublicInfo/PublicAffairs/Welcome_Info/IHSintro.asp

Jonas, S. (2003). *An introduction to the U.S. health care system* (pp. 17–45). New York: Springer Publishing.

Mays, G. (2008). Organization of the public health delivery system. In L. Novick & C. Morrow (Eds.), *Public health administration*: *Principles for population-based management* (pp. 69–126). Sudbury, MA: Jones and Bartlett.

NACCHO. (2010). 2010 national profile of local health departments. Retrieved from http://www.naccho.org/topics/infrastructure/profile/resources/index.cfm#anchor7

NACCHO. (2013). NAACHO applauds eleven public health departments receiving national accreditation. Retrieved from http://www.naacho.org/press/releases/accreditation.cfm

National Institutes of Health (NIH). (2013). Retrieved from http://www.nih.gov/about/mission.htm

Occupational Safety and Health Administration (OSHA). (2013). Retrieved from http://www.osha.gov/about.html

Office of the Surgeon General. (2013). Retrieved from http://www.surgeongeneral.gov/about/index.html

OSHA Quicktakes. (2013). Blood borne Pathogens. Retrieved from http://www.osha.gov/pls/oshaweb/owadisp.show_document?p_table=standards&p_id=10051

Substance Abuse and Mental Health Services Administration (SAMHSA). (2013). Retrieved from http://www.oas.samhsa.gov

The Joint Commission. (2013). About The Joint Commission. Retrieved from http://www.jointcommission.org/about_us/about_the_joint_commission_main.aspx

Turnock, B. (2007). *Essentials of public health*. Sudbury, MA: Jones and Bartlett.

U.S. Food and Drug Administration (FDA). (2013). Retrieved from http://www.fda.gov/AboutFDA/WhatWeDo/WhatFDARegulates/default.htm

NOTES

STUDENT ACTIVITY 4-1

IN YOUR OWN WORDS

Based on this chapter, please provide a description of the following concepts in your own words. DO NOT RECITE the text description.

Hazard Communication Standard (HCS): _____

_____

_____

National Response Network (NRF): _____

_____

_____

Regionalization of public health departments: _____

_____

_____

Coalition for Health Services Research (CHSR): _____

_____

_____

National Network on Aging: _____

_____

_____

U.S. Public Health Service Corps: _____

_____

_____

Morbidity and Mortality Weekly Report (MMWR): _____

_____

_____

National Incident Management System: _____

_____

_____

Public Health Accreditation Board: _____

_____

_____

Social Security Act of 1935: _____

_____

_____

Association of State and Territorial Health Officials (ASTHO): _____

_____

_____

U.S. Surgeon General: _____

_____

_____

REAL LIFE APPLICATIONS: CASE SCENARIOS

You will be graduating from college soon with a degree in healthcare management. You are considering different career choices and would like to work for the government. You are thinking of applying to both state and local health departments but are unsure of what types of activities you may be involved with as a healthcare manager.

ACTIVITY

(1) Discuss the role that state and local health departments have in health care, (2) identify the services that are provided by both levels, (3) using the Internet, look up the state and local health departments in your state and provide an overview of their activities, and (4) decide on where you are going to apply and explain your decision.

RESPONSES

_____

_____

_____

_____

_____

_____

_____

_____

_____

_____

_____

CASE SCENARIO TWO

You have been assigned as an intern at FEMA for the summer. You are not familiar with this governmental organization but want to be familiar with their mission and activities. Prior to your start date.

ACTIVITY

Perform an Internet search and prepare a report for the class on FEMA and their activities. Be specific about their role in the healthcare system.

RESPONSES

_____

_____

_____

_____

_____

_____

_____

_____

_____

_____

_____

_____

_____

_____

CASE SCENARIO THREE

You are thinking about continuing your education but are not sure what area of healthcare is of interest to you. Your friend just obtained her master of public health. Before you decide what degree you want to obtain, you think you should make contact with your local public health department.

ACTIVITY

Visit your state's health department website and find your local public department. Make contact with them to find out what activities they perform for the county. Visit their website or call the department and speak to an employee. Write up a report on your findings.

RESPONSES

_____

_____

_____

_____

_____

_____

_____

_____

_____

_____

_____

_____

_____

_____

CASE SCENARIO FOUR

You have decided you would like to become a federal government worker in the healthcare industry but are unsure of which organization would be of interest to you.

ACTIVITY

Select three of the federal government organizations identified in this chapter and provide a summary of their activities.

RESPONSES

_____

_____

_____

_____

_____

_____

_____

_____

_____

_____

_____

_____

_____

_____

_____

_____

STUDENT ACTIVITY 4-3

INTERNET EXERCISES

Write your answers in the space provided.

- Visit each of the websites listed here.
- Name the organization.
- Locate their mission statement on their website.
- Provide a brief overview of the activities of the organization.
- How do these organizations participate in the U.S. healthcare system?

Websites

http://www.atsdr.cdc.gov

Organization Name: _____

Mission Statement:

_____

_____

_____

Overview of Activities: _____

_____

_____

Importance of organization to U.S. health care:

_____

_____

_____

http://www.hrsa.gov

Organization Name: _____

Mission Statement:

_____

_____

_____

Overview of Activities: _____

_____

_____

Importance of organization to U.S. health care:

_____

_____

_____

http://www.fda.gov

Organization Name: _____

Mission Statement:

_____

_____

_____

Overview of Activities: _____

_____

_____

Importance of organization to U.S. health care:

_____

_____

_____

http:// www.ihs.gov

Organization Name: _____

Mission Statement:

_____

_____

_____

Overview of Activities: _____

_____

_____

Importance of organization to U.S. health care:

_____

_____

_____

http://www.acl.gov

Organization Name: _____

Mission Statement:

_____

_____

_____

Overview of Activities: _____

_____

_____

Importance of organization to U.S. health care:

_____

_____

_____

http://www.acf.hhs.gov

Organization Name: _____

Mission Statement:

_____

_____

_____

Overview of Activities: _____

_____

_____

Importance of organization to U.S. health care:

_____

_____

_____

STUDENT ACTIVITY 4-4

DISCUSSION QUESTIONS

The following are suggested discussion questions for this chapter.

(1) Discuss the role of the FDA in the healthcare industry.

_____

_____

_____

_____

_____

(2) Why was the Department of Homeland Security (DHS) established? Why was FEMA integrated into DHS?

_____

_____

_____

_____

_____

(3) What is the difference between the role of the state health department and the local health department in providing health services?

_____

_____

_____

_____

_____

(4) Go to the ASTHO website. Based on your research, why is it important to state agencies?

_____

_____

_____

_____

(5) What is the purpose of the Public Health Accreditation Board? Do you feel it has been successful in its goals?

_____

_____

_____

_____

_____

The Navigate Companion Website for this text is a great source for additional information on the U.S. healthcare system. You can gain a new perspective on many of the topics presented in this chapter by visiting http://go.jblearning.com/Niles2e. You'll find additional student activities, further reading, and interactive study tools that explore:

- History of government role in U.S. health care
- Discussion of important federal government healthcare organizations
- Role of state and local health departments in U.S. health care
- And much more.

Chapter 5

Public Health's Role in Health Care

LEARNING OBJECTIVES

The student will be able to:

- Define and discuss the determinants of health.

- Describe the core public health functions of assessment, policy, and assurance and their role in public health organizations.

- Define and discuss the epidemiology triangle and its importance to public health.

- Discuss the importance of the Prevention and Public Health Fund

- Evaluate the roles of John Snow, Lemuel Shattuck, and Edwin Chadwick in the development of public health.

- Analyze the importance of data and surveillance systems in public health policy.

DID YOU KNOW THAT?

- In 1842, Edwin Chadwick reported that the poor had higher rates of disease—a fact that still exists today.

- Established in 1905, the civic organization Rotary International has played a huge role in eradicating polio through international vaccine programs.

- In 1916, the Johns Hopkins University, located in Baltimore, Maryland, established the first school of public health.

- In 1992, a national exercise program for Medicare patients, Silver Sneakers, was created to provide free access to organized exercise at national fitness chains.

- A newer form of surveillance is called biosurveillance, which monitors patterns of unusual disease that may be the result of human intervention.

- Public health marketing is an innovative approach to public health practice because it draws from the business discipline of marketing and adds science-based health strategies of promotion and prevention.

INTRODUCTION

There are two important definitions of public health. In 1920, **public health** was defined by Charles Winslow as the science and art of preventing disease, prolonging life, and promoting physical health and efficiency through organized community efforts for the sanitation of the environment, control of community infections, and education of individuals regarding hygiene to ensure a standard of living for health maintenance (Winslow, 1920). Sixty years later, the **Institute of Medicine (IOM)**, in its 1988 *Future of Public Health* report, defined public health as an organized community effort to address public health by applying scientific and technical knowledge to promote health (IOM, 1988). Both definitions point to broad community efforts to promote health activities to protect the population's health status. The Affordable Care Act is also emphasizing the importance of prevention and wellness. The establishment of the Prevention and Public Health Fund has supported several community-based public health programs (APHA, 2013 a).

The development of public health is important to note as part of the basics of the U.S. healthcare system because its development was separate from the development of private medical practices. Public health specialists view health from a collectivist and preventative care viewpoint: to protect as many citizens as possible from health issues and to provide strategies to prevent health issues from occurring. The definitions cited in the previous paragraph emphasize this viewpoint. Public health concepts were in stark contrast to traditional medicine, which focused on the sole relationship between a provider and patient. Private practitioners held an individualistic viewpoint—citizens more often would be paying for their services from their health insurance or

from their own pockets. Physicians would be providing their patients guidance on how to cure their diseases, not preventing disease. This chapter will discuss the concept of health and healthcare delivery and the role of public health in delivering health care. The concepts of primary, secondary, and tertiary prevention and the role of public health in those delivery activities will be highlighted. Discussion will also focus on the origins of public health, the major role epidemiology plays in public health, the role of public health in disasters, core public health activities, the collaboration of public health and private medicine, and the importance of public health consumers.

WHAT IS HEALTH?

The World Health Organization (WHO) defines **health** as the state of complete physical, mental, and social well-being and not merely the absence of disease or infirmity (WHO, 1942). IOM defines health as a state of well-being and the capability to function in the face of changing circumstances. It is a positive concept emphasizing social and personal resources as well as physical capabilities (IOM, 1997). According to the Society for Academic Emergency Medicine (SAEM), health is a state of physical and mental well-being that facilitates the achievement of individual and societal goals (SAEM, 1992). All of these

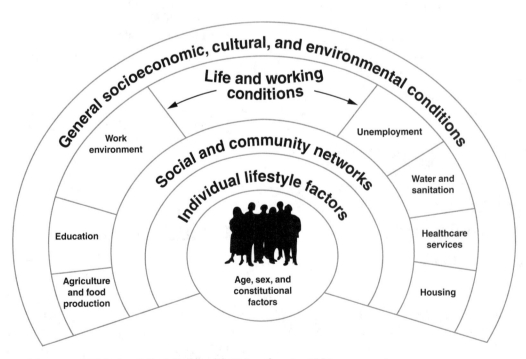

Figure 5-1 Dahlgren and Whitehead Model of Health Determinants, 1991
Source: Dahlgren, G., & Whitehead, M. (1991). *Policies and Strategies to Promote Social Equity in Health*. Stockholm, Sweden: Institute for Future Studies. Reprinted by permission.

definitions focus on the impact an individual's health status has on his or her quality of life.

Health has several determinants or influences that impact the status of an individual's health. The individual lifestyle factors such as age, sex, and **constitutional factors** are direct determinants of a person's health. Within the immediate environment of an individual, there are social and community networks—external influences on health. In addition to the **social and community networks** there are also the general **macroenvironmental conditions** of socioeconomic, cultural, and environmental conditions that impact health, such as education, work environment, living and working conditions, healthcare services, food production, unemployment, water and sanitation, and housing. These **determinants of health** depicted in **Figure 5-1** tie into the role of public health in the healthcare delivery system because public health focuses on the impact of these determinants on an individual's health. Public health provides health education and other preventive activities to consumers so they will understand the negative impact these determinants may have on their health status. These activities are often categorized as primary, secondary, and occasionally tertiary prevention (Determinants of Health, 2013).

PRIMARY, SECONDARY, AND TERTIARY PREVENTION

Primary prevention activities focus on reducing disease development. Smoking cessation programs, immunization programs, educational programs for pregnancy, and employee safety education are all examples of primary prevention programs. **Secondary prevention** activities refer to early detection and treatment of diseases. The goal of secondary prevention is to stop the progression of disease. Blood pressure screenings, colonoscopies, and mammograms are examples of secondary prevention. **Tertiary prevention** activities focus on activities to rehabilitate and monitor individuals during disease progression. Activities may also include patient behavior education to limit disease impact and reduce progression (Shi & Singh, 2008). Although public health professionals may participate in each area of prevention activities, they focus primarily on primary and secondary prevention. See **Table 5-1**.

ORIGINS OF PUBLIC HEALTH

During the 18th and 19th centuries, the concept of public health was born. Edwin Chadwick, Dr. John Snow, and Lemuel Shattuck demonstrated a relationship

TABLE 5-1	Primary, Secondary, and Tertiary Prevention		
	Primary	**Secondary**	**Tertiary**
Aim	Reduce disease development	Prevent disease progression by early detection and intervention	Disease management to reduce progress
Disease Phase	Specific risk factors associated with disease onset Factors associated with protection against disease	Early disease stage	Later disease stages
Target	Total population, selected groups and healthy individuals	Early disease individuals with established high risk factors	Patients
Examples	– Immunization programs – Education programs for pregnancy – Smoking cessation programs	– Blood pressure screenings – Mammograms – Colonoscopies	– Rehabilitation of stroke patients – Self management programs for chronic individuals – Patient behavior education

between the environment and disease that established the foundation of public health.

In 1842, **Edwin Chadwick** published the *Report on the Sanitary Condition of the Labouring Population of Great Britain*. His report highlighted the relationship between unsanitary conditions and disease (Rosen, 1958). As Chief Commissioner of the Poor Law Commission, Chadwick was responsible for relief to the poor in England and Wales. He became the champion of reform for working conditions. His report illustrated that the poor had higher rates of disease than the upper class, a fact that still exists today. His activities became the basis for U.S. public health activities (Rosen, 1958). He was also responsible for the implementation of the 1848 Public Health Act, which created England's first national board of health. Unfortunately, in 1854, the Parliament did not renew the Act, which consequently dissolved the board of health. Although dissolved, the concept of public health was born because this act, using data, identified several public health issues that were assigned to national and local boards. Public health issues such as water, sewerage, environment, safety, and food were a focus of the act. By identifying these community issues, people began to focus on improving the community's health status (Ashton & Sram, 1998).

Dr. John Snow, a famed British anesthesiologist, is more famous for investigating the cholera epidemics in London in the 1800s. He made the connection between contaminated water and the spread of cholera. Dr. Snow surveyed local London residents and discovered that those who were ill had retrieved water from a specific neighborhood pump on Broad Street. When the pump handle was removed, the disease ceased. This famous Broad Street pump incident became a classic example of an epidemiologic investigation that studies the causes between disease and external sources (Ellis, 2008).

Lemuel Shattuck, who has been called the architect of the public health infrastructure, wrote the landmark report, *Report of the Sanitary Commission of Massachusetts*. It was ignored for many years but finally in the 19th century, it was central to the development of state and local public health activities (Rosen, 1958).

As a result of their work, public health law was enacted and, by the 1900s, public health departments were focused on the environment and its relationship to disease outbreaks. Disease control and health education also became integral components of public health departments.

WHAT IS PUBLIC HEALTH?

Overview of the Public Health System

The Public Health System

According to the Centers for Disease Control and Prevention, public health systems are commonly defined as "all public, private, and voluntary entities that contribute to the delivery of essential public health services within a jurisdiction." **Figure 5-2** provides an overview of the components of public health, which include (CDC, 2013a):

- Public health agencies at state and local levels
- Healthcare providers
- Public safety agencies
- Human service and charity organizations
- Education and youth development organizations
- Recreation and arts-related organizations
- Economic and philanthropic organizations
- Environmental agencies and organizations

In 1945, in conjunction with Haven Emerson and C.E.A Winslow, the American Public Health Association (APHA) issued a set of guidelines for the basic functions of the local health department, including (Emerson, 1945):

- Vital statistics: data management of the essential facts on births, deaths, and reportable diseases
- Communicable disease control: management of tuberculosis, venereal disease, and malaria
- Sanitation: management of the environment, including milk, water, and dining
- Laboratory services
- Maternal and child health: management of school-aged children's health
- Health education of the general public

These functions remained the cornerstone of public health until the 1960s when the APHA, reacting to cultural and political changes, revised the definition of the core public health functions. The APHA issued the following guidelines for the core public health functions (APHA, 2013b):

- Health surveillance, planning, and program development
- Health promotion of local health activities
- Development and enforcement of sanitation standards
- Health services provisions

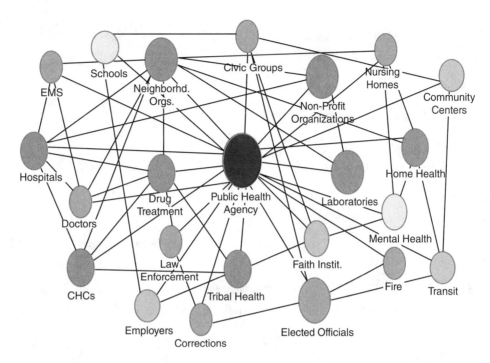

Figure 5-2 Public Health System Participants
Source: Reproduced from Centers for Disease Control and Prevention. (2013). The public health system and the 10 essential public health services. Retrieved from http://www.cdc.gov/nphpsp/essentialservices.html

The IOM, as a result of an in-depth study of public health, stated that the three **core public health functions** of public health are (IOM, 1988):

■ Assessment, which includes surveillance, identifying problems, data collection, and analysis

■ Policy development, which includes developing policies to address public problems

■ Assurance, which includes evaluating policies that meet program goals

These core public health functions became accepted by public health departments; however, there was some confusion about the terminology. In 1994, the Public Health Steering Committee, as part of the U.S. Public Health Service, issued a list of essential public health services that provided specific information on the implementation of the core public health functions and how they should be implemented (see **Table 5-2**).

THE EPIDEMIOLOGY TRIANGLE

Epidemiology is the study of disease distribution and patterns among populations. Epidemiologists search for the relationship of those patterns of disease to the causes of the disease. They scientifically collect data to determine what has caused the spread of the disease. Epidemiology is the foundation for public health because its focus is to prevent disease from reoccurring. Epidemiologists identify three major risk factor categories for disease. These three factors are called the **epidemiology triangle** (see **Figure 5-3**), which consists of the host, which is the population that has the disease; the agent or organism, which is causing the disease; and the environment, or where the disease is occurring (CDC, 2013b). Public health workers attempt to assess each factor's role in why a disease occurs. Based on this research, public health workers develop prevention strategies to alter the interaction between the host, the disease, and the environment so the disease occurrences will be less severe or will not occur again.

For example, a person (host) can be vaccinated against a disease to prevent the host from carrying the disease (agent). Procedures can be implemented such as sanitary regulations to protect the community condition (environment) from contamination.

EPIDEMIOLOGIC SURVEILLANCE

An important component of epidemiology is **surveillance**, which is the monitoring of patterns of disease and investigating disease outbreaks to develop public health intervention strategies to combat disease. A new

TABLE 5-2	**10 Essential Public Health Services Describing the Public Health Activities That All Communities Should Undertake**

1. Monitor health status to identify and solve community health problems.

2. Diagnose and investigate health problems and health hazards in the community.

3. Inform, educate, and empower people about health issues.

4. Mobilize community partnerships and action to identify and solve health problems.

5. Develop policies and plans that support individual and community health efforts.

6. Enforce laws and regulations that protect health and ensure safety.

7. Link people to needed personal health services and assure the provision of health care when otherwise unavailable.

8. Assure competent public and personal healthcare workforce.

9. Evaluate effectiveness, accessibility, and quality of personal and population-based health services.

10. Research for new insights and innovative solutions to health problems.

Source: Reproduced from Centers for Disease Control and Prevention. (2011). Core Functions of Public Health and How They Relate to the 10 Essential Services. Retrieved from http://www.cdc.gov/nceh/ehs/ephli/core_ess.htm

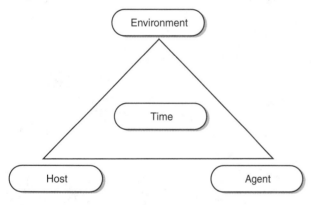

Figure 5-3 Epidemiological Triangle
Source: Reproduced from Centers for Disease Control and Prevention. (2013). Understanding the Epidemiologic Triangle through Infectious Disease. Retrieved from http://www.cdc.gov/bam/teachers/epi-triangle.html

form of surveillance involves **biosurveillance**, which focuses on early detection of unusual disease patterns that may be due to human intervention. Historically, surveillance activities have been passive and been initiated by public health workers through routine disease reports. However, public health has become more proactive by initiating contact with providers to assess any unusual disease pattern. New surveillance techniques can include pattern recognition software and geographic information systems to determine disease patterns (Turnock, 2007). Depending on the severity of the disease outbreaks, these activities will be investigated by the CDC, a federal public health agency, although public health mostly remains a state responsibility.

ENVIRONMENTAL HEALTH

Since John Snow linked disease with environmental factors, the field of **environmental health** is an integral component of public health. Environmental health workers often are responsible for investigating environmental hazards in the community and monitoring and enforcing environmental regulations. A subset of environmental health workers is occupational health workers who focus on ensuring employees' environments have safe working conditions. Both state and local health departments have environmental health departments that are responsible for investigating and enforcing local regulations. The Centers for Disease Control and Prevention have identified 10 essential environmental health services that relate to the core functions of public health assessment, policy development, and assurance (CDC, 2013c) (see **Table 5-3**).

TABLE 5-3	Essential Health Services and Core Public Health Functions of Environmental Health

Assessment

Monitor environmental and health status to identify and solve community environmental health problems

Diagnose and investigate environmental health problems and health hazards in the community

Policy Development

Inform, educate, and empower people about environmental health issues

Mobilize community partnerships and actions to identify and solve environmental health problems

Develop policies and plans that support individual and community environmental health efforts

Assurance

Enforce laws and regulations that protect environmental health and ensure safety

Link people to needed environmental health services and assure the provision of environmental health services when otherwise unavailable

Assure a competent environmental health workforce

Evaluate effectiveness, accessibility, and quality of personal and population-based environmental health services

Research for new insights and innovative solutions to environmental health problems

Source: Centers for Disease Control and Prevention. (2011). Core Functions of Public Health and How They Relate to the 10 Essential Services. Retrieved from http://www.cdc.gov/nceh/ehs/ephli/core_ess.htm

EMERGENCY PREPAREDNESS

Federal Response

Public health emergency preparedness is a term used for planning protocols that are in place to manage a large scale event such as a natural disaster like a hurricane or massive flooding, chemical or oil spills, or a manmade disaster such as the Boston Marathon bombing in 2013 or the terrorist attack of September 11, 2001. During a public health emergency, such as the California wildfires, Superstorm Sandy in New Jersey, and the tornados in Oklahoma, risk communication protocols are implemented to inform the public regarding the health issue and what should be done during a severe situation. Dissemination of information is handled through multimedia efforts such as the radio, television, and print media. Depending on the level of disease threat, the federal government may intervene in a disease outbreak. If not, state and local public health departments are responsible for monitoring the disease threat. Unfortunately, severe public health crises can create secondary disease threats. These crises also can have an extreme psychological impact on the public. The public needs to be informed. Since the terrorist attacks in 2001, simulations of public health

emergencies have been staged across vulnerable areas of the United States, including large urban areas such as New York City and Las Vegas, to plan for these possible events. Public health funding for state activities such as these are largely from CDC grants and budget allocations (Turnock, 2007).

September 11, 2001, Terrorist Attack Impact on Public Health

As result of the terrorist attacks on the United States in 2001, the Department of Homeland Security (DHS) was created from 23 federal agencies, programs, and offices to coordinate an approach to emergencies and disasters. Several public health functions were transferred to the DHS in 2003 (Turnock, 2007). Within the DHS, the Emergency Preparedness and Response Directorate coordinates emergency medical response in the event of a public health emergency. Some states have created their own Homeland Security offices that coordinate with the federal DHS. The **National Response Framework (NRF)**, created by DHS, presents the guiding principles that enable all response partners to prepare for and provide a unified national response to disasters and emergencies. It establishes a comprehensive, national, all-hazards approach to domestic incident response. The National Response Plan was replaced by the NRF effective March 22, 2008. The NRF defines the principles, roles, and structures that organize how we respond as a nation. It also describes how communities, states, the federal government, the private sector, and nongovernment partners collaborate to coordinate national response. Further, it describes "best practices" for managing incidents and builds on the **National Incident Management System (NIMS)**, which provides a framework for managing incidents. Information on the NRF, including documents, annexes, references, and briefings/trainings, can be accessed from the NRF Resource Center (FEMA, 2013).

STATE AND LOCAL RESPONSE TO DISASTERS

State and Local Health Department Planning in Emergency Preparedness

The state and local health departments play a major role in managing emergencies. The CDC has developed national standards for both state and local health departments to develop capabilities to deal with emergencies as part of their strategic plan. The following are the capabilities as outlined by the CDC (2013d):

- Capability 1: **Community preparedness**: The local health department has to assess the capability of the community and itself to respond quickly to a threat. It is also important to assess the impact of the threat.

- Capability 2: **Community recovery**: The ability to collaborate with community partners, (e.g., healthcare organizations, business, education, and emergency management) to plan and advocate for the rebuilding of public health, medical, and mental/behavioral health systems to at least a level of functioning comparable to pre-incident levels, and improved levels where possible.

- Capability 3: **Emergency operations coordination**: The ability to direct and support an event or incident with public health or medical implications by establishing a standardized, scalable system of oversight, organization, and supervision consistent with jurisdictional standards and practices and with the National Incident Management System.

- Capability 4: **Emergency public information and warning system**: The ability to develop, coordinate, and disseminate information, alerts,

warnings, and notifications to the public and incident management responders.

- Capability 5: **Fatality management**: The ability to coordinate with other organizations (e.g., law enforcement, healthcare, emergency management, and medical examiner/coroner) to ensure the proper recovery, handling, identification, transportation, tracking, storage, and disposal of human remains and personal effects; certify cause of death; and facilitate access to mental/behavioral health services to the family members, responders, and survivors of an incident.

- Capability 6: **Information sharing**: The ability to conduct multijurisdictional, multidisciplinary exchange of health-related information and situational awareness data among federal, state, local, territorial, and tribal levels of government, and the private sector. This capability includes the routine sharing of information as well as issuing of public health alerts to federal, state, local, territorial, and tribal levels of government and the private sector in preparation for, and in response to, events or incidents of public health.

- Capability 7: **Mass care**: The ability to coordinate with partner agencies to address the public health, medical, and mental/behavioral health needs of those impacted by an incident at a congregate location. This capability includes the coordination of ongoing surveillance and assessment to ensure that health needs continue to be met as the incident evolves.

- Capability 8: **Medical countermeasure dispensing**: The ability to provide medical countermeasures (including vaccines, antiviral drugs, antibiotics, antitoxin, etc.) in support of treatment or prophylaxis (oral or vaccination) to the identified population in accordance with public health guidelines and/or recommendations.

- Capability 9: **Medical materiel management and distribution**: The ability to acquire, maintain (e.g., cold chain storage or other storage protocol), transport, distribute, and track medical materiel (e.g., pharmaceuticals, gloves, masks, and ventilators) during an incident and to recover and account for unused medical materiel, as necessary, after an incident.

- Capability 10: **Medical surge**: The ability to provide adequate medical evaluation and care during events that exceed the limits of the normal medical infrastructure of an affected community. It encompasses the ability of the healthcare system to survive a hazard impact and maintain or rapidly recover operations that were compromised.

- Capability 11: **Non pharmaceutical interventions**: The ability to recommend to the applicable agency (if not public health) and implement, if applicable, strategies for disease, injury, and exposure control. Strategies include the following:
  - Isolation and quarantine
  - Restrictions on movement and travel advisory/warnings
  - Social distancing
  - External decontamination
  - Hygiene
  - Precautionary protective behaviors

- Capability 12: **Public health laboratory testing**: The ability to conduct rapid and conventional detection, characterization, confirmatory testing, data reporting, investigative support, and laboratory networking to address actual or potential exposure to all hazards. Hazards include chemical, radiological, and biological agents in multiple matrices that may include clinical samples, food, and environmental samples (e.g., water, air, and soil). This capability supports routine surveillance, including pre-event or pre-incident and post-exposure activities.

- Capability 13: **Public health surveillance and epidemiological investigation**: The ability to create, maintain, support, and strengthen routine surveillance and detection systems and epidemiological investigation processes, as well as to expand these systems and processes in response to incidents of public health significance.

- Capability 14: **Responder safety and health**: The ability to protect public health agency staff responding to an incident and the ability to support the health and safety needs of hospital and medical facility personnel, if requested.

- Capability 15: **Volunteer management**: The ability to coordinate the identification, recruitment, registration, credential verification, training, and engagement of volunteers to support the jurisdictional public health agency's response to incidents of public health significance.

Incident Command System and Public Health

Incident Command System (ICS) is used by police, fire, and emergency management agencies. ICS eliminates many communication problems, spans of control,

organizational structures, and differences in terminology when multiple agencies respond to an emergency event. The ICS is a coordinator for an emergency event. They are in control of a situation and make decisions about how to manage an emergency. They coordinate all responders to the event, which increases management effectiveness. Local public health agencies work with first responders such as fire and rescue, emergency medical service, law enforcement, physicians, and hospitals in managing health-related emergencies. Most local public health agencies provide epidemiology and surveillance, food safety, communicable disease control, and health inspections. Many state public health agencies provide laboratory services. Because public health is now considered an integral component to battling terrorism and, consequently, a matter of national security, federal funding has dramatically increased (FEMA, 2013).

BIOTERRORISM

According to the CDC, **bioterrorism** is an attack on a population by deliberately releasing viruses, bacteria, or other germs or agents that will contribute to illness or death in people (CDC, 2013e). These can be spread throughout the environment through the air, water, or in food. These agents can be difficult to detect and may take a period of time to spread. DHS, American Red Cross (ARC), the American Medical Association (AMA), and the Environmental Protection Agency (EPA) have developed educational campaigns regarding the U.S. response to bioterrorism. Since the September 11, 2001, terrorist attack on the United States, bioterrorism has become a reality.

More than 20 federal departments and agencies have roles in preparing for a bioterrorist attack. In 2002, the **Public Health Security and Bioterrorism Preparedness and Response Act** provided grants to hospitals and public health organizations to prepare for bioterrorism as a result of September 11, 2001. Funding supports increased public health infrastructures and programs, supports increased laboratory testing, and developed programs to detect bioterrorist threats. The **U.S. Food and Drug Administration (FDA)** also has additional responsibilities in the detection of food as a threat to community health (USFDA, 2013). Bioterrorism preparedness involves federal, state, and local health departments as well as input from other organizations. When a disaster occurs such as a bioterrorist attack, responses from both the federal and state level may take 24 hours; therefore, it is vital that local health departments, because they are at the front line of public health interventions, need to have a plan in place for immediate intervention. In terms of emergency responders, local health departments are the frontline organizations to assess an emergency situation (Turnock, 2007).

PUBLIC HEALTH FUNCTIONS AND ADMINISTRATION

Accreditation of Public Health Departments

The 2003 IOM report discussed previously recommends a national accreditation system for public health agencies because there is no national accrediting body to institute standards. In 2004, the CDC and the Robert Wood Johnson Foundation (RWJF) funded a study, the **Exploring Accreditation Project (EAP)**, to assess accreditation of public health agencies. Based on this information, in 2007, the **Public Health Accreditation Board (PHAB)** was formed as a nonprofit organization dedicated to improving and protecting the health of the public by advancing the quality and performance of tribal, state, local, and territorial public health departments. Since its inception, the PHAB has been working on a set of national accreditation standards for local health departments. In 2011, the PHAB has awarded 5-year accreditation to 11 public health departments. Accreditation status was awarded February 28, 2013 to:

- Comanche County Health Department (Lawton, OK)
- Franklin County Health Department (Frankfort, KY)
- Livingston County Department of Health (Mt. Morris, NY)
- Northern Kentucky Independent District Health Department (Edgewood, KY)
- Oklahoma City-County Health Department (Oklahoma City, OK)
- Oklahoma State Department of Health (Oklahoma City, OK)
- Spokane Regional Health District (Spokane, WA)
- The Public Health Authority of Cabarrus County, Inc. d/b/a Cabarrus Health Alliance (Kannapolis, NC)
- Three Rivers District Health Department (Owenton, KY)

- Washington State Department of Health (Olympia, WA)
- West Allis Health Department (West Allis, WI)

In 2013, the PHAB has awarded 5-year accreditation status to three public health departments. Accreditation status was awarded May 30 to Polk County Health Department in Balsam Lake, Wisconsin; Summit County Combined General Health District in Stow, Ohio; and Wood County Health Department in Wisconsin Rapids, Wisconsin.

The decisions bring the number of public health agencies now recognized by PHAB as high-performing health departments to 14. More than 130 health departments are currently preparing to seek national accreditation through the program, which aims to improve and protect the health of the public by advancing the quality and performance of the nation's tribal, state, local, and territorial health departments. (PHAB, 2013).

National Association of Local Boards of Health

Established in 1992, as a membership organization, the **National Association of Local Boards of Health (NALBOH)** informs, guides, and is the national voice for boards of health. In today's public health system, the leadership role of boards of health makes them an essential link between public health services and a healthy community. NALBOH provides technical expertise in governance and leadership, board development, health priorities, and public health policy at the local level (About NALBOH, 2013).

The Influence of the Institute of Medicine Reports on Public Health Functions

Published in 1988, the IOM published a report, *The Future of Public Health*, which indicated that although the health of the American people has been accomplished through public health measures such as consumer food regulations, water safety standards, and epidemic control of disease, the public has come to take public health measures for granted. The report indicated that there was an attrition of public health activities in protecting the community because of this attitude (IOM, 1988). The report established recommendations for reorganizing public health that emphasized population-based strategies rather than personal healthcare delivery. There was poor collaboration between public health and private medicine, no strong mission statement, weak leadership, and politicized decision making. Three core public health functions were identified: **assessment**, **policy development**, and **assurance**. Assessment was recommended because it focused on systematic continuous data collection of health issues, which would ensure that public health agencies were vigilant in protecting the public. Policy development was also mentioned but the recommendation was to ensure that any policies were based on valid data to avoid any political decision making. Policy development was recommended to include planning at all health levels, not just at the federal level. Federal agencies should support local health planning. Assurance focused on evaluating any processes that had been put in place to assure that the programs were being implemented appropriately (IOM, 1988). These core functions will ensure that public health remains focused on the community, has programs in place that are effective, and has an evaluation process in place to ensure that the programs do work.

In 2002, the IOM published a second, more in-depth report, *The Future of the Public's Health in the 21st Century*, based on the 1988 report that analyzed public health as a system and discussed several deficiencies first noted in their 1988 report. Deficiencies included:

- Fragmented government public health infrastructures
- Passive community participation in public health activities
- Lack of healthcare delivery coordination
- Lack of participation of businesses in influencing health activities
- Lack of coordination of media with the health arena
- Lack of academic institutions in community-based health activities

Recommendations to rectify these deficiencies included:

- Development of a national commission to establish a framework for state public health law reform
- Development of active partnerships between public health agencies and communities
- Insurance plans should offer preventive services as part of their plans

- Businesses should collaborate with communities to develop health promotion programs
- Media outlets should increase their public service announcements to include health promotion marketing
- Increased funding for researchers who are interested in public health practice research (IOM, 2002)

HEALTHY PEOPLE REPORTS

The *Healthy People* series is a federal public health planning tool produced by the CDC that assesses the most significant health threats and sets objectives to challenge these threats (Novick & Morrow, 2008). The first major report, published in 1979, *Healthy People: The Surgeon General's Report on Health Promotion and Disease Prevention*, discussed five goals of public health: reduce mortality rates among children, adolescents, young adults, and adults and increase independence among older adults. Objectives were set for 1990 to accomplish these goals (U.S. Department of Health and Human Services [HHS], 1979).

The **Healthy People 2000** report released in 1990, the *National Health Promotion and Disease Prevention Objectives*, was created to implement a new national prevention strategy with three major goals: increase life expectancy, reduce health disparities, and increase access to preventive services. Three categories (health promotion, health prevention, and preventive services) and surveillance activities were emphasized. *Healthy People 2000* provided a vision to reduce preventable disabilities and death. Year 2000 target objectives were set throughout the years to measure progress. An evaluation report in 2002 found that only 21% of the objectives were met with an additional 41% indicating progress. Unfortunately, in the critical areas of mental health, there were significant reversals in any progress. There was also minor progress in the areas of chronic diseases and diabetes (CDC, 2013f).

The **Healthy People 2010** report, *Understanding and Improving Health*, based on the previous *Healthy People* reports and their progress, was released in 2000 (HHS, 2000). The report contained a health promotion and disease prevention focus to identify preventable threats to public health and to set goals to reduce the threats. They had two major goals: to increase the quality and years of healthy life and to eliminate health disparities.

Nearly 500 objectives were developed according to 28 focus areas. Focus areas ranged from access to care, food safety, education, and environmental health, to tobacco and substance abuse. An important component of the *Healthy People 2010* was the development of an infrastructure to ensure public health services are provided in a systematic approach. Infrastructure includes skilled labor, information technology, organizations, and research (CDC, 2013g). Like Healthy People 2000, its major goals were to increase quality and life expectancy and to reduce health disparities. The goals for these reports are consistent with both Winslow's and the IOM's definitions of public health. In 2010, **Healthy People 2020** was released. It contains 1,200 objectives that focus on 42 topic areas. According to the CDC, a smaller set of *Healthy People 2020* objectives, called Leading Health Indicators (LHIs), has been targeted to communicate high-priority health issues (CDC, 2013h).

PUBLIC HEALTH INFRASTRUCTURE

U.S. public health activities are delivered by many organizations, including government agencies at the federal, state, and local levels and nongovernment organizations including healthcare providers, community organizations, educational institutions, charitable organizations, philanthropic organizations, and businesses (Mays, 2008).

GOVERNMENT CONTRIBUTIONS TO PUBLIC HEALTH

Federal

The federal government has the ability to formulate and implement a national policy agenda for public health (Lee, 1994). It also has the power to allocate funding to both government and nongovernment organizations for public health programs at the state government level. If there is a major health threat in a community, direct federal activity may occur such as investigating a disease outbreak or providing assistance during a major disaster. The majority of their activities focus on policy and regulatory development and funding allocation to public health programs. The major federal agency responsible for public health activities is HHS, which is responsible for the following activities (Pointer, Williams, Isaacs, & Knickman, 2007):

- Data gathering and analysis, and surveillance and control
- Conducting and funding research

- Providing assistance to state and local government programs
- Formulating health policy
- Ensuring food and drug safety
- Ensuring access to health services for the poor and elderly
- Providing direct services to special populations

State

State public health agencies follow two basic models: a freestanding agency structure that reports directly to the state's governor or an organizational unit with a larger agency structure that includes other healthcare activities. The key feature of state agencies is their relationship with their local public health agencies that are responsible for implementing state policy and regulations. Most states have public health activities distributed across many agencies that include environmental protection, human services, labor, insurance, transportation, housing, and agriculture (Mays, 2008).

Additional activities include (Pointer et al., 2007):

- Licensure of healthcare professionals
- Inspection and licensure of healthcare facilities
- Collection of vital statistics
- Epidemiologic studies
- Crisis management of disease outbreaks
- Disease registry
- Laboratory services
- Implementation and analysis of health policy
- Community health education

Local

Local government agencies are directly responsible for performing the majority of community public health services. **The National Association of County and City Officials (NACCHO),** which is the national advocacy organization for local health departments, released the operational definition of a local health department, which is defined as "what people in any community can reasonably expect from their local governmental public health presence. It sets forth a series of standards based on the Ten Essential Public Health Services and serves as the framework for the standards of the national voluntary accreditation program operated by the Public Health Accreditation Board (PHAB)" (NACCHO, 2013c).

NONGOVERNMENT PUBLIC HEALTH ACTIVITIES

Community hospitals have been important to public health. The Hill-Burton Act of 1943, which financed hospital construction projects, required them to provide charitable services, which established a tradition of charitable services among community hospitals. Hospitals may operate primary care clinics and sponsor health education programs and health screening fairs. The Joint Commission (TJC) requires hospitals to participate in community health assessment activities (TJC, 2013).

Ambulatory or outpatient care providers such as physician practices also contribute to community public health. Physicians may serve on local public health organizations or provide services to the uninsured for reduced fees. Hospitals, clinics, and nursing homes may also contribute to public health. Health insurers and managed care providers also make important public health contributions. All types of healthcare providers cooperate with state and local health departments by providing immunizations, offering patient education, screening for communicable diseases, and reporting disease information to health departments (Pointer et al., 2007). Health insurers and managed care providers have a large network of clients to encourage health promotion and health education activities. For example, a physical activity program for senior citizens, **Silver Sneakers**, was developed in 1992 and encouraged the elderly to participate in organized exercise at national fitness chains. Data is being collected to assess if those seniors visited their providers less because their health status increased. It is a free program to Medicare or Medicare supplement participants (Healthways Silver Sneakers Fitness Program, 2013). The Affordable Care Act of 2010's focus is on primary and preventive care as well as increased access and improving the quality of healthcare services.

Nonprofit agencies such as the **American Cancer Society**, **American Heath Association**, and **American Lung Association** have active health promotion and health screening programs at the national, state, and local levels. The **United Way** is a civic organization that is active in identifying health risks and implementing community public health programs to target these risks. Established in 1905, the civic organization **Rotary International** is responsible for efforts to eradicate polio through vaccine programs throughout the world (Rotary International, 2013). Philanthropic organizations such as RWJF have provided funding for public health activities, including community education and intervention programs. The RWJF's goal is to improve the health of all Americans and have provided substantial funds for research activities to combat public health issues such as obesity and smoking (RWJF, 2013).

Council of State and Territorial Epidemiologists (CSTE)

Established in 1992 and headquartered in Atlanta, Georgia, the **Council of State and Territorial Epidemiologists** (CSTE) is a professional organization of over 1,000 public health epidemiologists that work in state and local health departments who provide technical assistance to the **Association of State and Territorial Health Officials (ASTHO)** and to the CDC for research and policy issues. They provide expertise in the areas of maternal child health, infectious diseases, environmental health, injury epidemiology, occupational health, and public health informatics (CSTE, 2013).

The Association of State and Territorial Health Officials (ASTHO)

ASTHO is a not-for-profit organization that provides support for state and territorial health agencies. They provide research, expertise, and guidance for health policy issues. The federal government looks to ASTHO for their expertise in developing health policy. They frequently testify in front of Congress regarding major health issues. They advocate for increased public health funding and campaign against any funding reductions. ASTHO provides training opportunities for state public health leaders. All states and U.S. territories and the District of Columbia belong to ASTHO (ASTHO, 2013).

National Association for County and City Health Officials (NACCHO)

NACCHO is the advocacy organization for local health departments. Established in 1993 and located in Washington, D.C., NACCHO provides support to nearly 3,000 local health department members that include city, county, district, metro, and tribal agencies. They are staffed by nearly 100 physicians and public health experts and a 32-member board of directors that lobbies Congress for their public health agenda, promotes public health, and provides support for their members (NACCHO, 2013a).

135

NACCHO has recently focused on providing guidance to local health departments on ways to market public health activities and their role in public health. As discussed earlier, in collaboration with the CDC, they provide support for **Mobilizing for Action through Planning and Partnerships (MAPP)**, which is a community-driven strategic planning process for improving community health. In collaboration with World Ways Social Marketing, NACCHO has developed a logo with the tagline of "Prevent, Promote, Protect," which can be used nationally by local health departments to help the public understand their role. NACCHO has also developed a communications toolkit with fact sheets regarding public health departments. **Table 5-4** is a fact sheet that is used to market the importance of public health departments to the community (NACCHO, 2013b).

Public health, nursing, and medical schools are also major contributors to public health activities. Faculty from these schools often provide technical assistance to local public health organizations and often partner with organizations to establish health programs. The schools may also provide specific educational programs that are tailored to community needs. Educational accreditation organizations are also encouraging educational programs to participate in community health activities. Harvard University's School of Public Health has established several centers to advance research in public health, such as health communication, injury control, AIDS, health promotion, and population and development studies (Harvard School of Public Health, 2013).

PUBLIC HEALTH EDUCATION AND HEALTH PROMOTION

Public health educational strategies are a crucial component to public health interventions. **Health education** focuses on changing health behavior through educational interventions such as multimedia education and classes. **Health promotion** is a broader intervention term in public health that encompasses not only educational objectives and activities but also organizational, environmental, and economic interventions to support activities conducive to healthy behavior (Pointer et al., 2007).

Public Health Education Campaign

Educational strategies inform the community about positive health behavior, targeting those at risk to change or maintain positive health behavior. Many public health campaigns are performed by the local public health department and in collaboration with community organizations.

There are several steps to planning and developing a successful **public health educational** campaign **(Minnesota Department of Health, 2013)**.

- The first step in implementing a public health education campaign is to perform a community assessment to determine at-risk populations. Developing an effective educational campaign to target high-risk populations requires community participation.
- The next step is collaborating with the community for their input on health issues and prioritizing target health issues.
- The third step is performing surveillance activities for specific data related to mortality and morbidity rates.
- The fourth step is to develop a pilot study to assess the effectiveness of the proposed campaign.
- The fifth step is to revise the campaign based on the pilot study.
- The sixth step is to implement the chosen campaign for a period of time.
- The seventh step is to perform an evaluation of the impact of the campaign and revise, if needed.

Public Health Education Evaluation

Educational activities can be difficult to measure because of their abstract nature. It is important that specific outcome measures are developed prior to the campaign. Each measure should address the following parameters: (1) specific target group, (2) change in and type of behavior, (3) time frame for change, and (4) defined geographic area of change (Novick & Morrow, 2008).

Health Promotion Activities

Most health promotion campaigns have more community health objectives than health educational campaigns that focus on specific target populations. Health promotion focuses on a comprehensive coordinated approach to long-term health behavior changes by influencing the community through educational activities (Minnesota Department of Health, 2013). When a focus is at the community level, it is necessary to address **lifestyle behaviors** that includes cultural, economic, psychological, and environmental factors. Examples of health promotion include nutritional, genetic, or family counseling that would encompass health education activities. Health promotion may also include other community development activities such as occupational and environmental control and immunization programs (Turnock, 2007).

TABLE 5-4	What Does the Local Public Health Department Do in Your Community?

Your local health department (LHD)—you may know it as your local "health department" or "public health department"—is a leader in improving the health and well being of your community. This fact sheet describes the roles performed by LHDs in communities throughout the United States.

- **<u>Protects</u> you from health threats, the everyday and the exceptional.** Your LHD guards multiple fronts to defend you from any health threat, regardless of the source, and works tirelessly to prevent disease outbreaks. Your LHD makes sure the tap water you drink, the restaurant food you eat, and the air you breathe are all safe. It's ready to respond to any health emergency—be it bioterrorism, SARS, West Nile Virus, or an environmental hazard.

"Not content with merely a "clipboard" role, checking for compliance with regulations, Marquette County (MI) food service health inspectors organize and conduct classes to advise restaurant managers how best to meet current food safety standards. These inspectors are resources as well as enforcers."

- **<u>Educates</u> you and your neighbors about health issues.** Your LHD gives you information that allows you to make healthy decisions every day, like exercising more, eating right, quitting smoking, or simply washing your hands to keep from spreading illness. They provide this information through public forums in your community, public service announcements in the media, programs in schools, health education in homes and clinics, and detailed websites. During a public health emergency, your LHD provides important alerts and warnings to protect your health.

"Effective health education can be fun and can promote creativity and self-esteem. Marquette County (MI)'s Health Education Division sponsors annual school-based tobacco control billboard contests. Kids' winning designs are displayed on highway billboards throughout the county."

- **<u>Provides</u> healthy solutions for everyone.** Your LHD offers the preventive care you need to avoid chronic disease and to help maintain your health. It provides flu shots for the elderly and helps mothers obtain prenatal care that gives their babies a healthy start. Your LHD also helps provide children with regular check-ups, immunizations, and good nutrition to help them grow and learn.

"Health professionals and seniors know that foot problems are a major source of disability. Every month, public health nurses hold foot care clinics at every senior center in Marquette County (MI). The nurses examine feet for problems, refer clients for assistance, and provide counseling on how to avoid disease complications and discomfort and "be a friend to your feet."

- **<u>Advances</u> community health.** Your LHD plays a vital role in developing new policies and standards that address existing and emerging challenges to your community's health while enforcing a range of laws intended to keep you safe. Your LHD is constantly working—through research and rigorous staff training—to maintain its unique expertise and deliver up-to-date, cutting-edge health programs.

"Treatment for HIV/AIDS has evolved rapidly during the last several years. The staff of the Marquette County (MI) health department keeps up to date in preventing the spread of this awful epidemic through periodic, state-run training sessions."

Source: Adapted with permission from the National Association for County and City Officials (NACCHO). http://www.naccho.org/advocacy/marketing/toolkit/upload/Fact_Sheet_1.doc

Public Health Marketing

According to the CDC, **health marketing** is an innovative approach to public health practice. Public health marketing draws from the business discipline of marketing theory and adds science-based health strategies of promotion and prevention. It involves creating, communicating, and delivering health information and interventions using customer-oriented and science-based strategies to protect and promote health in diverse populations

(CDC, 2013i). Marketing research is used to deliver messages to educate the public on priority health issues.

Social media is electronic communications dedicated to community-based input, interaction, content-sharing, and collaboration. Websites and applications dedicated to forums, microblogging, social networking, social bookmarking, social curation, and wikis are among the different types of social media (Social Media, 2013). The most famous example is Facebook. Social media is the new media tool that can be easily used as part of a health communications program.

Social media has also become a communication tool for patient engagement, employees, and providers. According to a September 2011 employee survey of IT professionals, administrators, and physicians, 75% use social media for professional purposes within their employment. The Mayo Clinic and the U.S. Department of Veterans Affairs are exploring ways to use social media for patient engagement, including education (Most Health IT Pros Use Social Media, 2011). Hospitals and academic medical centers are establishing more YouTube channels and Twitter accounts nationwide. Physicians use Twitter to communicate easily and quickly with other physicians. YouTube provides an opportunity for brief videos regarding certain healthcare education.

Because of the continued increase in social media use, the Centers for Disease Control and Prevention Health Communicator's Social Media Toolkit (2011) contains recommendations for social media use in the healthcare industry:

1. Perform market research to determine key educational messages.

2. Review social media sites by user statistics and demographics.

3. Start a social media campaign by using low-risk tools such as podcasts and videos.

4. The educational messages must be based in science.

5. Develop a system of easy viral sharing by patients so everyone can benefit from the message.

6. Social media users should listen to each other. If patients are voicing concerns or questions, they need to be answered.

7. Leverage social networks to expand the message. An average Facebook user has 130 friends with whom he or she can easily share a health message.

In addition to these recommendations, the federal government has established two websites for social media's best practices and governance policies:

http://govsocmed.pbworks.com/Web-2-0-Governance-Policies-and-Best-Practices

http://socialmediagovernance.com/policies.php (CDC 2013i).

COLLABORATION OF PUBLIC HEALTH AND PRIVATE MEDICINE

Public health and private medicine have traditionally focused on different aspects of U.S. health. Public health focuses on primary prevention, specifically on the prevention of disease. Public health practitioners' approach is to develop strategies to promote community health. Private medicine has traditionally focused on tertiary care or providing a cure to individuals or patients. These approaches have traditionally been in conflict. In the 1920s, when public health clinics were treating the poor, private medicine felt threatened because these clinics were viewed as competitors (Reiser, 1996).

Prior to these activities, there were some collaborative activities in the early 1800s and early 1900s—many physicians were involved in public health. They realized the importance of public health in the role of infectious diseases. However, public health efforts were later resisted by physicians. They resented mandatory tuberculosis reporting, as well as immunization programs (Council on Scientific Affairs, 1990). When antibiotics were developed to combat diseases and the financial benefit of reimbursement of tertiary care by health insurance companies was realized, physicians' interest in public health dissipated (Lasker, 1997). They became more hostile because public health was viewed as a direct competitor.

Over the last decade, there has been an increase in the collaboration between public health and private medicine. In 1994, there was a long-term commitment established between the AMA and the APHA that instituted the following initiatives to formalize a partnership: creation of joint research and local and national networks, development of a strategic plan, and development of a shared vision of health care. There has been an increase in collaborative efforts between the AMA and the CDC to develop healthcare programs to combat disease. The AMA is recognizing that obesity is a disease and should be treated as a disease rather than a behavior (AMA, 2013). With the increased prevalence of obesity, diabetes, and other chronic health conditions, this collaboration is crucial to develop strategies to reduce the rates of these diseases in the United States.

CONCLUSION

Public health is challenged by its very success because consumers now take public health measures for granted. There are several successful vaccines that have targeted all childhood diseases, tobacco use has decreased significantly, accident prevention has increased, there are safer workplaces because of Occupational Safety and Health Administration (OSHA), the fluoridation of water is established, and there is a decrease in mortality from heart attacks (Novick & Morrow, 2008). NACCHO and ASTHO are important support organizations for both state and local governments by providing policy expertise, technical advice, and lobbying at the federal level for appropriate funding and regulations. When some major event occurs like a natural disaster, people immediately think that public health will automatically control these problems. The public may not realize how much effort and dedication and research takes place to protect the public.

As a healthcare consumer, it is important to recognize the role that public health plays in our health care.

If you are sick, you go to your physician for medical advice, which may mean providing you with a prescription. However, there are often times that you may not go see your physician because you do not have health insurance or you do not feel that sick or you would like to change one of your lifestyle behaviors. Public health surrounds consumers with educational opportunities to change a health condition or behavior. You can visit the CDC's website, which provides information about different diseases and health conditions. You can also visit your local health department.

The concept of public health has been more publicized over a decade because of the terrorist attacks of 2001, the anthrax attacks in post offices, the natural disasters of Hurricane Katrina and Superstorm Sandy, the Boston Marathon bombing, and the flooding in the Midwest. Funding has increased for public health activities because of these events. The concept of bioterrorism is now a reality. Because public health is now considered an integral component to battling terrorism and consequently a matter of national security, federal funding dramatically increased. In addition to these major public health issues, the goal of the Affordable Care Act is to improve the accessibility and quality of the U.S. healthcare system. There are nearly 50 healthcare reform initiatives that are being implemented during 2010–2017 and beyond. Many of these initiatives focus on public health activities.

VOCABULARY

American Cancer Society

American Public Health Association

American Lung Association

Assessment

Association of State and Territorial Health Officials (ASTHO)

Assurance

Biosurveillance

Bioterrorism

Community preparedness

Community recovery

Constitutional factors

Core public health functions

Determinants of health

Edwin Chadwick

Emergency operations coordination

Emergency public information and warning system

Environmental health

Epidemiology

Epidemiology triangle

Exploring Accreditation Project (EAP)

Fatality management

Health

Health education

Health marketing

Health promotion

Healthy People 2000 report

Healthy People 2010 report

Healthy People 2020 report

Incident Command System (ICS)

Information sharing

Institute of Medicine (IOM)

John Snow

Lemuel Shattuck

Lifestyle behaviors

Macroenvironmental conditions

Mass care

Medical countermeasure dispensing

Medical materiel management and distribution

Medical surge

Mobilizing for Action through Planning and Partnership (MAPP)

National Association of County and City Health Officials (NACCHO)

National Association of Local Boards of Health (NALBOH)

National Incident Management System (NIMS)

National Response Framework (NRF)

Nonpharmaceutical interventions

Policy development

Primary prevention

Public health

Public Health Accreditation Board (PHAB)

Public health education

Public health emergency preparedness

Public health laboratory testing

Public Health Security and Bioterrorism Preparedness and Response Act

Public health surveillance and epidemiological investigation

Responder safety and health

Rotary International

Secondary prevention

Silver Sneakers

Social media

Social and community networks

Surveillance

Tertiary prevention

U.S. Food and Drug Administration (FDA)

United Way

Volunteer management

REFERENCES

About NALBOH. (2013). Retrieved from http://www.nalboh.org/About.htm

American Medical Association (AMA). (2013). Retrieved from http://www.ama-assn.org/ama/pub/advocacy/current-topics-advocacy.shtml

American Public Health Association (APHA). (2013a). The Prevention and Public Health Fund. Retrieved from http://healthypeople.gov/2020/implement/assess.aspx

APHA. (2013b). 10 essential public health services. Retrieved from http://www.apha.org/about/news/pressreleases/2013/Historic+Affordable+Care+Act+offers+great+promise+for+protecting+nation's+health.htm

Ashton, J., & Sram, I. (1998). Millennium report to Sir Edwin Chadwick. *British Medical Journal, 317,* 592–596.

Association of State and Territorial Health Officials. (2013). Retrieved from http://www.astho.org/about/

Centers for Disease Control and Prevention (CDC). (2011). The health communicator's social media toolkit. Retrieved from http://www.cdc.gov/socialmedia/tools/guidelines/pdf/socialmediatoolkit_bm.pdf

CDC. (2013a). Core functions and capabilities of state public health laboratories. Retrieved from http://www.cdc.gov/mmwr/preview/mmwrhtml/rr5114a1.htm

CDC. (2013b). Understanding the epidemiologic triangle through infectious disease. Retrieved from http://www.bam.gov/teachers/activities/epi_1_triangle.pdf

CDC. (2013c). Environmental health services. Retrieved from http://www.cdc.gov/nceh/ehs/ephli/core_ess.htm

CDC. (2013d). Public health emergency response guide for state, local, and tribal public health directors. Retrieved from http://www.bt.cdc.gov/planning/responseguide.asp

CDC. (2013e). Bioterrorism. Retrieved from http://emergency.cdc.gov/bioterrorism/

CDC. (2013f). *Healthy People 2000*. Retrieved from http://www.cdc.gov/nchs/healthy_people/hp2000.htm

CDC. (2013g). *Healthy People 2010*. Retrieved from http://www.cdc.gov/nchs/healthy_people/hp2010.htm

CDC. (2013h). *Healthy People 2020*. Retrieved from http://www.cdc.gov/nchs/healthy_people/hp2020.htm

CDC. (2013i). What is health marketing? Retrieved from http://www.cdc.gov/healthmarketing/whatishm.htm

Council of State and Territorial Epidemiologists. (2013). About CSTE. Retrieved from http://www.cste.org/?page=About_CSTE

Council on Scientific Affairs. (1990). The IOM report and public health. *Journal of American Medical Association*, *264*, 4, 508–509.

Determinants of health. (2013). Retrieved from http://healthypeople.gov/2020/implement/assess.aspx

Ellis, H. (2008). John Snow: Early anesthetist and pioneer of public health. *British Journal of Hospital Medicine*, *69*, 2, 113.

Emerson, H. (1945). *Local health units for the nation* (p. viii). New York: The Commonwealth Fund.

Federal Emergency Management Agency (FEMA). (2013). NRF Resource Center. Retrieved from http://www.fema.gov/nrf

Harvard School of Public Health. (2013). Research centers. Retrieved from www.hsph.harvard.edu/research/

Healthways Silver Sneakers Fitness Program. (2013). Retrieved from http://www.silversneakers.com

Institute of Medicine (IOM). (1988). *The future of public health*. Washington, DC: National Academies Press.

IOM. (1997). *Improving health in the community*. Washington, DC: National Academies Press.

IOM. (2002). *The future of the public's health in the 21st century*. Washington, DC: National Academies Press.

The Joint Commission (TJC). (2013). Hospital Accreditation. Retrieved from http://www.jointcommission.org/AccreditationPrograms/Hospitals/

Lasker, R. (1997). *Medicine & public health: The power of collaboration*. New York: Academy of Medicine.

Lee, B. (1994). *Health policy and the politics of health care: Nation's health* (4th ed.). Sudbury, MA: Jones and Bartlett.

Mays, G. (2008). Organization of the public health delivery system. In L. Novick & C. Morrow (Eds.), *Public health administration: Principles for population-based management* (pp. 69–126). Sudbury, MA: Jones and Bartlett.

Minnesota Department of Health. (2013). *Community health promotion*. Retrieved from http://www.health.state.mn.us/divs/hpcd/chp/hpkit/index.htm

Most health IT pros use Social Media (2011). Retrieved from http://www.informationweek.com/healthcare/mobile-wireless/most-health-it-pros-use-social-media/231601331

National Association of County and City Health Officials (NACCHO). (2013a). About NACCHO. Retrieved from http://www.naccho.org/about/.

NACCHO. (2013b). Mobilizing for action through planning and partnerships. Retrieved from http://naccho.org/topics/infrastructure/mapp/index.cfm?&render

NACCHO. (2013c). Operational Definition of a Functional Local Health Department. Retrieved from http://www.naccho.org/topics/infrastructure/accreditation/OpDef.cfm

Novick, L., & Morrow, C. (2008). A framework for public health administration and practice. In L. Novick & C. Morrow (Eds.), *Public health administration: Principles for population-based management* (pp. 35–68). Sudbury, MA: Jones and Bartlett.

Pointer, D., Williams, S., Isaacs, S., & Knickman, J. (2007). *Introduction to U.S. health care*. Hoboken, NJ: Wiley Publishing.

Public Health Accreditation Board (PHAB). (2013). Retrieved from http://www.phaboard.org/

Reiser, S. (1996). Medicine and public health. *Journal of American Medical Association*, *276*, 17, 1429–1430.

Robert Wood Johnson Foundation (RWJF). (2013). Retrieved from http://www.rwjf.org/about/

Rosen, G. (1958). *A history of public health*. New York: MD Publications.

Rotary International. (2013). Retrieved from http://www.rotary.org

Shi, L., & Singh, D. (2008). *Essentials of the U.S. health care system*. Sudbury, MA: Jones and Bartlett.

Social Media. (2013). Retrieved from http://whatis.techtarget.com/definition/social-media

Society for Academic Emergency Medicine (SAEM), Ethics Committee. (1992). An ethical foundation for health care: An emergency medicine perspective. *Annals of Emergency Medicine*, *21*, 11, 1381–1387.

Turnock, B. (2007). *Essentials of public health*. Sudbury, MA: Jones and Bartlett.

U.S. Department of Health and Human Services (HHS). (1979). *Healthy people: The Surgeon General report on health promotion and disease prevention*. Publication no. 79-55071. Washington, DC: Public Health Service.

U.S. Department of Health and Human Services (HHS. (2000). *Healthy people 1979*. Retrieved from http://www.healthypeople.gov/document/html/uih/uih_bw/uih_2.htm#determanats

U.S. Food and Drug Administration. (2013). *Counterterrorism legislation*. Retrieved from http://www.fda.gov/EmergencyPreparedness/Counterterrorism/BioterrorismAct/default.htm

World Health Organization (WHO) (1942). Retrieved from http://www.who.int/about/definition/en/print.html.

WHO. (2013). *Health promotion*. Retrieved from http://www.who.int/healthpromotion/en/

Winslow, C. (1920). The untitled fields of public health. *Science*, *51*, 23.

NOTES

STUDENT ACTIVITY 5-1

IN YOUR OWN WORDS

Based on this chapter, please provide a description of the following concepts in your own words. DO NOT RECITE the text description.

Exploring Accreditation Project (EAP): _____

_____

_____

Determinants of health: _____

_____

_____

Mobilizing for Action through Planning and Partnership (MAPP): _____

_____

_____

Healthy People Reports: _____

_____

_____

Incident Command System (ICS): _____

_____

_____

Institute of Medicine (IOM): _____

_____

_____

Health promotion: _____

_____

_____

National Response Framework (NRF): _____

_____

_____

Health marketing: _____

_____

_____

STUDENT ACTIVITY 5-2

REAL LIFE APPLICATIONS: CASE SCENARIO ONE

Because of all of the media attention on terrorism, your grandparents, who are elderly, are very concerned about terrorist attacks on the United States. They hear the concept of "bioterrorism" and are worried they will be poisoned. They do not understand the role public health departments play in protecting the public from terrorism. As the director of the local health department, you explain that you have a disaster plan prepared in case there is a natural or manmade disaster in the community.

ACTIVITY

(1) Define bioterrorism and how it can impact a community; (2) describe the coordination of the federal, state, and local health departments in a catastrophic event such as bioterrorism; and (3) explain the role that the public health department has in protecting special groups such as the disabled and elderly.

RESPONSES

_____

_____

_____

_____

_____

_____

_____

_____

_____

_____

_____

_____

_____

_____

CASE SCENARIO TWO

You are a business marketing major. You want to provide your expertise to your friend who is a public health nurse. She feels the need to market health strategies on reducing cigarette smoking in teens.

ACTIVITY

Develop a social media campaign for your friend using three forms of social media.

RESPONSES

_____

_____

_____

_____

_____

_____

_____

_____

_____

_____

_____

_____

_____

_____

_____

CASE SCENARIO THREE

You have been offered a position with the American Public Health Association. You were not sure if it was a for-profit or nonprofit organization and whether their mission is to make money or help people. You want to be sure that this will be a good fit for you.

ACTIVITY

Visit the American Public Health Association website and review their mission statement and their level of activities. Develop a pros and cons list to determine if you should take the job.

RESPONSES

_____

_____

_____

_____

_____

_____

_____

_____

_____

_____

_____

_____

_____

_____

_____

CASE SCENARIO FOUR

You are working in a restaurant and are concerned about some safety issues. You mentioned it to the manager but the manager was not concerned. You feel you need to look for answers in another direction.

ACTIVITY

Visit the Occupational Safety and Health Administration website to find out what you can do regarding the issues in your workplace.

RESPONSES

_____

_____

_____

_____

_____

_____

_____

_____

_____

_____

_____

_____

_____

STUDENT ACTIVITY 5-3

INTERNET EXERCISES

Write your answers in the space provided.

- Visit each of the websites listed here.
- Name the organization.
- Locate their mission statement on their website.
- Provide a brief overview of the activities of the organization.
- How do these organizations participate in the U.S. healthcare system?

Websites

http://www.fema.gov/nrf

Organization Name: _____

Mission Statement:

_____

_____

_____

Overview of Activities: _____

_____

_____

Importance of organization to U.S. health care:

_____

_____

_____

http://www.saem.org

Organization Name: _____

Mission Statement:

_____

_____

_____

Overview of Activities: _____

_____

_____

Importance of organization to U.S. health care:

_____

_____

_____

http://www.apha.org

Organization Name: _____

Mission Statement:

_____

_____

_____

Overview of Activities: _____

_____

_____

Importance of organization to U.S. health care:

_____

_____

_____

http://www.hsph.harvard.edu/research

Organization Name: _____

Mission Statement:

_____

_____

_____

Overview of Activities: _____

_____

_____

Importance of organization to U.S. health care:

_____

_____

_____

http://www.silversneakers.com

Organization Name: _____

Mission Statement:

_____

_____

_____

Overview of Activities: _____

_____

_____

Importance of organization to U.S. health care:

_____

_____

_____

http://www.naccho.org

Organization Name: _____

Mission Statement:

_____

_____

_____

Overview of Activities: _____

_____

_____

Importance of organization to U.S. health care:

_____

_____

_____

DISCUSSION QUESTIONS

The following are suggested discussion questions for this chapter.

(1) Define public health marketing. Do you think it will help change people's unhealthy behaviors?

_____

_____

_____

_____

_____

(2) What is the difference between the role of the state health department and the local health department in providing health services?

_____

_____

_____

_____

_____

(3) Go to the ASTHO website. Based on your research, why is it important to state health departments?

_____

_____

_____

_____

_____

(4) What is the purpose of the Public Health Accreditation Board? Do you feel it has been successful in its goals?

_____

_____

_____

_____

(5) Discuss three of the capabilities developed by the CDC as national standards for emergency preparedness.

_____

_____

_____

_____

_____

The Navigate Companion Website for this text is a great source for additional information on the U.S. healthcare system. You can gain a new perspective on many of the topics presented in this chapter by visiting http://go.jblearning.com/Niles2e. You'll find additional student activities, further reading, and interactive study tools that explore:

- History of public health
- Importance of emergency preparedness in the United States
- Government contributions to U.S. public health
- and much more.

Chapter 6

Inpatient and Outpatient Services

LEARNING OBJECTIVES

The student will be able to:

- Identify and discuss three milestones of the history of the hospital.

- Define and discuss the different hospitals by their ownership classification.

- Describe the difference between hospitals by who they serve.

- Identify the different types of outpatient care settings.

- Analyze the utilization trends of both inpatient and outpatient services.

- Evaluate the difference between inpatient and outpatient services.

DID YOU KNOW THAT?

- Hospitals are the foundation of our healthcare system.

- Other terms related to "hospital" include hospitality, host, hotel, and hospice.

- Voluntary hospitals are called voluntary because their funding comes from the community voluntarily.

- According to the Urgent Care Association, ownership of urgent care centers is split fairly evenly among physicians (35.4%), corporations such as private investors and insurers (30.5%), and hospitals (25.2%). Women seek healthcare services more frequently than men.

- Public hospitals are the oldest type of hospital and are government owned.

- Religious hospitals were developed as a way to perform spiritual work.

INTRODUCTION

Inpatient services are services that involve an overnight stay of a patient. Historically, the U.S. healthcare industry was based on the provision of inpatient services provided by hospitals and outpatient services provided by physicians. As our healthcare system evolved, hospitals became the mainstay of the healthcare system, offering primarily inpatient with limited outpatient services. Over the past 2 centuries, hospitals have evolved from serving the poor and homeless to providing the latest medical technology to serve the seriously ill and injured (Shi & Singh, 2008). Although their original focus was inpatient services, as a result of cost containment and consumer preferences, more outpatient services are now being offered by hospitals. Hospitals have evolved into medical centers that provide the most advanced service. Hospitals can be classified by who owns them, length of stay, and the type of services they provide. Inpatient services typically focus on acute care, which includes secondary and tertiary care levels that most likely require inpatient care. Inpatient care is very expensive and, throughout the years, has been targeted for cost containment measures. Hospitals have begun offering more outpatient services that do not require an overnight stay and are less financially taxing on the healthcare system. U.S. healthcare expenditures have increased as part of the gross domestic product, and consequently, more cost containment measures have evolved. Outpatient services have become more popular because they are less expensive and they are preferred by consumers. This chapter will discuss the evolution of outpatient and inpatient healthcare services in the United States.

HISTORY OF HOSPITALS

The word hospital comes from the Latin word *hospes*, which means a visitor or host who receives a visitor. From this root word, the Latin *hospitalia* evolved, which means an apartment for strangers or guests. The word hospital was a word in the Old French language. As it evolved, in the 15th century, England shifted the meaning to a home for the infirm, poor, or elderly. The modern definition of "an institution where sick or injured are given medical or surgical care" was developed in the 16th century. The name Hôtel-Dieu, "the hotel of God," was commonly given to hospitals in France during the Middle Ages (American Hospital Association, 2013).

Over 5,000 years ago, Greek temples were the first type of hospital with similar institutions in Egyptian, Hindu, and Roman cultures (Longest & Darr, 2008). They were the precursor of the **almshouses** or **poorhouses** that were developed in the 1820s to primarily serve the poor. Hospitals provided food and shelter to the poor and consequently treated the ill. **Pesthouses**, operated by local governments, were used to quarantine people who had contagious diseases such as cholera. The framework of these institutions set up the concept of the hospital. Initially, wealthy people did not want to go to hospitals because the conditions were deplorable and the providers were not skilled, so hospitals, which were first built in urban areas, were used by the poor. In 1789, the Public Hospital of Baltimore was established for the indigent and, in 1889, it became Johns Hopkins Hospital, which exists today as one of the best hospitals in the world (Sultz & Young, 2006). In the 1850s, a hospital system was finally developed, but the conditions were deplorable because of the staff of unskilled providers.

Hospitals were owned primarily by the physicians who practiced in them (Relman, 2007), and therefore became more cohesive among providers because they had to rely on each other for referrals and access to hospitals, which gave them more professional power (Rosen, 1983).

In the early 20th century, with the establishment of standardized medical education, hospitals became accepted across socioeconomic classes and developed into the symbol of medicine. With the establishment of the American Medical Association (AMA) that protected the interests of providers, the reputation of providers became more prestigious. In the 1920s, because of the development of medical technological advances, increases in the quality of medical training and specialization, and the economic development of the United States, the establishment of hospitals became the symbol of the institutionalization of health care and the acknowledgment of the medical profession as a powerful presence (Torrens, 1993). During the 1930s and 1940s, the ownership of hospitals changed from physician-owned to church-related and government operated (Starr, 1982). Religious orders viewed hospitals as an opportunity to perform their spiritual good works, so religion played a major role in the development of hospitals. Several religious orders established hospitals that still exist today.

In 1973, the first Patient Bill of Rights was introduced to represent the healthcare consumer in hospital care (AHA, 2013a). In 1972, the AHA had all hospitals display a "Patient Bill of Rights" in their institutions (Sultz & Young, 2006). In 1974, the National Health Planning and Resources Development Act required states to have **certificate of need (CON)** laws to ensure the state approved any capital expenditures associated with hospital/medical facilities' construction and expansion. The Act was repealed in 1987, but as of December 2011, 36 states still have some type of CON mechanism (National Conference of State Legislatures, 2013). The concept of CON was important because it encouraged state planning to ensure their medical system was based on need.

Hospitals are the foundation of our healthcare system. As our health insurance system evolved, the first type of insurance was hospital insurance. As society's health needs increased, expansion of different medical facilities increased. There was more of a focus on ambulatory or outpatient services because U.S. healthcare consumers prefered outpatient services and, secondly, it was more cost-effective. In 1980, the AHA estimated that 87% of hospitals offered outpatient surgery (Duke University Libraries, 2013). Although hospitals are still an integral part of our healthcare delivery system, the method of their delivery has changed. "Hospitalists," created in 1996, are providers that focus specifically on the care of patients when they are hospitalized (Nabili, 2013). This new type of provider recognized the need of providing quality hospital care. More hospitals have recognized the trend of outpatient services and have integrated those types of services into their delivery. In 2000, as a result of the Balanced Budget Act cuts of 1997, the federal government authorized an outpatient Medicare reimbursement system, which has supported hospital outpatient services efforts. In 2010, hospitals employed approximately 5 million employees, received over 600 million outpatient visits and 130 million visits to their emergency departments, and performed 27 million surgeries of which 60% were outpatient surgeries (American Hospital Association, 2012a).

HOSPITAL TYPES BY OWNERSHIP

There are three major types of hospitals by ownership: (1) public, (2) voluntary or community, and (3) proprietary hospitals. **Public hospitals** are the oldest type of hospital and are owned by the federal, state, or local government. **Federal hospitals** generally do not serve the general public but operate for federal beneficiaries such as military personnel, veterans, and Native Americans. The Veterans Affairs (VA) hospitals are the largest group of federal hospitals. They have high utilization rates by veterans. Taxes support part of their operations. In 2011, there were 208 federal hospitals. County and city hospitals are open to the general population and are supported by taxes. Many of these hospitals are located in urban areas to serve the poor and the elderly. Larger public hospitals may be affiliated with medical schools and are involved in training medical students and other healthcare professionals (Shi & Singh, 2008). Their services are primarily reimbursed by Medicare and Medicaid services and have high utilization rates. In 2011, there were 1,045 state and local hospitals (AHA, 2013b).

Voluntary hospitals are not government owned, private, and not-for-profit. They are considered voluntary because their financial support is the result of community organizational efforts. Their focus is their community. Private, not-for-profit hospitals are the largest group of hospitals. In 2011, there were nearly 3,000 not-for-profit hospitals. **Proprietary hospitals** or investor-owned hospitals are for-profit institutions and are owned by corporations, individuals, or partnerships. Their primary goal is to generate a profit. They have the lowest utilization rates. In 2011, there were 1,025 proprietary hospitals (AHA, 2013b).

HOSPITAL TYPES BY SPECIALTY

Hospitals may be classified by what type of services they provide and their target population. A general hospital provides many different types of services to meet the general needs of its population. Most hospitals are general hospitals. Specialty hospitals provide services for a specific disease or target population. Some examples are psychiatric, children's, women's, cardiac, cancer, rehabilitation, and orthopedic hospitals.

OTHER HOSPITAL CLASSIFICATIONS

Hospitals can be classified by single- or multiunit operations. Two or more hospitals may be owned by a central corporation. Multiunit hospitals are the result of the merging or acquiring of other hospitals that have financial problems. These chains can be operated as for-profit, not-for-profit, or government owned. These hospitals often formed systems because it was more cost-efficient. In 2011, there were over 3,000 hospital systems. Hospitals can also be classified by length of stay. A short stay or **acute care hospital** focuses on patients who stay on an average of less than 30 days. Community hospitals are short term. A **long-term care hospital** focuses on patients who stay on an average of more than 30 days. Rehabilitation and chronic disease hospitals are examples of long-term care hospitals. More than 90% of hospitals are acute or short-term (AHA, 2013b).

Hospitals can be classified by geographic location—rural or urban. Urban hospitals are located in a county with designated urban or city geographic areas. Rural hospitals are located in a county that has no urban areas. In 2011, there were 1,984 rural community hospitals. Urban hospitals tend to pay higher salaries and consequently offer more complex care because of the highly trained providers and staff. In 2011, there were nearly 3,000 urban hospitals. Rural hospitals tend to see more poor and elderly and, consequently, have financial issues (AHA, 2013b). As a result of this issue, the **Medicare Rural Hospital Flexibility Program** (MRHFP) was created as part of the Balanced Budget Act of 1997. The MRHFP allows some rural hospitals to be classified as critical access hospitals if they have no more than 25 acute care beds and provide emergency care and are eligible for grants to increase access to consumers. This classification enables them to receive additional Medicare reimbursement called cost plus. **Cost plus reimbursement** allows for capital costs, which enables these facilities to expand (Centers for Medicare & Medicaid Services [CMS], 2013).

Teaching hospitals are hospitals that have one or more graduate resident programs approved by the AMA. **Academic medical centers** are hospitals organized around a medical school. There are approximately 400 teaching hospitals that are members of the **Council of Teaching Hospitals and Health Systems** in the United States and Canada. These institutions offer substantial programs and are considered elite teaching and research institutions affiliated with large medical schools (Association of American Medical Colleges, 2013).

As discussed previously, **church-related hospitals** are developed as a way to perform spiritual work. The first church-affiliated hospitals were established by Catholic nuns. These hospitals are community general hospitals. They could be affiliated with a medical school. **Osteopathic hospitals** focus on a holistic approach to care. They emphasize diet and environmental factors that influence health as well as the manipulation of the body. Their focus is preventive care. Historically, osteopathic hospitals were developed as a result of the antagonism between the different approaches to medicine—traditional or allopathic medicine versus holistic. Current trends indicate that both branches of medicine now serve in each others' hospitals and respect the focus of each others' treatment (Shi & Singh, 2008).

HOSPITAL GOVERNANCE

Hospitals are governed by a **chief executive officer** (CEO), a board of trustees or board of directors, and the chief of medical staff. The CEO or president is ultimately responsible for the day-to-day operations of the hospital and is a board of trustee's member. CEOs provide leadership to achieve their mission and vision. The **board of trustees** is legally responsible for hospital operations. It approves strategic plans and budgets and has authority for appointing, evaluating, and terminating the CEO. Boards often form different committees such as quality assurance, finance, and planning. In a recent AHA survey, the CEOs indicated the two standing committees were **finance** and **quality**. Economic conditions and legal requirements have forced boards to become more goal oriented and have developed very specific objectives that also focus on quality and safety as well as finances. Hospital governance has evolved as hospital structures have changed. There are more hospitals that belong to a system of hospitals with one board that oversees the system making the individual hospital boards' subsidiary boards (Totten, 2012).

The **chief of medical staff** or **medical director** is in charge of the medical staff/physicians that provide clinical services to the hospital. The physicians may be in private practice and have admitting privileges to the hospital and are accountable to the board of trustees. The medical staff is divided according to specialty or department, such as obstetrics, cardiology, radiology, etc. There may be a **chief of service** that leads each of these specialties. There is also the **operational staff** that is a parallel line of staff with the medical staff. They are responsible for managing nonmedical staff and performing nonclinical, administrative, and service work (Longest & Darr, 2008; Pointer et al., 2007). It is in the best interest of the institution that both the operational staff and medical staff collaborate to ensure smooth management of the facility.

The medical staff also have committees such as a **credentials committee** that reviews and grants admitting privileges to physicians, a **medical records committee** that oversees patient records, a **utilization review committee** that ensures inpatient stays are clinically appropriate, an **infection control committee** that focuses on minimizing infections in the hospital, and a **quality improvement committee** that is responsible for quality improvement programs (Shi & Singh, 2008).

HOSPITAL LICENSURE, CERTIFICATION, AND ACCREDITATION

State governments oversee the licensure of healthcare facilities including hospitals. States set their own standards. It is important to note that all facilities must be licensed but do not have to be accredited. **State licensure** focuses on building codes, sanitation, equipment, and personnel. Hospitals must be licensed to operate with a certain number of beds.

Certification of hospitals enables them to obtain Medicare and Medicaid reimbursement. This type of certification is mandated by the Department of Health and Human Services (DHHS). All hospitals that receive Medicare and Medicaid reimbursement must adhere to **conditions of participation** that emphasize patient health and safety. **Accreditation** is a private standard developed by accepted organizations as a way to meet certain standards. For example, accreditation of a hospital by The Joint Commission (TJC) means that hospitals have met Medicare and Medicaid standards and do not have to be certified. Medicare and Medicaid have also authorized the American Osteopathic Organization to jointly accredit their types of hospitals with TJC (TJC, 2013 a). It is important to mention that TJC has had tremendous impact on how healthcare organizations are accredited. Since its formation in 1951, TJC has expanded its accreditation beyond hospitals. They accredit ambulatory care, assisted living, behavioral health care, home care, hospitals, laboratory services, long-term care, and office-based surgery centers. Accreditation of managed care organizations such as preferred providers and managed behavioral organizations ended in 2006 (The Joint Commission, 2013b).

International Organization for Standardization

Established in 1947 in Geneva, Switzerland, the **International Organization for Standardization (ISO)** is a worldwide organization that promotes standards from different countries. Although this is not an accrediting organization, those organizations that register with the ISO are promoted as having higher standards. ISO 9000 (quality management focus) and ISO 14000 (environmental management focus) are management standards that are applicable to any organization, including healthcare organizations, and many healthcare organizations are registered with the ISO. For example, the ISO has standards for healthcare informatics and medical devices (ISO, 2013).

PATIENT RIGHTS

The **Patient Self-Determination Act of 1990** requires hospitals and other facilities that participate in the Medicare and Medicaid programs to provide patients, upon admission, with information on their rights; it is also referred to as the Patient Bill of Rights. If you enter any hospital, you will see the Bill of Rights posted on its walls. This law requires that the hospital maintain

confidentiality of its personal and medical information. Patients also have the right to be provided accurate and easy-to-understand information about their medical condition so they may give **informed consent** for any of their medical care.

The Affordable Care Act (ACA) created an additional Patient Bill of Rights that focuses on implementing consumer-oriented practices from insurance companies, which will help children and adults with pre-existing conditions to obtain and keep insurance coverage, to end lifetime reimbursement limits on healthcare insurance reimbursements, and to increase the opportunities for consumers to choose their physicians (Fact Sheet, 2013).

CURRENT STATUS OF HOSPITALS

Many hospitals have experienced financial problems. As a result of the increased competition of outpatient services (which are often more cost-effective, efficient, and consumer friendly) and reduced reimbursement from Medicare and Medicaid, many hospitals have developed strategies to increase their financial stability. Due to pressure to develop cost containment measures, hospitals are forming huge systems and building large physician workforces. In order to compete with the ACA's mandated state health insurance marketplaces where consumers can purchase health insurance, health insurance companies are developing relationships with hospitals, creating joint marketing plans, and sharing patient data (Matthews, 2011).

Over the years, outpatient services have become the major competitors of hospitals. Advanced technology has enabled more ambulatory surgeries and testing, which has resulted in the development of many specialty centers for radiology and imaging, chemotherapy treatment, kidney dialysis, etc. These services were often performed in a hospital. What is even more interesting is that physicians or physician groups own some of the centers. They are receiving revenue that used to be hospital revenue. Hospitals have recognized that fact and have embraced outpatient services as part of their patient care. Hospitals have to continue to focus on revenue generation by operating more outpatient service opportunities; they own 25% of urgent care centers in the United States, 21% have ownership interest in ambulatory surgery centers, and 3% have sole ownership of outpatient centers (ASCA, 2013a).

Cost Containment Approaches

Hospitals are employing different methods to improve quality and control costs.

They use the following models:

- Lean: Based on the Toyota model, this model focuses on increasing efficiency while reducing waste. Staff identify patient care processes that are inefficient and revise them to improve patient care.
- Six Sigma: A Motorola approach that uses statistics to identify and eliminate defects in patient care.
- Plan Do Study Act (PDSA): Developed by the Institute for Healthcare Improvement, a four-step cycle that focuses on improvement of workflow.

Providers plan a change in a workflow, and once the change is implemented, they describe what happened with the change, describe the impact of the change, observe and learn from the change, and act upon the change.

Many of the large U.S. hospitals are working with the Joint Commission Center for Transforming Healthcare to implement processes that target safe and quality patient care. For example, the PSDA can be used to reduce medication errors by analyzing the process of providing medications, determining what changes need to be made, and assessing if the changes were successful by the reduction of medication errors (American Hospital Association, 2012b).

OUTPATIENT SERVICES

As discussed previously, **outpatient services** are services that are provided that do not require an overnight stay. Often, the term **ambulatory care** is used interchangeably with outpatient services. Ambulatory literally means a person is able to walk to receive a service, which may not always be necessarily true. The term outpatient is a more general term for services other than inpatient services (Jonas, 2003). Hospitals also offer outpatients service in their emergency departments and their outpatient clinics.

Physician Offices

The basic form of an outpatient service is a patient seeing his or her physician in the physician's office. Both general practitioners and specialists offer ambulatory care as either solitary practitioners or in group practice.

Traditionally, physicians established solitary practices, but the cost of running a practice became too expensive so more physicians have established group practices (Pointer et al., 2007).

Hospital Emergency Services

Hospital emergency medical services are an integral part of the American healthcare system. Emergency departments provide care for patients with emergency healthcare needs. There were 130 million emergency department visits in 2010, accounting for about 4% of all healthcare spending in the United States (CDC, 2013a). Emergency department use is more likely among the poor, those in fair or poor health, the elderly, infants and young children, and those with Medicaid coverage (CDC, 2013b,). Hospitals traditionally provide inpatient services, though nearly all community hospitals provide emergency services that are considered outpatient services. Although emergency departments have the technology to treat emergency situations, many emergency rooms are used for nonemergency issues.

Hospital-Based Outpatient Clinics

Many outpatient clinics are found in teaching hospitals. They use outpatient clinics as an opportunity to teach and perform research. The clinics are categorized as surgical, medical, and other. Larger teaching hospitals may have 100 specialty and subspecialty clinics (Jonas, 2003). They may operate as part of the hospital or as a hospital-owned entity.

Urgent/Emergent Care Centers

Urgent/emergent care centers were first established in the 1970s, and are used for consumers who need medical care but their situation is not life-threatening. This would take the place of the hospital emergency room visit. The medical issue usually occurs outside traditional physician office hours so they see patients in the evenings and on weekends and holidays. Many of these centers are both walk-in and appointment facilities. They do not take the place of a patient's primary care provider. These centers are conveniently located and may be in strip malls or medical buildings so they are accessible for consumers. It is important to note that many managed care organizations will reimburse member visits because they are less expensive than an emergency room visit (Sultz & Young, 2006). The urgent care centers relieve the emergency departments from seeing patients who do not have life-threatening situations. It is anticipated that there will be an increase in urgent care centers because of this need.

The number of new urgent care centers has increased for a total of 9,000 nationwide in 2012. Physicians (35.4%), private investors and insurers (30.5%), and hospitals (25.2%) are the top three owners of urgent care centers. Private equity firms have invested nearly $4 billion in healthcare services in 2013, fueled predominantly by urgent care centers. This type of medical care has become the consumer preference because there is less wait time than an emergency room visit (Dolan, 2013). According to an Urgent Care Association of America (UCAOA) survey, approximately 85% of the centers have a physician on site at all times, and 75% of the physicians are board certified in a primary specialty (UCAOA, 2013).

Ambulatory Surgery Centers

Ambulatory surgery centers (ASCs) are for surgeries that do not require an overnight stay. Physicians have taken the lead in developing ASCs. The first ASC was established in 1970. It provided an opportunity for physicians to have more control over their surgical practices as they grew frustrated by hospital policies, wait times for surgical rooms, and delays in new equipment. Advances in technology and newer anesthesia drugs to help patients recover more quickly from grogginess have enabled more surgeries to be performed on an outpatient basis. ASCs may focus on general surgical procedures that involve the abdomen, whereas specialized surgical centers focus on orthopedic surgery, plastic surgery, and gynecologic surgery. Some centers offer a combination of both general and specialized surgeries. Outpatient surgery is a major contributor to growth in ambulatory care. Approximately 8 million surgeries are performed in 4,000 ASCs annually. The most common procedures include ophthalmology; gastroenterology; orthopedic; ear, nose, and throat; gynecology; and plastic surgery. ASCs contribute to healthcare cost containment. Procedures at ASCs cost nearly 50% less than inpatient surgeries. Hospitals have ownership interest in 21% of ASCs and have sole ownership in 3% of ASCs. Patient surveys indicate over 90% customer satisfaction with their care and service (ASCA, 2013). **Health Centers** (HCs), which originated in the 1960s as part of the war on poverty, are organizations that provide culturally competent primary healthcare services to the uninsured or indigent population such as minorities, infants and children, patients with HIV, substance abusers, the homeless, and migrant workers. They are supported by the Health Resources and Services Administration (HRSA) and operate on four fundamentals:

1. Location in high service need community
2. Governed by a community board
3. Provide comprehensive primary care
4. Must achieve performance objectives (HRSA, 2013b)

HCs often are located in urban and rural areas where there is a designated need. They enter a contract with the state or local health department to provide services to these populations. They also provide links with social workers, Medicaid, and Health Insurance Program (HIP). As part of the ACA, funding increased for HCs. Grants were awarded to 219 health centers to expand access to care for more than 1.25 million additional patients and create approximately 5,640 jobs by establishing new health center service delivery sites (DHHS, 2012a). HCs may be organized as part of the local health department or other health service; they also operate at schools. In 2011, over 1,000 HCs received federal funding, providing care to over 20 million patients. HCs provide more preventive services than primary care providers such as healthcare education, mammograms, pap smears, and adult immunizations (DHHS, 2013b).

Home Health Agencies

Home health agencies and **visiting nurse agencies** provide medical services in a patient's home. The earliest form of home health care was developed by Lillian Wald, who created the Visiting Nurse Service of New York in 1893 to service the poor. In 1909, she persuaded the Metropolitan Life Insurance Company to include nursing home care in their policies (Longest & Darr, 2008). This care is often provided to the elderly, disabled, or a patient who is too weak to come to the hospital or physician's office or has just been released from the hospital. Contemporary home health services include both medical and social services, incorporating skilled nursing care and home health aide care such as dispensing medications, assisting with activities of daily living, and meal planning. Physical, speech, and occupational therapy can also be provided at home. Medical equipment such as oxygen tanks, hospital beds, etc., may also be provided. Annually, approximately 7 million people receive home health services that are provided by approximately 20,000 agencies. These agencies can be private not-for-profit, government, or private for-profit (Longest & Darr, 2008).

Although the home healthcare industry is very popular with patients, there have been continued problems with the quality of home health care being offered, as well as issues with fraudulent Medicare reimbursement for services not needed. Although most states offer licensing for home health agencies, it is important that home health agencies are Medicare certified because they are required to comply with CMS regulations. In 2011, about 3.4 million Medicare beneficiaries received home health services from almost 11,900 home health agencies. Access to home health care is generally adequate: 99% of beneficiaries live in a ZIP code where a Medicare home health agency operates, and 98% live in an area with two or more agencies. There were 12,000 agencies in 2011. In 2011, Medicare implemented two major changes to strengthen program integrity for Medicare home health services. In April 2011, CMS implemented an ACA requirement for a face-to-face encounter with a physician or nurse practitioner when home health care is ordered. They can also receive accreditation from the Community Health Accreditation Program (CHAP) (Medpac, 2012).

Employee Assistance Programs

Employee assistance programs (EAPs) are a type of occupational health program. Established in the 1970s as an intervention for employee drug and alcohol abuse, the program has expanded to offer other services such as tobacco cessation programs and mental health counseling and referrals. EAP services have expanded to include disease management and prevention health (Employee Assistance Programs, 2013).

OTHER HEALTH SERVICES

Respite Care

Often, family and friends of chronically ill patients become the major caregivers of their friends and family. This continuous care can become stressful for those caregivers. These caregivers may still be working full-time and have other family members that need their attention. As a result of this issue, **respite care** or **temporary care programs** were formally established in the 1970s to provide systematic relief to those caregivers who need a mental break. It also forestalls the ill patient from being placed in a facility. There are a variety of programs that are considered respite programs, such as adult day care, furloughs to facilities for the

patient, and in-home aides. Long-term care insurance may pay for a portion of respite care (DHHS, 2010).

Hospice

Hospice care provides care for patients who have a life-threatening illness and comfort for the patient's family. Medicare, private health insurance, and Medicaid (in 43 states) cover hospice care for qualified patients. Some hospice programs offer healthcare services on a sliding fee scale basis for patients with limited resources. A typical hospice care team includes the following:

- Doctors
- Nurses
- Home health aides
- Clergy or other spiritual counselors (e.g., minister, priest, rabbi)
- Social workers
- Volunteers
- Occupational, physical, and/or speech therapists

The family of the terminally ill patient is also involved in the care giving. Hospice services can be offered both as inpatient and outpatient services. Hospitals may have designated hospice units. Home health agencies may also offer a hospice program. Medicare, Medicaid, Department of Veterans Affairs, and private insurance plans will pay for hospice services. Donations allow hospice care facilities to provide care at no cost to those who cannot afford it (WebMD, 2012).

Adult Day Care

Adult day care centers are day programs that provide a medical model of care with medical and therapeutic services; a social model that provides meals, recreation, and some basic medical health; or a medical–social model that provides social interaction and intensive medical-related activities, all depending on the needs of the patients. Adult day care centers were developed in the 1960s based on research that indicated that they were an opportunity to provide a break for informal caregivers as well as provide an opportunity to prolong the patient's life at home. The average age of the adult day care center recipient is 72 years old and two-thirds are female (DHHS, 2012).

In 1979, the **National Adult Day Services Association (NADSA)** was formed to promote these types of community services. They established national standard criteria for the operation of adult day care centers. Many adult day care centers are regulated by state licensing and may be certified by a particular community agency. In 2010, there were 5,000 adult day care centers, with a national average rate of $61 per day (includes 8–10 hours on average) compared to an average rate for home health aides of $19 per hour. They are often affiliated with larger formal healthcare or skilled nursing care facilities, medical centers, or senior organizations (NADSA, 2013).

Senior Centers

Established by the Older American Act of 1965, **senior centers** provide a broad array of services for the older population. Services provided include meal and nutrition programs, education, recreational programs, health and wellness programs, transportation services, volunteer opportunities, counseling, and other services.

According to 2010 statistics, there are 11,000 senior centers in the United States, serving approximately 1 million seniors every day; users spend 3 hours per day, 1 to 3 times per week, at the centers; 70% of users are women; and the average age of attendees is 75 years of age (National Council on Aging [NCOA], 2013). Funding is received from state and local governments, grants, and private donations.

Located in Washington, D.C., NCOA is a not-for-profit advocacy agency for the senior population. As part of the NCOA, the **National Institute of Senior Centers (NISC)** is a network of senior center professionals that promote senior centers. It is the only national program dedicated to the welfare of senior centers. It sponsors a national voluntary accreditation program for senior centers (NCOA, 2013). With the estimated increase in life expectancy, senior centers will continue to expand and offer more services to seniors who have chronic disease that can be managed on an outpatient basis.

Women's Health Center

Women have unique health needs that require specialized medical facilities. Recognizing this need, in 1991, HHS established an **Office of Women's Health (OWH)**. There are currently 10 regional offices that oversee women's health activities nationwide. Women's life expectancy is approximately 7 years longer than

men's and will represent a larger portion of the elder population. The OWH mission is to promote women's and girls' health by gender-specific health activities (DHHS, 2013a).

Meals on Wheels of America

Established in 1954, the **Meals on Wheels Association of America (MOWAA)** is the oldest and largest national organization composed of and representing 5,000 community-based Senior Nutrition Programs that are members of the association. These programs provide well over 1 million meals to seniors who need them each day. Some programs serve meals at senior centers, some deliver meals directly to the homes of seniors whose mobility is limited, and many provide both services. Federal funding for Meals on Wheels is provided by the Senior Nutrition Program that was authorized by the 1972 Older Americans Act. In October of 2011, the U.S. Administration on Aging (AoA) entered into a cooperative agreement with MOWAA to establish a new National Resource Center on Nutrition and Aging. The primary role of the National Resource Center's (NRC) AoA-MOWAA is to cultivate innovative ideas related to nutrition and aging in the United States (MOWAA, 2013).

In 2010, MOWAA received a large donation of $5 million from the Walmart Foundation in the fall of 2010 for the We Are Meals on Wheels Project. The We Are Meals on Wheels Project consists of four major components: (1) Walmart Foundation—MOWAA Building the Future Grants Program, (2) We Are Meals on Wheels National Multimedia Public Awareness Campaign, (3) Walmart Foundation Institute for Senior Nutrition Education, and (4) MOWAA State-Affiliate Training Wheels Program (Walmart, 2013).

Planned Parenthood Federation of America

Planned Parenthood Federation of America (PPFA) is a 90-year-old organization that provides family services to men, women, and teens in local communities regarding sexual health, family planning, and more, both online and at sites across the United States. PPFA also provides important health education to over 1 million individuals. They accept Medicaid but also offer services based on a sliding fee scale (PPFA, 2013). PPFA is a founding member of the International Planned Parenthood Federation.

American Red Cross

Founded in 1881 and headquartered in Washington, D.C., the **American Red Cross (ARC)** provides emergency response to victims of war and natural and man-made disasters. They also offer services to the indigent and the military, analyze and distribute blood products, provide education, and organize international relief programs. Approximately 91 cents of every dollar spent is invested in humanitarian programs. There are over 700 local chapters with 35,000 employees supported by 500,000 volunteers (ARC, 2013).

PPFA and ARC are examples of the types of outpatient services offered in different communities across the United States. Organizations have recognized that outpatient services are preferred by healthcare consumers and are cost effective. Many physicians have established outpatient services as a way to satisfy consumer preference.

Doctors Without Borders

Established in 1971 by physicians and journalists in France, **Doctors Without Borders** is an international medical organization that provides quality medical care to those individuals threatened by violence, catastrophe, lack of health care, natural disasters, epidemics, or wars in 60 countries. Nearly 90% of their funding is from private sources. Staff is derived from the communities where the crises are occurring as well as U.S. aid workers. The organization won the Nobel Peace Prize in 1999. A U.S. component of this organization was established in 1990, and recently raised $133 million in funding. In 2010, it sent U.S.-based aid workers on more than 430 assignments overseas (Doctors Without Borders, 2013).

Remote Area Medical Volunteer Corps

Remote Area Medical (RAM) was founded in 1985 to develop a mobile efficient workforce to provide free health care to areas of need worldwide. The first services delivered by Remote Area Medical Volunteer Corps in the United States were in the Appalachian Mountains of the Southeast, where 42% of the population is classified as rural, as compared to the national average of 20%. Volunteer physicians, nurses, and other healthcare professionals provide general medical, surgical, eye, dental, and veterinary care to thousands of individuals worldwide. However, 60% of their services are provided to the United States. RAM determines where the centers are needed the most and set up a mobile healthcare unit for weekend services only.

RAM established a foundation in 1996 for the sole purpose of raising funds for RAM activities (RAM, 2013).

Telemedicine

According to the HRSA Rural Health, **telemedicine** or telehealth uses technology for providing healthcare services and is an efficient method of providing outpatient care. Telemedicine is a new model for delivering health care—it moves information electronically to consumers quickly and efficiently without a patient physically seeing a healthcare provider. Telemedicine uses electronic information and telecommunication technologies to support long-distance clinical health care, patient and professional health-related education, public health, and health administration. The Office for the Advancement of Telehealth (OAT) promotes the use of telehealth technologies for healthcare delivery, education, and health information services. The office is part of the Office of Rural Health Policy, located within HRSA at the U.S. Department of Health and Human Services. HRSA's mission is to assure quality health care for underserved, vulnerable, and special needs populations (HRSA, 2013a).

Blue Cross Blue Shield of Louisiana and Blue Cross Blue Shield of Massachusetts announced partnerships with American Well, a telehealth provider that also works with WellPoint. American Well will provide physician consultation to policyholders of those companies through iPads, iPhones, Android devices, and webcam-equipped PCs. Humana is planning a pilot telehealth initiative with Medicare Advantage patients (Golia, 2013).

CONCLUSION

Although hospitals admit 35 million individuals annually, the healthcare industry has recognized that outpatient services are a cost-effective method of providing quality health care and has therefore evolved into providing quality outpatient care. This type of service is the preferred method of receiving health care by the consumer. In 2013, there were over 900 million visits to doctor's offices, which is the traditional method of ambulatory care (CDC, 2013b). However, as medicine has evolved and more procedures, such as surgeries, can be performed on an outpatient basis, different types of outpatient care have evolved. As discussed previously, there are more outpatient surgical centers, imaging centers, urgent/emergent care centers, and other services that used to be offered on an inpatient basis. There will continue to be an increase in outpatient services being offered. As a consumer, technology will only increase the quality and efficiency of your health care. Telemedicine will also become a more widely used model for health care because of the continued advances in technology. The implementation of the patient's electronic health record nationwide will be the impetus for the development of more electronic healthcare services.

VOCABULARY

Academic medical centers

Accreditation

Acute care hospital

Adult day care centers

Almshouses

Ambulatory care

Ambulatory surgery centers

American Red Cross (ARC)

Board of trustees

Certificate of need (CON)

Certification

Chief executive officer

Chief of medical staff

Chief of service

Church-related hospitals

Conditions of participation

Cost plus reimbursement

Council of Teaching Hospitals and Health Systems

Credentials committee

Doctors Without Borders

Employee assistance programs

Federal hospitals

Finance committee

Health Center

Home health agencies

Hospice care

Hospital emergency medical services

Infection control committee

Informed consent

Inpatient services

International Organization for Standardization (ISO)

Long-term care hospital

Meals on Wheels Association of America (MOWAA)

Medical director

Medical records committee

Medicare Rural Hospital Flexibility Program (MRHFP)

National Adult Day Services Association (NADSA)

National Institute of Senior Centers (NISC)

Office of Women's Health

Operational staff

Osteopathic hospitals

Outpatient services

Patient Self-Determination Act of 1990

Pesthouses

Planned Parenthood Federation of America (PPFA)

Poorhouses

Proprietary hospitals

Public hospitals

Quality committee

Quality improvement committee

Remote Area Medical (RAM)

Respite care

Senior centers

State licensure

Teaching hospitals

Telemedicine

Temporary care programs

Urgent/emergent care centers

Utilization review committee

Visiting nurse agencies

Voluntary hospitals

REFERENCES

AHA (2013a). A patient bill of rights. Retrieved from http://www.patienttalk.info/AHA-Patient_Bill_of_Rights.htm

AHA. (2013b). 2013 Health and hospital trends. Retrieved from http://www.aha.org/aha/research-and-trends/health-and-hospital-trends/2013.html

Ambulatory Surgery Center Association (ASCA). (2013). Retrieved from http://www.ascassociation.org/faqs/faqaboutascs/#1

American Hospital Association. (2012a). Trends affecting hospitals and health systems. Retrieved from http://www.aha.org/research/reports/tw/chartbook/index.shtml

American Hospital Association (AHA). (2013). Center for hospital and health administration history. Retrieved from http://www.aha.org/research/rc/chhah/index.shtml

American Red Cross (ARC). (2013). Our history. Retrieved from http://www.redcross.org/about-us/history

ASCA. (2013b). A positive trend in health care. Retrieved from http://www.ascassociation.org/ASCA/Resources/ViewDocument/?DocumentKey=7d8441a1-82dd-47b9-b626-8563dc31930c.

Association of American Medical Colleges (AAMC). (2013). Council of Teaching Hospitals and Health Systems. Retrieved from https://www.aamc.org/members/coth/DHHS. (2013a). *Hospice care*. Retrieved from http://www.eldercare.gov/ELDERCARE.NET/Public/Resources/Factsheets/Hospice_Care.aspx

Buchbinder, S., & Shanks, N. (2007). *Introduction to health care management*. Sudbury, MA: Jones and Bartlett.

CDC. (2013a). National hospital medical care ambulatory survey. Retrieved from http://www.cdc.gov/Nchs/ahcd.htm

Centers for Disease Control and Prevention (CDC). (2013b). Ambulatory care use and physician visits. Retrieved from http://www.cdc.gov/nchs/fastats/docvisit.htm

Centers for Medicare and Medicaid Services (CMS). Home Health Agency (HHA) Center. (2013). Retrieved from http://www.cms.hhs.gov/center/hha.asp

Community health centers and rural health clinics. Retreived from http://www.aha.org/advocacy-issues/rural/CHCandRHC.shtml

Department of Health and Human Services (DHHS). (2010). Respite care. Retrieved from http://www.eldercare.gov/ELDERCARE.NET/Public/Resources/Factsheets/Respite_Care.aspx

DHHS. (2012b). Adult day care Retrieved from http://www.eldercare.gov/ELDERCARE.NET/Public/Resources/Factsheets/Adult_Day_Care.aspx

DHHS. (2013b). Recovery act: Community health centers. Retrieved from http://www.hhs.gov/recovery/hrsa/healthcentergrants.html

Doctors Without Borders. (2013). History & principles. Retrieved from http://www.doctorswithoutborders.org/aboutus/?ref=nav-footer

Dolan, P. (2013). Urgent care surge fueled by pressures on health system. Retrieved from http://www.amednews.com/article/20130415/business/130419964/2/

Duke University Libraries. (2013). Timeline of medicine. Retrieved from http://library.duke.edu/digitalcollections/mma/timeline.html

Fact Sheet: The Affordable Care Act's new patient Bill of Rights. (2013). Retrieved from http://www.healthreform.gov/newsroom/new_patients_bill_of_rights.html

Golia, N. (2013). Three insurers take the plunge into telehealth. Retrieved from DHHS. (2012a).

Health care law expands community health centers, services more patients. (2012, July 1). Retrieved from http://www.hhs.gov/news/press/2012pres/06/20120620a.html

Health Resources and Services Administration. (2013a). Telehealth. Retrieved from http://www.hrsa.gov/ruralhealth/about/telehealth/

Health Resources and Services Administration. (2013b). What is a health center? Retrieved from http://bphc.hrsa.gov/about/

International Organization for Standardization (ISO). (2013). Retrieved from http://www.iso.org

Jonas, S. (2003). *An introduction to the U.S. health care system*. New York: Springer Publishing.

Longest, B., & Darr, K. (2008). *Managing health services organizations and systems*. Baltimore: Health Professions Press.

Mathews, A. W. (2011, Dec. 12). The future of U.S. healthcare. Retrieved from http://online.wsj.com/article/SB10001424052970204319004577084553869990554.html

Meals on Wheels Association of America (MOWAA). (2013). Key initiatives, projects and grants. Retrieved from http://www.mowaa.org/page.aspx?pid=296

Medpac. (2012). Home health care services, Chapter 8. Retrieved from http://www.medpac.gov/chapters/Mar12_Ch08.pdf

Nabili, S. (2013). What is a hospitalist? Retrieved from http://www.medicinenet.com/script/main/art.asp?articlekey=93946

National Adult Day Services Association (NADSA). (2013). Adult day services: Overview and facts. Retrieved from http://www.nadsa.org/adsfacts/default.asp

National Conference of State Legislatures. (2013). Certificate of need: State health laws and programs. Retrieved from http://www.ncsl.org/default.aspx?tabid=14373

National Council on Aging. (2013). Retrieved from http://www.ncoa.org/content.cfm?sectionID=46

Office of Disability Employment Policy. (2013). Employee Assistance Programs for a new generation of employees. Retrieved from http://www.dol.gov/odep/documents/employeeassistance.pdf

Planned Parenthood Federation of America (PPFA). (2013). Retrieved from http://www.plannedparenthood.org/about-us/index.htm

Pointer, D., Williams, S., Isaacs, S., & Knickman, J. (2007). *Introduction to U.S. health care*. Hoboken, NJ: Wiley Publishing.

Relman, A. (2007). *A second opinion: Rescuing America's health care* (pp. 15–67). New York: Public Affairs.

Remote Area Medical Volunteer Corps (RAM). (2013). Retrieved from http://www.ramusa.org/about/history.htm

Rosen, G. (1983). *The structure of American medical practice 1875–1941*. Philadelphia: University of Pennsylvania Press.

Shi, L., & Singh, D. (2008). *Delivering health care in America*. Sudbury, MA: Jones and Bartlett.

Starr, P. (1982). *The social transformation of American medicine*. Cambridge, MA: Basic Books.

Substance Abuse and Mental Health Services Administration (SAMHSA). (2013). Retrieved from http://www.samhsa.gov

Sultz, H., & Young, K. (2006). *Health care USA: Understanding its organization and delivery* (5th ed.). Sudbury, MA: Jones and Bartlett.

The Joint Commission (TJC). (2013a). Accreditation and certification preparation. Retrieved from http://www .jointcommissioninternational.org/Quality-and-Safety-Risk-Areas/Accreditation-and-Certification/

The Joint Commission. (2013b). Ambulatory health care Retrieved from http://www.jointcommission.org /accreditation/ambulatory_healthcare.aspx

Torrens, P. R. (1993). Historical evolution and overview of health services in the United States. In S. J. Williams & P. R. Torrens (Eds.), *Introduction to health services* (4th ed.). Clifton Park, NY: Delmar Publishers.

Totten, M. (2012). Hospital governance in the US: An evolving landscape. Issue 1, Spring. Retrieved from http://www.greatboards.org/newsletter/2012/greatboards-newsletter-spring-2012.pdf

Urgent Care Association of America (UCAA). (2013). Retrieved from http://www.ucaoa.org/home_abouturgentcare .php

Walmart. (2013). Hunger relief & healthy eating. Retrieved from http://walmartstores.com/CommunityGiving/9054 .aspx

WebMD. (2013). Hospice care. Retrieved from http://www.webmd.com/balance/tc/hospice-care-topic-overview? page=2

NOTES

STUDENT ACTIVITY 6-1

IN YOUR OWN WORDS

Based on this chapter, please provide an explanation of the following concepts in your own words. DO NOT RECITE the text.

Cost plus reimbursement: _____

_____

_____

Respite care: _____

_____

_____

Patient Self-Determination Act of 1990: _____

Public hospitals: _____

_____

_____

Voluntary hospitals: _____

_____

_____

Proprietary hospitals: _____

_____

_____

Certification: _____

_____

_____

Accreditation: _____

_____

_____

Ambulatory care: _____

_____

_____

STUDENT ACTIVITY 6-2

REAL LIFE APPLICATIONS: CASE SCENARIO ONE

You just received your Master of Health Administration degree and decided you would like to pursue a career in hospital management. You cannot decide what type of hospital you would like to apply to and decide to investigate the different types of hospitals that are available.

ACTIVITY

(1) Identify three different types of hospitals that are available for your employment, (2) based on your research, select a hospital type and state why you chose this type of hospital.

RESPONSES

_____

_____

_____

_____

_____

_____

_____

_____

_____

_____

_____

_____

_____

_____

CASE SCENARIO TWO

One of your friends was just released. She was pleased with her care but was not sure about her physician who told her she was a 'hospitalist.' You had not heard of the term before as well.

ACTIVITY

Perform an Internet search on the term 'hospitalist.' Define the term and find out if there are any current statistics on hospitalist use.

RESPONSES

_____

_____

_____

_____

_____

_____

_____

_____

_____

_____

_____

_____

_____

_____

CASE SCENARIO THREE

Your mother is a volunteer at a hospice facility. She often comes home emotionally exhausted. You have never visited a hospice and asked if you could go with her next time. She agrees. Prior to your visit, you want to understand the concept of a hospice.

ACTIVITY

Perform an Internet search on the subject to understand their mission and goals. Write up your research and share it with your mother.

RESPONSES

_____

_____

_____

_____

_____

_____

_____

_____

_____

_____

_____

_____

_____

_____

_____

CASE SCENARIO FOUR

As part of your internship, you will be assigned this semester to an adult day care center. You are only familiar with child day care centers so you decide to do some research before you start your internship.

ACTIVITY

Perform an Internet search on adult day care centers in your area and develop an information report to share with your classmates.

RESPONSES

_____

_____

_____

_____

_____

_____

_____

_____

_____

_____

_____

_____

_____

_____

INTERNET EXERCISES

Write your answers in the space provided.

- Visit each of the websites listed here.
- Name the organization.
- Locate their mission statement on their website.
- Provide a brief overview of the activities of the organization.
- How do these organizations participate in the U.S. healthcare system?

Websites

http://www.doctorswithoutborders.org

Organization Name: _____

Mission Statement:

_____

_____

_____

Overview of Activities: _____

_____

_____

Importance of organization to U.S. health care:

_____

_____

_____

http://www.4woman.gov

Organization Name: _____

Mission Statement:

_____

_____

_____

Overview of Activities: _____

_____

_____

Importance of organization to U.S. health care:

_____

_____

_____

Organization Name: _____

Mission Statement:

_____

_____

_____

Overview of Activities: _____

_____

_____

Importance of organization to U.S. health care:

_____

_____

_____

http://www.swiftmd.com

Organization Name: _____

Mission Statement:

_____

_____

_____

Overview of Activities: _____

_____

_____

Importance of organization to U.S. health care:

_____

_____

_____

http://www.ncoa.org

Organization Name: _____

Mission Statement:

_____

_____

_____

Overview of Activities: _____

_____

_____

Importance of organization to U.S. health care:

_____

_____

_____

http://www.ascassociation.org

Organization Name: _____

Mission Statement:

_____

_____

_____

Overview of Activities: _____

_____

_____

Importance of organization to U.S. health care:

_____

_____

_____

STUDENT ACTIVITY 6-4

DISCUSSION QUESTIONS

The following are suggested discussion questions for this chapter.

(1) Why do you think impatient services are so popular with healthcare consumers? Discuss your experience with outpatient services.

_____

_____

_____

_____

(2) What are urgent care centers? Have you or someone you know used these centers?

_____

_____

_____

_____

(3) Research an employee assistance program and report back to the types of services they provide.

_____

_____

_____

_____

(4) Visit the Doctors Without Borders website. Report back to the discussion board on one of their recent activities.

_____

_____

_____

_____

(5) What is telemedicine? Give examples of telemedicine. Would you use telemedicine to receive care from your healthcare provider?

_____

_____

_____

_____

The Navigate Companion Website for this text is a great source for additional information on the U.S. healthcare system. You can gain a new perspective on many of the topics presented in this chapter by visiting http://go.jblearning.com/Niles2e. You'll find additional student activities, further reading, and interactive study tools that explore:

- Discussion of hospitals, the foundation of the U.S. healthcare system
- Discussion of the different types of outpatient services
- Contribution of civic organizations to healthcare services
- And much more.

Chapter 7

U.S. Healthcare Workforce

LEARNING OBJECTIVES

The student will be able to:

- Describe five types of physicians and their roles in health care.

- Describe six types of nurse professionals and their roles in health care.

- Describe six types of other health professionals and their roles in health care.

- Discuss the issue of geographic maldistribution of physicians and its impact on access to care.

- Describe the difference between primary, secondary, tertiary, and quartenary care.

- Define allied health professionals and their role in the healthcare industry.

DID YOU KNOW THAT?

- The healthcare industry is one of the largest employers in the United States with a workforce of 18 million workers.

- Approximately 65% of U.S. physicians are specialists, which includes surgeons, cardiologists, and psychiatrists.

- Quarternary care is an extension of tertiary care and is considered cutting edge specialty medicine.

- Since the 1990s, physicians who specialize in the care of hospitalized patients are called "hospitalists."

- Women represent nearly 80% of the healthcare workforce.

- A consumer is eligible to view a physicians's credentials in the National Practitioner Data Bank.

INTRODUCTION

The healthcare industry is the fastest growing industry in the U.S. economy, employing a workforce of 18 million healthcare workers. Considering the aging of the U.S. population and the impact of the Affordable Care Act, it is expected that the healthcare industry will continue to experience strong job growth (Centers for Disease Control and Prevention [CDC], 2013). When we think of healthcare providers, we automatically think of physicians and nurses. However, the healthcare industry is composed of many different health service professionals, including dentists, optometrists, psychologists, chiropractors, podiatrists, nonphysician practitioners (NPPs), administrators, and allied health professionals. It is important to identify allied health professionals because they provide a range of essential healthcare services that complement the services provided by physicians and nurses. This category of health professionals is an integral component of providing quality health.

Health care can occur in varied settings. Physicians have traditionally operated in their own practices but they also work in hospitals, mental health facilities, managed care organizations, or community health centers. They may also hold government positions or teach at a university. They could be employed by an insurance company. Health professionals, in general, may work at many different organizations, both for profit and nonprofit. Although the healthcare industry is one of the largest employers in the United States, there continues to be shortages of physicians in geographic areas of the country. Rural areas continue to suffer physician shortages, which limits consumer access to health care. There have been different incentive programs to encourage physicians to relocate to rural areas, but shortages still exist. In most states, only physicians, dentists, and a few other practitioners may serve patients directly without the authorization of another licensed independent health professional. Those categories authorized include chiropractic, optometry, psychotherapy, and podiatry. Some states authorize midwifery and physical therapy (Jonas, 2003). There also continues to be a shortage of registered nurses nationwide. The American Association of Colleges of Nursing (AACN) is publicizing this issue with policy makers (AACN, 2013).

With the passage of the Affordable Care Act, it is anticipated there will continue to be a shortage of physicians in certain areas. The Association of American Medical Colleges estimates that by 2015 there will be a shortage of over 60,000 physicians. The number will double by 2025 because of the aging of the population as well as the impact of the Affordable Care Act. Medicare officials predict that Medicare enrollment will increase by nearly 45% by 2025, which will further place strain on physician shortages (Lowrey & Pear, 2012). This chapter will provide a description of the different types of healthcare professionals and their role in providing care in the U.S. system.

PRIMARY, SECONDARY, AND TERTIARY CARE

There are three important concepts of care that need to be emphasized: primary, secondary, and tertiary care. **Primary care** is the essential component of the U.S. healthcare system because it is the point of entry into the system—where the patient makes first contact with the system. Primary care focuses on continuous and routine care of an individual. It may be delivered by a physician, nurse practitioner, midwife, or physician's assistant. Categories of primary care practitioners usually include family practitioners, pediatricians, internal medicine providers, obstetricians and gynecologists, psychiatrists, and emergency medicine physicians (Jonas, 2003). The focus of a primary care provider is to ensure patient access to the system by coordinating the delivery of healthcare services. Primary care is often referred to as essential health care, and could include health education, counseling, and other preventive services. **Secondary care** focuses on short-term interventions that may require a specialist's intervention. Examples of secondary care include hospitalizations, routine surgery, specialty consultation, and rehabilitation. **Tertiary care** is a complex level of medical care, typically done by surgeons—physicians that perform operations to treat disease, physical problems, and injuries. This type of care is usually based on a referral from a primary care provider. Examples of tertiary care are orthopedic surgeons who operate on broken bones, oncology surgeons who removed cancerous bodies, and cardiac surgeons who operate on the heart. A new term, **quaternary care**, is an extension of tertiary care and refers to highly specialized, cutting edge tertiary care. This is performed in research facilities and highly specialized facilities. An example of this type of care is proton beam therapy, which is cutting edge technology used to treat prostate cancer (Torrey, 2011).

PHYSICIAN EDUCATION

Physicians play a major role in providing healthcare services. They have been trained to diagnose and treat patient illnesses. Depending on their training, physicians have participated in primary, secondary, and tertiary care. All states require a license to practice medicine. Physicians must receive their medical education from an accredited school that awards either a **Doctor of Medicine (MD)** or a **Doctor of Osteopathic Medicine (DO)**. Many students prepare for medical school by majoring in a premedical undergraduate program, which often consists of science and mathematics. Undergraduate students are also required to take the MCAT—the Medical College Admission Test.

In order to provide direct patient care, physicians must take a licensing examination in the desired state of practice once they complete a residency. State licensing requirements may vary. This residency or training may take 3–8 years. The residency is important because it allows physicians to learn about a certain specialty of interest while providing them with on-the-job training. The length of the residency program can be as short as 3 years for a family practice and as long as 10 years for different surgery specialties. Most states require physicians to participate in continuing medical education (CME) activities to maintain state licensure.

The major difference between an MD and a DO is their approach to treatment. DOs tend to stress preventive treatments and use a **holistic approach** to treating a patient, which means they focus not only on the disease, but also on the entire person. Most DOs are generalists. MDs use an **allopathic approach**, which means MDs actively intervene in attacking and eradicating disease and focus their efforts on the disease (BLS, 2013a).

In 2010, there were 691,000 jobs for physicians. Growth between 2010 and 2020 is estimated at 24%, which is an estimated 860,000. Wages of physicians are among the highest of all occupations. According to the Medical Group Management Association, in 2010, physicians practicing primary care received total median annual compensation of $202,392, and physicians practicing in medical specialties received total median annual compensation of $356,885. Due to the difference in wages, there are less primary care physicians in the overall physician population—32.2%. Specialists represent over 65% of the overall physician population (BLS, 2013b).

GENERALISTS AND SPECIALISTS

Generalists can be primary care physicians, family care practitioners, general internal medicine physicians, or general pediatricians. Their focus is preventive services such as immunizations and health examinations. They treat less severe medical problems and often serve as a gatekeeper for a patient, which means they coordinate patient care if the patient needs to see a specialist for more complex medical problems. **Specialists** are required to be certified in their area of specialization. This may require additional years of training, as discussed in the previous paragraph, and require a **board certifying or credentialing examination**. The most common specialties are dermatology, cardiology, pediatrics, pathology, psychiatry, obstetrics, anesthesiology, specialized internal medicine, gynecology, ophthalmology, radiology, and surgery (Shi & Singh, 2008). The

board certification is often associated with the quality of the healthcare provider's services because board certification requires more training. A consumer is eligible to view a physician's credentials in the **National Practitioner Data Bank** (NPDB). The database was created to provide a nationwide system to prohibit any incompetent healthcare practitioners from moving state to state without disclosing any previous issues.

The database is a depository of negative actions against licenses, or clinical privileges. It also provides information about any medical liability settlements (AMA, 2013). Located on the Centers for Medicare and Medicaid (CMS) website, the **Physician Compare website** helps consumers with research about physicians who accept Medicare. It provides basic information about their address and contact information, education, languages spoken, gender, hospital affiliation, Medicare acceptance, and specialty (CMS, 2013).

DIFFERENCES BETWEEN PRIMARY AND SPECIALTY CARE

Primary care is the initial contact between the healthcare provider and the patient. If needed, **specialty care** will be a result of a primary care evaluation. The primary care physician will ultimately coordinate the health care of the patient if additional specialty care is required. If a patient has a chronic condition, the primary care provider will coordinate the overall care of the individual (Torrey, 2011). In a managed care environment, which focuses on cost containment, the primary care physician becomes the gatekeeper of the patient's care by referring a patient to a specialist for additional care. Primary care students spend most of their focus in ambulatory settings learning about different diseases, whereas specialty care students spend time in an inpatient setting focusing on special patient conditions.

PATTERNS OF PHYSICIAN SUPPLY

The concept of **geographic maldistribution** has occurred because physicians prefer to practice in urban and suburban areas where there is a higher probability of increased income. Recruiting physicians to rural areas is difficult because of the working conditions, reduced income, and reduced access to technology, which is more available in urban and suburban areas. Another issue in physician supply is the increasing number of specialists to generalists, which is called **specialty maldistribution**. The supply of specialists has increased more than 100% over the last 20 years, while the supply of generalists has increased only 18%. The Affordable Care Act mandate of expanding health insurance coverage will add an additional 34 million consumers to the healthcare system. President Obama has called for an increase in primary care physicians, nurse practitioners, and physician assistants to manage this huge increase (Petterson et al. 2012).

TYPES OF HEALTHCARE PROVIDERS

Hospitalists

A **hospitalist** is a physician that provides care to hospitalized patients. This new type of physician, which evolved in the 1990s, is usually a general practitioner and is becoming more popular—because they spend so much time in the hospital setting, they can provide more efficient care. They replace a patient's primary care physician while the patient is hospitalized. A hospitalist monitors the patient from admittance to discharge, acting as a primary care provider for inpatient medicine. However, they normally do not have a relationship with the patient prior to admittance. They coordinate the care within the hospital among the specialty physicians and other healthcare practitioners. Hospitalists comprise 9% of the primary care workforce and 4% of the overall physician workforce, which approximates 30,000 in the United States (Association of American Medical Colleges [AAMC], 2012).

Nonphysician Practitioners

It is important to mention the general term **nonphysician practitioner (NPP)**, which includes nonphysician clinicians (NPCs) and midlevel practitioners (MLPs). The specific professionals of this category will be discussed in depth in this chapter, but it is important to mention their importance generally in providing health care. They are sometimes called **physician extenders** because they often are used as a substitute for physicians. They are not involved in total care of a patient so they collaborate closely with physicians. Categories of NPPs include physician assistants (PAs), nurse practitioners (NPs), and certified nurse practitioners (CNPs). NPPs have been favorably received by patients because they tend to spend more time with patients (Shi & Singh, 2008).

Physician Assistants

Physician assistants (PAs), a category of NPPs, provide a range of diagnostic and therapeutic services to patients. They take medical histories, conduct patient examinations, analyze tests, make diagnoses, and perform basic medical procedures. They are able to prescribe medicines in all but three states. They must be associated with and supervised by a physician but the supervision does not need to be direct. In many areas where there is a shortage of physicians, PAs act as primary care providers. They collaborate with physicians by telephone and onsite visits. Students take classes and participate in clinical settings. They are required to pass a national certification exam and may take additional education in surgery, pediatrics, emergency medicine, primary care, and occupational medicine. Their average salary is $86,410 (BLS, 2013c).

Nurses

Nurses constitute the largest group of healthcare professionals and provide the majority of care to patients. They are the patient's advocate. There are several different types of nurses that provide patient care and several different levels of nursing care based on education and training.

Although nursing supply and demand is cyclical, during recent years there has been a continued nursing shortage. According to the American Society of Registered Nurses, the recession has minimized the nursing shortage. Nurses who were expecting to retire remained on the job and many former nurses returned to the workforce to recover lost savings, although there has been a shortage of **registered nurses** nationwide (Casselman, 2013). It is expected that the impact of the Affordable Care Act will create another supply shortage. The following is a summary of each type of nurse.

Licensed Practical Nurse/Licensed Vocational Nurse

- There are approximately 700,000 **licensed practical nurses (LPNs; or licensed vocational nurses [LVNs] in California and Texas)** in the United States. They are the largest group of nurses and provide basic nursing care.

- Education is offered by community colleges or technical schools. Training takes approximately 12–14 months and includes both education and supervised clinical practice. LPNs have a high school diploma and take a licensing exam. The 2010 median salary is approximately $40,380.

- Their job responsibilities include patient observation, taking vital signs, keeping records, assisting patients with personal hygiene, and feeding and dressing patients, which are considered **activities of daily living (ADLs)**.

- In some states, LPNs administer some medications.

- They work primarily in hospitals, home health agencies, and nursing homes.

- Many LPNs work full time and earn their Bachelor of Science in Nursing (BSN) degree to increase their career choices (BLS, 2013d).

Registered Nurse

- A registered nurse (RN) is a trained nurse who has been licensed by a state board after passing the national nursing examination. They can be registered in more than one state.

- There are different levels of registered nursing based on education.

- **Associate Degree in Nursing (ADN)**: Two-year program offered by community colleges.

- Diploma programs: Three-year programs offered by hospitals. There is no degree offered but undergraduate credit may be earned. They are very expensive and are being offered less often.

- **Bachelor of Science in Nursing (BSN)**: The most rigorous of the nursing programs. Programs offered by colleges and universities normally take 4–5 years. They perform both classroom activity and clinical practice activity.

- Their job responsibilities include recording symptoms of any disease, implementing care plans, assisting physicians in examinations and the treatment of patients, administering medications and performing medical procedures, supervising other personnel such as LPNs, and educating patients and families about follow-up care.

- The majority of RNs work in hospitals. Depending on the level of education, the average annual income is $64,900.

- **Advanced practice nurse (APN)** or midlevel practitioners are nurses who have experience and education beyond the requirements of an RN. They operate between the RN and MD, which is why they are called **midlevel practitioners**. They normally obtain a Master of Science in Nursing (MSN) with a specialty in the field of practice. There are four areas of specialization: clinical nurse specialist (CNS), certified registered nurse anesthetist (CRNA), nurse practitioners (NP), and certified nurse–midwives (CNM). The 2010 median salary is $81,000.

- Many of these certifications allow for a nurse to provide direct care including writing prescriptions (BLS, 2013e).

Nurse Practitioners and Certified Nurse–Midwives

As stated earlier, NPPs are an integral component of providing quality health care in the United States. **nurse practitioners (NPs)** are the largest categories of advanced practice nurses (APNs). The first group of NPs was trained in 1965 at the University of Colorado. In 1974, the American Nursing Association developed the Council of Primary Care Nurse Practitioners, which helped substantiate the role of NPs in patient care. Over the last 2 decades, several specialty NP boards have been established, such as pediatrics and reproductive health for certification of NPs. On January 1, 2013, the American Academy of Nurse Practitioners (founded in 1985) and the American College of Nurse Practitioners (founded in 1995) merged to form the American Association of Nurse Practitioners (AANP), the largest full-service national professional membership organization for NPs.

They are required to obtain an RN and a master's degree or doctoral degree. They may receive a certificate program and complete direct patient care clinical training. NPs emphasize health education and promotion as well as disease treatment—referred to as care and cure. NPs spend more time with patients and, as a result, patient surveys indicate satisfaction with NPs' care. NPs may specialize in pediatrics, family, geriatric, or psychiatric care. Most states allow NPs to prescribe medications. They practice in ambulatory, acute, and long-term settings. Their 2010 median salary was $97,345 (AANP, 2013). They are a very cost-effective alternative to a physician. They will play a role in the expanded health services prescribed by the Affordable Care Act.

Certified nurse–midwives (CNMs) are RNs who have graduated from a nurse–midwifery education program that has been accredited by the American College of Nurse–Midwives' Division of Accreditation. Nurse–midwives have been practicing in the United States for nearly 90 years. They must pass the national certification exam to receive the designation of CNM. Nurse–midwives are primary care providers for women who are pregnant. They must be recertified every 8 years. Recent average salaries are reported at $64,000. The **certified midwives (CMs)** are individuals who do not have a nursing degree but have a related health background. They must take the midwifery education program, which is accredited by the same organization. They must also pass the same national certification exam to be given the designation of CM. The recent average salary is $70,000 (American College of Nurse–Midwives, 2013).

Certified Nursing Assistants or Aides

Certified nursing assistants (CNAs) are unlicensed patient attendants who work under the supervision of physicians and nurses. They answer patient call bells that need their service; assist patients with personal hygiene, changing beds, ordering their meals; and assist patients with their ADLs. Most CNAs are employed by nursing care facilities. There are approximately 1.5 million CNAs in the healthcare industry. They are required to receive 75 hours of training and are required to pass a competency examination. Their average pay is extremely low and they are often overlooked for pay and advancement, creating a high turnover in their field despite the fact that they provide needed services to the patient (Pointer et al., 2007; Shi & Singh, 2008).

OTHER INDEPENDENT HEALTHCARE PROFESSIONALS

Dentists

Dentists prevent, diagnose, and treat teeth, gum, and mouth diseases. They are required to complete 4 years of education from an accredited dental school once a bachelor's degree is completed. They are awarded a Doctor of Dental Surgery (DDS) or Doctor of Dental Medicine (DDM). Some states may require a specialty license. The first 2 years of dental school are focused on dental sciences. The last 2 years are spent in a clinical environment. Dentists may take an additional 2–4 years of postgraduate education in orthodontics (teeth straightening), oral surgery, public health dentistry, etc. In 2010, there are over 155,000 dentists in the United States—over 90% are private practice and are primarily general practitioners. Job growth is approximately 21% between 2010 and 2020. The 2010 median salary average is $146,920. There is no industry priority to target this population (BLS, 2013f).

Dentists are often helped by **dental assistants**. Dental hygienists clean patients' teeth and educate patients on proper dental care. Dental assistants work directly with dentists in the preparation and treatment of patients. Some states require assistants to graduate from an

accredited program and pass a state exam. Some states have no formal educational requirements. Dental assistants who do not have formal education may learn their duties through on-the-job training. They do not have to be licensed but there are certification programs available. The 2010 median pay was $33,470. Job growth is projected at 31% from 2010 to 2020 (BLS, 2013g).

Dental hygienists clean teeth, examine patients for oral diseases, and provide other preventative dental care. They educate patients on ways to improve and maintain oral health. Dental hygienists typically need an associate's degree in dental hygiene. Every state requires dental hygienists to be licensed; but requirements vary by state. Employment is expected to grow by 38% from 2010 to 2020, much faster than the average for all occupations. Ongoing research linking oral health and general health will continue to spur the demand for preventative dental services provided by dental hygienists. The 2010 median pay was $68,250 (BLS, 2013h).

Pharmacists

Pharmacists are responsible for dispensing medication that has been prescribed by physicians. They also advise both patients and healthcare providers on potential side effects of medications. All Doctor of Pharmacy programs require applicants to have taken postsecondary courses such as chemistry, biology, and anatomy. Applicants need at least 2–3 years of undergraduate study; for some programs, applicants must have a bachelor's degree. For most programs, applicants also must take the Pharmacy College Admissions Test (PCAT). All states license pharmacists. After they finish the PharmD, prospective pharmacists must pass two exams to get a license. One in pharmacy skills and knowledge and the other in pharmacy law. In May 2010, the median wage of pharmacists was $111,570. Employment of pharmacists is expected to increase by 25% from 2010 to 2020 (BLS, 2013i).

Chiropractors

Chiropractors have a holistic approach to treating their patients, which means they focus on the entire body with emphasis on the spine. They believe the body can heal itself with no medication or surgery. Chiropractors treat patients with musculoskeletal system health issues, which are made up of bones, muscles, ligaments, and tendons. They manipulate the body with their hands or with a machine. Becoming a chiropractor requires earning a Doctor of Chiropractic (DC) degree and getting a state license. Doctor of Chiropractic programs take 4 years to complete and require 3 years of previous undergraduate college education for admission. Although specific requirements vary by state, all jurisdictions require the completion of an accredited Doctor of Chiropractic program to be licensed in the state. In May 2010, the median annual wage of chiropractors was $67,200. Employment of chiropractors is expected to increase by 28% from 2010 to 2020 (BLS, 2013j).

Optometrists

Optometrists, also known as Doctors of Optometry or ODs, are the main providers of vision care. They examine people's eyes to diagnose vision problems. Optometrists may prescribe eyeglasses or contact lenses. Optometrists also test for glaucoma and other eye diseases and diagnose conditions caused by systemic diseases, such as diabetes and high blood pressure, and refer patients to other health practitioner. Optometrists often provide preoperative and postoperative care to cataract patients, as well as to patients who have had laser vision correction or other eye surgery.

Optometrists need a Doctor of Optometry (OD) degree. In 2011, there were 20 accredited Doctor of Optometry programs in the United States, one of which was in Puerto Rico. All states require optometrists to be licensed. All prospective optometrist must have an OD from an accredited optometry school and must complete all sections of the National Boards in Optometry to be licensed in a state. Some states require an additional exam. Employment of optometrists is expected to grow by 33% from 2010 to 2020. In 2010, the median annual wage of optometrists was $94,990 (BLS, 2013k).

Psychologists

Psychologists study the human mind and human behavior. Some psychologists work independently, doing research or working only with patients. Others work as part of a healthcare team, collaborating with physicians, social workers, and others to treat illness and promote overall wellness. Most clinical, counseling, and research psychologists need a doctoral degree. Psychologists can complete a PhD in psychology or a Doctor of Psychology (PsyD) degree. A PhD in psychology is a research degree that culminates in a comprehensive exam and a dissertation based on original research. In clinical, counseling, school, or health

service settings, students usually complete a 1-year internship as part of the doctoral program. The PsyD is a clinical degree and is often based on practical work and examinations rather than a dissertation. In most states, practicing psychology or using the title of "psychologist" requires licensure or certification. The American Board of Professional Psychology awards specialty certification in 13 areas of psychology, such as clinical health, couple and family, psychoanalysis, or rehabilitation. Although board certification is not required for most psychologists, it can demonstrate professional expertise in a specialty area. Some hospitals and clinics do require certification. In those cases, candidates must have a doctoral degree in psychology, state license or certification, and any additional criteria of the specialty field. In May 2010, the median annual wage of psychologists was $68,640. Overall employment of psychologists is expected to grow 22% from 2010 to 2020 (BLS, 2013l).

Podiatrists

Podiatrists provide medical and surgical care for people suffering from foot, ankle, and lower leg problems. They diagnose illnesses, treat injuries, and perform surgery. Podiatrists must have a Doctor of Podiatric Medicine (DPM) degree, which is a 4-year degree after earning a bachelor's degree. Admission to DPM programs usually also requires taking the Medical College Admission Test (MCAT). In 2011, there were nine colleges of podiatric medicine in the United States. The 2010 median annual wage of podiatrists was $118,030. Employment of podiatrists is expected to increase 20% from 2010 to 2020 (BLS, 2013m).

ALLIED HEALTH PROFESSIONALS

In the early 20th century, healthcare providers consisted of physicians, nurses, pharmacists, and optometrists. As the healthcare industry evolved with increased use of technology and sophisticated interventions, increased time demands were placed on these healthcare providers. As a result, a broader spectrum of healthcare professionals with skills that complemented these primary healthcare providers evolved. These **allied health professionals** assist physicians and nurses in providing care to their patients. The impact of technology has increased the number of different specialties available. They can be divided into four main categories: laboratory technologists and technicians, therapeutic science practitioners, behavioral scientists, and support services (The Association of Schools of Allied Health Professionals [ASAHP], 2013).

Laboratory or clinical laboratory technologists and technicians have a major role in diagnosing disease, assessing the impact of interventions, and applying highly technical procedures. Examples of this category include radiologic technology and nuclear medicine technology. Therapeutic science practitioners focus on the rehabilitation of patients with diseases and injuries. Examples of this category include physical therapists, radiation therapists, respiratory therapists, dieticians, and dental hygienists.

Behavioral scientists such as social workers and rehabilitation counselors provide social, psychological, and community and patient educational activities (Sultz & Young, 2006). This chapter cannot list all allied health professionals but a list of those allied health careers that have accredited education programs will be discussed.

The **Commission on Accreditation of Allied Health Education Programs (CAAHEP)** accredits 2,000 U.S. programs that offer allied health specialties. This section will provide a brief summary of the different allied healthcare jobs that contribute to providing quality health care. This information was obtained from the CAAHEP website and the Bureau of Labor Statistics (CAAHEP, 2013a).

Anesthesiologist Assistant

Under the direction of an anesthesiologist and as a team member of the anesthesia care component of surgical procedures, this specialty physician assistant assists with implementing an anesthesia care plan. Activities would include performing presurgical and surgical tasks and may also assist in administrative and educational activities. The **anesthesiologist assistant (AA)** primarily is employed by medical centers. In 2012, median salaries ranged from $110,000 to $120,000 for 40 hours per week. Acceptance into an AA educational program requires an undergraduate premedical education, which consists of sciences such as biology, chemistry, physics, and mathematics. The AA program length of duration is 24–27 months (CAAHEP, 2013b).

Cardiovascular Technologist

At the request of a physician, a **cardiovascular technologist** performs diagnostic examinations for cardiovascular issues. Basically, they assist physicians in treating cardiac (heart) and peripheral vascular (blood vessels) problems. They may also review and or record clinical data, perform procedures, and obtain data for physician review. They may provide services in any medical setting but are primarily in hospitals. They also operate and maintain testing equipment and may explain test procedures. These allied health professionals generally work a 5-day, 40-hour week that may include weekends. In 2010, their wages averaged $51,000. Employment of cardiovascular technologists and technicians is expected to increase by 26% through the year 2016. A high school diploma or qualifications in a clinically-related allied position is required to enter an education program which may last from 1 to 4 years depending on the background of the student (CAAHEP, 2013c).

Cytotechnologist

Cytology is the study of the how cells function and their structure. **Cytotechnologists**, a category of clinical laboratory technologists, are specialists who collaborate with pathologists to evaluate cellular material. This material is used by pathologists to diagnose diseases such as cancer and other diseases. Cytotechnologists prepare slides of body cells and examine these cells microscopically for abnormalities that may signal the beginning of a cancerous growth. Most cytotechnologists work in hospitals. In 2012, cytotechnologists averaged $64,000. In order to enter into their educational program, applicants should have a background in the biological sciences. Applicants must have an undergraduate degree in order to quality for national certification (CAAHEP, 2013d).

Diagnostic Medical Sonographer

Under the supervision of a physician, this specialist provides patient services using medical ultrasound, which photographs internal structures. **Sonography** uses sound waves to generate images of the body for the assessment and diagnosis of various medical conditions. Sonography commonly is associated with obstetrics and the use of ultrasound imaging during pregnancy. This specialist gathers data to assist with disease management in a variety of medical facilities including hospitals, clinics, and private practices. They may assist with patient education. In addition to working directly with patients, **diagnostic medical sonographers** keep patient records. They also may prepare work schedules, evaluate equipment purchases, or manage a sonography or imaging department.

Diagnostic medical sonographers may specialize in obstetric and gynecologic sonography (the female reproductive system), abdominal sonography (the liver, kidneys, gallbladder, spleen, and pancreas), neurosonography (the brain), breast sonography, vascular sonography, or cardiac sonography.

Employment of diagnostic medical sonographers is expected to increase by about 19% through 2016. Sonographers work approximately 40 hours per week but may have weekend and evening hours. In 2011, the median salaries averaged $60,000. Colleges and universities offer formal training in both 2- and 4-year programs, culminating in an associate or a bachelor's degree. Applicants to a 1-year educational program must have relevant clinical experience. There are 2-year programs, which are the most prevalent, that will accept high school graduates with an education in basic sciences (CAAHEP, 2013e).

Emergency Medical Technician and Paramedic

People who are ill, have had an accident, or have been wounded often depend on the competent care of **emergency medical technicians (EMTs) and paramedics**. All EMT and paramedic patients require immediate medical attention. EMTs and paramedics provide this vital service as they care for and transport the sick or injured to a medical facility for appropriate medical care.

In general, EMTs and EMT–paramedics (EMT-Ps) provide emergency medical assistance because of an accident or illness that has occurred outside the medical setting. EMTs and paramedics work under guidelines approved by the physician medical director of a healthcare organization to assess and manage medical emergencies. They are trained to provide lifesaving measures. EMTs provide basic life support and EMT–Ps provide advanced life support measures. They may be employed by an ambulance company, fire department, public emergency medical services company, hospital, or a combination thereof. They may be paid or be volunteers from the community. Both EMTs and EMT–Ps must be proficient in cardiopulmonary resuscitation (CPR). They learn the basics of different types of medical emergencies. EMT–ps perform more sophisticated procedures. They also receive extensive training in patient assessment. The work is not only physically demanding but can also be stressful, sometimes involving life or death situations. In 2011, their average salaries were approximately $30,360.

Firefighters may also be trained as EMTs. EMT training is offered at community colleges, technical schools, hospitals, and academies. EMTs require 40 hours of training, whereas EMT–Ps require 200–400 hours of training. Applicants for the programs are expected to have a high school diploma or the equivalent. The National Registry of Emergency Medical Technicians (NREMT) certifies emergency medical service providers at five levels: First Responder, EMT-Basic, EMT-Intermediate (which has two levels called 1985 and 1999), and Paramedic. All 50 states require certification for each of the EMT levels (CAAHEP, 2013f).

Exercise Physiologists

Exercise physiologists assess, design, and manage individual exercise programs for both healthy and unhealthy individuals. Clinical exercise physiologists work with a physician when applying programs for patients that have demonstrated a therapeutic benefit for the patient. In 2013, their median wages, depending on geographic area and experience, was $42,264. These allied health professionals may work with fitness trainers, exercise science professionals, or physicians in cardiac rehabilitation in hospital settings. Applicants for their 2-year program should have an undergraduate degree in exercise science (CAAHEP, 2013g).

Medical Assistant

Supervised by physicians, **medical assistants** must have the ability to multitask. Over 60% of medical assistants work in medical offices and clinics. They perform both administrative and clinical duties. Medical assistants are employed by physicians more than any other allied health assistant. In 2010, their median salary was $38,000. Their educational program consists of an associate degree, certificate, or diploma program (CAAHEP, 2013h).

Medical Illustrator

Medical illustrators are trained artists that portray visually scientific information to teach both the professionals and the public about medical issues. They may work digitally or traditionally to create images of human anatomy and surgical procedures as well as three-dimensional models and animations. Medical illustrators may be self-employed, work for pharmaceutical companies or advertising agencies, or be employed by medical schools. In 2010, median salaries were $63,000. Applicants must have an undergraduate degree with a focus on art and premedical education. The program is 2 years and results in a master's degree (CAAHEP, 2013i).

Orthotist and Prosthetist

These specialists address neuromuscular/skeletal issues and develop a plan and a device to rectify any issues. The **orthotist** develops devices called "othoses" that focus on the limbs and spines of individuals to increase function. The **prosthetist** designs "prostheses" or devices for patients who have limb amputations to replace the limb function. Most of these allied health professionals work in hospitals, clinics, colleges, and medical schools. In 2011, their median salaries were $70,000. Their education may be achieved through a 4-year program or a certificate program that varies from 6 months to 2 years. Applicants for the 4-year program should have a high school diploma. Applicants for the certificate programs must have a 4-year degree (CAAHEP, 2013j).

Perfusionist

A **perfusionist** operates equipment to support or replace a patient's circulatory or respiratory function. Perfusion involves advance life support techniques. They may be responsible for administering blood byproducts or anesthetic products during a surgical procedure. They may be employed by hospitals, surgeons, or group practices. The 2011 median salary range was $65,000. The prerequisites for their educational programs vary depending on the length of the program, which can range from 1 to 4 years, depending on the individual's experience (CAAHEP, 2013k).

Personal Fitness Trainer

Personal fitness trainers are familiar with different forms of exercise. They have a variety of clients who they serve one-on-one or in a group activity. They may work with exercise science professionals or physiologists in corporate, clinical, commercial fitness, country clubs, or wellness centers. In 2010, their median pay was $32,000. Their educational programs consist of a 1-year certificate or a 2-year associate degree program. Applicants must have a high school diploma or equivalent for program entry (CAAHEP, 2013l).

Polysomnographic Technologist

Polysomnographic technologists perform sleep tests and work with physicians to provide diagnoses of sleep disorders. They monitor brain waves, eye movements, and other physiological activity during sleep, analyze this information, and provide it to the patient's physician. They work in sleep disorder centers that may be affiliated with a hospital or operate independently. In 2010, their median salary was $50,000. Applicants for their education programs should have a high school diploma or equivalent. Their educational program can range from a 2-year associate degree or a 1-year certificate program (CAAHEP, 2013m).

Recreational Therapist

Recreational therapists provide individualized and group recreational therapy for individuals experiencing limitations in life activities as a result of a disabling condition, illness or disease, aging, and/or developmental factors. Recreational therapists use a variety of educational, behavioral, recreational, and activity-oriented strategies with clients to enhance functional performance and improve positive lifestyle behaviors designed to increase independence, effective community participation, and well-being.

Recreational therapists work in clinical settings, such as hospitals, psychiatric or skilled nursing facilities, substance abuse programs, and rehabilitation centers. Recreational therapists treat and rehabilitate individuals with specific medical, social, and behavioral problems, usually in cooperation with physicians; nurses; psychologists; social workers; and speech, physical, and occupational therapists.

A bachelor's degree with a major in recreational therapy or therapeutic recreation, or a major in recreation with a specialization in recreational therapy or therapeutic recreation, is required for national certification. Specific requirements can be obtained from the National Council for Therapeutic Recreation Certification. Job growth is expected to increase 15% by 2018 due to the aging of the U.S. population. Median pay for 2009 for certified therapists was $39,000 (CAAHEP, 2013n).

Transfusion Medicine Specialist/Specialists in Blood Banking Technology

Transfusion medicine specialists or specialists in blood bank (SBB) technology provide routine and specialized tests for blood donor centers, transfusion centers, laboratories, and research centers. In 2011, the median salary was $55,000. Applicants for their educational programs must be certified in medical technology and have an undergraduate degree from an accredited educational institution. If they are not certified, they must have a degree from an accredited institution with a major in a biological or physical science and have appropriate work experience. This allied health program ranges from 1 to 2 years (CAAHEP, 2013o).

Surgical Assistant

A **surgical assistant** is a specialized physician's assistant. Their main goal is to ensure the surgeon has safe and sterile environment to perform. They determine the appropriate equipment for the procedure, select radiographs for a surgeon's reference, assist in moving the patient, confirm procedures with the surgeon, and assist with the procedure as directed by the surgeon. Their educational programs range from 10 to 22 months. In 2012, median annual pay was $75,000. Applicants must have a bachelor of science or higher or an associate degree in an allied health field with 3 years of recent experience, current CPR/basic life support certification, acceptable health and immunization records, and computer literacy (CAAHEP, 2013p).

Surgeon Technologist

Surgeon technologists are key team members of the medical practitioners providing surgery. They are responsible for preparing the operating room by equipping the room with the appropriate sterile supplies and verifying the equipment is working properly. Prior to surgery, they also interact with the patient to ensure they are comfortable, monitor their vital signs, and review patient charts. During surgery, they are responsible for ensuring all surgery team members maintain a sterile environment and providing instruments to the surgeons. Post surgery, they prepare the room for the next patient. They may also provide follow-up care in the postoperative room. They work in hospitals, outpatient settings, or may be self-employed. In 2010, the median pay was $39,920 per year. Applicants for their educational programs must have a high school diploma or equivalent. The programs range from 12 to 24 months (CAAHEP, 2013q).

NON-CAAHEP ALLIED HEALTH PROFESSIONALS

The following job descriptions are important allied health professionals but are not a CAAHEP program:

Pharmacy Technicians

Pharmacy technicians typically do the following:

- Take from customers or health professionals the information needed to fill a prescription
- Count tablets and measure amounts of other medication for prescriptions
- Compound or mix medications, such as preparing ointments
- Package and label prescriptions
- Accept payment for prescriptions and process insurance claims
- Do routine pharmacy tasks, such as answering phone calls from customers

Many pharmacy technicians learn how to perform their duties through on-the-job training. Others attend postsecondary education programs in pharmacy technology at vocational schools or community colleges, which award certificates. These programs typically last 1 year or less and cover a variety of subjects, such as arithmetic used in pharmacies, recordkeeping, ways of dispensing medications, and pharmacy law and ethics. Technicians also learn the names, actions, uses, and doses of medications. Many training programs include internships, in which students get hands-on experience in a pharmacy. The median annual wage of pharmacy technicians was $28,400 in 2012, and employment is expected to grow by 32% from 2010 to 2020 (BLS, 2013n).

Psychiatric Technicians and Aides

Psychiatric technicians and aides care for people who have mental illness and developmental disabilities. The two occupations are related, but technicians typically provide therapeutic care, and aides help patients in their daily activities. Psychiatric technicians typically enter the occupation with a postsecondary certificate. Programs in psychiatric or mental health technology are commonly offered by community colleges and technical schools. Psychiatric technician programs include courses in biology, psychology, and counseling. The programs also may include supervised work experience or cooperative programs, in which students gain academic credit for structured work experience. The median annual wage of psychiatric technicians was $28,710 in 2010. Employment of psychiatric technicians is expected to increase 15% from 2010 to 2020 (BLS, 2013o).

Respiratory Therapist

There are two levels of **respiratory therapists**: the certified respiratory therapist and registered respiratory therapist. The entry level respiratory therapist performs basic respiratory care procedures under the supervision of a physician or an advance level therapist. They review patient data, including tests and previous medical history; implement and monitor any respiratory therapy under the supervision of a physician; and may be involved in the home care of a patient. Entry level therapists are employed in hospitals, nursing care facilities, clinics, sleep labs, and home care organizations. In 2013, the median pay was $60,000. Applicants are required to have a high school degree or equivalent. Their educational program consists of a 2-year program leading to an associate's degree. An advanced level respiratory therapist participates in clinical decision making such as diagnosing lung and breathing disorders, recommending treatment methods, providing patient education, and developing and recommending care plans in collaboration with a physician. Becoming an advanced level therapist can be achieved through increased education such as a bachelor's or master's degree (BLS, 2013p).

Health Services Administrators

It is important to discuss the importance of **health services administrators** and their role in health care. They can be found at all levels of a healthcare organization. They may be managing hospitals, clinics, nursing homes, community health centers, and other types of healthcare facilities. At the top of the organization, they are responsible for strategic planning and the overall success of the organization. They are responsible for financial, clinical, and operational outcomes of an organization. Midlevel administrators also play a leadership role in departments and are responsible for managing their area of responsibility. They may manage departments or individual programs. Administrators at all levels work with top administration to achieve organizational goals. As healthcare costs continue to increase, it is important that health services administrators focus on efficiency and effectiveness at all levels of management (Shi & Singh, 2008).

Health services administration is taught at both the undergraduate and master's levels. The most common undergraduate degree is a degree in healthcare administration, although most generalist managers require a master's degree. Undergraduate degrees may be acceptable for entry-level management positions. Salaries vary by administration level. In 2010, the median pay was $84,229. Approximately 40% of hospitals employ health services administrators.

The most common master's degrees are the Master of Health Services Administration (MHA), Master of Business Administration (MBA) with a healthcare emphasis, or a Master of Public Health (MPH). The MHA or MBA degree provides a more business oriented education that health administrators need for managing healthcare organizations. However, having an MPH degree also provides insight into the importance of public health as an integral component of our healthcare system (BLS, 2013q).

Home Health and Personal Care Aides

Home health and personal care aides help people who are disabled, chronically ill, or cognitively impaired, as well as older adults who may need assistance. They assist with activities such as bathing and dressing, and they provide services such as light housekeeping. In some states, home health aides may be able to give a client medication or check the client's vital signs under the direction of a nurse or other healthcare practitioner. Home health and personal care aides work most often in a client's home or small group homes. There is no formal education required; however, if they work in a certified home health agency or hospice facility, they must receive formal training. The 2010 median pay was $20,560. The projected growth of this occupation between 2010 and 2020 is nearly 70%, due to the increased popularity of home health care (BLS, 2013r).

CONCLUSION

Healthcare personnel represent one of the largest labor forces in the United States. As a healthcare consumer and potential employee of the healthcare industry, this chapter provided an overview of the different types of employees in the healthcare industry. Some of them require many years of education; however, some of these positions can be achieved through 1–2 year programs. There are more than 200 occupations and professions among the 13 million healthcare workers (Sultz & Young, 2006). The healthcare industry will continue to progress as the United States trends in demographics, disease, and public health pattern change, and cost and efficiency issues, insurance issues, technological influences, and economic factors continue to evolve. More occupations and professions will develop as a result of these trends. The major trend that will impact the healthcare industry is the aging of the U.S. population. The BLS predicts that half of the next decades' fastest growing jobs will be in the healthcare industry. The Affordable Care Act will have an impact on the continued positive growth for this industry.

VOCABULARY

Activities of daily living (ADLs)

Advanced practice nurse (APN)

Allied health professionals

Allopathic approach

Anesthesiologist assistant (AA)

Associate degree in nursing (ADN)

Bachelor of Science in Nursing (BSN)

Board certifying or credentialing examination

Cardiovascular technologist

Certified nursing assistants (CNAs)

Certified nurse–midwives (CNMs)

Certified midwives (CMs)

Chiropractors

Cytotechnologists

Dental assistants

Dental hygienists

Dentists

Diagnostic medical sonographer

Doctor of Medicine (MD)

Doctor of Osteopathic Medicine (DO)

Emergency medical technician (EMT)

Emergency medical technician-paramedic (EMT-P)

Exercise physiologists

Generalists

Geographic maldistribution

Health services administrator

Holistic approach

Home health and personal care aides

Hospitalists

Licensed practical nurse

Licensed vocation nurse

Medical assistant

Medical illustrator

Midlevel practitioners

National Practitioner Data Bank

Nonphysician practitioner

Nurse practitioner (NP)

Optometrists

Orthotist

Perfusionists

Personal fitness trainer

Pharmacists

Pharmacy technician

Physician assistant (PA)

Physician Compare website

Physician extender

Podiatrists

Polysomnographic technologist

Primary care

Prosthetist

Psychiatric technicians and aides

Psychologists

Quarternary care

Recreational therapists

Registered nurse

Respiratory therapist

Secondary care

Sonography

Specialists

Specialty care

Specialty maldistribution

Surgeon technologist

Surgical assistant

Tertiary care

Transfusion medicine specialist

REFERENCES

American Academy of Nurse Practitioners (AANP). (2013). Retrieved from http://www.aanp.org/AANPCMS2/AboutAANP

American Association of Colleges of Nursing (AACN). (2013). Nursing shortage. Retrieved from http://www.aacn.nche.edu/media-relations/fact-sheets/nursing-shortage

American College of Nurse-Midwives (ACNM). (2013). The credentials CNM and CM. (2013). Retrieved from http://www.midwife.org/The-Credential-CNM-and-CM

American Medical Association (AMA). (2013). National Practitioner Data Bank. Retrieved from http://www.ama-assn.org/ama/pub/physician-resources/legal-topics/business-management-topics/national-practitioner-data-bank.page

Association of American Medical Colleges (AAMC). (2012). Analysis in brief: Estimating the number and characteristics of hospitalist physicians in the U.S. and their possible workforce implications. Retrieved from https://www.aamc.org/download/300620/data/aibvol12_no3-hospitalist.pdf

Association of Schools of Allied Health Professionals (ASAHP). (2013). Allied health professionals. Retrieved from http://www.asahp.org/definition.htm

Bureau of Labor Statistics (BLS). (2013a). Occupational outlook handbook: Physicians and surgeons: What physicians and surgeons do. Retrieved from http://www.bls.gov/ooh/healthcare/physicians-and-surgeons.htm#tab-2

BLS. (2013b). Occupational outlook handbook: Physicians and surgeons: Pay. Retrieved from http://www.bls.gov/ooh/healthcare/physicians-and-surgeons.htm#tab-5

BLS. (2013c). Occupational outlook handbook: Physician assistant. Retrieved from http://www.bls.gov/ooh/healthcare/physician-assistants.htm

BLS. (2013d). Occupational outlook handbook: Licensed practical nurses and licensed vocational nurses. Retrieved from http://www.bls.gov/ooh/healthcare/licensed-practical-and-licensed-vocational-nurses.htm

BLS. (2013e). Occupational outlook handbook: Registered nurses. Retrieved from http://www.bls.gov/ooh/healthcare/registered-nurses.htm

BLS. (2013f). Occupational outlook handbook: Dentists. Retrieved from http://www.bls.gov/ooh/healthcare/dentists.htm

BLS. (2013g). Occupational outlook handbook: Dental assistants. Retrieved from http://www.bls.gov/ooh/Healthcare/Dental-assistants.htm

BLS. (2013h). Occupational outlook handbook: Dental hygienists. Retrieved from http://www.bls.gov/ooh/healthcare/dental-hygienists.htm

BLS. (2013i). Occupational outlook handbook: Pharmacists. Retrieved from http://www.bls.gov/ooh/Healthcare/Pharmacists.htm

BlS. (2013j). Occupational outlook handbook: Chiropractors. Retrieved from http://www.bls.gov/ooh/healthcare/chiropractors.htm

BLS. (2013k). Occupational outlook handbook: Optometrists. Retrieved from http://www.bls.gov/ooh/healthcare/optometrists.htm

BLS. (2013l). Occupational outlook handbook: Psychologists. Retrieved from http://www.bls.gov/ooh/Life-Physical-and-Social-Science/Psychologists.htm

BLS. (2013m). Occupational outlook handbook: Podiatrists. Retrieved from http://www.bls.gov/ooh/healthcare/podiatrists.htm

BLS. (2013n). Occupational outlook handbook: Pharmacy technicians. Retrieved from http://www.bls.gov/ooh/healthcare/pharmacy-technicians.htm

BLS. (2013o). Occupational outlook handbook: Psychiatric technicians and aides. Retrieved from http://www.bls.gov/ooh/healthcare/psychiatric-technicians-and-aides.htm/

BLS. (2013p). Occupational outlook handbook: Respiratory therapist. Retrieved from http://www.bls.gov/ooh/healthcare/respiratory-therapists.htm/

BLS. (2013q). Occupational outlook handbook: Medical and health services managers. Retrieved from http://www.bls.gov/ooh/Management/Medical-and-health-services-managers.htm

BLS. (2013r). Occupational outlook handbook: Home health and personal care aides. Retrieved from http://www.bls.gov/ooh/healthcare/home-health-and-personal-care-aides.htm

Casselman, B. (2013, April 25). The myth of the Nursing Shortage. Retrieved from http://blogs.wsj.com/economics/2013/04/25/the-myth-of-the-nursing-shortage/

CAAHEP. (2013b). Anesthesiologist assistant. Retrieved from http://www.caahep.org/Content.aspx?ID=20

CAAHEP. (2013c). Cardiovascular technology. Retrieved from http://www.caahep.org/Content.aspx?ID=21

CAAHEP. (2013d). Cytotechnology. Retrieved from http://www.caahep.org/Content.aspx?ID=22

CAAHEP. (2013e). Diagnostic medical sonography. Retrieved from http://www.caahep.org/Content.aspx?ID=23

CAAHEP. (2013f). Emergency medicine technician–paramedic. Retrieved from http://www.caahep.org/Content.aspx?ID=39

CAAHEP. (2013g). Exercise physiology. Retrieved from http://www.caahep.org/Content.aspx?ID=40

CAAHEP. (2013h). Medical assisting. Retrieved from http://www.caahep.org/Content.aspx?ID=43

CAAHEP. (2013i). Medical illustration. Retrieved from http://www.caahep.org/Content.aspx?ID=44

CAAHEP. (2013j). Orthotist/prosthetist. Retrieved from http://www.caahep.org/Content.aspx?ID=65

CAAHEP. (2013k). Perfusion. Retrieved from http://www.caahep.org/Content.aspx?ID=46

CAAHEP. (2013l). Personal fitness training. Retrieved from http://www.caahep.org/Content.aspx?ID=47

CAAHEP. (2013m). Polysomnographic technology. Retrieved from http://www.caahep.org/Content.aspx?ID=48

CAAHEP. (2013n). Recreational therapy. Retrieved from http://www.caahep.org/Content.aspx?ID=61

CAAHEP. (2013o). Specialist in blood bank technology/transfusion medicine. Retrieved from http://www.caahep.org/Content.aspx?ID=51

CAAHEP. (2013p). Surgical assisting. Retrieved from http://www.caahep.org/Content.aspx?ID=52

CAAHEP. (2013q). Surgeon technology. Retrieved from http://www.caahep.org/Content.aspx?ID=53

Centers for Disease Control and Prevention (CDC). (2013). Workplace safety & health topics: Healthcare workers. Retrieved from http://www.cdc.gov/niosh/topics/healthcare/

Centers for Medicare & Medicaid Services (CMS). (2013). About physician compare. Retrieved from http://www.medicare.gov/physiciancompare/staticpages/aboutphysiciancompare/about.html

Commission on Accreditation of Allied Health Education Programs (CAAHEP). (2013a). About CAAHEP. Retrieved from http://www.caahep.org/Content.aspx?ID=63

Jonas, S. (2003). *An introduction to the U.S. health care system*. New York: Springer.

Lowery, A., & Pear, R. (2012). Doctor shortage likely to increase with health law. Retrieved from http://www.nytimes.com/2012/07/29/health/policy/too-few-doctors-in-many-us-communities.html?_r=0&pagewanted=print

Petterson, S., Liaw, W., Phillips, R., Rabin, D., Meyers, D., & Bazemore, A. (2012). Projecting U.S. primary care physician workforce needs: 2010–2015. *Annals of Family Medicine, 10*(6): 503–509.

Pointer, D., Williams, S., Isaacs, S., & Knickman, J. (2007). *Introduction to health care*. New York: Wiley & Sons.

Shi, L., & Singh, D. (2008). *An introduction to health care in America: A systems approach*. Sudbury, MA: Jones and Bartlett.

Sultz, H., & Young, K. (2006). *Health care USA*. Sudbury, MA: Jones and Bartlett.

Torrey, T. (2011). Levels of medical care: Primary, secondary, tertiary and quaternary care. Retrieved from http://patients.about.com/od/moreprovidersbeyonddocs/a/Stages-Of-Care-Primary-Secondary-Tertiary-And-Quaternary-Care.htm

NOTES

STUDENT ACTIVITY 7-1

IN YOUR OWN WORDS

Based on this chapter, please provide an explanation of the following concepts in your own words. DO NOT RECITE the text.

Doctor of Medicine: _____

_____

_____

Doctor of Osteopathic Medicine: _____

_____

_____

Allopathic approach: _____

_____

_____

Psychologist: _____

_____

_____

Respiratory therapist: _____

_____

_____

Medical illustrator: _____

_____

_____

Emergency medical technician: _____

_____

_____

Transfusion medicine specialist: _____

_____

_____

Certified midwives: _____

_____

_____

Board certifying or credentialing examination: _____

_____

_____

STUDENT ACTIVITY 7-2

REAL LIFE APPLICATIONS: CASE SCENARIO ONE

You have heard that the healthcare industry is a growing industry for employment. You are unsure of the types of careers available to you.

ACTIVITY

You have chosen to explore the area of nursing and have provided the information here regarding nursing opportunities. For each of these opportunities, you will provide (1) educational requirements, (2) job responsibilities, and (3) average wages.

Nursing Options

Licensed practical nurse: _____

_____

_____

_____

_____

Registered nurse: _____

_____

_____

_____

_____

CASE SCENARIO TWO

Your friend has decided to research the area of allied health professionals as an opportunity for a career in healthcare and has provided the information here regarding two opportunities in this area. He will provide (1) educational requirements and (2) job responsibilities and (3) average wages.

ACTIVITY

Your friend has decided to visit the CAAHEP website to research two accredited allied health professional jobs that are of interest to him and has added his research below.

Allied Health Professionals

Surgical assistant: _____

_____

_____

_____

_____

Transfusion medical specialist: _____

_____

_____

_____

_____

CASE SCENARIO THREE

You just moved to a rural community from an urban community and you want to establish relationships with physicians at your new home. You were surprised to find out how few choices you have. You decide to investigate why this is occurring.

ACTIVITY

Look on the Internet to find out information on geographic maldistribution. Write up a report for your family and friends regarding this major issue.

RESPONSES

_____

_____

_____

_____

_____

_____

_____

_____

_____

_____

_____

_____

_____

_____

_____

CASE SCENARIO FOUR

You have just been introduced to the different types of healthcare typically provided by physicians and other healthcare providers.

ACTIVITY

You ask your older sister, who is in medical school, to explain the differences and provide examples of primary, secondary, tertiary, and quarternary care.

RESPONSES

_____

_____

_____

_____

_____

_____

_____

_____

_____

_____

_____

_____

_____

STUDENT ACTIVITY 7-3

INTERNET EXERCISES

Write your answers in the space provided.

- ■ Visit each of the websites here.
- ■ Name the organization.
- ■ Locate their mission statement on their websites.
- ■ Provide a brief overview of the activities of the organization.
- ■ How do these organizations participate in the U.S. healthcare system?

Websites

http://www.aanp.org

Organization Name: _____

Mission Statement:

_____

_____

_____

Overview of Activities: _____

_____

_____

Importance of organization to U.S. health care:

_____

_____

_____

_____

http://www.asahp.org

Organization Name: _____

Mission Statement:

_____

_____

_____

Overview of Activities: _____

_____

_____

Importance of organization to U.S. health care:

_____

_____

_____

http://www.caahep.org

Organization Name: _____

Mission Statement:

_____

_____

_____

Overview of Activities: _____

_____

_____

Importance of organization to U.S. health care:

_____

_____

_____

http://www.aamc.org

Organization Name: _____

Mission Statement:

_____

_____

_____

Overview of Activities: _____

_____

_____

Importance of organization to U.S. health care:

_____

_____

_____

http://bhpr.hrsa.gov

Organization Name: _____

Mission Statement:

_____

_____

_____

Overview of Activities: _____

_____

_____

Importance of organization to U.S. health care:

_____

_____

_____

http://www.aapa.org

Organization Name: _____

Mission Statement:

_____

_____

_____

Overview of Activities: _____

_____

_____

Importance of organization to U.S. health care:

_____

_____

_____

STUDENT ACTIVITY 7-4

DISCUSSION QUESTIONS

The following are suggested discussion questions for this chapter.

(1) Which of the allied health professional jobs would you like to choose as a career and why?

_____

_____

_____

_____

(2) What is a physician extender? Would you as a patient use a physician extender? Defend your decision.

_____

_____

_____

_____

(3) What is geographic maldistribution? Do you believe it is a problem?

_____

_____

_____

_____

(4) What is specialty maldistribution?

_____

_____

_____

_____

(5) Discuss the different nurse career options. Which one would you choose and why?

_____

_____

_____

_____

The Navigate Companion Website for this text is a great source for additional information on the U.S. healthcare system. You can gain a new perspective on many of the topics presented in this chapter by visiting http://go.jblearning.com/Niles2e. You'll find additional student activities, further reading, and interactive study tools that explore:

- Importance of physicians and nurses to healthcare services
- Contribution of allied healthcare professionals to the industry
- Overview of different healthcare career opportunities
- And much more.

Chapter 8

Healthcare Financing

LEARNING OBJECTIVES

The student will be able to:

- Discuss the different cost-sharing strategies in health insurance plans.
- Analyze the different types of consumer-driven health plans.
- Discuss the importance of Medicare and Medicaid to health care.
- Identify the different government and private health insurance reimbursement methods.
- Evaluate the different types of health insurance policies.
- Describe PACE, TRICARE, and SCHIP and their importance to health care.

DID YOU KNOW THAT?

- Nearly 60% of Medicare enrollees are female, which corresponds to the longer life expectancy of a U.S. female.
- The state of Massachusetts has the highest per capita of personal healthcare spending at nearly $7,000.

- Medicare and Medicaid are the two largest government-sponsored health insurance programs in the United States.
- Approximately 84% of the U.S. population is covered by some form of health insurance.

INTRODUCTION

The percentage of the U.S. gross domestic product (GDP) devoted to healthcare expenditures has increased over the past several decades. In 2010, the United States spent $2.6 trillion on health care or 17.6% of the GDP, which is the highest in the world. In 2011, U.S. Census data indicates there were 48.6 million uninsured U.S. citizens, which is a decrease from 50 million in 2010. The Centers for Medicare and Medicaid Services (CMS) predicts annual healthcare costs will be $4.64 trillion by 2020, which represents nearly 20% of the U.S. GDP (CMS, 2011a). The increase in healthcare spending can be attributed to three causes: (1) When prices increase in an economy overall, the cost of medical care will increase and, even when prices are adjusted for inflation, medical prices have increased; (2) as life expectancy increases in the United States, more individuals will require more medical care for chronic diseases, which means there will be more healthcare expenses; and (3) as healthcare technology and research provide for more sophisticated and more expensive procedures, there will be an increase in healthcare expenses (Pointer, Williams, Isaacs, & Knickman, 2007). There are four areas that account for a large percentage of national healthcare expenditures: hospital care, physician and clinical services, prescription drugs, and nursing and home healthcare expenditures (Longest & Darr, 2008). Unlike countries that have universal healthcare systems, payment of healthcare services in the United States is derived from (1) **out-of-pocket payments** from patients who pay entirely or partially for services rendered; (2) health insurance plans, such as indemnity plans or managed care organizations; (3) public/ government funding such as Medicare, Medicaid, and other government programs; and (4) health savings accounts (HSAs) (Buchbinder & Shanks, 2007; Shi & Singh, 2008; Sultz & Young, 2006). Much of the burden of healthcare expenditures has been borne by private sources—employers and their health insurance programs. Employers are offering less healthcare benefits. In 2002, 72% offered health insurance benefits, which has dropped to 67.5% in 2010 (Kliff, 2012). When people are downsized, individuals may continue to pay their health insurance premiums through the Consolidated Omnibus Budget Reconciliation Act (COBRA) once they are unemployed, but most individuals cannot afford to pay the expensive premiums. As a result of the passage of the Affordable Care Act (ACA) of 2010, the government is playing a proactive role in developing a healthcare system that is consumer oriented. The Act is requiring more employers to offer health insurance benefits and requiring individuals to purchase healthcare insurance if they can afford it, so these statistics may increase.

To understand the complexity of the U.S. healthcare system, this chapter will provide a breakdown of U.S. healthcare spending by source of funds, state, and the major private and public sources of funding for these expenditures. It is important to reemphasize that there are three parties involved in providing health care: the provider, the patient, and the fiscal intermediary such as a health insurance company or the government. Therefore, included in the chapter is also a description of how healthcare providers are reimbursed for their services and how reimbursement rates were developed for both private and public funds.

HEALTHCARE SPENDING BY SERVICE TYPE

These data are a summary from the Centers for Medicare and Medicaid Services website of the different healthcare spending categories.

Overview

In 2010, hospital spending accounted for nearly 36% of personal healthcare expenditures, prescription drugs for 12%, physician care for 24%, and nursing care and continuing care communities for 7%. In 2010, private health insurance paid 46.4% of total personal health care, the federal government 34%, state and local governments 11%, and out-of-pocket payments 15%. In 2011, private health insurance premiums on a per enrollee basis grew only 3.2%, which was a decrease from 4.6% in 2010. The 4.6% growth rate was due to the increased enrollment of the under 26 age demographic due to the new mandate from the Affordable Care Act.

Out-of-pocket payments grew 2.8% in 2011 to $307.7 billion, which was a result of higher cost sharing for healthcare services (CMS, 2013c). In 2011, Medicare spending was $554 billion, 21% of national health spending, and grew 6.2%, an increase from 4.3% in 2010. The spending increase is attributed to skilled nursing facility and physician service reimbursements. Medicaid spending was $407.7 billion (2.5%), a decrease from a 5.9% growth rate in 2010. This was due to a slower enrollment rate in Medicaid in 2011.

Hospital

According to CMS, hospital spending increased 4.3% to $851 billion compared to a 4.9% growth in 2010. There was slower growth in 2011 due to price growth slowdown and less use of hospital services. Medicaid spending for hospital use decreased while Medicare and private health insurance hospital spending and physician spending increased.

Clinical and Other Professional Services

Private health insurance and Medicare spending on clinical services increased in 2011 because there was an increase in clinical service usage by consumers with a 4.3% growth rate from 2010, which had experienced a 3.1% growth rate. Spending on specialty care such as chiropractic services, podiatry, and optometry increased nearly 5% compared to a growth rate of 4.6% in 2010. Dental services increased 3% in 2011, which was a slight increase of 0.3% from 2010. Out-of-pocket spending for dental services, which accounts for 40% of dental spending, increased 4.1% in 2011, compared to a growth rate of 0.7% in 2010.

Home Health Care

Home health-care agency spending slowed from a 5.3% growth rate in 2010 to a 4.5% growth rate ($74.3 billion) in 2011. In 2011, Medicare and Medicaid spending for home health care, which account for over 80% of home healthcare spending, increased slightly from 2010.

Nursing Care and Continuing Care Retirement Community Spending

Nursing care and continuing care spending increased 4.4% in 2011 compared to 3.2% in 2010. These statistics can be attributed to Medicare spending, which increased in 2011 to 16.5% compared to 7.2% growth in 2010.

Prescription Drugs

Prescription drug spending grew nearly 3% in 2011, a stark increase from a growth rate of 0.4% in 2010. The difference in the growth rates were due to prescription drug price increases for brand name drugs, although consumers are continuing to purchase more generic drugs (CMS, 2011a).

HEALTHCARE SPENDING BY STATE

In 2009, the highest per capita of personal healthcare spending was the District of Columbia at $10,349, compared to a low of $5,031 in Utah. The highest per capita spending was in the 10 states that had the highest levels of total personal healthcare spending per capita: Massachusetts, Alaska, Connecticut, Maine, Delaware, New York, Rhode Island, New Hampshire, North Dakota, Pennsylvania, and the District of Columbia. In 2009, the 10 states that had the lowest levels of total personal healthcare spending per capita were Utah, Arizona, Georgia, Idaho, Nevada, Texas, Colorado, Arkansas, California, and Alabama. Personal healthcare spending per capita for these states ranged from 8% to 26% below the national average and varied from $6,272 (Alabama) to $5,031 (Utah) (CMS, 2009).

The states with the highest Medicare spending per enrollee were New Jersey and Florida, with each state's spending levels at nearly $12,000 per enrollee in 2009, or 15% above the national average. Florida also had the highest share of its overall health spending in 2009 accounted for by Medicare, at 29.5%, which correlates with the large percentage of seniors living in Florida. In 2009, Montana, the state with the lowest per enrollee Medicare personal healthcare spending, spent roughly two-thirds of New Jersey's per enrollee amount. This finding is likely related to a relatively higher share of younger beneficiaries enrolled in Montana compared to enrollees in New Jersey. Nine of the fourteen states with higher than average per enrollee Medicare spending had a share of female enrollees higher than the national average (55.4%) (CMS, 2009).

According to CMS, the improving economy, the ACA mandate of individual health insurance coverage and the graying of our population are expected to increase healthcare expending from 2014 and beyond. With the 2014 implementation of the Health Insurance Marketplaces, as well as the mandate of increased state Medicaid coverage, it is estimated between 8–11 million Americans will have insurance coverage (CMS, 2011b).

HEALTH INSURANCE AS A PAYER FOR HEALTHCARE SERVICES

Like life insurance or homeowner's insurance, **health insurance** was developed to provide protection should a covered individual experience an event that required health care. In 1847, a Boston insurance company offered sickness insurance to consumers. During the 19th century, large employers such as coal mining and railroad companies offered medical services to their employees by providing company doctors. Fees were taken from their pay to cover the service. In 1913, union-provided health insurance was administered by the International Ladies Garment Workers, where health insurance was negotiated as part of their employment contract. During this period, there were several proposals for a national health insurance program, but the efforts failed. The American Medical Association (AMA) was worried that any national health insurance would impact the financial security of their providers. The AMA persuaded the federal government to support private insurance efforts. Employer-based health insurance grew rapidly post–World War II for 3 decades with some stability for 1 decade and an eventual decline in coverage since the late 1980s (Enthoven

& Fuchs, 2006). However, it is still the major method of providing health care in the United States.

In 1929, a group hospital insurance plan was offered to teachers at a hospital in Texas. The teachers contracted for 21 days of hospital care for a $6.00 premium. This was the basic concept from which prepaid healthcare plans evolved. This also became the foundation of the nonprofit Blue Cross Blue Shield (BCBS) plans. In order to placate the AMA, BCBS initially offered only hospital insurance in order to avoid infringement of physicians' incomes (BCBS, 2013; Thomasson, 2013).

In 1935, the Social Security Act was created and was considered "old age" insurance. During this period, there was continued discussion of a national health insurance program. But with the impact of World War II and the Depression, there was no funding for this program. The government felt that the Social Security Act was a sufficient program to protect consumers. These events were a catalyst for the development of a health insurance program that included private participation. Although a universal health coverage program was proposed during President Clinton's administration in the 1990s, it was never passed. In 2006, Massachusetts passed mandatory health coverage for all citizens. State data from 2010 indicates that Massachusetts had the lowest uninsured resident rates in the country because of this initiative, although their healthcare premiums were also one of the highest (Kaiser Family Foundation, 2012; Thomasson, 2013). In the 1960s, President Johnson signed Medicare and Medicaid into law, which protects the elderly, disabled, and indigent. President Nixon signed into law the Health Maintenance Act of 1973, which focused on effective cost measures for health delivery and was the basis for the current health maintenance organizations (HMOs). Also, in the 1980s, diagnosis-related groups (DRGs) and prospective payment guidelines were established to provide directions for treatment. These DRGs were attached to appropriate insurance reimbursement categories for treatment. Also, in the 1980s and 1990s, several consumer laws were passed. COBRA was passed to provide health insurance protection if an individual changes jobs. In 1993, the Family and Medical Leave Act (FMLA) was passed to protect an employee in the event of a family illness. Employees can receive up to 12 weeks of unpaid leave and their health insurance is covered during this period. Also, in 1996, the Health Insurance Portability and Accountability Act (HIPAA) was passed, which provided stricter confidentiality regarding the health

information of individuals. The Affordable Care Act of 2010 eliminated lifetime and unreasonable annual caps or limits on healthcare reimbursement with annual limitations, provided assistance for the uninsured with pre-existing conditions, prohibited denial of insurance coverage for pre-existing conditions for children, created a temporary national high risk pool for health insurance for individuals with pre-existing conditions who have no insurance, and extended dependent coverage up to age 26 (Niles, 2011).

TYPES OF HEALTH INSURANCE

Health insurance, particularly employer-provided health insurance, is the primary source of payment of healthcare services in the United States. Unfortunately, employer-provided health insurance has become very expensive for businesses, resulting in the increase in cost sharing by employees (Emanuel, 2008). There are four types of private insurance: group insurance, individual private health insurance, self-insurance, and managed care plans. **Group insurance** anticipates that a large group of individuals will purchase insurance through their employer and the risk is spread among those paying individuals. If an individual is self-employed, such as a small business owner or farmer, he or she may purchase **individual private health insurance**. Unlike group insurance, the risk is determined by the individual's health. Premiums, deductibles, and copayments are much higher for this type of insurance. Established in the 1970s, **self-funded or self-insurance** programs are health insurance programs that are implemented and controlled by the company itself. **Managed care plans** are a type of health program that combines administrative costs and service costs for cost control.

Health insurance is a financing mechanism that protects the insured from using their personal funds when expensive care is required. Having insurance also decreases the risks of delays in seeking treatment that may result in increased costs disease (Sultz & Young, 2006). Approximately 84% of the population is covered by some form of health insurance. All insurance plans fall into three categories: **voluntary health insurance (VHI)**, social insurance, and public welfare insurance. VHI is a type of private health insurance that is provided by nonprofit and for-profit health plans such as BCBS. **Social insurance** is provided by the government at all levels: federal, state, and local. An example of this type of insurance is Medicare. **Public welfare insurance** is based on financial need.

The primary example of public welfare insurance is **Medicaid**. All insurance plans define a contract among the beneficiaries, the purchasers (the employers and government), the health plan organizations, and the providers who deliver the services (Pointer et al., 2007). There are also self-insurance programs that are administered by employers who bear the financial risk of providing their own health insurance to their employees. The funds to operate the program are derived from employee premiums. Reimbursement of health services are taken from this pool of funds rather than from another health insurance company.

There are two forms of payment, fee for service and prepayment, which provide the basis for all health insurance coverage. **Fee for service**, developed by BCBS, is based on the concept of a person purchasing coverage for certain benefits, using the health insurance coverage for these designated benefits, and paying the provider for the services provided. The provider may be paid by the insurance coverage or out of pocket by the patient. In a **prepayment** concept, the individual pays a fixed, predetermined amount for the services rendered. Managed care organizations follow a prepayment model (Sultz & Young, 2006).

COST SHARING OF HEALTH SERVICES

Most insurance policies require a contribution from the covered individual in the form of a copayment, deductible, and/or coinsurance. This concept is called **cost sharing**. Used in both fee-for-service and prepaid plans, **copayments** are costs that patients must pay at the time they receive the services. It is a designated dollar amount. For, **coinsurance**, a type of copayment that is part of a fee-for-service policy, the patient pays a percentage of the cost of the services. A typical coinsurance portion is 20% paid by the individual, with the remaining 80% paid by the health insurance plan. **Deductibles** are payments that are required prior to the insurance paying for services rendered in a fee-for-service plan. Deductible amounts vary from individual and family health insurance coverage and cover one calendar year. For example, an individual may have a $250 deductible per calendar year, which means they must pay the $250 before their health insurance covers the services, unfortunately. The growth in health insurance premiums is an excellent barometer to measure changes in private health insurance costs. Since 2007, health insurance premiums have increased approximately 6% annually. The rise in premium costs has increased the percentage

of health insurance cost sharing on the employee (Miller, 2012). The main issue with the increase in cost sharing is its impact on individuals utilizing healthcare services. A study published in the *New England Journal of Medicine* concluded that adding an additional cost-sharing measure, such as a copayment of $10, reduces the number of women who received a mammography. These results concur with similar studies that examine cost sharing for health screening services (Bach, 2008). Recognizing this trend, the ACA mandated that several types of preventive screenings will no longer require cost sharing.

TYPES OF HEALTH INSURANCE POLICIES

Comprehensive health insurance policies provide benefits that include outpatient and inpatient services, surgery, laboratory testing, medical equipment purchases, therapies, and other services such as mental health, rehabilitation, and prescription drugs. Most comprehensive policies have some exclusion attached to their policies. The opposite of comprehensive health insurance policies is basic or **major medical policies**, which reimburse hospital services such as surgeries and any expenses related to any hospitalization. There are limits on hospital stays. **Catastrophic health insurance** policies cover unusual illnesses with a high deductible and have lifetime reimbursement caps. There are also specific health insurance policies such as **disease-specific policies** for cancer and **medigap or Medicare supplement or medsup policies** that provide supplemental insurance coverage for Medicare patients (Shi & Singh, 2008).

TYPES OF HEALTH INSURANCE PLANS

There are two basic types of insurance plans: **indemnity plans,** which are fee-for-service plans, and managed care plans, which include health maintenance organizations, preferred provider organizations (PPOs), and point-of-service (POS) plans. Indemnity plans or fee-for-service plans are contracts between a beneficiary and a health plan but there is no contract between the health plan and providers. The beneficiary pays a premium to the health plan. When the beneficiary receives a healthcare service, the plan will reimburse the beneficiary based on an established fee for a particular service regardless of the provider's fees. The beneficiary will then reimburse the provider directly (Sultz & Young, 2006).

The managed care plan is a special type of health plan that focuses on cost containment of health services. The first type of managed care organization was the HMO, which evolved in the 1970s. As managed care organizations evolved, different types of managed care organizations developed.

Managed care plans combine health services and health insurance functions to reduce administrative costs. For example, employers contract with a health plan for services on behalf of their employees. The employer is required to pay a set amount per the enrolled employee on a monthly basis. The contracted health plan has a contract with certain providers to whom it pays a fixed rate per member on a monthly basis for certain services. Enrolled employees may cost share with a copayment. There is no deductible. The enrolled employees have restrictions on their choice of providers or incur larger copayments if they choose a provider out of the network.

A recent trend in health insurance plans is **consumer-driven health plans** (CDHPs) that are tax advantage plans with high deductible coverage. The most common CDHPs are **health reimbursement arrangements (HRAs)** and HSAs. HRAs, or **personal care accounts**, began in 2001 as a result of an Internal Revenue Service (IRS) regulation. An HRA is funded by the employer but owned by the employees and remains with the company if the employee leaves. This has been an issue because it has no portability (Wilensky, 2006).

A **health savings account (HSA)**, which was authorized by the **Medicare Prescription Drug, Improvement, and Modernization Act of 2003,** pairs high deductible plans with fully portable employee-owned tax-advantaged accounts. This plan encourages consumers to become more cost conscious when using the healthcare system because they are using their own funds for healthcare services. The HSA, unlike the HRA, is a portable account, which means it can be transferred to another employer when the employee changes jobs. HSAs encourage consumers to understand healthcare service pricing because these accounts are paired with a high deductible. America's Health Insurance Plans (AHIP), an industry trade association, estimates that 4% of firms that offered benefits also offered an HSA or HRA (Wilensky, 2006).

Other types of CDHPs include **flexible spending accounts (FSAs)** and **medical savings accounts (MSAs)**. FSAs provide employees with the option of setting aside pretax income to pay for out-of-pocket medical expenses. Employees must submit claims for these expenses and are reimbursed from their spending accounts. The drawback is that the amount set aside must be spent within 1 year. Any unspent dollars cannot be rolled over so it is very important to be specific about the projected medical expenses. Mandated as part of HIPAA, the MSA allows workers employed in firms with 50 or less employees, and who have high deductible health insurance plans, to set aside pretax dollars to be used for healthcare premiums and non reimbursed healthcare expenses (Buchbinder & Shanks, 2007).

As discussed previously, self-funded or self-insurance programs are health insurance programs that are implemented and controlled by the company itself. They retain all of the risk in providing health insurance to their employees by paying any claims from their employees. Both the employee and employer pay into the fund. The employer maintains a trust that is overseen by federal regulation. All claims are paid from the trust. The company will purchase reinsurance from another insurance company to protect itself from any catastrophic losses. The **reinsurance** sets a **stop–loss measure** that limits the amount the company will pay for claims (CMS, 2013i).

Long-Term Care Insurance

As life expectancy continues to increase in the United States, more people will require more healthcare services for chronic conditions. Unfortunately, Medicare and traditional health insurance policies do not pay for long-term care. Medicaid will pay for long-term care if you qualify for their program. **Long-term care insurance** was developed to cover services such as assistance with **activities of daily living** (personal hygiene, feeding and dressing oneself) as well as care in an organizational setting. The cost of long-term care insurance can vary based on the type and amount of services selected as well as the age at time of purchase and healthcare status. If an individual is already receiving long-term care or is in ill health, a person may not qualify for long-term care insurance. Most long-term care insurance policies are comprehensive, which means they will cover expenses from home health care, hospice, respite care, assisted living and nursing homes, Alzheimer's special care, and adult day care centers. Long-term care policy costs vary greatly based on age and type of policy. The **National Clearinghouse for Long-Term Care Information** has provided the following information for purchasing long-term care insurance:

- The policyholder can select a daily benefit amount and how much is paid on a daily basis, depending on the healthcare setting. The type of healthcare setting can also be identified such as home health care or skilled nursing facility.

- The policyholder can select a lifetime amount the policy will provide, which can range from $100,000 to $300,000. More expensive policies will allow unlimited coverage with no dollar limit, which is unusual. Most policies will provide long-term coverage from 2 to 5 years.

- The policyholder can also select an inflation option, which adjusts the coverage amount as you age.

- Some policies may pay for family/friend long-term care for the policyholder. The policy may also provide reimbursement for equipment or transportation.

More employees are now offering long-term care insurance as an option to their employees. Employers do not contribute to the premium cost but may negotiate a better group rate. Long-term care insurance is becoming more popular because individuals are recognizing that Medicare will not pay for long-term care unless it is a medical necessity. Medicaid will pay for long-term care, but only for those individuals who qualify for the program (DHHS, 2013b).

PUBLIC FINANCING OF HEALTHCARE SERVICES

Since 1965, public financing has played a large role in providing healthcare services to the elderly, disabled, and the indigent. Medicare and Medicaid are the two largest government-sponsored health insurance programs in the United States. Medicare, Title XVIII of the Social Security Act, provides medical care for (1) individuals who are 65 years and older, (2) disabled individuals who are entitled to Social Security benefits, and (3) people who have end-stage renal disease (Shi & Singh, 2008). Medicare is an **entitlement program** because people, after paying into the program for years, are entitled to receive benefits. It is important

to emphasize that Medicare and Medicaid have provided access to healthcare services through their programs. The number of uninsured in the United States would be much higher if these programs did not exist (Enthoven & Fuchs, 2006).

Medicare

CMS has oversight of Medicare. There are currently 50 million Medicare enrollees. Projections are expected to increase to 60 million by 2050. Medicare is the healthcare industry's largest payer. It was originally designed as a two-part structure: Part A for hospital insurance and Part B for supplemental or voluntary medical insurance. Recently, two additional parts were added: Part C/Medicare Advantage and Part D, which is a prescription drug plan benefit. The following summary information is from the medicare.gov website.

Medicare Part A: Hospital Insurance

Medicare Part A is primarily financed from payroll taxes and is considered hospital insurance. The employer and employee contribute to the Social Security (Medicare) fund. Employees contribute 1.45% of wages that are matched by employers. Self-employed individuals pay 2.9% of earnings. You pay no premium if you or your spouse paid Medicare taxes for at least 10 years. In general, Part A covers: hospital care, skilled nursing facility care, nursing home care (as long as custodial care is not the only care you need), hospice, and home health services (CMS, 2013a).

Medicare Part B: Original Medicare—Voluntary Medical Insurance

Medicare Part B is a supplemental health plan to cover physician services. It is financed 24% from enrollee premiums and 76% from federal treasury funds. Part B covers two types of services: medically necessary services—services or supplies that are needed to diagnose or treat your medical condition and that meet accepted standards of medical practice; and preventive services—health care to prevent illness (like the flu) or detect it at an early stage, when treatment is most likely to work best. The ACA has mandated there is no cost sharing for many preventive services. Part B covers things like clinical research, ambulance services, durable medical equipment (DME), mental health, inpatient, outpatient, partial hospitalization, getting a second opinion before surgery, and limited outpatient prescription drugs. Part B is made available when enrollees sign up for Part A (CMS, 2013a).

Medicare Part C: Medicare Advantage

Medicare Part C is also referred to as Medicare Advantage and it can be considered a managed care model. It covers all services in Parts A and B. It is voluntary and aailable when an individual enrolls in Parts A and B. This program was designed to move Medicare patients into more cost-effective health insurance programs such as HMOs or PPOs. Medicare pays a fixed amount for your care every month to the companies offering Medicare Advantage Plans. These companies must follow rules set by Medicare. However, each Medicare Advantage Plan can charge different out-of-pocket costs and have different rules for how you get services (CMS, 2013b).

Medicare Part D: Prescription Drug Benefit

The Medicare Prescription Drug Improvement and Modernization Act of 2003 (MMA), which authorized **Medicare Part D,** produced the largest additions and changes to Medicare. Tax revenues of the federal government support the majority of the program costs. Its purpose was to provide relief from costly prescription costs for seniors. Like Part B, it is a voluntary program because enrollees pay a premium for coverage. Medicare Part C has Part D benefits rolled in to their program. Private health insurance companies contract with Medicare to provide services. Effective January 1, 2006, this program developed a prescription drug program for enrollees. The following is a summary of Part D benefits (CMS 2013c):

- ■ Affordable prescription drug plans were made available for Medicare Advantage plan enrollees and traditional Medicare health plans.

- ■ For seniors who are considered indigent, the MMA established a low-income subsidy for the costs of Part D.

There is an issue with the Medicare Part D coverage gap, more commonly known as the "**donut hole**" for Medicare Part D beneficiaries that this Act should remedy. A typical beneficiary for Part D pays 25% of drug costs, including the deductible during the first part of the drug coverage phase. Once you reach the threshold of $2,830, the donut hole is activated, which means the beneficiary pays 100% of the drug costs until both the plan and beneficiary costs reach the maximum of $6,440. This maximum changes annually.

Once this threshold, called the catastrophic threshold limit is reached, Medicare Part D will cover the costs of the drugs (approximately 95%) with the beneficiary paying $2.40 for generic drugs and $6.00 for brand drugs for the remainder of the year (Allsup, Inc., 2013). However, this donut hole restarts every year. This increase in beneficiary payout was very expensive for those enrolled and often resulted in individuals not obtaining necessary medication because of cost. In 2010, those beneficiaries that fall into the donut hole received a $250 rebate check from Medicare (Bihari, 2010). Since the passage of the ACA, 6.6 million Medicare enrollees who were impacted by the donut hole have saved over $7 billion on prescription drugs, which averages $1,061 per beneficiary. In addition to the $250 rebate check, those impacted received discounts and increased coverage. They will continue to receive these benefits until the coverage gap is closed in 2020 (CMS 2013h).

Medigap or Medicare Supplement Plan or Medsup

Medicare covers less than half of total healthcare costs for enrollees, which leaves them with substantial out-of-pocket expenses. To cover these expenses, Medicare enrollees can receive additional coverage from: (1) Medicaid if the Medicare enrollee is eligible, (2) enrollment in Medicare Advantage, which can provide supplemental coverage, (3) employer-sponsored retiree insurance, or (4) purchase supplemental insurance policies from private insurance companies, which are called medigap or medsup policies. Medsup plans cover copays, deductibles, and coinsurance, which can be very expensive. Medicare has created 10 medsup plans that vary by state. Depending on the selected plan, the premiums will vary. Medicare Part C (Medicare Advantage) enrollees are not eligible for medsup plans (Medicare.gov, 2013).

Medicaid

Medicaid, Title XIX of the Social Security Act, provides health insurance to the medically indigent. It is a welfare program that is administered at the state government level. The program serves 45 million low income Americans. Individuals who meet the requirements of both Medicare and Medicaid programs can be dually enrolled. Medicaid spending varies based on the status of the U.S. economy. It is not a federally mandated program; however, all states have Medicaid except Arizona. Managed care enrollment has controlled Medicaid spending. Eligible people include

(1) families with children receiving support under the Temporary Assistance for Needy Families (TANF), (2) people receiving Supplemental Security Income (SSI), and (3) children and pregnant women with income at or below 133% of the federal poverty level, and (4) children whose parents have income too high for Medicaid but too low for private insurance (CMS, 2013d).

The ACA has requested that states expand their Medicaid programs to provide more coverage to individuals. The ACA created **Community First Choice** as an optional Medicaid benefit, which focuses on community health services to Medicaid enrollees with disabilities. This will enable consumers to receive care at home or at community health centers rather than going to a hospital or their facility. This option became available on October 1, 2011 and provides a 6% increase in federal matching payments to states for expenditures related to this option (CMS, 2013g). These mandates will enable lower income consumers and children to have access to health care at an affordable cost.

All states administer their own program so eligibility varies by state. State programs must match federal funding and must provide the following: inpatient and outpatient hospital services, physician care, nursing facility services, home health services, prenatal care, family planning services, health services for children under 21, midwife services, and pediatric and family nurse practitioner services. State programs are responsible for at least 40% of the costs for provider services and must equally share the administrative costs of the Medicaid programs (CMS, 2013d). States have the right to determine the eligibility criteria for Medicaid enrollment, optional services to provide, methods and rates for provider payments, and utilization limits for services (Pointer et al., 2007).

Children's Health Insurance Program

Authorized by the Balanced Budget Act of 1997, and codified as Title XXI of the Social Security Act, the State Children's Health Insurance Program (SCHIP), now **Children's Health Insurance Program (CHIP)**, was initiated in response to the number of children who are uninsured in the United States. The CHIP gave states $40 billion over a decade to provide health care for these children. This program offers additional funds to states to expand Medicaid benefits to children younger than 19 years of age who otherwise may not qualify because their family income exceeds Medicaid levels.

The ACA of 2010 maintains the CHIP eligibility standards in place as of enactment through 2019. The law extends CHIP funding until October 1, 2015, when the already enhanced CHIP federal matching rate will be increased by 23%, bringing the average federal matching rate for CHIP to 93%. The ACA also provided an additional $40 million in federal funding to continue efforts to promote enrollment in Medicaid and CHIP (DHHS, 2013a).

Program of All-Inclusive Care for the Elderly

Also authorized by the Balanced Budget Act of 1997, **Program of All-Inclusive Care for the Elderly (PACE)** is a comprehensive healthcare delivery system funded by Medicare and Medicaid. Oversight is provided by CMS, and it is modeled from a San Francisco, California, senior healthcare center, On Lok Senior Health Services. The PACE model focuses on providing community-based care and services to people who otherwise need nursing home levels of care. Their philosophy is that seniors with chronic care needs are better served in the community when possible. PACE organizations provide care and services in the home, the community, and the PACE center. They have contracts with many specialists and other providers in the community to make sure that patients get the care they need. Many PACE participants get most of their care from staff employed by the PACE organization in the PACE center. PACE centers meet state and federal safety requirements.

Implemented at the state level, PACE can be offered as a Medicaid option. Participants must be Medicare eligible or 55 years or older with a disability, live in a PACE area, and be certified for nursing home care. An interdisciplinary team assesses the needs of the patient and develops a long-term plan. The PACE model provides services of Medicaid and Medicare but in an integrated manner. The National Pace Association Primary Care Committee has developed care models specifically for PACE patients who have diabetes, chronic heart failure, kidney disease, and pulmonary disease and prevention guidelines. PACE providers are reimbursed from Medicare and Medicaid payments. As of 2013, there were 93 PACE programs operational in 31 states. CMS has issued guidelines for PACE programs to market their services (National PACE Association, 2002).

Worker's Compensation

The employer is financially liable for employees who become injured or ill as a result of working conditions. **Worker's compensation** is a state administered program. Employees may receive cash for lost wages, payment for medical treatment, survivor's death benefits, and indemnification for loss of skills. Although worker's compensation is not a traditional health insurance program, it does provide medical benefits. The main difference between employer health insurance programs and worker's compensation is that the employer must cover the full cost of the benefits (DOL, 2013).

The worker's compensation program protects both the employer and employee if there is a job-related injury and illness. Worker's compensation is a state program so benefits vary by state. Employees are eligible for this program for the following issues: (1) medical care, (2) death, (3) disability, and (4) rehabilitation services. Most employees receive approximately 66.66% of their earnings, which are tax-free. Workers compensation programs are funded by the employer who contracts with a commercial insurer or they self-insure. Depending on the industry and the risk of injury, rates can vary from 1% of the payroll to 100% of the payroll. Like unemployment insurance, rates can also vary based on the **experience rating** of the company, meaning how often they have used the workmen's compensation program for employees who have been injured on the job. If the experience rating is high, their rates will be high (Noe et al., 2009).

These laws fall under **no-fault liability** or no-fault insurance, developed to avoid costly legal fees because there is no process to assess blame. The employee does not have to demonstrate that the employer was in the wrong and the employer is protected from lawsuits unless it can be demonstrated they were grossly negligent in the working conditions (Nolo, 2013). Unfortunately, there are disparities of how workers' compensation programs are implemented in each state. States often differ on the scope of permanent disability benefits and mental health coverage resulting from work. Experts estimate that 1 out of 20 occupational disease victims receive workers' compensation benefits and 1 out of 100 for occupational cancer. The American Public Health Association recommends that a national database be established on worker injuries, illnesses, toxic exposures, and diseases (APHA, 2009). As of this writing, workers' compensation is not reformed.

Other Prospective Reimbursement Methods
Tricare

The U.S. Department of Defense operates the Military Health Services System (MHHS), which provides medical services to active duty and retired members of the armed services. As the active duty numbers increased, a special medical care program called **TRICARE** was developed to respond to the growing needs of retired members. As a major component of the Military Health System, TRICARE combines the healthcare resources of the uniformed services with networks of civilian healthcare professionals, institutions, pharmacies, and suppliers to provide access to high-quality healthcare services while maintaining the capability to support military operations. TRICARE is regionally managed, structured after managed care, and coordinates the efforts of the Navy, Army, and Air Force. They have an HMO-type operation, a PPO-type organization, and a traditional fee-for-service program. There are 11 TRICARE regions in the United States with other TRICARE operations in Europe, Latin America, and the Pacific (TRICARE, 2009).

Indian Health Service

The Indian Health Service (IHS) is the principal federal healthcare provider and health advocate for Indian people, and its goal is to raise their health status to the highest possible level. The IHS provides a comprehensive health service delivery system for American Indians and Alaska Natives who are members of 566 federally recognized tribes across the United States. The IHS is staffed by approximately 15,000 employees made up of a mixture of Civil Service, federal employees, and United States Public Health Services (USPHS) commissioned officers (IHS, 2013).

REIMBURSEMENT METHODS OF PRIVATE HEALTH INSURANCE PLANS

As healthcare costs have escalated, the government has developed various mechanisms aimed at standardizing reimbursement for healthcare services. Later, insurance companies developed standards for **usual, customary, and reasonable (UCR) services** based on community and state surveys of provider charges. If there was a difference in the reimbursement rates, the provider asked the patient to pay the difference. The problem with fee-for-service reimbursement methods is that it may have become a tool for some physicians to increase the number of services provided to the patient as a way to increase their income (Shi & Singh, 2008).

Insurance companies, managed care organizations, and the government are referred to as **third-party payers**. The other parties are the patient and the healthcare provider. The payment function in health care determines how much is reimbursed for the services. Fee for service, which was discussed previously, is the preferred method of reimbursement by providers. Historically, providers set the rate for their services that the government and health insurance companies paid without question. This type of **retrospective reimbursement** determines the amount of reimbursement after the delivery of services and provides little financial risk to providers. This method contributed to the increase in healthcare costs (Feldstein, 2005).

The most common type of reimbursement is a **service benefit plan**. This type of **prospective reimbursement** method was developed and used primarily by managed care organizations. The employer has a contract with a benefit plan and pays a premium for each of its employees. Employees usually also pay a portion of the premium to the health plan. The health plan contracts with certain providers and facilities to provide services to their beneficiaries at a specified rate and makes payments directly to the providers for their services (McLean, 2003).

Beneficiaries/employees and families may have a cost-sharing arrangement with their employer for these services, such as deductibles and coinsurance payments, that supply payment to providers upon the receipt of a service. HMOs are examples of service benefit plans. In a managed care organization, the organization reimburses the provider at a **capitated rate**, which means they receive a set rate for serving enrolled patients regardless of how much care the provider gives. This type of capitation is also used by Medicaid and Medicare for their managed care programs (Pointer et al., 2007).

Per diem rates or per patient per day rates is a defined dollar amount per day for care provided. This is the most common form of reimbursement to hospitals. **Cost–plus reimbursement**, a type of retrospective reimbursement, was the traditional method used by Medicare and Medicaid to establish per diem rates for inpatient services. Under this method, reimbursement rates for institutions are based on the total costs incurred in operating the institution that are used to calculate the per diem or per patient day rate. The method is called cost–plus because, in addition to the operating costs, the reimbursement rate allows a portion of the capital costs to determine the rate (Buchbinder & Shanks, 2007; Shi & Singh, 2008; Sultz & Young, 2006).

GOVERNMENT REIMBURSEMENT METHODS FOR HEALTHCARE SERVICES

The federal government has sought to control healthcare expenditures through programs such **as diagnosis-related groups, (DRGs), ambulatory patient groups (APGs), ambulatory payment categories (APCs), home health resource groups (HHRGs), resource utilization groups (RUGs)**, and **resource-based relative value scales (RBRVSs)**. States also used regulatory efforts such as a **certificate of need (CON)** to control expenditures by requiring an assessment to certify that a hospital is needed for a designated area. Also, Medicaid growth costs have been limited by hospital preadmission screening, limiting hospital stays, reducing per diem rates, increasing copayments, and decreasing service coverage. Reducing Medicaid reimbursements creates issues of **cost shifting**. Healthcare organizations must find other ways to be reimbursed or they will not be profitable so they cost shift by raising the prices to privately insured patients to offset the small reimbursement charges of Medicaid and Medicare (Feldstein, 2005).

Hospital Reimbursement

In 1982, Congress passed the **Tax Equity and Fiscal Responsibility Act (TEFRA)** and the **Social Security Amendments of 1983** to manage Medicare cost controls. There was a mandate to hospitals for a **prospective payment system** (PPS) to establish reimbursement rates for certain conditions. CMS reimburses hospitals per admission and per diagnosis, which is based on a DRG—a prospective payment system for hospitals established through the Social Security Amendments of 1983. Each DRG group represents similar diagnoses of diseases that are expected to have similar use of hospital services. The amount of reimbursement is set per discharge of a patient. Hospitals that can provide services at lower costs may keep the difference in the reimbursement rates (Longest & Darr, 2008).

Resource-Based Relative Value Scale

Under the Omnibus Budget Reconciliation Act of 1989, Medicare developed a new initiative of RBRVS to reimburse physicians according to a relative value assigned to a service. This reimbursement is divided into three components: physician work, practice expenses, and malpractice insurance. Medicare pays a flat fee for physician visits and is based on the Healthcare Common Procedure Coding

System, which is used to code professional services. The RBRVS, implemented in 1992, has become a standard Medicare Part B reimbursement method. This system increased reimbursement for family and general practice by about 15%. Also, physicians who had not signed a Medicare participation agreement, meaning they do accept Medicare reimbursement as the full payment for services, were prevented from **balance billing** so the physician is not able to bill the patient the difference between Medicare payments and the physician charges. The statute limited the amount the physician could balance bill the patient (Longest & Darr, 2008).

Ambulatory Patient Groups/Ambulatory Payment Categories

Ambulatory Patient Groups (APGs) were developed in the 1980s and are a system of codes that explained the number and types of services used in an ambulatory visit. Similar to the DRG classification, patients per APG had similar clinical classifications, resource use, and costs. Implemented in August 2000, Ambulatory Payment Categories (APCs) were adapted from the APGs. The APC divides all outpatient services into 300 procedural groups/classifications based on similar clinical content such as surgery, medical, and ancillary services. Each APC is assigned a payment weight based on the median cost of services within the APC. The rates are also adjusted for wage differential by location. This type of rate is a bundled rate established by Medicare (CMS, 2009).

Resource Utilization Groups

This type of prospective payment system for skilled nursing facilities, used by Medicare, provides for a per diem based on the clinical severity of patients. A classification system called Resource Utilization Groups (RUG), a type of DRG, was designed to differentiate patients based on how much they use the resources of the facility. As the patient's condition changes, the rate of reimbursement changes. A per diem rate was established using these classifications (Longest & Darr, 2008; Shi & Singh, 2008).

Home Health Resource Groups

Implemented in October 2000, the Home Health Resource Group (HHRG), which is a prospective payment used by Medicare, pays a fixed predetermined rate for each 60-day episode of care, regardless of the services. All services are bundled under a home health agency.

The HHRG uses 80 distinct groups to classify patients' conditions (Longest & Darr, 2008).

The Center for Medicare and Medicaid Innovation's goal is to support the development and testing of innovative healthcare payment and service delivery models. Effective January 2013 are 41 demonstration projects for payment and care models, including accountable care organizations, value-based purchasing, and coordinated and prevention care. The following are proposed models for innovative care. These initiatives will be run for a 3-year period.

Traditionally, Medicare makes separate payments to providers for each of the individual services they furnish to beneficiaries for a single illness or course of treatment. This approach can result in fragmented care with minimal coordination across providers and healthcare settings. Payment rewards the quantity of services offered by providers rather than the quality of care furnished. Research has shown that bundled payments can align incentives for providers—hospitals, post-acute care providers, physicians, and other practitioners—allowing them to work closely together across all specialties and settings (CMS, 2013e).

The 4 Models

The **Bundled Payments Initiative** is composed of four broadly defined models of care, which link payments that multiple service beneficiaries receive during an episode of care. Model 1 includes an episode of care focused on the acute care inpatient hospitalization. Awardees agree to provide a standard discount to Medicare from the usual Part A hospital inpatient payments.

Models 2 and 3 involve a **retrospective bundled payment** arrangement where actual expenditures are reconciled against a target price for an episode of care. Model 4 involves a prospective bundled payment arrangement, where a lump sum payment is made to a provider for the entire episode of care. Over the course of the 3-year initiative, CMS will work with participating organizations to assess whether the models being tested result in improved patient care and lower costs to Medicare (see Table 8-1).

Accountable Care Organizations

According to the CMS website, **accountable care organizations (ACOs)** are groups of providers and hospitals who volunteer to give coordinated care to Medicare patients. The goal of ACOs is to ensure that patients, especially with chronic conditions, receive

TABLE 8-1	Bundled Payments Models Initiative

Model 1: Retrospective Acute Care Hospital Stay Only

Under Model 1, the episode of care is defined as the inpatient stay in the acute care hospital. Medicare will pay the hospital a discounted amount based on the payment rates established under the Inpatient Prospective Payment System used in the original Medicare program. Medicare will continue to pay physicians separately for their services under the Medicare Physician Fee Schedule. Under certain circumstances, hospitals and physicians will be permitted to share gains arising from the providers' care redesign efforts. Participation will begin as early as April 2013 and no later than January 2014 and will include most Medicare fee-for-service discharges for the participating hospitals.

Model 2: Retrospective Acute Care Hospital Stay plus Post-Acute Care

In Model 2, the episode of care will include the inpatient stay in the acute care hospital and all related services during the episode. The episode will end either 30, 60, or 90 days after hospital discharge. Participants can select up to 48 different clinical condition episodes.

Model 3: Retrospective Post-Acute Care Only

For Model 3, the episode of care will be triggered by an acute care hospital stay and will begin at initiation of post-acute care services with a participating skilled nursing facility, inpatient rehabilitation facility, long-term care hospital, or home health agency. The post-acute care services included in the episode must begin within 30 days of discharge from the inpatient stay and will end either a minimum of 30, 60, or 90 days after the initiation of the episode. Participants can select up to 48 different clinical condition episodes.

Model 4: Acute Care Hospital Stay Only

Under Model 4, CMS will make a single, prospectively determined bundled payment to the hospital that would encompass all services furnished during the inpatient stay by the hospital, physicians, and other practitioners. Physicians and other practitioners will submit "no-pay" claims to Medicare and will be paid by the hospital out of the bundled payment. Related readmissions for 30 days after hospital discharge will be included in the bundled payment amount. Participants can select up to 48 different clinical condition episodes.

Source: Modified from the Centers for Medicare and Medicaid Services. (2013). Bundled Payments for Care Improvement (BPCI) initiative: General information. Retrieved from http://innovation.cms.gov/initiatives/bundled-payments/

timely care while avoiding duplication of services and preventing medical errors. Medicare has developed three major programs for providers to become ACOs:

- **Medicare Shared Savings Program**—a program that helps Medicare fee-for-service program providers becomes an ACO.

- **Advance Payment ACO Model**—a supplementary incentive program for smaller practices and, physician-based and rural providers in the Shared Savings Program. They receive monthly payments to use for coordinated care. There are currently 35 who participate in the program.

- **Pioneer ACO Model**—a program designed for early adopters of coordinated care. Any monetary savings are shared with Medicare (CMS, 2013f)

There are 32 ACOs enrolled in the Pioneer ACO model. According to recent results, only 13 of the ACOs improved patient quality of healthcare services and patient satisfaction and saved money. Two of the ACOs owe Medicare $4 million because they spent more on their patients than the traditional Medicare fee-for-service rates (Bleach, 2013). As of July 2013, seven ACOs have opted to leave the Pioneer Model and enter the Medicare Shared Savings Program and two will be leaving the Medicare ACO program entirely. The 13 that saved money while improving quality of care saved $87.6 million in 2012, saving about $33 million for Medicare (Zigmond, 2013).

HEALTHCARE FINANCIAL MANAGEMENT

Although for-profit and not-for-profit healthcare organizations have different missions, both types of organizations have financial objectives to achieve. The most common are: (1) generating a reasonable net income to continue effective operations, (2) setting prices for services, (3) contracting management of third-party payers such as Medicare and Medicaid and health service providers, (4) analyzing information for cost control, (5) adhering to governmental regulations such as reimbursement methods, and (6) minimizing financial risk (Buchbinder & Shanks, 2007). To ensure these objectives are met, many healthcare organizational structures include the following positions to supervise the financial management function. The **chief financial officer (CFO)** supervises the **comptroller** who is charged with accounting and reporting functions. The CFO may also supervise the **treasurer,** who is responsible for cash management, banking relations, accounts payable, etc. An **internal auditor** who reports to the CFO ensures that accounting procedures are performed in accordance with appropriate regulations (McLean, 2003). All of these positions ensure that the organization is focusing on its mission to provide quality healthcare services. If there is no strong financial management system in place, the organization will fail.

FUNDS DISBURSEMENT

After services are delivered, the agency has to verify and pay the claims received from the providers. Disbursement of funds, which is often called **claims processing**, is carried out in accordance to the administrative procedures of the program. Most insurance companies and managed care organizations have a claims department to process payments. Self-funded insurance programs often hire a third-party administrator to process claims. Medicare and Medicaid contract with commercial insurance companies to process claims for them (Pointer et al., 2007).

CONCLUSION

As healthcare expenditures continue to increase, the major focus of the healthcare industry is cost control in both the public and private sector. For years, healthcare costs were unchecked. The concept of retrospective reimbursement methods for healthcare services, which mean that a provider submitted a bill to a health insurance company that automatically reimbursed the provider, had no incentive to control costs in health care. This type of reimbursement method contributed to expensive health care for both the healthcare insurance companies and the individual who was paying out of pocket for their services. The establishment of a prospective reimbursement system for Medicare—developed based on care criteria for certain conditions regardless of provider costs— was an incentive system for providers to manage how they were providing services. The DRGs, RUGs, and RBRVSs are examples of this type of reimbursement method. The focus now is efficiency and quality.

Also, the implementation of managed care organizations has focused on cost control. Although healthcare spending decreased in the 1990s, healthcare costs have continued to increase since. The implementation of CDHPs have assisted individuals with controlling healthcare costs by providing opportunities to save money for health care while obtaining a tax advantage. The Center for Medicare and Medicaid Innovation's new demonstration projects may provide data that supports new effective payment models that tie quality care with reimbursement.

VOCABULARY

Accountable care organizations (ACOs)

Activities of daily living (ADLs)

Advance Payment ACO Model

Ambulatory patient groups (APGs)

Ambulatory payment categories (APCs)

Balance billing

Bundled Payments Initiative

Capitated rate

Catastrophic health insurance

Center for Medicare and Medicaid Innovation

Certificate of Need (CON)

Chief financial officer (CFO)

Children's Health Insurance Program (CHIP)

Claims processing

Coinsurance

Community First Choice

Comprehensive health insurance policies

Comptroller

Consumer-driven health plans

Copayments

Cost–plus reimbursement

Cost sharing

Cost shifting

Deductibles

Diagnosis-related group (DRG)

Disease-specific policies

Donut hole

Entitlement program

Experience rating

Fee for service

Flexible spending accounts (FSAs)

Group insurance

Health insurance

Health reimbursement arrangements (HRAs)

Health savings accounts (HSAs)

Home health resource group (HHRG)

Indemnity plans

Individual private health insurance

Internal auditor

Long-term care insurance

Major medical policies

Managed care plans

Medicaid

Medical saving accounts (MSAs)

Medicare Part A

Medicare Part B

Medicare Part C

Medicare Part D

Medicare Prescription Drug Improvement and Modernization Act of 2003

Medicare Shared Savings program

Medigap or Medicare supplemental or medsup policies

National Clearinghouse for Long-Term Care Information

No-fault liability

Out-of-pocket payments

Personal care accounts

Per diem rates

Pioneer ACO Model

Prepayment

Program of All-Inclusive Care for the Elderly (PACE)

Prospective reimbursement

Prospective payment system

Public welfare insurance

Reinsurance

Resource-based relative value scales (RBRVSs)

Resource utilization group (RUG)

Retrospective bundled payments

Retrospective reimbursement

Self-funded or self-insurance

Service benefit plan

Social insurance

Social Security Amendments of 1983

Stop–loss measure

Tax Equity and Fiscal Responsibility Act (TEFRA)

Third-party payer

Treasurer

TRICARE

Usual, customary, and reasonable (UCR) services

Voluntary health insurance (VHI)

Workers' compensation

REFERENCES

Allsup, Inc. (2013). Making the most of Social Security and Medicare benefits. Retrieved from https://www.allsup .com/personal-finance/financial-planning/financial-planning-for-family-caregivers/make-the-most-of-social-security -and-medicare

American Public Health Association (APHA). (2009). Workmen's compensation reform. Retrieved from http:// www.apha.org/NR/rdonlyres/B240302E-94EF-4456-966F-6AEF329C289E/0/WorkersCompDraftNov102009.pdf

Bach, P. (2008). Cost sharing for health care: Whose skin? Which game? *New England Journal of Medicine*, *358*, 4, 411–413.

Bihari, M. (2010). Understanding the Medicare Part D donut hole. Retrieved from http://healthinsurance .about.com /od/medicare/a/understanding_part_d.htm?p=1

Bleach, G. (2013). All Pioneer ACOs improved quality; only a third lowered costs. Retrieved from http://www .modernhealthcare.com/article/20130716/NEWS/307169958/all-pioneer-acos-improved-quality-only-third -lowered-costs

Blue Cross Blue Shield (BCBS). (2013). Retrieved from http://www.bcbs.com/about-the-association/

Buchbinder, S., & Shanks, N. (2007). *Introduction to health care management*. Sudbury, MA: Jones and Bartlett.

Centers for Medicare and Medicaid Services (CMS). (2013a). Medicare program—general information. Retrieved from http://www.cms.gov/Medicare/Medicare-General-Information/MedicareGenInfo/index.html

CMS. (2011a). National health expenditures 2011 highlights. Retrieved from http://www.cms.gov/Research-Statistics -Data-and-Systems/Statistics-Trends-and-Reports/NationalHealthExpendData/Downloads/highlights.pdf

CMS. (2011b). National health expenditures projections2012–2022. Retrieved from http://www.cms.gov/Research -Statistics-Data-and-Systems/Statistics-Trends-and-Reports/NationalHealthExpendData/Downloads/Proj2012.pdf

CMS. (2013b). How Medicare Advantage plans work? Retrieved from http://www.medicare.gov/sign-up-change -plans/medicare-health-plans/medicare-advantage-plans/how-medicare-advantage-plans-work.html

CMS. (2013c). Drug coverage (Part D). Retrieved from http://www.medicare.gov/part-d/

CMS. (2013d). Medicaid information by topic. Retrieved from http://www.medicaid.gov/Medicaid-CHIP -Program-Information/By-Topics/By-Topic.html

CMS. (2013e). Center for Medicare and Medicaid Innovation. Retrieved from http://innovation.cms.gov

CMS. (2013f). Innovation models. Retrieved from http://innovation.cms.gov/initiatives/index.html#views=models

CMS. (2013g). Community First Choice. Retrieved from http://www.medicaid.gov/Medicaid-CHIP-Program -Information/By-Topics/Long-Term-Services-and-Support/Home-and-Community-Based-Services/Community -First-Choice-1915-k.html

CMS. (2013h). Details for title: On eve of Medicare anniversary, over 6.6 million seniors save over $7 billion on drugs (2013, July 29). Retrieved from http://cms.gov/Newsroom/MediaReleaseDatabase/Press-Releases/2013 -Press-Releases-Items/2013-07-29.html

CMS. (2013i). Self-insured plan. Retrieved from https://www.healthcare.gov/glossary/self-insured-plan/

CMS. (2009). National health expenditure data. Retrieved from http://www.cms.gov/Research-Statistics -Data-and-Systems/Statistics-Trends-and-Reports/NationalHealthExpendData/index.html?redirect= /nationalhealthexpenddata

Department of Health and Human Services (DHHS). (2013a). Long-term care insurance. Retrieved from http:// www.longtermcare.gov/LTC/Main_Site/Paying_LTC/Private_Programs/LTC_Insurance/index.aspx

Department of Labor (DOL). (2013). Office of Worker's Compensation Programs. Retrieved from http://www .dol.gov/esa/owcp/dfec/regs/compliance/wc.htm

DHHS. (2013b). Long term care : Where you live matters. Retrieved from http://longtermcare.gov/where-you-live-matters/

Emanuel, E. (2008). *Health care, guaranteed*. New York: Public Affairs.

Enthoven, A. & Fuchs, V. (2006). Employment-based health insurance: Past, present and future. *Health Affairs, 25*, 6, 1538–1547.

Feldstein, P. (2005). *Health care economics*. Clifton Park, NY: Thomson/Delmar Learning.

Judson, K., & Harrison, C. (2006). *Law & ethics for medical careers*. New York: McGraw-Hill.

Kaiser Family Foundation. (2012, May). Focus on health reform: Massachusetts health care reform: Six years later. Retrieved http://kaiserfamilyfoundation.files.wordpress.com/2013/01/8311.pdf

Indian Health Services (IHS). (2013). Retrieved from http://www.ihs.gov/index.cfm?module=About

Kliff, S. (2012). Study: Fewer employers are offering health insurance. Retrieved from http://www.washingtonpost.com/blogs/wonkblog/post/study-fewer-employers-are-offering-health-insurance/2012/04/24/gIQAfGH6eT_print.html

Longest Jr., B., & Darr, K. (2008). *Managing health services organizations and systems*. Baltimore: Health Professions Press.

McLean, R. (2003). *Financial management in health care organizations* (pp. 12–19). Clifton Park, NY: Thomson/Delmar Learning.

Medicare.gov. (2013). What's Medicare supplement (Medigap) insurance? Retrieved from http://www.medicare.gov/supplement-other-insurance/medigap/whats-medigap.html

Miller, S. (2012). 6.3% health premium increases projected for 2013. Retrieved from http://www.shrm.org//hrdisciplines/benefits/articles/pages/health-premiums-2013.aspx

National PACE Association. (2002). *About NPA*. Retrieved from http://www.npaonline.org/website/article.asp?id=5

Niles, N. (2011). *Basics of U.S. healthcare reform*. Sudbury, MA: Jones and Bartlett.

Noe, R., Hollenbeck, J., Gerhart B., & Wright, P. (2009). *Fundamentals of human resource management* (3rd ed.). McGraw-Hill/Irwin: 29–30.

Nolo. (2013). Workers' compensation benefits FAQ. Retrieved from http://www.nolo.com/legal-encyclopedia/your-right-to-workers-comp-benefits-faq-29093.html

Pointer, D., Williams, S., Isaacs, S., & Knickman, J. (2007). *Introduction to U.S. health care*. Hoboken, NJ: Wiley Publishing.

Shi, L., & Singh, D. (2008). *Delivering health care in America* (4th ed.). Sudbury, MA: Jones and Bartlett.

Starr, P. (1982). *The social transformation of American medicine*. Cambridge, MA: Basic Books.

Sultz, H., & Young, K. (2006). *Health care USA: Understanding its organization and delivery* (5th ed.). Sudbury, MA: Jones and Bartlett.

Thomasson, M. (2013). Health insurance in the United States. Retrieved from http://eh.net/encyclopedia/article/thomasson.insurance.health.us

TRICARE. (2009). Retrieved from http://tricare.mil/tma/AboutTMA.aspx

Wilensky, G. (2006). Consumer driven health plans: Early evidence and potential impact on hospitals. *Health Affairs, 25*, 1, 174–186.

Zigmond, J. (2013). CMS names 9 ACOs leaving the Pioneer program. Retrieved from http://www.modernhealthcare.com/article/20130716/NEWS/307169945/cms-names-acos-leaving-pioneer-program/

NOTES

STUDENT ACTIVITY 8-1

Based on this chapter, please provide an explanation of the following concepts in your own words. DO NOT RECITE the text.

Reinsurance: _____

_____

_____

Flexible spending accounts (FSAs): _____

_____

_____

Prospective reimbursement: _____

_____

_____

Diagnosis-related group (DRG): _____

_____

_____

Resource utilization group (RUG): _____

_____

_____

Coinsurance: _____

_____

_____

Consumer-driven health plans: _____

_____

_____

Cost sharing: _____

_____

_____

Entitlement program: _____

_____

_____

STUDENT ACTIVITY 8-2

REAL LIFE APPLICATIONS: CASE SCENARIO ONE

Your grandmother just turned 65 and is very confused about Medicare. She doesn't understand why there are four parts to this health insurance program. She has asked you to help her with enrolling in Medicare.

ACTIVITY

(1) List the different parts of Medicare and (2) explain what each part is and why it may be important to your grandmother.

RESPONSES

_____

_____

_____

_____

_____

_____

_____

_____

_____

_____

_____

_____

_____

_____

CASE SCENARIO TWO

Your health insurance is paid for by your family. You continually hear your parents complain about cost sharing in their health insurance costs. You are not familiar with the term.

ACTIVITY

Perform research to identify cost sharing in the U.S. healthcare system. Define cost sharing and how the cost is shared with the employer and employees like your parents. Develop a report and share it with your parents.

RESPONSES

_____

_____

_____

_____

_____

_____

_____

_____

_____

_____

_____

_____

_____

_____

CASE SCENARIO THREE

As life expectancy continues to increase in the United States, you are encouraging your older siblings to start planning ahead. You indicate to them they should think about long-term care insurance. They said they have never heard of it.

ACTIVITY

You decide to perform research on long-term care insurance and how it is used. You prepare a report for your siblings.

RESPONSES

_____

_____

_____

_____

_____

_____

_____

_____

_____

_____

_____

_____

_____

_____

CASE SCENARIO FOUR

One of your friends recently left the military. He is happy that he has medical benefits under TRICARE. You are not familiar with this program.

ACTIVITY

You decide to research TRICARE and what type of benefits it provides to military members. Write your results and present to the class.

RESPONSES

_____

_____

_____

_____

_____

_____

_____

_____

_____

_____

_____

_____

_____

_____

_____

_____

STUDENT ACTIVITY 8-3

INTERNET EXERCISES

Write your answers in the space provided.

- Visit each of the websites listed here.
- Name the organization.
- Locate their mission statement on their website.
- Provide a brief overview of the activities of the organization.
- How do these organizations participate in the U.S. healthcare system?

Websites

http://www.tricare.mil

Organization Name: _____

Mission Statement:

_____

_____

_____

Overview of Activities: _____

_____

_____

Importance of organization to U.S. health care:

_____

_____

_____

http://www.npaonline.org

Organization Name: _____

Mission Statement:

_____

_____

_____

Overview of Activities: _____

_____

_____

Importance of organization to U.S. health care:

_____

_____

_____

Organization Name: _____

Mission Statement:

_____

_____

_____

Overview of Activities: _____

_____

_____

Importance of organization to U.S. health care:

_____

_____

_____

http://www.innovations.ahrq.gov

Organization Name: _____

Mission Statement:

_____

_____

_____

Overview of Activities: _____

_____

_____

Importance of organization to U.S. health care:

_____

_____

_____

http://www.schip-info.org

Organization Name: _____

Mission Statement:

_____

_____

_____

Overview of Activities: _____

_____

_____

Importance of organization to U.S. health care:

_____

_____

_____

http://www.ebms.com

Organization Name: _____

Mission Statement:

_____

_____

_____

Overview of Activities: _____

_____

_____

Importance of organization to U.S. health care:

_____

_____

_____

STUDENT ACTIVITY 8-4

DISCUSSION QUESTIONS

The following are suggested discussion questions for this chapter.

(1) What is long-term care insurance? Do you think this is a useful tool? Would you buy it?

_____

_____

_____

_____

_____

(2) Discuss the three types of Medicare accountable care organizations. Do you think these are a great way to provide care? Defend your answer.

_____

_____

_____

_____

_____

(3) What is the donut hole? How would you fix this?

_____

_____

_____

_____

_____

(4) Visit the www.cms.gov website and go to the innovation center. Discuss one of the innovation methods you found on the website and its potential contribution to healthcare.

_____

_____

_____

_____

_____

(5) Review the PACE website. What do you think of this association?

_____

_____

_____

_____

_____

The Navigate Companion Website for this text is a great source for additional information on the U.S. healthcare system. You can gain a new perspective on many of the topics presented in this chapter by visiting http://go.jblearning.com/Niles2e. You'll find additional student activities, further reading, and interactive study tools that explore:

- Analysis of how we spend our healthcare dollars in the United States
- Overview of U.S. cost sharing in health care
- Discussion of the different types of health insurance plans
- And much more.

Chapter 9

Managed Care Impact on Healthcare Delivery

LEARNING OBJECTIVES

The student will be able to:

- Define managed care.
- Describe the network-based types of managed care organizations (MCOs).
- Discuss the history of managed care.
- Discuss four major goals of managed care.
- Assess the relationship of managed care with providers.
- Identify four cost control methods of MCOs.

DID YOU KNOW THAT?

- The concept of managed care has been evolving since the early 1930s.
- The oldest form of managed care is the health maintenance organization (HMO).
- Carve outs are healthcare services that will not be paid by MCOs and could include experimental treatment, drug costs, and behavioral health costs.
- The Health Plan Employer Data and Information Set (HEDIS) is a data set of healthcare plans' service activities and is used to evaluate healthcare plans. Although there is a voluntary submission process, nearly 100% of all health plans submit their data to HEDIS.

- According to *Fortune* magazine's analysis of industries, managed care had the highest growth rate of the five major healthcare sectors.
- The Affordable Care Act of 2010 mandates that health insurance companies must spend 80%–85% of their premium revenues on quality health care.

INTRODUCTION

Managed care refers to the cost management of healthcare services by controlling who the consumer sees and how much the service costs. MCOs were introduced 40 years ago, but became more entrenched in the healthcare system when the Health Maintenance Organization Act of 1973 was signed into law by President Nixon (Buchbinder & Shanks, 2007). Healthcare costs were spiraling out of control during that period. Encouraging the increase in the development of HMOs, the first widely used managed care model, would help to control the healthcare costs. MCOs' integration of the financial industry with the medical service industry resulted in controlling the reimbursement rate of services, which allowed them more control over the health insurance portion of health care (Sultz & Young, 2006). Physicians were initially resistant to managed care models because they were threatened by loss of income. As the number of managed care models increased, physicians realized they had to accept this new form of healthcare delivery and, if they participated in a managed care organization, it was guaranteed income. Managed care health plans have become a standard option for consumers. Medicare Part C or Medicare Advantage offers managed care options to their enrollees. Many employers offer managed care plans to their employees. This chapter will discuss the evolution of managed care and why it developed, the different types of managed care, the MCO assessment measures used for cost control, the issues regarding managed care, and how managed care has impacted the delivery of healthcare services.

HISTORY OF MANAGED CARE

The delivery of health care traditionally evolved around the individual relationship between the provider and the patient/consumer. The payment was either provided by a health insurance company or paid out of pocket by the consumer. This **fee-for-service (FFS)** system or **indemnity plan** increased the cost of health care because there were no controls on how much to charge for the provider's service. As healthcare costs continued to spiral out of control throughout the decades, more experiments with contract practice and prepaid service occurred randomly across the U.S. healthcare system (Shi & Singh, 2008).

According to the Tufts Managed Care Institute, from 1850 to 1900, railroad, mining, and lumber companies provided their employees with healthcare services. The companies contracted with a physician to provide services to their employees at a rate per worker (which is a capitation rate because it limits the amount the provider will be paid per service). The reason these companies had to contract with a physician was because of the remote areas of work locations.

A managed care pioneer, Dr. Michael Shadid, started a farmer cooperative health plan in 1929 in Oklahoma. He enrolled several hundred families who paid a set fee and Dr. Shadid provided them with care. Also, in 1929, the Los Angeles Department of Health contracted with physicians to provide healthcare services to 2,000 workers and families. In 1933, Dr. Sidney Garfield contracted with 5,000 construction workers to prepay for their healthcare. In 1938, he contracted with Henry Kaiser to provide medical care to his workers for a dam project.

When group health insurance programs were formed in the 1940s, it reduced the power of the corporations over managing the healthcare coverage and increased the power of the health insurance companies. The health insurance companies and providers had no incentives to control the costs of services. The concept of contractual practices and capitation were not adopted nationwide, which pleased the American Medical Association (AMA) because providers could increase their income with a traditional FFS practice. As a result of this system, healthcare costs continued to increase dramatically (Tufts Managed Care Institute, 2013).

The concept of managed care has been evolving seriously since the early 1930s. The Committee on the Costs of Medicare Care recommended in 1932 that health care should be reorganized into a type of prepaid formula to control costs of services (Committee on the Costs of Medical Care, 1932). The FFS system was recognized even then as inefficient because there was no patient care coordination between the primary care provider and other providers. There was also no focus on minimizing cost of services.

In the early 1930s and 1940s, several health plans adopted the concept of prepaid practice plans: the Group Health Association of Washington, the Group Health Cooperative of Puget Sound, the Health Insurance Plan of Greater New York, the Group Health Plan of Minneapolis, and the Kaiser Permanente Medical Care program, which became the model for HMOs. According to the Kaiser Permanente website, the Kaiser Permanente Plan was developed in 1933 as a result of providing care to construction, shipyard, and steel workers for Kaiser Industries, which they owned during this period. Dr. Sidney Garfield, a surgeon, recognized the potential to provide care to the thousands of workers involved in extensive projects, so he built a hospital and set up a practice to care for these workers. Unfortunately, he often did not receive pay for his services because the insurance companies were not timely in their reimbursement and some workers were uninsured. Harold Hatch, an insurance agent, developed the prepaid concept of medical care. Dr. Garfield would receive insurance remuneration up front per day for each worker. This system worked extremely well and was used for several different industrial projects until 1945, when many of these large projects were completed. Kaiser Permanente opened this type of managed care system to the public in 1945. Membership increased to 300,000 members as a result of union membership. Kaiser Permanente, located in Oakland, CA, has continued this type of concept successfully. It is the largest nonprofit health plan today, with 9.1 million members and nearly $51 billion in operating revenue (Kaiser Permanente, 2013).

Legislative Influence on Managed Care Development

In 1973, President Nixon signed into law the HMO Act. This Act authorized $375 million in funding (loans and grants) for HMO expansion of existing facilities, which rewarded them for focusing on cost control. The Act also required that any business that had 25 or more employees offer an HMO option if available. According to a 2004 report by AMA's Council on Medical Services on managed care, over the next 30 years, several legislative acts were passed that impacted how managed care developed (Hoven, 2004).

The HMO Act of 1973 was amended in 1976 and 1978, which relaxed requirements for HMOs and restricted funding for HMO assistance programs for 2 years. In 1988, the HMO Act was amended to allow employees to contribute less to HMO plans than to traditional FFS plans. In 1982, the Tax Equity and Fiscal Responsibility Act cut more federal funding for health care, including HMOs. The Balanced Budget Act of 1997 established Medicare+Choice (M+C; Part C) which developed different structures for managed care plans. In 2003, the Medicare Prescription Drug, Improvement, and Modernization Act of 2003 replaced M+C with Medicare Advantage (Hoven, 2004).

Over 3 decades, MCOs' strategies have increased their exposure. More companies have become interested in controlling healthcare costs and routinely offer managed care plans to their employees.

MANAGED CARE CHARACTERISTICS

Regardless of the type of MCO, all MCOs have five common characteristics (Knight, 1998):

- They all establish relationships with organizations and providers to offer a designated set of services to their members.
- They all establish criteria for their members to utilize the MCO.
- They all establish measures to estimate cost control.

- They all provide incentives to encourage health service resources.
- They all provide and encourage utilization of programs to improve the health status of their enrollees.

The MCO provides comprehensive services that include primary, secondary, and tertiary care. Depending on the type of MCO, physicians may work exclusively for the MCO or may be under contract with the MCO. MCOs will also contract with hospitals and outpatient clinics to ensure they provide comprehensive services.

Different Types of Managed Care Models

There are six organizational structures of MCOs.

1. **Health maintenance organizations (HMOs):** HMOs are the oldest type of managed care. Members must see their primary care provider first in order to see a specialist. There are four types of HMOs: staff model, group model, network model, and the independent practice association (Bihari, 2010).

   - The **staff model** hires providers to work at a physical location. The **group model** negotiates with a group of physicians exclusively to perform services. This was the first type of HMO model introduced by Kaiser Permanente.

   - The **network model** is similar to the group model but these providers may see other patients who are not members of the HMO. There is a negotiated rate for service for members to see providers who belong to the network.

   - The **independent practice associations (IPAs)** contract with a group of physicians who are in private practice to see MCO members at a prepaid rate per visit. The physicians may sign contracts with many HMOs. The physicians may also see non-HMO patients. This type of HMO was a result of the HMO Act of 1973.

2. **Preferred provider organizations (PPOs):** These providers agree to a relative value-based fee schedule or a discounted fee to see members. They do not have a gatekeeper like the HMO so a member does not need a referral to see a specialist. The PPO does not have a copay but does have a deductible. This plan was developed by providers and hospitals to ensure that nonmembers could still be served while providing a discount to MCOs for their members. A member may see a provider not in the network but

they may pay more out of pocket for their services. The bill could be as much as 50% of the total bill. They are currently the most popular type of plan (American Heart Association, 2013).

3. **Exclusive provider organizations (EPOs):** These are similar to PPOs but they restrict members to the list of preferred or exclusive providers members can use.

4. **Physician hospital organizations (PHOs):** These organizations include physician hospitals, surgical centers, and other medical providers that contract with a managed care plan to provide health services (Judson & Harrison, 2006).

5. **Point-of-service (POS) plans:** The POS plans are a blend of the other MCOs—a type of HMO/ PPO hybrid. They encourage but do not require that plan members use a primary care provider who will become the gatekeeper of services. Members will receive lower fees if they use a gatekeeper model. They may also see an out-of-network provider at any time but will be charged a higher rate. This type of plan was developed as a result of complaints about the inability of members to choose their provider (American Heart Association, 2013).

6. **Provider-sponsored organizations (PSOs):** These organizations are owned or controlled by healthcare providers. This is an emerging term that describes provider organizations that are formed to directly contract with purchasers to deliver healthcare services. PSOs are formed by organizations such as IPAs. However, unlike IPAs, they assume insurance risk for their beneficiaries (Bihari, 2010).

THE MANAGED CARE ORGANIZATION PAYMENT PLAN

Depending on the type of MCO structure, their financing structure with providers may differ as well.

There are three major types of provider remuneration: capitation, discounted fees, and salaries. With a **capitation policy** or per member per month policy, the provider is paid a fixed monthly amount per member, often called a **Per Member Per Month (PMPM) payment.** This member fee is given to the provider regardless of how often the members use the service and the types of services used. The provider is responsible for providing all services deemed necessary.

Discounted fees are a type of FFS but are discounted based on a fee schedule. The provider supplies the service and then can bill the MCO based on the fee schedule developed by the MCO. Each service can be billed separately. The provider anticipates a large referral pool from the MCO so they will accept the discounted rates.

Salaries are the third method of payment. In this instance, the provider is actually an employer of the MCO. Annually, a type of bonus is distributed among the providers based on how often services have been used by members. So although they receive a salary, they will be rewarded by additional performance measures (The Geometry Center, 2013).

COST CONTROL MEASURES OF MANAGED CARE ORGANIZATIONS

Restriction on Provider Choice

Members of an MCO often have restrictions on their choice for a provider. As the types of MCOs have evolved over the years, the restrictions have lessened, but there is a financial penalty such as a higher copayment or higher deductible for choosing a provider outside of the network.

Gatekeeper

In some MCOs, the primary care provider is the **gatekeeper** of all of the care for the patient member. Any secondary or tertiary care would be coordinated by the gatekeeper or primary care provider. The primary care provider is responsible for the case management of a member patient. If additional medical services are needed, the primary care provider must refer the member patient for additional services. Some members do not like having a gatekeeper and would prefer to make these decisions themselves. As a result of this model, some MCOs require a preauthorization of services by the MCO. Many MCOs have clinical guidelines to determine service approval (Buchbinder & Shanks, 2007).

Services Review

Utilization review evaluates the appropriateness of the types of services provided. According to Shi and Singh (2008), there are three types of utilization reviews: prospective, concurrent, and retrospective. **Prospective utilization review** is implemented before the service is actually performed by having the procedure authorized by the MCO, having the primary care provider decide to refer the member for the service, or assessing the service based on the clinical guidelines. **Concurrent utilization reviews** are decisions that are made during the actual course of service such as length of inpatient stay and additional surgery. **Retrospective utilization review** is an evaluation of services once the services have been provided. This may occur to assess treatment patterns of certain diseases. This type of review may include a financial review to assure accuracy of billing. **Practice profiling**, an offshoot of retrospective utilization review, examines specific provider patterns of practice. This is a type of employee performance review because the focus is to determine which provider also fits in with the organizational culture of the MCO (Spector, 2004).

MEDICARE AND MEDICAID MANAGED CARE

Medicare Managed Care

As stated previously, the M+C program was created as a result of the Balanced Budget Act of 1997. Implemented in 2000, the purpose of M+C was to encourage Medicare enrollees to use managed care services. Medicare offered risk plans and cost plans for their enrollees. **Risk plans** pay a premium per member that is based on the member's county of residence. Members could use both in-network and out-of-network providers. The risk plans covers all Medicare services and vision and prescription care. **Medicare cost plans** are a type of HMO and have similar rules to Medicare Advantage plans. CMS reimburses the MCOs on a preset monthly basis per enrollee based on a forecasted budget. The reimbursement rate is based on the reasonable cost of providing services. Cost plans allow members to pursue care outside the network. If that occurs, the services are covered under the original Medicare (CMS, 2013a).

In 2003, the Medicare Prescription Drug, Improvement, and Modernization Act (MMA) renamed the program **Medicare Advantage** (MA) and allowed PPOs as an option. It also allowed enrollees to participate in private fee-for-service (PFFS) plans as part of the MA. CMS evaluated the administration of the MA program and, based on that evaluation, they developed strategies to recruit more MCO participation. Despite these improvements, managed care enrollment initially dropped nearly 2 million in 2004. With changes in MA, 2006 enrollment surpassed the M+C enrollment. As a result of the MMA, the newly revamped MA program has been a financial boost to MCOs. Enrollment in MA

has increased 7% in 2012, which is unusual because many enrollees may lose the ability to use their same healthcare provider and are therefore typically hesitant to switch. But the increase in MA enrollment is indicating that more users are willing to switch plans if a plan fits their healthcare needs. The following are the five largest MA healthcare providers according to market share percentage: UnitedHealthGroup (19%), Humana (17%), Kaiser (8%), Wellpoint (5%), and Aetna (3%). This data may change because the Affordable Care Act will be implementing Medicare reimbursement reductions over the next several years in order to reduce the Medicare administrative costs (Moeller, 2012).

Medicaid Managed Care

According to the Medicaid website, states have traditionally provided people Medicaid benefits using a fee-for-service system; however, in the past 15 years, states have more frequently implemented a managed care delivery system for Medicaid benefits. More states are requiring people to enroll in a managed care program. Increasing numbers of states (16 in 2012) are using **Managed Long Term Services and Supports (MLTSS)**, a CMS Medicaid program, as a strategy for expanding home- and community-based services to ensure quality and increase efficiency. When states implement an MLTSS program, they can use any one of the following types of entities:

- **Managed Care Organizations (MCOs)**—like HMOs, these companies agree to provide most Medicaid benefits to people in exchange for a monthly payment from the state.

- **Limited benefit plans**—these companies may look like HMOs but only provide one or two Medicaid benefits (like mental health or dental services).

- **Primary care case managers**—these individual providers (or groups of providers) agree to act as an individual's primary care provider, and receive a small monthly payment for helping to coordinate referrals and other medical services (CMS, 2013c).

According to CMS, of the total Medicaid enrollment in 2011, approximately 74% were receiving Medicaid managed care benefits. All states except Alaska, New Hampshire, U.S. Virgin Islands, and Wyoming have Medicaid managed care. Managed care plans use the gatekeeper model, HMOs, and prepaid health plans. **Carve outs** are services that Medicaid is not obligated to pay for under an MCO contract. Carve outs have occurred because the MCO cannot provide the service or it is too expensive. Unfortunately, mental health services and substance abuse treatment services are often categorized as carve out services (CMS, 2013b).

According to the Medicaid Managed Care website, as of 2012, those states that have a Medicaid managed care program must have a written CMS approved strategy for improving their programs and to perform an external quality review to ensure they are providing quality care. To assist in these efforts, CMS has updated the State Quality Strategy Toolkit available at: http://www.medicaid.gov/Medicaid-CHIP-Program-Information/By-Topics/Quality-of-Care/Downloads/Quality-Strategy-Toolkit-for-States.pdf. The External Quality Review analyzes the program on quality, timeliness, and access to the healthcare services that a MCO, prepaid inpatient health plan, or their contractors furnish to Medicaid beneficiaries. CMS has created a new External Quality Review (EQR) Toolkit to assist states and external quality review organizations in completing the annual EQR technical report. This toolkit is available at http://www.medicaid.gov/Medicaid-CHIP-Program-Information/By-Topics/Quality-of-Care/Quality-of-Care-External-Quality-Review.html. This type of quality assurance activity is in concert with the goals of the Affordable Care Act to improve the quality of the U.S. healthcare system.

ASSESSMENT OF MANAGED CARE MODELS

National Committee on Quality Assurance

From a healthcare consumer perspective, when an organization's top priority is cost control, there may be concerns about losing a level of quality. As managed care was integrated into Medicaid and Medicare, the government also became more involved in the evaluation of managed care providers. Also, as competition increased in the managed care arena, there was fear that more services would be reduced to maintain lower premiums (Sultz & Young, 2006). As a result of these issues, the **National Committee on Quality Assurance (NCQA)** was established to maintain the quality of care in health plans.

NCQA was established in 1990 to monitor health plans and improve healthcare quality. Their focus is to measure, analyze, and improve healthcare programs. The NCQA accredits MCOs and, although a voluntary

review process, the process includes surveys completed by managed care experts and physicians. They evaluate access and service and quality of the MCO's providers, primary prevention activities, and case management for the chronically ill. An organization can be accredited at three levels: excellent, commendable, and accredited. This accreditation, although voluntary, has alleviated concerns of the MCOs' focus on cost control. The NCQA has developed a report card of accredited health plans that consumers can access on their website. In the past, the NCQA had developed different criteria for the different types of MCOs. The NCQA developed standards and guidelines for all MCOs, regardless of their organizational structure. Since 2006, the NCQA has developed standards specifically for Medicaid Managed Care accreditation. There are currently 41 states that recognize the NCQA accreditation for both their Medicaid Managed care and commercial managed care programs. Additionally, the NCQA has a physician directory that recognizes quality practices. As the MCO industry has become very competitive, it is to the benefit of an MCO to become accredited. The Affordable Care Act has many quality assurance initiatives connected with the NCQA (NCQA, 2013a).

Health Plan Employer Data and Information Set

Health Plan Employer Data and Information Set (HEDIS) was established by the NCQA in 1989. It is used by over 90% of all health plans to measure service and quality of care. The reported data is available to MCOs and physicians. HEDIS uses 75 measures from different areas of health care. Because so many health plans submit data to this HEDIS database and because the measures are so specifically defined, one can create comparisons of health plan performance. Health plans also use HEDIS results to assess performance and calculate physician and healthcare plan rankings (HEDIS, 2013b).

HEDIS measures health issues such as medication use patterns, breast cancer rates, rates of chronic diseases such as diabetes, childhood health issues, high blood pressure issues, heart disease and mental health disease, and health plans' treatment of these major health issues. Healthcare plans and providers use this database for performance assessment and consumers may access this information through the State of the Health Care Quality Report, which analyzes the healthcare system. The Committee on Performance Measurement has members that represent the consumers, providers, health plans, employers, and other stakeholders who decide what type of data should be collected by the HEDIS and what type of measures should be used (HEDIS, 2013b). There are four standards that are the focus of a NCQA review: quality management, utilization standards, members' rights and responsibilities, and services. The NCQA will also be involved with the quality assurance of the new initiatives designated by the Affordable Care Act, including the State Health Insurance Marketplaces, the Accountable Care Organizations, and the Patient Centered Home models (NCQA, 2013b).

MANAGED CARE ACCREDITATION

Although the Joint Commission and the NCQA can accredit different types of managed care organizations, since 1983, the **Accreditation Association for Ambulatory Health Care (AAAHC)** has been reviewing and accrediting managed care organizations. In 2012, their standards were revised to focus on managed care principles, including members' rights, care coordination, enrollee records accuracy, credentialing of provider networks, quality improvement, and health education. They have received **Medicare Deemed Status** from CMS, which means that the AAAHC can survey Medicare Advantage HMO and PPO plans (AAAHC, 2013).

ISSUES WITH MANAGED CARE OPERATIONS

Several years ago, survey results indicated that physicians who contract with several MCOs were concerned with providing quality care to their patients because the MCOs' focuses are on cost. However, managed care options have become an integral component of the healthcare system, so assurance of quality and cost measures have been implemented to assist with managed care quality of care while maintaining cost effective care. The AMA has developed a **National Managed Care Contract (NMCC)**, which is designed to comply with the managed care laws of all 50 states and the District of Columbia, as well as with federal requirements. The comprehensive information it provides covers the business relationship between physicians and managed care organizations. Using the NMCC, physicians can better understand, evaluate, and negotiate managed care contracts.

Physicians are also concerned with physician network rentals or **silent PPOs**, which are unauthorized third parties outside the contract between the MCO and the physician that gain access to the MCO discount rates. Examples of these network rentals are automobile insurers or workmen's compensations insurers. They obtain the physician's rates from a database. The main insurer who has the contract with the physician does not provide the information to the physician and the third parties continue to benefit from the discounted rates. This scheme takes money from the physicians because they are obtaining discounts fraudulently. Physicians have pursued legal action against MCOs due to issues with reimbursement such as the abuse of these discounted rates by unauthorized users. The AMA has an educational service for physicians to determine if a silent PPO is being implemented (Advocacy Resource Center, 2012).

The concept of **medical loss ratio** or the minimum amount of dollars a healthcare plan spends on providing care rather than administration has been targeted by the Affordable Care Act. Under the Affordable Care Act, insurance companies must spend 80–85% of member premium revenues on medical care and healthcare quality improvement. If they do not meet that minimum percentage, the insurance companies must provide a rebate to their customers. In 2012, over 13 million consumers received $1.1 billion in rebates—the average consumer rebate was around $151. In a recent Kaiser Foundation study, researchers found that the average medical loss ratio in the individual market went from 78% in 2010 to 83% in 2012. Had medical loss ratios remained at 2010 levels, premiums would have been much higher (Lambrew, 2013).

CONCLUSION

The managed care model for healthcare delivery was developed for the primary purpose of containing healthcare costs. By administering both the healthcare services and the reimbursement of these services, and therefore eliminating a third party health insurer, the industry felt that this model would be very cost-effective. Both the consumer/patient and the physician's concerns were the same—providing quality care while focusing predominantly on cost. Consumers were also worried about losing freedom to chose their primary care provider. Physicians were concerned about loss of income.

As managed care evolved, managed care models developed that allowed more choice for both the consumer and the physician. Eventually, there were models such as PPOs and POS plans that allowed consumers to more freely choose their providers. There is a financial disincentive to use a provider outside the network of the MCO. From a provider perspective, providers are also able to see non-MCO patients, which increases their income. The provider also receives a financial disincentive because any MCO patient was given health care at a discounted rate.

There also have been issues with how MCOs have reimbursed physicians. As discussed in chapter, the issue with silent PPOs has financially hurt physicians. Physicians have also had problems with timely reimbursement from MCOs. There were issues with fraudulent reimbursement rates of out-of-network services, which resulted in members paying exorbitant out-of-pocket expenses. However, the American Medical Association has developed tools to assist physicians with managed care contracting and reimbursement processes. The Affordable Care Act mandate that insurance companies must spend 80–85% of their premium revenues on quality care or be penalized with fines and/or give rebates to their members will be an incentive for managed care organizations to provide quality and affordable care.

VOCABULARY

Accreditation Association for Ambulatory Health Care

Capitation policy

Carve outs

Concurrent utilization reviews

Discounted fees

Exclusive provider organizations (EPOs)

Fee-for-service (FFS)

Gatekeeper

Group model

Health maintenance organization (HMO)

Health Plan Employer Data and Information Set (HEDIS)

Indemnity plan

Independent practice associations (IPAs)

Limited benefit plans

Managed Care Long Term Services and Support (MLTSS)

Managed care organizations (MCOs)

Medical loss ratio

Medicare Advantage

Medicare cost plans

Medicare Deemed Status

National Committee on Quality Assurance (NCQA)

National Managed Care Contract (NMCC)

Network model

Per Member Per Month (PMPM) payment

Physician hospital organizations (PHOs)

Point-of-service (POS) plans

Practice profiling

Preferred provider organizations (PPOs)

Primary care case managers

Prospective utilization review

Provider sponsored organizations (PSOs)

Retrospective utilization review

Risk plans

Salaries

Silent PPOs

Staff model

Utilization review

REFERENCES

Accreditation Association for Ambulatory Health Care (AAAHC). (2013). About AAAHC. Retrieved from http://www.aaahc.org/about/

Advocacy Resource Center. (2012). Retrieved from http://www.ama-assn.org/resources/doc/arc/x-ama/reg-rental -network-ppos-issue-brief.pdf

American Heart Association. (2013). Managed health care plans. Retrieved from http://www.americanheart.org /presenter.jhtml?identifier=4663

Buchbinder, S., & Shanks, N. (2007). *Introduction to health care management*. Sudbury, MA: Jones and Bartlett.

Centers for Medicare & Medicaid Services (CMS). (2013a). Other Medicare managed plans. Retrieved from http://www.medicare.gov/sign-up-change-plans/medicare-health-plans/other-health-plans/other-medicare -health-plans.html

CMS. (2013b). Managed care. Retrieved from http://www.medicaid.gov/Medicaid-CHIP-Program-Information /By-Topics/Delivery-Systems/Managed-Care/Managed-Care.html

CMS. (2013c). Medicaid Managed Long Term Services and Support. Retrieved from http://www.medicaid.gov /Medicaid-CHIP-Program-Information/By-Topics/Delivery-Systems/Medicaid-Managed-Long-Term-Services -and-Supports-MLTSS.html

Committee on the Costs of Medical Care. (1932). *Medical care for the American people: The final report*. Chicago: University of Chicago Press.

Healthcare Effectiveness Data and Information Set (HEDIS). (2013a). HEDIS and performance management. Retrieved from http://www.ncqa.org/HEDISQualityMeasurement.aspx

HEDIS. (2013b). HEDIS and quality compass. Retrieved from http://www.ncqa.org/HEDISQualityMeasurement /WhatisHEDIS.aspx

Hoven, A. (2004). Impact of the health maintenance act of 1973. *Report of the Council on Medical Services*, CMS Report 4-A-04.

Judson, K., & Harrison, C. (2006). *Law & ethics for medical careers*. New York: McGraw-Hill.

Kaiser Permanente. (2013). *Our history*. Retrieved from http://xnet.kp.org/newscenter/aboutkp/historyofkp.html

Knight, W. (1998). *Managed care: What it is and how it works*. Gaithersburg, MD: Aspen Publishers.

Lambrew, J. (2013). Good news: Americans saved billions thanks to the Affordable Care Act. Retrieved from http://www.potusnews.net/category/Jeanne-Lambrew.aspx

Mann, C. (2012). CMCS informational bulletin: November 19th. Retrieved from http://www.medicaid.gov/Federal -Policy-Guidance/downloads/CIB-11-19-12.pdf

Moeller, P. (2012). Lower Medicare Advantage premiums attract seniors. Retrieved from http://money.usnews .com/money/blogs/the-best-life/2012/02/07/lower-medicare-advantage-premiums-attract-seniors_print.html

National Committee for Quality Assurance (NCQA). (2013a). About the NCQA. Retrieved from http://www .ncqa.org/AboutNCQA.aspx

NCQA. (2013b). NCQA accreditation for health insurance exchanges and alignment with ACA. Retrieved from http://www.ncqa.org/Programs/Accreditation/HealthPlanHP/Accreditation/AlignmentwithACA.aspx

Shi, L., & Singh, D. (2008). *An Introduction to Healthcare in America: A systems approach*. Sudbury, MA: Jones and Bartlett.

Spector, R. (2004). Utilization Review and Managed Health Care Liability. *Southern Medical Journal, 97* (3): 284–286.

Sultz, H., & Young, K. (2006). *Health care USA: Understanding its organization and delivery* (5th ed.). Sudbury, MA: Jones and Bartlett.

The Geometry Center. (2013). How do health care plans pay for physicians? Retrieved from http://www.geom.uiuc.edu/usenate/payreport/how.html

Tufts Managed Care Institute. (2013). A brief history of managed care. Retrieved from http://www.thci.org/downloads/BriefHist.pdf

NOTES

STUDENT ACTIVITY 9-1

IN YOUR OWN WORDS

Based on this chapter, please provide an explanation of the following concepts in your own words. DO NOT RECITE the text.

Managed care: _____

_____

_____

Health maintenance organizations: _____

_____

_____

Preferred provider organizations: _____

_____

_____

Medicare Deemed Status: _____

_____

_____

Point-of-service plans: _____

_____

_____

Indemnity plan: _____

_____

_____

Carve outs: _____

_____

_____

Fee-for-service plans: _____

_____

_____

Medical loss ratio: _____

_____

_____

Silent PPOs: _____

_____

_____

STUDENT ACTIVITY 9-2

REAL LIFE APPLICATIONS: CASE STUDY

A friend, who had been a dependent on her parents' insurance, recently graduated from college and was offered a full-time healthcare management position. When she started to complete her human resource (HR) application, the HR manager asked her what type of healthcare plan she chose. Her new employer offered several different healthcare plans: fee-for-service, HMO, PPO, and POS plans. She was very confused and asked you to explain the managed care plans to her.

ACTIVITY

(1) Describe the characteristics of these healthcare plans and (2) identify the differences between the HMO and PPO plans.

RESPONSES

_____

_____

_____

_____

_____

_____

_____

_____

_____

_____

_____

_____

_____

_____

_____

_____

_____

CASE SCENARIO TWO

You had heard that the premiums for your health insurance plan may decrease as result of the Affordable Care Act's requirement that insurance companies spend a certain amount of their premium revenue on their plans. You were interested to find out if this was true.

ACTIVITY

Perform an Internet search on medical loss ratios. Describe the concept and why it could decrease the cost sharing of your health insurance coverage.

RESPONSES

_____

_____

_____

_____

_____

_____

_____

_____

_____

_____

_____

_____

_____

_____

CASE SCENARIO THREE

For years, your parents had a traditional fee-for-service health insurance. They are now required to switch to a managed care product. They are very upset because they love their physicians. However, their physicians did tell them they had contracted with certain MCOs to provide services. Your parents were still confused.

ACTIVITY

Explain the managed care principle, and which program would enable them to still use their practitioners.

RESPONSES

_____

_____

_____

_____

_____

_____

_____

_____

_____

_____

_____

_____

_____

CASE SCENARIO FOUR

As a healthcare consumer that recently switched to a managed care health plan, you were very worried about the quality of the care provided to you. You were wondering if there were any reviews of these types of programs to determine the quality of healthcare services offered.

ACTIVITY

Discuss the different types of reviews used to assess managed care organizations.

RESPONSES

_____

_____

_____

_____

_____

_____

_____

_____

_____

_____

_____

_____

_____

_____

STUDENT ACTIVITY 9-3

INTERNET EXERCISES

Write your answers in the space provided.

- Visit each of the websites listed here.
- Name the organization.
- Locate their mission statement/values statement on their website.
- Provide a brief overview of the activities of the organization.
- How do these organizations participate in the U.S. healthcare system?

Websites

http://www.ncqa.org

Organization Name: _____

Mission Statement:

_____

_____

_____

Overview of Activities: _____

_____

_____

Importance of organization to U.S. health care:

_____

_____

_____

http://www.aaahc.org

Organization Name: _____

Mission Statement:

_____

_____

_____

Overview of Activities: _____

_____

_____

Importance of organization to U.S. health care:

_____

_____

_____

http://www.americanheart.org

Organization Name: _____

Mission Statement:

_____

_____

_____

Overview of Activities: _____

_____

_____

Importance of organization to U.S. health care:

_____

_____

_____

http://managedhealthcareexecutive.modernmedicine.com

Organization Name: _____

Mission Statement:

_____

_____

_____

Overview of Activities: _____

_____

_____

Importance of organization to U.S. health care:

_____

_____

_____

http://www.managedcare.com

Organization Name: _____

Mission Statement:

_____

_____

_____

Overview of Activities: _____

_____

_____

Importance of organization to U.S. health care:

_____

_____

_____

http://www.amednews.com

Organization Name: _____

Mission Statement:

_____

_____

_____

Overview of Activities: _____

_____

_____

Importance of organization to U.S. health care:

_____

_____

_____

STUDENT ACTIVITY 9-4

DISCUSSION QUESTIONS

The following are suggested discussion questions for this chapter.

(1) Why was managed care developed? Do you think managed care is a good way to provide healthcare services? Why or why not?

_____

_____

_____

_____

_____

(2) What is the difference between an HMO and PPO? Which one do you prefer? Search the Internet to find one HMO and one PPO.

_____

_____

_____

_____

_____

(3) What is a medical loss ratio? How does it impact healthcare consumers?

_____

_____

_____

_____

_____

(4) Discuss the importance of the National Committee on Quality Assurance on U.S. health care.

_____

_____

_____

_____

(5) Select one of the new initiatives that NCQA will be administering. Which one do you think is the most valuable for healthcare services? Defend your answer.

_____

_____

_____

_____

_____

The Navigate Companion Website for this text is a great source for additional information on the U.S. healthcare system. You can gain a new perspective on many of the topics presented in this chapter by visiting http://go.jblearning.com/Niles2e. You'll find additional student activities, further reading, and interactive study tools that explore:

- History of managed care
- Overview of managed care plans
- Analysis of managed care models
- And much more.

Chapter 10

Information Technology Impact on Health Care

LEARNING OBJECTIVES

The student will be able to:

- Define and discuss health information technology, health information systems, and health/medical informatics.

- Evaluate the importance of the Office of the National Coordinator for Health Information Technology to health care.

- Assess the importance of the National eHealth Collaborative to health information technology policy.

- Discuss the importance of Dr. Octo Barnett to healthcare technology.

- Evaluate the impact of information technology on healthcare stakeholders.

- Discuss the difference between an EMR and an EHR.

DID YOU KNOW THAT?

- Both President Bush and President Obama have supported the initiative for electronic health records.

- E-prescribing is a form of a clinical decision support system.

- The Veterans Health Administration's health information technology system is one of the best in the nation.

- There is a new product called electronic aspirin, which is an implant on the side of the head normally impacted by a headache.

- The Food and Drug Administration (FDA) has approved a medical robot that can make rounds, checking on patients in different rooms.

- The Microsoft HealthVault, Microsoft's version of an electronic patient record, now has a feature that allows a patient to preregister for hospital procedures and admissions.

INTRODUCTION

The general term of **informatics** refers to the science of computer application to data in different industries. **Health** or **medical informatics** is the science of computer application that supports clinical and research data in different areas of health care. It is a methodology of how the healthcare industry thinks about patients and how their treatments are defined and evolved. For example, **imaging informatics** applies computer technology to organs and tissue (Coiera, 2003;

Open Clinical, 2013). **Health information systems** are systems that store, transmit, collect, and retrieve these data (Anderson, Rice, & Kominski, 2007). **Health information technology's** (HIT) goal is to manage the health data that can be used by patients/consumers, insurance companies, healthcare providers, healthcare administrators, and any stakeholder that has an interest in health care (Goldstein & Blumenthal, 2008).

HIT impacts every aspect of the healthcare industry. All of the stakeholders in the healthcare industry use HIT. **Information technology (IT)** has had a tremendous impact on the healthcare industry because it allows faster documentation of every transaction. When an industry focuses on saving lives, it is important that all activity has a written document that describes the activity. Computerization of documentation has increased the management efficiency and accuracy of healthcare data. The main focus of HIT is the national implementation of an electronic patient record. Both Presidents Bush and Obama have supported this initiative.

This is the foundation of many IT systems because it will enable different systems to share patient information, which will increase the quality and efficiency of health care. This chapter will discuss the history of IT, different applications of IT health care, and the status of electronic health records and barriers for its national implementation.

HISTORY OF INFORMATION TECHNOLOGY IN THE HEALTHCARE INDUSTRY

Computers' first widespread use was in the 1960s as a result of the implementation of Medicaid and Medicare. Healthcare providers were inundated with forms to complete for both programs. In order to receive reimbursement from both programs, services needed to be tracked and forms needed to be completed and submitted to these programs. Therefore, computers were used to assist with the financial management of these programs (Buchbinder & Shanks, 2007). As a result of computer integration, more healthcare providers recognized the efficiency of computers to manage programs. Hospitals particularly recognized the efficiency of electronic billing. During the 1960s, hospitals developed their own computer systems that housed their financial information. The hospitals were responsible for the maintenance of these systems. These systems, which were large mainframe systems,

required a large staff to maintain their operations. All of the hospitals' data was stored on these mainframe computers. Computer programs were developed by the hospitals to extract data reports. These mainframe computers were very expensive. They were eventually replaced in the 1970s with minicomputers, which were more efficient, more cost-effective, and easier to maintain. These minicomputers were connected to a main computer that stored all of the data. They were also used to enter information. Eventually, specific computer systems were developed for laboratories and clinics. It is important to mention Dr. G. Octo Barnett, who is a Professor of Medicine at Harvard Medical School and the senior director at the Laboratory of Computer Science at Massachusetts General Hospital (Appleby, 2008). He developed the first computer program for healthcare applications, called MUMPS, in 1964, which became the basis of very sophisticated programs used today.

During the 1980s and 1990s, the development and widespread use of personal computers (PCs) revolutionized information systems and technology. PCs were not reliant on a main computer for analyses. They were able to generate more sophisticated reports. PCs were often linked as a network to share information among different departments in hospitals. The development of the PC also enabled more computerization of physician practices. In the 2000s, the application of IT has increased in the healthcare industry with cutting edge new applications such as electronic aspirin and needle-free insulin injections and the national implementation of electronic health information.

The establishment of a **chief information officer (CIO)** in healthcare organizations emphasized how important information systems and technology had become to healthcare organizations. The U.S. healthcare system has been the world leader for developing cutting edge technology in health care. It has impacted how diagnostic procedures are performed, how data is collected and disseminated, how medicine is delivered, how providers treat their patients, and how surgeries are performed. There are several healthcare stakeholders that are impacted by technology. Consumers, providers, employers, researchers, all governmental levels, nonprofit and for-profit healthcare organizations, and insurance payers have all been impacted by technology (eJobDescription, 2013). Technological advances have been blamed, in part, for the continued rise of healthcare expenditures, but the results of technological advances cannot be disputed.

ELECTRONIC PATIENT RECORDS

History

The Institute of Medicine (IOM) has published a series of reports over the past several years that focus on improving the quality of health care in the United States. In 2001, they published the report *Crossing the Quality Chasm: A New Health System for the 21st Century*, which stresses the importance of improving IT infrastructure. IOM emphasized the importance of an electronic health record (EHR), an electronic record of patients' medical history. The report also discussed the importance of patient safety by establishing data standards for collecting patient information (IOM, 2001).

In 1991 and 1997, the IOM issued reports that focused on the impact of computer-based patients' records as important technology for improving health care (Vreeman, Taggard, Rhine, & Wornell, 2006). There are two concepts in electronic patient records that are used interchangeably but are different—the **electronic medical record** (EMR/EHR) and the **electronic health record** (EHR). The **National Alliance for Health Information Technology** (NAHIT) defines the EHR as the electronic record of health-related information on an individual that is accumulated from one health system and is utilized by the health organization that is providing patient care while the EMR accumulates more patient medical information from many health organizations that have been involved in the patient care. Simply, the EHR is an EMR that can be integrated with other systems (MNT, 2008b). The IOM has been urging the healthcare industry to adopt the electronic patient record but initially costs were too high and the health community did not embrace the recommendation. This discussion will focus on the EHR.

As software costs have declined, more healthcare providers have adopted the use of the EHR system. The EHR system can be used in hospitals, healthcare provider offices, and other types of healthcare facilities. It enables healthcare organizations to monitor patient safety and care. In 2003, the Department of Health and Human Services (DHHS) began to promote the use of HIT, including the use of the EHR. The IOM was asked to identify essential elements for the establishment of an EHR. The IOM broadly defined an EHR to include (IOM, 2013):

- The collection of longitudinal data on a person's health
- Immediate electronic access to this information
- Establishment of a system that provides decision support to ensure the quality, safety, and efficiency of patient care

According to DHHS, the Health Information Technology for Economic and Clinical Health (HITECH) Act, which was enacted as part of the 2009 American Recovery and Reinvestment Act, was designed to stimulate the adoption of health information technology in the United States. The HITECH Act, until 2015, offers incentives for physicians and other healthcare professionals to adopt health IT. After that, the act spells out penalties for noncompliance of health IT.

The Office of the National Coordinator (ONC) for Health Information Technology is responsible for implementing the incentives and penalties program. The ONC has been working to create "meaningful use" guidelines for physicians and others that will help them receive incentive payments and avoid penalties in the future (DHHS, 2013).

Benefits of Electronic Health Records

Several studies have been performed to assess the impact of the EHR on healthcare delivery. Administrators of several healthcare delivery systems reported many benefits to the implementation of an EHR. Many administrators cited the capability of more comprehensive reporting that integrated both clinical and administrative data. It also provided an opportunity to analyze and review patient outcomes because of the standardization of the clinical assessments. Also noted was the development of electronic automated reports that improved the discharge of a patient. The reports also provided an opportunity for the administrator to assess the workload of a department. The EHR also improved operational efficiency. The EHR had excellent capabilities to process and store data. Administrators further reported that the computerized documentation took 30% less time than the previous handwritten notes (Shields et al., 2007).

Several studies indicated there was an improvement in interdepartmental communication. The EHR provided aggregate data in the patient records to other departments and the information about the patient was legible. The actual design and implementation of an

EHR system contributed to the development of a more interdisciplinary approach to patient care (Ventres & Shah, 2007; Whitman & David, 2007). The implementation of an EHR system led to improved data accuracy because it reduced the need to replicate data. The EHR system also provided a platform for routine data quality assessments, which was important to maintain the accuracy of the EHR data. The EHR system provides an opportunity for future research. The data captured in the database could be used to analyze outcomes and develop baseline data for future research.

Incentives to Use Electronic Health Records: Meaningful Use

In accordance with the HITECH Act, the Centers for Medicaid and Medicare established incentives to encourage "**meaningful use**" of EHRs to increase patient care quality and safety. Meaningful use, as defined by the CMS, has established core measures that healthcare providers must meet to determine the EHR system is being adequately used. For example, providers must have entered one medication using the CPOE for at least 30% of their patients (Centers for Medicare and Medicaid Services [CMS], 2013c). In order to qualify for the incentive program, their EHR system must store data in a structured format that adheres to the standards developed by the Centers for Medicare and Medicaid and must be certified specifically for the incentive program. Both healthcare professionals and hospitals are eligible for the program. They can participate in the Medicare, Medicare Advantage, or Medicaid program but cannot receive incentives for all of the programs. They must choose which program.

The program started in 2011 and will conclude in 2016. Eligible healthcare professionals can participate for up to 5 continuous years and receive up to $44,000 for those years. Providers must demonstrate meaningful use on an annual basis. The last year for provider enrollment is 2014; however, to receive maximum participation, providers must have enrolled by 2012. Effective 2015, providers who do not demonstrate meaningful use will be subject to a fine up to 5% of their incentive amount. Medicaid professionals can also be involved in the meaningful use EHR system. Nearly all states are administering the program. Medicaid incentives are higher than the Medicare program—up to $63,750 over 6 years. Specified criteria for meaningful use for

hospitals was established to review their EHR systems. As of March 2012, nearly 2,700 hospitals have received incentives of $3 billion (CMS, 2013d).

An example of a leader in EHR adoption is Geisinger Wyoming Valley Hospital. It is 1 of 3 hospitals, and 63 primary and specialty care clinics in a not-for-profit healthcare system. In 1995, Geisinger was moving towards an EHR system and integrating it across both inpatient and outpatient services. Community physicians who are not part of the system can view the patient electronic record through a connect software. Any doctor with privileges can view the records and add additional information off site. To further enhance the system, Geisinger added a Modified Early Warning System score, which alerts that monitoring and intervention may be needed based on vital statistics. They also developed a Discharge Navigator system to coordinate patient discharges more efficiently (Walker, 2013).

BARRIERS TO ELECTRONIC HEALTH RECORD IMPLEMENTATION

From a user perspective such as a physician's office, a major issue with EHR implementation is the cost of implementing the system. Software purchases, hardware, network upgrades, training, and computer personnel must be considered in the purchase of the system. The average cost of installation for a practice is $55,000 (Daigrepont & McGrath, 2011).

According to Valerius (2007), migrating from a hard copy system to an electronic system requires several components, including a physician order communication/results retrieval, electronic document/control management, point of care charting, electronic physician order entry and prescribing, clinical decision support system, provider patient portals, personal health records, and population health. When an organization implements an electronic system, there are changes in the workflow because much of the process was previously manual. Training is required for both healthcare professionals and staff to fully utilize the system.

When purchasing a system for patient electronic records, it was found that there were equipment or software inadequacies that created a much slower system for processing data. If the system failed, it created frustration for healthcare professionals and administrators. Both of these problems emphasized the need for adequate training for both the providers and staff. Much of the initial training required overtime for the staff. Most of the training lasted approximately 4 months. Continued training was also required for maintenance of the system (Valerius, 2007).

The critical success factors medical practices need to consider for successful HIT implementation include **(Daigrepont & McGrath, 2011)**:

- Uniform adoption of technology by all participants
- Reliable HIT infrastructure
- A system that is appropriate for the practice
- A plan that details the milestones of the implementation of the system
- Ongoing training of all employees to ensure optimal use of the HER

A focus of EHR implementation is the development of standards for the type of data collected so it can be exchanged between two systems. However, the American Academy of Pediatrics has indicated that that EHRs lack specific functions for pediatric patients such as child abuse reporting and newborn screening. The AAP has developed additional standards that EHR vendors could integrate into their products (Robeznieks, 2013).

In October 2008, Microsoft announced their **HealthVault** website (HealthVault, 2013) that enables patients to develop **electronic patient records** free of charge. These electronic health records are the patient component of the electronic health record. It is up to the individual as to how much medical information the person wants to store online with this website. The website also has links to several health websites that can assist with exercise programs, heart issues, drug reactions, software that allows users to share their medical information with their providers, etc. In November 2008, the Cleveland Clinic agreed to pilot data exchanges between HealthVault and the Cleveland Clinic's personal health record system. The Clinic enrolled 250 patients in the areas of diabetes, hypertension, and heart disease to test the system. The patients tested their health status at home using blood pressure monitors, weight scales, heart rate monitors, and glucometers. The patients tested themselves and the reports were uploaded to the clinic using HealthVault. They were also able to access health education material on HealthVault regarding their

diseases. This is the first pilot study in the country to assess this tool. The 2010 results of the pilot study indicated that there was a 26–71% increase in time intervals between doctor appointments. Heart patients made more appointments with their physicians as well (iMedicalApps, 2013). In 2010, Microsoft released a new version of HealthVault, Healthvault Community Connect, which allows patients to preregister for hospital procedures and admissions via the hospital's Web portal. Patients can create a HealthVault personal e-health record account. When patients are discharged from the hospital, copies of their hospital care are uploaded to the patient's HealthVault account for the patient's accessibility. Microsoft Healthvault can now communicate with many healthcare websites, mobile applications, and personal health devices, which enable patients to more quickly upload their health data (HealthVault, 2013).

PRIMARY CARE INFORMATION PROJECT IN NEW YORK CITY MODEL

In 2008, the New York City Department of Health and Mental Hygiene (DOHMH), as part of a $27 million mayoral initiative to improve the quality and efficiency of health care in New York City, developed the **Primary Care Information Project** (PCIP) to support the adoption and use of prevention-oriented EHRs primarily among providers who care for the city's underserved and vulnerable populations. DOHMH is working with a vendor, eClinicalWorks—a leading provider of integrated end-to-end EHRs and practice management systems for multilocation, multispecialty medical practices. PCIP involved primary care practices located in underserved communities (including family medicine, pediatrics, internal medicine, and obstetrics/gynecology). In order to participate in the project and receive the eClinicalWorks software, physicians contributed $4,000 and a commitment to bring their technology and infrastructure up to market standards. The project recruited more than 1,600 physicians who serve 200,000 patients in New York City in locations including outpatient clinics, community health centers, small group physician practices, and a women's jail. It is a difficult process because it is a major change, but it has been cost effective and efficient. As of 2013, the PCIP has helped more than 3,200 providers implement EHRs, and also has provided technical assistance to more than 7,700 providers in New York City. PCIP offers demonstrable evidence of the potential for health IT. The sooner everyone understands that implementing EHRs in physicians' offices is the starting line, not the finish line, the sooner EHRs can realize their potential as a tool to lower cost and improve care. Future plans are to use the PCIP data to understand the population health of New York City as a whole, not just patients in participating PCIP practices. They are working in partnership with the City University of New York School of Public Health with funding from the Robert Wood Johnson Foundation, the de Beaumont Foundation, the Robin Hood Foundation, and the New York State Health Foundation to benchmark the PCIP data against other data sources and calling the new EHR-based population health surveillance system "The NYC Macroscope." They also hope to help other regions and organizations learn from the work using EHRs for population health surveillance (Singer, 2013; New York City DOHMH, 2009).

Computerized information systems that are seen in finance, manufacturing, and retail have not achieved the same penetration in health care. EHRs have captured the attention of politicians, insurance companies, and practitioners as a way to improve patient safety because patient information will be more complete and standardized, which will enhance the decision-making process of a practitioner (Murer, 2007). Major barriers to EHR implementation have been discussed, including training and financial impact of an organization as the system becomes integrated with daily operations. However, there are legal issues associated with the implementation of an EHR.

There may be medical malpractice concerns when a physician initially adopts an EHR due to errors when transferring patient data from a paper system to an electronic system. Another legal issue is the electronic definition of a legal patient record. A traditional patient record is a folder containing a paper trail of patient visits, prescriptions, and tests. During a trial, what constitutes an electronic patient record? A report is generated by the EHR software that does not look like the actual screen data of the patient. As with patient paper files, there are certainly issues with medical errors related to entering the patient information into the system. For example, a family physician using an EHR system nearly prescribed the incorrect medication because of an incorrect click of the mouse. Lastly, the other issue is the protection of the data. Depending on who has access to the patient data in the healthcare facility, there may be breaches of confidentiality (Gamble, 2012).

CLINICAL DECISION SUPPORT SYSTEMS

Artificial intelligence (AI) is a field of computerized methods and technologies created to imitate human decision making. A technique of AI is **expert systems** (ESs), which were developed to imitate experts' knowledge in decision making (Coiera, 2003). **Electronic clinical decision support systems** (CDSSs) are systems that are designed to integrate medical information, patient information, and a decision-making tool to generate information to assist with cases. They are a type of knowledgebase system. The key functions of a CDSS are (1) administrative, (2) case management, (3) cost control, and (4) decision support. Administrative protocols consist of clinical coding and documentation for procedure approval and patient referrals if necessary. Case management control focuses on the management of patients to ensure they are receiving timely interventions. Cost control is a focus because the system monitors orders for tests and medication, which reduces unnecessary interventions (Perreault & Metzger, 1999).

Specifically, ESs can be used to alert and remind healthcare providers of a patient's condition change, or to have a laboratory test or an intervention performed. An ES can also assist with a diagnosis using the system's database. The system can expose any weaknesses in a treatment plan or check for drug interactions and allergies. A system can also interpret imaging tests routinely to flag any abnormalities. It is important to note that the more complex duties of a system require the integration of an EHR system so the system can interface with the patient data (Coiera, 2003).

Research over the past several years has indicated that CDSSs have many potential benefits that can be classified into three categories: (1) improved patient safety, (2) improved quality of care, and (3) improved efficiency in healthcare delivery. Although the barriers to implementation were identified previously, the benefits for many institutions have outweighed those barriers so they have found ways to utilize these CDSSs. More CDSSs are being developed to provide information for various types of diseases (Open Clinical, 2013).

COMPUTERIZED PHYSICIAN ORDER ENTRY

Computerized physician order entry (CPOE) systems are CDSSs that enable a patient's provider to enter a prescription order or order for a lab or diagnostic test in a computer system. The order entry has four components: (1) information can be entered from a handheld device, laptop, or desktop computer; (2) it enables the provider to order a test, prescription, or procedure; (3) it is connected to a decision support system that alerts providers to any problems with their orders; and (4) it can be integrated into the overall computer system of the organization. The CPOE first appeared in 1971 when NASA Space Center and Lockheed Corporation developed a system for a hospital in California. It improves quality assurance in patient care, thus reducing medical errors, (Ash, Gorman, Seshardri, & Hersch, 2004). Similar to the EHR, barriers to implementing a CPOE system are the initial financial investment, the customization requirement with the current organization's computer system, medical and administrative training to use this system, and staff's fear of change. These barriers can be addressed before successful implementation of a CPOE.

E-prescribing, a form of CPOE, consists of medication history, benefits information, and processing new and existing prescriptions. According to the 2012 *National Progress Report on E-Prescribing and Safe-Rx Rankings*, 93% of internists, 85% of cardiovascular specialists, and 84% of family practice providers have adopted e-prescribing. Nearly 70% of physicians' offices prescribe and nearly 90% of prescribers also use an electronic health record. Over 90% of pharmacies can accept electronic prescriptions (Surescripts, 2012). Medication ordering and the administration of these medications can be incorrectly given to a patient because of similar sounding names, similar dosages, and similar labeling. E-prescibing can be performed on a desk computer, laptop, or handheld device that will record physicians' prescription orders, which eliminates having an individual read a handwritten prescription. CPOE also includes a decision support system that includes possible drug interactions and dosage information that assist with the physician making the best decision possible for a patient.

Section 132 of the Medicare Improvements for Patients and Providers Act of 2008 (MIPPA) authorized incentives to encourage physicians to e-prescibe. In January 2009, Medicare and some private healthcare plans began paying a bonus to physicians who e-prescibe to their Medicare patients. Since 2012, Medicare has also penalized physicians who do not e-prescibe by reducing their reimbursement rates by 1%, 1.5% for 2013, and 2% for 2014 and all subsequent years (CMS, 2013b). IT companies are providing free software to physicians to encourage them to electronically prescribe. This system can be used alone but it is best used with the EHR system because it integrates the information from the patient's EHR into its decision making.

PHARMACY BENEFIT MANAGERS

Technology-based tools provide exceptional value to the prescription benefits of a health insurance program. E-presicing will become more commonplace with the mandates of Medicare. In order to manage this technology effectively and efficiently, a **pharmacy benefit manager** (PBM) uses technology-based tools to assess and evaluate the management of the prescription component so it can be customized to address the needs of the organization. PBMs are companies that administer drug benefits for employers and health insurance carriers. They contract with managed care organizations, self-insured employers, Medicaid and Medicare managed care plans, federal health insurance programs, and local government organizations. Approximately 95% of all patients with drug coverage received benefits through a PBM. They manage approximately 70% of more than 3 billion prescriptions in the United States each year. The PBM integrates medical and pharmacy data of the population to determine which interventions are the most cost-effective and clinically appropriate (Federal Trade Commission, 2011).

DRUG–DRUG INTERACTIONS

Drug–drug interactions (DDIs) are used by software programs to alert pharmacists and clinicians about potential drug interactions. These alerts can be notifying the provider that two drugs may interact or there may be management strategies provided regarding the DDIs. DDI software programs can be very beneficial to providers but must be updated continually to ensure there is current information provided regarding drug interactions (Murphy et al., 2009).

TELEHEALTH

Telehealth is the broad term that encompasses the use of IT to deliver education, research, and clinical care. An important activity of telehealth is the use of email between providers and their patients. In an American Medical Association 2004 survey, approximately 25% of physicians reported that they communicated with their patients via email. Telehealth also includes communication between healthcare providers. **E-health** refers to the use of the Internet by both individuals and healthcare professionals to access education, research, and products and services. There are several websites such as WebMD and Healthline that provide consumers with general healthcare information. A 2008 study that examined why consumers access the Internet found that consumers perceived the Internet as an alternative source for health information. Consumers used the Internet as a way to avoid visiting a provider and to increase their access to health care. It also provided a way of obtaining information discreetly and anonymously, as well as a source of support groups. It is important to emphasize that consumers must be conscious of the quality of the websites they access to ensure the information they are receiving is accurate (Leung, 2008).

Telemedicine refers to the use of IT to enable healthcare providers to communicate with rural care providers regarding patient care or to communicate directly with patients regarding treatment. The ultimate goal of telemedicine is to improve the patient's health status. The basic form of telemedicine is a telephone consultation. There are growing IT applications for telemedicine, including smart phones, video conferencing, and email (American Telemedicine Association, 2012). Telemedicine is most frequently used in pathology and radiology because images can be transmitted to a distant location where a specialist will read the results. Telemedicine is becoming more common because it increases healthcare access to remote locations such as rural areas. It is also a cost-effective mode of treatment. Telemedicine includes:

1. Synchronous consulting between primary care providers and specialists electronically

2. Remote patient monitoring, which includes sending patient data to a remote location electronically

3. Providing electronic health consumer information

4. Medical education to healthcare professionals

The information can be sent electronically via networks and websites (American Telemedicine Association, 2012).

For example, eEmergency, established in 2009, provides electronic immediate access of emergency certified physicians and nurses to rural providers to help them with diagnosis of patients with critical conditions. Since its inception in 2009, eEmergency has served more than 15,000 patients at 70 locations. Rural clinicians and administrators agreed that eEmergency services

have demonstrated significant impact on the quality of clinical services provided in rural areas (American Telemedicine Association, 2013).

As EHRs are used more frequently, it will be possible to provide more comprehensive services. A limitation may be how to reimburse a provider for providing an electronic consultation. Another limitation may also be if there are issues with reimbursement across state lines (Anderson, Rice, & Kominski, 2007).

CHIEF INFORMATION OFFICER

As more healthcare services are delivered electronically, many healthcare organizations have designated a chief information officer (CIO) to manage the organization's information systems. Some organizations may also refer to this position as a **chief technology officer (CTO)** or they may have both. Normally, the CIO is a vice president of the organization and the CTO reports to that position. The CIO also integrates HIT into the organization's strategic plan. The CIO must have knowledge of current information technologies as they apply to the healthcare industry and how new technology can apply to the organization. The CIO is also responsible for motivating employees whenever there is any technological change (Oz, 2006). C. Martin Harris, who is the CIO of the Cleveland Clinic, feels that the challenge of the CIO (who he believes is a change agent) is to move from the implementing of the EHR to continuing to provide quality care to the patient by developing an integrated system model regardless of the size of the organization or the location of the organization. As more health care is being delivered by technology, it will be the responsibility of the CIO to develop a model that is patient-oriented rather than operations-oriented (Harris, 2008).

COUNCIL FOR AFFORDABLE QUALITY HEALTH CARE

The Council for Affordable Quality Health Care (CAQH), a nonprofit organization, consists of alliances of health plans and trade associations that discuss efficiency initiatives to streamline healthcare administration by working with healthcare plans, providers, the government, and consumers. As part of their initiative, they have created a **Committee on Operating Rules for Information Exchange** (CORE), which borrows from the banking industry's standards for one of the largest electronic payment systems in the world. Based on stakeholder input, CORE has set up standards and operating rules for streamlining processes between providers and healthcare plans. This system allows for real-time access to patient information pre- and post-care. Established by DHHS, the Health Information Technology Standards Panel (HITSP) utilized the CORE platform in its first set of data standards. HITSP is working toward the national integration of both public and private healthcare data standards for sharing among all organizations. As part of the required data standards mandated by the Affordable Care Act, the CORE is being used for data exchange of EHRs to ensure compliance with the Health Insurance Portability and Accountability Act (HIPAA) and other standards (CAQH, 2013).

OTHER APPLICATIONS

Enterprise Data Warehouse

Enterprise data warehouses (EDWs) are developed to provide information that helps organizations in strategic decision making. Data warehousing requires an integration of many computer systems across an organization. Older systems, often referred to as **legacy systems**, are difficult to integrate but worthwhile because they further supported strategic decision making. Business EDWs collect numeric data to assess trends. Retail, banking, and manufacturing use EDWs because these industries usually have repetitive actions that can be easily categorized. For example, banks have savings accounts, CDs, Roth IRAs, money markets, etc. It is very easy to analyze that type of data. Healthcare transactions can occur in the hospital, in community health centers, and in physicians' offices, and each transaction is unique. Other patient healthcare data may not be numeric (Inmon, 2007). There is written information that needs to be integrated into a system such as a physician's prognosis. Therefore, a healthcare EDW must be developed that acknowledges these differences. One of the first healthcare systems to utilize an EDW was the Veterans Health Administration (VHA) (VHA, 2013).

Veterans Health Administration's Corporate Data Warehouse

IOM has indicated that the VHA's HIT system is one of the best in the nation. However, VHA's system was once considered inefficient. VA's Office of Information and Technology's mission is to provide high performance clinical data that consist of one corporate enterprise warehouse and four regional data warehouses.

The purpose of the system is to improve healthcare quality and patient safety by providing data to support healthcare management decision making (Department of Veterans Affairs, 2013).

The Centers for Medicaid and Medicare Services Enterprise Data Warehouse

In 2006, CMS, as a pilot study, developed the largest EDW in history to gather hospital, prescription, and physician data to analyze the claims data for Medicare and Medicaid. They felt that the integration of their data would enable them to analyze the number of claims submitted by providers. It also assisted in identifying any potential fraud and abuse. It was determined that the EDW was successful but they were concerned that it was a claims oriented warehouse. Therefore, part of their EDW strategy is the Integrated Data Repository (IDR), which integrates data from CMS and their partners in a consistent, secure, multi-view environment that includes providers, patients, claims, drug information, and other data as needed (CMS, 2013a).

Radio Frequency Identification

Radio frequency identification (RFID) chips transmit data to receivers. Each of these chips is uniquely identified by a signal indicating where it is located. RFID has been used in the business industry for inventory management by placing a chip on each of the pieces of inventory. Walmart was one of the first retailers to use RFID technology to manage their massive inventory. Recently, RFID technology is being used in many aspects of healthcare industry operations. RFID can be used for the following **(GAO RFID, 2013)**:

- Tracking pharmaceuticals as they are shipped from the manufacturer to the customer
- Tracking pharmaceutical inventory in a healthcare facility
- Tracking wait time in emergency rooms
- Tracking the use of what is being used in surgeries
- Tracking costly medical equipment to ensure easy access
- Identifying providers in hospitals to ensure efficiency in care
- Identifying laboratory specimens to reduce medical errors
- Tracking patients, including infants, while they are hospitalized

- Tracking hazardous materials that pose a public health threat
- Tracking hand washing use to ensure employee compliance

For example, Sharpe Memorial Hospital, San Diego, California's largest emergency trauma center, in an 8-month pilot of the RFID system, tagged expensive, slow moving drugs with RFID chips. During the pilot period, Sharpe was able to reduce drug stock levels and no medications expired unused. Because of the benefits of the pilot, Sharpe is increasing the number of RFID-tagged items in the hospital. In 2012, the largest healthcare market for RFID technology is tracking healthcare equipment. It is anticipated that the worldwide market will increase to $2.1 billion in 2014 (GAO RFID, 2013).

APPLIED HEALTH INFORMATION TECHNOLOGY

The PhreesiaPad

Chaim Indig and Evan Roberts, both younger than 30 years old, spent a year examining the healthcare market. They felt, as entrepreneurs, that the healthcare industry was the best entry for them to start a business. They realized that patient check-in at doctors' offices was a problem. Backed by venture capital firms and with advice from medical professionals, they developed PhreesiaPad, a wireless digital device with a touch screen keyboard that allows patients to enter their demographic information and the reason they are visiting the doctor. This new technology eliminates the need for patients to replicate their information each time they pay a visit to the doctor. The software automatically verifies the patient insurance information. If they have a copay or balance, they can pay with a credit or debit card. As of 2011, Phreesia offers a payment plan for the patient on its pad to ensure that providers will be paid. When the patient is finished, a report is automatically generated for the doctor to review before seeing the patient. This increases office efficiency, shortens visit rates, and reduces error rates. This information can also be uploaded to an EHR (Phreesia, 2013).

According to a study conducted by the Medical Group Management Association (MGMA), approximately 30% of patients leave their clinician's office without making any payment, and it takes practices an average of 3.3 billing statements before a patient's outstanding balance is paid in full. The MGMA study also reports that practices wrote off an average of 11.3% of total accounts receivable in the 2010 fiscal year. Phreesia is a tool that can rectify these financial issues (Leatherbury, 2012).

PatientPoint (Formerly Healthy Advice Network)

PatientPoint provides education to patients electronically while in the waiting room or an exam room. Health education information is customized with brand advertising messages displayed on digital flat screens in physicians' waiting rooms. There are 25-minute loops of brand materials that focus on prevention and management of disease. More than 55,000 primary care and specialty physicians have chosen *Healthy Advice* programs for their practices. These offices represent over 435 million patient and caregiver visits annually. *Healthy Advice* programs are also in more than 500 hospitals across the United States (PatientPoint, 2013).

In 2012, **Healthy Advice Network** purchased PatientPoint, which expands their capabilities by providing care coordination, financial solutions, electronic check-ins, health outcomes support, and certification support for new healthcare models such as accountable care (Business Wire, 2012).

MelaFind Optical Scanner

The **MelaFind optical scanner** is not for definitive diagnosis but rather to provide additional information a doctor can use in determining whether or not to order a biopsy. The goal is to reduce the number of patients left with unnecessary biopsy scars, with the added benefit of eliminating the cost of unnecessary procedures. The MelaFind technology (MELA Sciences, Irvington, NY) uses missile navigation technologies originally paid for by the Department of Defense to optically scan the surface of a suspicious lesion at 10 electromagnetic wavelengths (MacRae, 2013).

Electronic Aspirin

A technology under clinical investigation at Autonomic Technologies, Inc., (Redwood City, CA) is a patient-powered tool for blocking pain-causing signals at the first sign of a headache. The system involves the permanent implant of a small nerve-stimulating device in the upper gum on the side of the head normally affected by the headache. When a patient senses the onset of a headache, he or she places a handheld remote controller on the cheek nearest the implant. The resulting signals block the pain-causing neurotransmitters (MacRae, 2013).

Needle-Free Diabetes Care

Echo Therapeutics (Philadelphia, PA) is developing technologies that would replace the patient self-injecting with a needle by using a patch. The company is working on a biosensor patch that reads blood analysis through the skin without drawing blood. The technology involves a handheld electric-toothbrush-like device that removes just enough top-layer skin cells to put the patient's blood chemistry within range of a biosensor. The sensor collects one reading per minute and sends the data wirelessly to a monitor. This monitor will emit audible alarms when there are issues with the patient's glucose levels (Diabetes Health, 2012).

Robotic Checkups

Medical robots can make rounds, checking on patients in different rooms and managing their individual charts and vital signs without direct human intervention. The RP-VITA Remote Presence Robot produced jointly by iRobot Corp. and InTouch Health is the first such autonomous navigation remote-presence robot to receive FDA clearance for hospital use. The device is a mobile cart with a two-way video screen and medical monitoring equipment, programmed to maneuver through healthcare facilities. This is an innovative method of telemedicine (iRobot, 2013).

Sapien Heart Valve

The **Sapien heart valve** is a life-saving alternative to open-heart surgery for patients who need a new valve but are at high risk for surgery. Manufactured by Edwards Life Sciences (Irvine, CA), the Sapien has been available in Europe but is now finding its first use in U.S. heart centers—where it is limited only to the highest at-risk patients. The Sapien valve is inserted by catheter from a small incision near the rib cage. The valve material is made of bovine tissue attached to a stainless-steel stent, which is expanded by inflating a small balloon in the valve space. A simpler procedure with much shorter hospitalizations could

have a positive impact on healthcare costs (Edwards Lifesciences Corporation, 2013).

Acuson P10

Siemens has introduced a pocket-sized ultrasound, **Acuson P10**, which can be used for traditional applications of diagnostic and screening tests. It can be used in outpatient areas, intensive care units, and rescue helicopters to provide instant information to make a diagnosis. The results can be viewed on the screen but can also be uploaded to a computer. This technology eliminates the need for the provider to send the patient to an imaging center (MNT, 2008a).

Piccolo Xpress Chemistry Analyzer

The size of a shoebox, Piccolo xpress is a compact, portable chemistry analyzer that delivers blood test results quickly. The provider places blood and the like on a small disc and slides the disc into the Piccolo xpress. The provider requests tests to be performed using its touch screen display that prints out a hardcopy report in approximately 12 minutes, or the information can be transferred to an EHR. This technology expedites the provider's ability to diagnose a patient (Piccolo xpress, 2013).

THE IMPORTANCE OF HEALTH INFORMATION TECHNOLOGY

A recent study focused on the implementation and management of IT in the hospital setting. Szydlowski and Smith (2009) interviewed six hospital CIOs (or their equivalents) and nurse managers to assess why they used HIT. The CIOs indicated they used HIT to streamline administrative processes in the organization. They all recognized the substantial cost to invest in HIT but understood that the investment was long term and that it would ultimately be very cost-efficient. The nurse managers focused on the ability to reduce medical errors as a result of HIT. They also indicated that having electronic patient data ultimately contributed to more efficient and effective clinical decision making. The barriers to successful implementation identified by both the CIOs and the nurse managers were inadequate training on HIT and the amount of time needed to become familiar with HIT. The concerns the CIOs indicate are also applicable to other healthcare providers such as physician offices and outpatient facilities. Technology can produce innovative ways to improve patient care, and for all of the providers that is the main goal.

CONCLUSION

The healthcare industry has lagged behind other industries utilizing IT as a form of communicating important data. Despite that fact, there have been specific applications developed for HIT such as e-prescibing, telemedicine, ehealth, and specific applied technologies such as the PatientPoint, MelaFind optical scanner, the Phreesia Pad, Sapien heart valve, robotic checkups, Electronic Aspirin, Accuson P10, and the Piccolo xpress, which were discussed in this chapter. Healthcare organizations have recognized the importance of IT and have hired CIOs and CTOs to manage their data. However, healthcare consumers need to embrace an electronic patient record, which is the basis for the Microsoft Health Vault. This will enable patients to be treated effectively and efficiently nationally. The patient health record can be integrated into the electronic health records that are being utilized nationwide. Having the ability to access a patient's health information could assist in reducing medical errors. As a consumer, utilizing a tool like HealthVault could provide an opportunity to consolidate all medical information electronically so, if there are any medical problems, the information will be readily available.

VOCABULARY

Accuson P10

Artificial intelligence

Chief information officer (CIO)

Chief technology officer (CTO)

Committee on Operating Rules for Information Exchange (CORE)

Computerized physician order entry

Corporate data warehouse

Drug–drug interactions

E-health

Electric aspirin

Electronic clinical decision support systems

Electronic health record

Electronic medical record

Electronic patient record

Enterprise data warehouse

E-prescribing

Expert system

Health information systems

Health information technology

HealthVault

Healthy Advice Network

Imaging informatics

Informatics

Information technology (IT)

Legacy systems

Meaningful use

Medical informatics

Melafind optical scanner

National Alliance for Health Information Technology (NAHIT)

Needle-free diabetes care

PatientPoint

Pharmacy benefit manager

Piccolo xpress Chemistry Analyzer

Primary Care Information Project

Radio frequency identification

Robotic checkups

Sapien heart valve

Telehealth

Telemedicine

REFERENCES

American Telemedicine Association. (2012). What is telemedicine? Retrieved from http://www.americantelemed.org/learn

American Telemedicine Association. (2013). Telemedicine case studies. Retrieved from http://www.americantelemed.org/learn/telemedicine-case-studies/case-study-full-page/avera-ecare-supports-675-rural-clinicians-in-the-delivery-of-highest-quality-care

Anderson, R., Rice, T., & Kominksi, G. (2007). *Changing the U.S. health care system*. San Francisco, CA: JosseyBass.

Appleby, C. (2008). IT visionary: G. Octo Barnett, MD. *Most Wired Magazine*. Retrieved from http://www.hhnmostwired.com/hhnmostwired_app/jsp/articledisplay.jsp?dcrpath=HHNM

Ash, J., Gorman, P., Seshadri, V., & Hersh, W. (2004). Computerized physician order entry in U.S. hospitals: Results of a 2002 survey. *Journal of the American Medical Informatics Association*, *11*(2), 95–99.

Buchbinder, S., & Shanks, N. (2007). *Introduction to health care management*. Sudbury, MA: Jones and Bartlett.

Business Wire. (2012). Healthy Advice Network acquires PatientPoint. Retrieved from http://www.businesswire.com/news/home/20120221006477/en/Healthy-Advice%C2%AE-Networks-Acquires-PatientPoint%E2%84%A2

CAQH. (2013). What are operating rules? Retrieved from http://www.caqh.org/CORE_rules.php

Centers for Medicare and Medicaid Services (CMS). (2013a). CMS Integrated Data Repository (IDR). Retrieved from http://www.cms.gov/Research-Statistics-Data-and-Systems/Computer-Data-and-Systems/IDR

Centers for Medicare and Medicaid Services (CMS). (2013b). Electronic prescribing (eRx) incentive program. Retrieved from http://www.cms.gov/Medicare/Quality-Initiatives-Patient-Assessment-Instruments/ERxIncentive/index.html?redirect=/erxincentive

Centers for Medicare and Medicaid Services (CMS). (2013c). Meaningful use. Retrieved from http://www.cms.gov/Regulations-and-Guidance/Legislation/EHRIncentivePrograms/Meaningful_Use.html

Centers for Medicare and Medicaid Services (CMS). (2013d). Medicare and Medicaid EHR incentive program basics. Retrieved from http://www.cms.gov/Regulations-and-Guidance/Legislation/EHRIncentivePrograms/Basics.html

Coiera, E. (2003). *The guide to health informatics* (2nd ed.). London: Hodder Arnold.

Daigrepont, J., & McGrath, J. (2011). EHR critical success factors. In *Complete guide and toolkit to successful EHR adoption* (pp. 13–21). Chicago, IL: HIMSS.

Department of Health and Human Services (DHHS). (2013). Health information technology. Retrieved from http://www.hhs.gov/healthit/onc/background

Department of Veterans Affairs (VA). (2013). Corporate data warehouse. Retrieved from http://www.hsrd.research.va.gov/for_researchers/vinci/cdw.cfm#.UoEl8Y1Fs8p

Diabetes Health. (2012). Needle-free CGM could be available in 2013. Retrieved from http://diabeteshealth.com/read/2012/09/26/7661/needle-free-cgm-could-be-available-in-2013

eJobDescription. (2013). Chief information officer job description. Retrieved from http://www.ejobdescription.com/CIO_Job_Description.html

Edwards Lifesciences Corporation. (2013). Edwards Sapien transcatheter heart valve. Retrieved from http://www.edwards.com/products/transcathetervalve/Pages/THVcategory.aspx

Federal Trade Commission. (2011). FTC and DOJ issue report on competition and health care. Retrieved from http://www.ftc.gov/opa/2004/07/healthcarerpt.shtm

Gamble, M. (2012). 5 legal issues surrounding electronic medical records. Retrieved from http://www .beckershospitalreview.com/legal-regulatory-issues/5-legal-issues-surrounding-electronic-medical-records.html

GAO RFID. (2013). RFID for healthcare industry. Retrieved from http://healthcare.gaorfid.com

Goldstein, M., & Blumenthal, D. (2008). Building an information technology infrastructure. *Journal of Law, Medicine & Ethics*, 709–715.

Harris, C. (2008). C. Martin Harris, CIO, Cleveland Clinic. *Health Management Technology*, *29*(7), 10.

HealthVault. (2013). Overview. Retrieved from https://www.healthvault.com/us/en/overview

iMedicalApps. (2013). Cleveland Clinic pilots Microsoft HealthVault. Retrieved from http://www.imedicalapps .com/2010/03/microsoft-healthvault-community-connect-cleveland-clini/

Inmon, B. (2007). Data warehousing in a health care environment. *The Data Newsletter*. Retrieved from http://tdan .com/print/4584

Institute of Medicine (IOM). (2001). Crossing the quality chasm: A new health system for the 21st century. Retrieved from http://www.iom.edu/Reports/2001/Crossing-the-Quality-Chasm-A-New-Health-System-for-the -21st-Century.aspx

iRobot. (2013). InTouch Health and iRobot announce first customers to install RP-VITA, the new face of telemedicine. Retrieved from http://www.irobot.com/us/Company/Press_Center/Press_Releases/Press_Release .aspx?n=050613

Leatherbury, L. (2012). Phreesia increases productivity, improves collections for medical practices. *South Florida Hospital News*. Retrieved from http://southfloridahospitalnews.com/page/Phreesia_Increases_Productivity _Improves_Collections_for_Medical_Practices/7158/1/

Leung, L. (2008). Internet embeddedness: Links with online health information seeking, expectancy value/quality of health information websites, and Internet usage patterns. *Cyber Psychology & Behavior*, *11*(5), 565–569.

MacRae, M. (2013). Top 5 Medical Technology Inventions. Retrieved from https://www.asme.org/engineering-topics /articles/bioengineering/top-5-medical-technology-innovations

MNT. (2008a). ACUSON P10 crosses healthcare boundaries: Handheld pocket ultrasound carries out essential obstetric scanning in Tanzania. Retrieved from http://www.medicalnewstoday.com/articles/114511.php

MNT. (2008b). The National Alliance for Health Information Technology explores next set of strategic initiatives. Retrieved from http://www.medicalnewstoday.com/articles/101878.php

Murer, C. (2007). EHRS: Issues preventing widespread adoption. *Rehab Management*, *20*, 38–39.

Murphy, J., Malone, D., Olson, B., Grizzle, A., Armstrong, E., & Skrepnek, G. (2009). Development of computerized alerts with management strategies for 25 serious drug-drug interactions. American Journal of Health-System Pharmacists, 66, 38–44.

New York City Department of Health and Mental Hygiene (DOHMH). (2009). EHR expansion initiative. Retrieved from http://www.nyc.gov/html/doh/html/pcip/pcipehrapp.shtml

Open Clinical. (2013). Health informatics. Retrieved from http://www.openclinical.org/healthinformatics. html

Oz, E. (2006). *Management information systems*. Mason, OH: Thomson Southwestern.

PatientPoint. (2013). About us. Retrieved from http://www.patientpoint.com/aboutus/formerly-healthy-advice.aspx

Perreault, L., & Metzger, J. (1999). A pragmatic framework for understanding clinical decision support. *Journal of Health care Information Management*, *13*, 2, 5–21.

Phreesia. (2013). Phreesia news. Retrieved from http://www.phreesia.com/news.asp.

Piccolo xpress. (2013). Overview. Retrieved from http://www.piccoloxpress.com/products/piccolo/overview

Robeznieks, A. (2013). Pediatricians offer model for kids' EHRs. Retrieved from http://www.modernphysician.com/article/20130404/MODERNPHYSICIAN/304049975

Shields, A., Shin, P., Leu, M., Levy, D., Betancourt, R., Hawkins, D., & Proser, M. (2007). Adoption of health information technology in community health centers: Results of a national survey. *Health Affairs, 26*(3), 1373–1383.

Singer, J. (2013). EHRs are a tool not a solution: The NYC primary care information project. Retrieved from http://healthaffairs.org/blog/2013/03/13/ehrs-are-a-tool-not-a-solution-the-nyc-primary-care-information-project

Surescripts. (2012). National Progress Report on EPrescribing and Safe-Rx Rankings. Retrieved from http://www.surescripts.com/about-e-prescribing/progress-reports/national-progress-reports#downloads

Szydlowski, S., & Smith, C. (2009). Perspectives from nurse leaders and chief information officers on health information technology implementation. *Hospital Topics: Research and Perspectives on Healthcare, 87*(1), 3–9.

Valerius, J. (2007). The electronic health record: What every information manager should know. *The Information Management Journal, 4*(1), 56–59.

Veterans Health Administration (VHA). (2013). VHA Corporate Data Warehouse (CDW). Retrieved from http://www.virec.research.va.gov/CDW/Overview.htm

Ventres, W., & Shah, A. (2007). How do EHRs affect the physician patient relationship? *American Family Physician, 75*(9), 1385–1390.

Vreeman, D., Taggard, S., Rhine, M., & Worrell, T. W. (2006). Evidence for electronic health record systems in physical therapy. *Physical Therapy, 86,* 3, 434–446.

Walker, J. M. (2013). Using the EHR to transform healthcare. Retrieved from http://www.ehcca.com/presentations/hitsymposium/walker_2a.pdf

Whitman, J. C., & David, S. (2007). Effectively integrating your EMR/EHR initiative. *The Physician Executive, 33*(5), 56–59.

NOTES

STUDENT ACTIVITY 10-1

IN YOUR OWN WORDS

Based on this chapter, please provide an explanation of the following concepts in your own words. DO NOT RECITE the text.

Health information technology: _____

_____

_____

Expert systems: _____

_____

_____

Electronic health records: _____

_____

_____

Legacy systems: _____

_____

_____

Enterprise data warehouse: _____

_____

_____

Radio frequency identification: _____

_____

_____

Healthy Advice Network: _____

_____

_____

Computerized physician order entry (CPOE) systems: _____

_____

_____

Phreesia Pad: _____

_____

_____

STUDENT ACTIVITY 10-2

Complete the following case scenarios based on the information provided in the chapter. Your answer must be IN YOUR OWN WORDS.

REAL LIFE APPLICATIONS: CASE SCENARIO ONE

As one of four physicians, you all are interested in implementing an EHR system. You heard there was an excellent project in New York City that has successfully implemented a system.

ACTIVITY

You schedule a visit to New York City to visit their project. You prepare a report for your physicians on the results of their project.

RESPONSES

_____

_____

_____

_____

_____

_____

_____

_____

_____

_____

_____

_____

_____

CASE SCENARIO TWO

As a new physician, one of your goals is to increase access to providing health care in the rural areas of your state. You have heard that telemedicine may be an opportunity for you.

ACTIVITY

You perform research on the advantages and disadvantages of telemedicine for your practice.

RESPONSES

_____

_____

_____

_____

_____

_____

_____

_____

_____

_____

_____

_____

_____

_____

_____

CASE SCENARIO THREE

You were just promoted to CIO of your hospital. One of your goals is to improve the efficiencies of hospital operation. You heard that RFID is a viable option to pursue.

ACTIVITY

Perform research on RFID technology and its application to the healthcare industry. Select three types of RFID applications that will work for your hospital and develop a report for your CEO.

RESPONSES

_____

_____

_____

_____

_____

_____

_____

_____

_____

_____

_____

_____

_____

_____

_____

CASE SCENARIO FOUR

You were just hired as the office manager of a six-physician office. As part of your responsibilities, one of the physicians asked you to investigate the possibility of an electronic health record (EHR) system. They had heard that the federal government has an incentive program to implement an EHR system.

ACTIVITY

Visit the www.cms.gov website and research the CMS incentive program. Prepare a report for your physicians.

RESPONSES

_____

_____

_____

_____

_____

_____

_____

_____

_____

_____

_____

_____

_____

_____

STUDENT ACTIVITY 10-3

INTERNET EXERCISES

Write your answers in the space provided.

- Visit each of the websites listed here.
- Name the organization.
- Locate their mission statement on their website.
- Provide a brief overview of the activities of the organization.
- How do these organizations participate in the U.S. healthcare system?

Websites

http://www.aap.org

Organization Name: _____

Mission Statement:

_____

_____

_____

Overview of Activities: _____

_____

_____

Importance of organization to U.S. health care:

_____

_____

_____

http://www.patientpoint.com

Organization Name: _____

Mission Statement:

_____

_____

_____

Overview of Activities: _____

_____

_____

Importance of organization to U.S. health care:

_____

_____

_____

Organization Name: _____

Mission Statement:

_____

_____

_____

Overview of Activities: _____

_____

_____

Importance of organization to U.S. health care:

_____

_____

_____

Organization Name: _____

Mission Statement:

_____

_____

_____

Overview of Activities: _____

_____

_____

Importance of organization to U.S. health care:

_____

_____

_____

Organization Name: _____

Mission Statement:

_____

_____

_____

Overview of Activities: _____

_____

_____

Importance of organization to U.S. health care:

_____

_____

_____

http://www.healthvault.com

Organization Name: _____

Mission Statement:

_____

_____

_____

Overview of Activities: _____

_____

_____

Importance of organization to U.S. health care:

_____

_____

_____

STUDENT ACTIVITY 10-4

DISCUSSION QUESTIONS

The following are suggested discussion questions for this chapter.

(1) What is radio frequency identification? Using the textbook and the Internet, discuss three ways this technology applies to healthcare.

_____

_____

_____

_____

(2) What is PatientPoint? Do you think this is an effective way to educate patients? Defend your answer.

_____

_____

_____

_____

(3) What is Electronic Aspirin? What are the advantages and disadvantages of this new product. Would you use this product? Defend your answer.

_____

_____

_____

_____

(4) What are two advantages and two disadvantages of EHR? What is meaningful use? What are the barriers to implementing an EHR system?

_____

_____

_____

_____

(5) What is the Primary Care Information Project? Do you think it has been successful?

_____

_____

_____

_____

_____

The Navigate Companion Website for this text is a great source for additional information on the U.S. healthcare system. You can gain a new perspective on many of the topics presented in this chapter by visiting http://go .jblearning.com/Niles2e. You'll find additional student activities, further reading, and interactive study tools that explore:

- Electronic health records
- New applications of technology in health care
- Reducing medical errors with technology
- And much more.

Chapter 11

Healthcare Law

LEARNING OBJECTIVES

The student will be able to:

- Describe the legal relationship between patient and provider.

- Apply civil and criminal liability concepts to healthcare providers and consumers.

- Analyze six employment laws and their importance to the healthcare workplace.

- Define and discuss the different contracts between a patient and healthcare provider.

- Analyze the purpose of antitrust law.

- Discuss the importance of the original Patient Bill of Rights.

DID YOU KNOW THAT?

- The Physician Referral Laws were passed because providers were referring patients to medical services in which they or family members had a financial interest.

- *Qui tam* provisions, a concept used in antitrust law, is Latin for *he who sues*. This provision enables individuals to sue providers for fraudulent activity against the federal government, recovering a portion of the funds returned to the government.

- In response to the Affordable Care Act antifraud initiatives, over 15,000 Medicare providers were expelled from the system for fraudulent activity.

- According to civil law, a surgeon performing surgery without consent could be considered assault and battery.

- The most important relationship in the healthcare system is the relationship between the patient—the healthcare consumer—and their provider, which could be a physician or an organization such as a clinic or hospital where the physician has a relationship.

- Defensive medicine occurs when clinicians order more tests and provide more services than necessary to protect themselves from malpractice lawsuits.

INTRODUCTION

To be an effective healthcare manager, it is important to understand basic legal and ethical principles that influence the work environment, including the legal relationship between the organization and the consumer—the healthcare provider and the patient. The basic concepts of law, both civil and criminal healthcare law, tort reform, employment-related legislation, safety in the workplace, the legal relationship between the provider and the patient will be discussed in this chapter.

BASIC CONCEPTS OF HEALTHCARE LAW

The healthcare industry is one of the most heavily regulated industries in the United States. Those who provide, receive, pay for, and regulate healthcare services are affected by the law (Miller, 2006). **Law** is a body of rules for the conduct of individuals and organizations. Law is created so there is a minimal standard of action required by individuals and organizations. There is law created by federal, state, and local governments. As the judiciary system interprets previous legal decisions regarding a case, they are creating **common law** (Buchbinder & Shanks, 2007). The minimal standard for action is federal law, although state law may be more stringent. Legislature creates laws that are called **statutes**. Both common law and statutes are then interpreted by administrative agencies by developing **rules and regulations** that interpret the law.

There are civil and criminal laws that affect the healthcare industry. **Civil law** focuses on the wrongful acts against individuals and organizations based on contractual violations. **Torts**, derived from the French word for *wrong*, is a category of wrongful acts, in civil law, which may not have a preexisting contract. To prove a civil infraction, you do not need as much evidence as in a criminal case. **Criminal law** is concerned with actions that are illegal based on court decisions. In order to convict someone of a criminal activity, it has to be proven without a reasonable doubt of guilt. Examples of criminal law infractions would be Medicare and Medicaid fraud (Miller 2006).

As stated earlier, torts are wrongdoings that occur to individuals or organizations regardless of whether a contract is in place. There are several different types of violations that can apply to health care. There are two basic healthcare torts: (1) negligence, which involves the unintentional act or omission of an act that would contribute to the positive health of a patient, and (2) intentional torts, such as assault and battery or invasion of privacy (Buchbinder & Shanks, 2007).

An example of **negligence** would be if a provider does not give appropriate care or withholds care that results in damages to the patient. In the healthcare industry, **intentional torts** such as assault and battery would be a surgeon performing surgery on a patient without his or her consent (Bal, 2009). Invasion of privacy would be the violation of patients' health records. Privacy issues relating to patient information is a major issue in the healthcare industry. These activities are categorized under the term *medical malpractice*.

According to the *American Heritage Dictionary* (2000), **medical malpractice** is the "improper or negligent treatment of a patient by a provider which results in injury, damage or loss" (p. 1060). According to the Institute of Medicine's (IOM) landmark report *To Err Is Human*, medical malpractice has resulted in approximately 80,000–100,000 deaths per year. Disputes over improper care of a patient have hurt both the providers and patients. Patients have sued physicians because they feel their provider has not provided them the proper level of care compared to the standard of care in the industry.

According to Bal (2009, p. 339), "the injured patient must show that the physician acted negligently in rendering care, and that such negligence resulted in injury. To do so, four legal elements must be proven: (1) a professional duty owed to the patient; (2) breach of such duty; (3) injury caused by the breach; and (4) resulting damages. Money damages, if awarded, typically take into account both actual economic loss and noneconomic loss, such as pain and suffering."

TORT REFORM DISCUSSION

As a result of the number of malpractice claims in the United States, malpractice insurance premiums have increased. This has resulted in the concept of **defensive medicine**, which means that providers often order more tests and provide more services than necessary to protect themselves from malpractice lawsuits (DefensiveMedicine, 2013). Historically, there have been continued malpractice insurance crises during the 1970s, 1980s, and, most recently, the beginning of this century (Danzon, 1995). The issues in the 1970s led to joint underwriting measures that required insurance companies to offer medical malpractice if the physician purchased other insurance. In some states, compensation funds were established to offset large award settlements. The level of malpractice suits lessened but the amount of awards were still huge. During the mid-1980s, the premiums were rising again—nearly 75%. It was determined that any initiatives established in the 1970s were not effective (Rosenbach & Stone, 1990). A third malpractice insurance crisis occurred in the 2000s. Issues with obtaining medical malpractice insurance in several states have increased, forcing physicians to join underwriting associations, which can charge exorbitant premiums.

As a result of the recent malpractice insurance crisis, more states have adopted statutory caps on monetary damages that a plaintiff can recover in malpractice claims. States felt that a cap on monetary damages would have less impact on malpractice insurance premiums because the less an insurance company has paid out in insurance claims, the less the insurance company would have to raise insurance rates. Many states have established caps on awards. For example, Florida, Kansas, Maryland, Massachusetts, Michigan, North Carolina, and Texas have established **noneconomic damages** for different medical cases (LaMance, 2012). Noneconomic damages means cases that are claiming damage for pain, emotional suffering, and loss of enjoyment (USLegal, 2013). However, the following states have no limits on awards for medical practice: Alabama, Arizona, Georgia, Illinois, Kentucky, New Hampshire, Missouri, Ohio, Pennsylvania, Washington, and Wyoming (LaMance, 2012). In 2012, New Hampshire proposed a patient-centered process that if the patients settle early, they will receive payment within months, instead of a year, which is typical (Pho, 2012). In 2012, Oregon was also pursuing an "early settlement" by having the physician and patient meet to discuss the alleged injury with an attempt to resolve it through a mediation process first, prior to a trial (Budnick, 2013). States have also developed other **tort reform** measures that relate to filing claims, standard of care, attorney fees, statute of limitations on claims, and alternatives to the court system to resolving disputes.

Many legal factors have contributed to the increase in claims. Voluntary hospitals are no longer exempt from malpractice suits. The fact that employers now have to take responsibility for their employees' wrongdoing has also increased claims. The concept of informed consent for the patient has expanded and therefore increased claims. The acceptable **standard of care**, which used to be strictly based on a locality rule, has now become a state or national standard, which has also resulted in increased claims (Bal, 2009). Statutes specifying the acceptable standard of care in a malpractice suit in a local setting were replaced by a national or state standard. This increased the ability to locate expert witnesses that would testify at a trial regarding the standard of care given to the plaintiff.

Expert witness qualifications are also specified to ensure that the witness is indeed an expert in his or her field. Clinical practice guidelines, which are developed to ensure an acceptable standard of care, are also used (Miller, 2006). The informed consent of a patient to receive care was also expanded in the 1970s to become a patient-friendly standard that specifies what information must be given to patients to ensure they are making an informed decision regarding their care (Office of Technology Assessment [OTA], 1993).

Some physicians are leaving private practice because they can no longer afford the premiums—they are now in administrative positions at all levels of government, are academicians, or are teaching at medical universities. The malpractice insurance issues have forced many states to review their malpractice guidelines. Some states' tort reform, which has imposed limits on the amount awarded, continues to cause controversy. However, recent federal studies have indicated that imposing caps on awards may be an effective method to reduce malpractice costs and to discourage frivolous lawsuits. In addition, the U.S. Supreme Court ruled that any awards must be included in an individual's taxed income (Miller, 2006).

THE LEGAL RELATIONSHIP BETWEEN THE PROVIDER AND CONSUMER

The most important relationship in the healthcare system is the relationship between the patient—the healthcare consumer—and his or her provider, which could be a physician or an organization such as a clinic or hospital where the physician has a relationship. A physician can establish a relationship with a patient in three ways: (1) establishing a **contractual relationship to care for a designated population**, (2) establishing an **express contract** with a patient under mutual agreement, and (3) establishing a relationship under an **implied contract** (Laws, 2013).

In order for a contract to exist, there must be four components of the contract: (1) agreement between two parties, (2) both parties must be competent to consent to the agreement, (3) the agreement must be of value, and (4) the agreement must be legal. If any of these components are missing, the parties are not bound by the agreement to comply with the terms. It is important to emphasize that the agreement does not have to be formally written (Buchbinder & Shanks, 2007). This chapter will discuss several types of contracts as they pertain to health care.

A contract to care for a designated population is indicative of a health maintenance organization (HMO) or managed care contract. A physician is contractually required to care for those member patients of a managed care organization. They may sign contracts to provide care for hospitals, schools, or long-term care facilities that have designated populations (Miller, 2006).

An express contract is a simple contract—merely a mutual agreement of care between the physician and patient. The physician may define the limitations of the contract, including the parameters of care. They may only decide to practice in a certain geographic area or, if they are a specialist, they would only provide services in that area of specialty. An implied contract can be implied from a physician's actions. If a physician gives advice regarding medical treatment, there is an implied contract (Laws, 2013). The relationship between a patient and hospital, a **contractual right to admission**, can be considered a contract if a hospital has contracted to treat certain members of an organization, like a managed care organization; if so, the hospital is required to treat those members. A second example of this type of contractual right to admission is if governmental hospitals, such as county hospitals, are required to provide care for patients regardless of ability to pay (Miller, 2006).

How Does a Relationship with a Provider End?

According to the American Medical Association (AMA), once a patient and physician relationship has started, the physician is legally and ethically obligated to continue the relationship until the patient no longer requires their care. There may be practical reason for a relationship to end such as geographic relocation or change of healthcare insurance. If a patient becomes noncompliant and abusive, the physician has the right to end a relationship. However, to protect the physician from being accused of "**patient abandonment**," the physicians must take steps to properly end the relationship. If a patient withdraws from the relationship with the provider, then the physician no longer has a duty to provide follow-up. Also, if medical care is no longer needed, the relationship naturally is completed. If a patient is transferred to another provider, the provider then establishes a relationship with the new patient. However, a physician could withdraw from a relationship by giving sufficient notice of their withdrawal or providing their patient with a referral. However, if a physician withdraws from a relationship without

sufficient reason, the provider may be liable for breach of contract or patient abandonment. The AMA (2013) provides the following five steps for a physician to terminate a relationship:

1. Giving the patient written notice, preferably certified mail

2. Providing the patient with a specific reason for termination

3. Continuing to provide care for a reasonable period of time so the patient can find other care

4. Providing assistance to the patient to find other care

5. Offering to transfer all medical records with patient permission

HEALTHCARE-RELATED LEGISLATION

Healthcare Consumer Laws

Other legislative acts will be discussed thoroughly throughout the text; however, these acts directly impact how health care is provided to consumers.

Hill-Burton Act

The **Hill-Burton Act** of 1946 was passed because the federal government recognized the lack of hospitals in the United States during the 1940s. They passed the Hospital Survey and Construction Act, more commonly known as the Hill-Burton Act. Federal grants were provided to states for hospital construction to ensure there were 4.5 beds per 1,000 people (Shi & Singh, 2008). This act had a huge influence on creating more hospitals nationally. If a hospital received federal funds from the Hill-Burton Act, it agreed to a community service requirement, so any person residing in the area of the hospital cannot be denied treatment in the portion of the hospital financed by the Hill-Burton Act (exceptions: lack of needed services, unavailability of the services needed, or the patient's ability to pay). Nursing homes are also eligible for Hill-Burton funding so the regulations also apply to them. Inability to pay cannot be a basis for denial when the person needs emergency services that the hospital can provide. There are several exclusions to these regulations:

- If hospitalization is not medically necessary, there is no right to admission.

- Scope of services: If the hospital does not provide the services needed by the patient, it does not have to admit the patient.

- Capacity: If space or staffing is not available, the hospital does not have to admit a patient; however, it has to stabilize the patient for transport to another facility (Shi & Singh, 2008).

- The facilities must provide free care to people in the amount of 10% of the amount of grants received or 3% of their annual operating costs (U.S. Department of Health & Human Services, 2013b).

Hospitals that are under the Hill-Burton Act are required to post notices about the program in their area of admission. These notices must be easy to read and in languages appropriate to the community.

Emergency Medical Treatment and Active Labor Act

The **Emergency Medical Treatment and Active Labor Act (EMTALA)** of 1986, enforced by the Centers for Medicare and Medicaid Services (CMS) and the Office of Inspector General (OIG), requires Medicare participants to receive emergency care from a hospital or medical entity that provides dedicated emergency services. This was passed as part of the Consolidated Omnibus Budget Reconciliation Act of 1985 (COBRA). This requirement is a type of fiduciary duty that means the healthcare provider or organization is obligated to provide care to someone who has placed his or her trust in them (CMS, 2013). This law is also called the "antidumping" statute because, prior to the enactment of this law, many hospitals dumped Medicare patients. Penalties for violating EMTALA include monetary fines, impact on their Joint Commission accreditation status, license suspension, and damage to their reputation (Ringholz, 2005). The original act was amended in 2000 and 2006 to strengthen the law. CMS issued guidelines that further explained the act. This legislation protects consumers to ensure they receive appropriate emergency care when they present themselves to regulated hospitals and medical organizations (CMS, 2013).

Children's Health Insurance Program

The **Children's Health Insurance Program (CHIP)** was enacted under the Balanced Budget Act of 1997, is Title XXI of the Social Security Act, and is jointly financed by federal and state funding and administered by the states. Administered by CMS, the purpose of this program is to provide coverage for low-income children younger than the age of 19 years who live above the income level requirements of Medicaid. They cannot be eligible for Medicaid or be covered by private health insurance (National Health Law Program, 2013). Approximately 8 million children who are uninsured and ineligible for public assistance have been positively impacted by this program. Children who are eligible for state health benefit plans are not eligible for CHIP. Studies have indicated that this program has improved access to insurance for children. Legislation was passed that extended the funding for the CHIP program through September 2015 (Kaiser Family Foundation, 2013).

Benefits Improvement and Protection Act

The **Benefits Improvement and Protection Act of 2000 (BIPA)**, formally called the Medicare, Medicaid, and CHIP Benefits Improvement and Protection Act, modifies Medicare payment rates for many services. It also adds coverage for preventive and therapeutic service. It increases federal funding to state programs. From a healthcare consumer perspective, it protects Medicare beneficiaries by granting them the ability to appeal provider termination of services (Congressional Budget Office, 2001). It requires providers to issue a written notice to the patient that coverage has been terminated, giving an end date for the termination. The patient has the right to appeal the decision.

The **HIPAA National Standards** of 2002 to protect patient's personal medical records further protected medical records and other personal health information maintained by healthcare providers, hospitals, insurance companies, and health plans. It gives patients new rights to access of their records, restricts the amount of patient information released, and establishes new restrictions to researchers' access (U.S. Department of Health & Human Services, 2013a).

ANTITRUST LAWS

The purpose of **antitrust law** is to protect the consumer by ensuring there is a market driven by competition so the consumer has a choice for health care. In a sense, antitrust laws protect the competition so the consumer has a choice. Antitrust laws apply to most healthcare organizations. Federal antitrust laws focus on interstate and foreign commerce, but the term "interstate commerce" has been interpreted by the U.S. Supreme Court to include local activities that impact interstate commerce (Miller, 2006).

There are both federal and state antitrust laws. Examples of antitrust issues would be large mergers that would encourage monopolies in health care and price fixing among competitors. There are four main antitrust federal laws that will be discussed in this chapter: the Sherman Antitrust Act, the Clayton Act, the Federal Trade Commission Act, and the Robinson-Patman Act (the amendment to the Clayton Act). These acts are important to know because they were developed to ultimately protect the healthcare consumer and those who provide healthcare services.

There are two federal agencies that enforce antitrust violations: the Federal Trade Commission and the Department of Justice. The **Federal Trade Commission** (FTC), established in 1914 by the **Federal Trade Commission Act**, is one of the oldest federal agencies and is charged with the oversight of commercial acts and practices. Two major activities of the FTC are to maintain free and fair competition in the economy and to protect consumers from misleading practices. They may issue "cease and desist orders" to companies to ensure they stop their practices until a court decides what the company may do (Carroll & Buchholtz, 2009). The **Department of Justice** (DOJ), headed by the U.S. Attorney General, was established in 1870 to handle U.S. legal issues, including the enforcement of federal laws. The DOJ and FTC collaborate on antitrust law enforcement (FTC, 2013).

The **Sherman Act of 1890** focuses on eliminating **monopolies**, which are healthcare organizations that control a market so that the consumer has no choice in health care. It also targets **price fixing** among competitors; price fixing prohibits the consumer from paying a fair price because competitors establish a certain price (by either increasing or lowering prices) among themselves to stabilize the market. Healthcare facilities may also have an agreement on **market division**. This illegal action occurs when one or more health organizations decide which type of services will be offered at each organization. **Tying** refers to healthcare providers that will only sell a product to a consumer who will also buy a second product from them. **Boycotts** are also illegal according to this act. When healthcare providers have an agreement to not deal with anyone outside their group, that is considered interfering with the consumers' rights to choose. **Price information exchange** of services between providers can also be illegal (Miller, 2006). Healthcare providers are protected under the act if it has been determined that hospitals have exclusive contracts with certain providers, which excludes other providers from use of the hospital.

This could be a violation of the act. Violations of the act are considered federal crimes.

The **Clayton Act of 1914** was passed to supplement the Sherman Act, as amended by the Robinson-Patman Act, which issues further restrictions on mergers and acquisitions. With the increasing development of hospital chains, this act has focused on hospitals. There are no criminal violations of this act, unlike the Sherman Act. Any organization considering a merger or acquisition above a certain size must notify both the Antitrust Division of the DOJ and FTC. The act also prohibits other business practices that, under certain circumstances, may harm competition. The act also allows individuals to sue for three times their actual damages plus legal costs.

The **Hart-Scott-Rodino Antitrust Improvement Act of 1976**, as an amendment to the Clayton Act, ensures those hospitals and other entities that entered mergers, acquisitions, and joint ventures must notify DOJ and FTC before any final decisions are made. This is a requirement for any hospitals with greater than $100 million in assets acquiring a hospital with more than $10 million in assets (Buchbinder & Shanks, 2007). The DOJ and FTC will make the final decision on these proposals. This ensures there will not be any type of monopoly within a certain geographic area.

INFORMED CONSENT

The concept of **informed consent** is based on the patient's right to make an informed decision regarding medical treatment. It is a legal requirement in all 50 states. It is more than a patient signing an informed consent form—it is the communication between the provider and patient regarding a specific medical treatment. The provider is responsible for discussing the following information with the patient: the diagnosis if it has been established; the nature of a proposed treatment or operation, including the risks and benefits, any alternatives, and the risks and benefits of the alternatives; and the risks and benefits of not agreeing to the procedure or treatment (AMA, 2013). If a patient did not provide informed consent for a procedure or treatment, it is considered a case of negligence.

The first case of informed consent occurred in the late 1950s. Earlier consent cases were based on **battery**, which is the physical touching of an individual without his or her permission that is considered harmful or offensive. The liability occurred as a result of the unpermitted touching. The patient did not consent to a procedure or treatment and therefore the provider was considered to have committed battery (Miller, 2006). Most cases now revolve around whether a patient was provided adequate information prior to the procedure or treatment being implemented. The second component of informed consent is what information should be given to the patient that will constitute informed consent.

To determine what constitutes informed consent, there are two legal standards that are applied: the reasonable patient and reasonable physician standard. The **reasonable patient standard** focuses on the patient's information needs, including the risks and benefits that allow the patient to make a decision. The **reasonable physician standard** focuses on the standard information that would be given by any physician to a patient contemplating the same procedure or treatment. Most states utilize the reasonable patient standard (Miller 2006).

PATIENT BILL OF RIGHTS

The **Patient Self-Determination Act of 1990** requires hospitals, nursing homes, home health providers, hospices, and managed care organizations that provide services to Medicare- and Medicaid-eligible patients to supply information on patient rights to patients upon admission. It virtually applies to every type of healthcare facility. The facility must provide adult patients with written information, under the state law, about making healthcare decisions. Based on the concept of informed consent, in 1972 the Board of Trustees of the American Hospital Association developed a Patient Bill of Rights. The **Patient Bill of Rights** states that the patient has the right to all information from this provider regarding any testing, diagnoses, and treatments. This information must be provided to the patient in terms that the patient will be able to understand (Rosner, 2004). Eligible health organizations will have the Patient Bill of Rights displayed.

HEALTHCARE FRAUD

Increasing healthcare costs that have impacted public health insurance programs have emphasized the need to combat fraud and abuse of the healthcare system. The U.S. government has estimated that fraud may account for 10% of healthcare expenditures. From 1995 to 2005, DOJ closed nearly 400 healthcare fraud cases worth $9.3 billion (Kesselheim & Studdert, 2008). The centerpiece for fraud recovery is the False Claims Act.

The **False Claims Act**, enacted in 1863, was originally passed to protect the federal government against defense contractors during the Civil War. The False Claims Act has been amended several times throughout the years; however, in the 1990s, the act focused on healthcare fraud, most notably Medicare and Medicaid fraud. The False Claims Act of 1995 imposes criminal penalties on anyone who tries to present fictitious claims for payment to the federal government. It is one of the most powerful government tools to combat civil fraud in health care (Memmott & Makwana, 2007). This act also provides financial incentives for whistleblowers— allowing employees to blow the whistle about contractor fraud against the federal government. Private plaintiffs fulfilling this role are pursuant to the *qui tam* provisions of the act, which means "he who sues" (Miller, 2006). The Deficit Reduction Act of 2005 introduced additional incentives for states to crack down on healthcare fraud by giving the states additional incentives under their own fraud law. What is controversial about this act is that whistle blowers may receive between 15% and 25% of proceeds in the case. As a result of the financial incentive program, the federal government has received $12 billion in returned funds (Carroll & Buchholtz, 2009). According to one report, in 2006, nearly 500 hospitals across the United States were the subject of Medicare fraud. The civil fines for each violation can be $5,500–$11,000. Healthcare organizations may have hundreds of fines so their penalties can be huge (Degnan & Scoggin, 2007).

In December 2001, the federal government, as a result of an administrator employed by a private health insurer and an employer at a pharmaceutical company (the whistle blowers), recovered $95 million from TAP, a pharmaceutical company that encouraged doctors to prescribe their product by providing the product free to doctors, who then billed Medicare for the cost of the product. In August 2001, several executives of a hospital chain, the physicians, and the auditors blew the whistle on Hospital Corporation of America, who submitted claims for unnecessary diagnostic services. The recovery was for nearly $72 million (Kesselheim & Studdert, 2008).

The Stark laws (named after Representative Pete Stark who authored the legislation), also known as the **Physician Self-Referral Laws** or the **Ethics in Patient Referral Act of 1989**, prohibits physicians, including dentists and chiropractors, from referring Medicare and Medicaid patients to other providers for **designated**

health services in which they have a financial interest. These laws directly prohibit many referrals that may increase a provider or family members' financial interest. Designated health services include clinical laboratory services, outpatient prescription drug services, physical and occupational therapy, and imaging services such as magnetic resonance imaging (MRI), and the like. The statute became effective on January 1, 1995, but the regulations interpreting the statute were not released until January 4, 2001 (Gosfield, 2003). Additional Stark amendments expanded the types of services a physician could not refer Medicare and Medicaid patients to if they or a family member has a financial interest. These regulations protect consumers by ensuring they will receive objective referrals for health services.

It is the responsibility of the human resource management department to ensure that employees, both direct and indirect providers of healthcare organizations, are aware of these litigious issues and are trained to deal with patients in accordance with these legal issues. Human resource management must train employees on the impact of employment-related healthcare legislation. The following section outlines major employment-related legislation that influences the healthcare industry.

EMPLOYMENT-RELATED LEGISLATION

Civil Rights Act of 1964, Title VII: This landmark act prohibits discrimination based on race, sex, color, religion, and national origin. Discrimination means making distinctions among people who are different. This legislation is the key legal piece to equal opportunity employment. Two components to this legislation, which will be discussed later, are disparate treatment and disparate impact. It applies to employers with 15 or more employees. This act is enforced by the Equal Employment Opportunity Commission (EEOC).

The Civil Rights Act of 1964, Title VII, created a concept of protected classes to protect these groups from employment discrimination of compensation, conditions, or privileges of employment. The protected classes include sex, age, national origin, race, and religion. A major current issue under the purview of discrimination legislation is sexual harassment. According to the EEOC, **sexual harassment** is defined as unwelcome sexual conduct that has a negative impact on the employee. There are two major distinctions in sexual

harassment: (1) quid pro quo sexual harassment, which occurs when sexual activities occur in return for an employment benefit and (2) when the behavior of coworkers is sexual in nature and creates an uncomfortable work environment. What is more prevalent in sexual harassment is the creation of a hostile work environment. Several court case judgments indicate that repeated suggestive joke telling and lewd photos on display can be legally constituted as a hostile work environment. In the healthcare industry, nurses experience sexual harassment from colleagues, physicians, and patients.

Civil Rights Act of 1991: Title VII only allowed damages for back pay. This act enables individuals to receive both **punitive damages**, which are damages that punish and defendant and **compensatory damages** for financial or psychological harm. This act applies to employers with 15 or more employees. The size of the damages is based on the size of the company: $50,000 for employers with 15 to 100 employees; $100,000 for companies with 101 to 200 employees; $200,000 for employers with 201 to 500 employers; and $300,000 for employers with more than 500 employees. This act is enforced by the EEOC.

The 1991 law extended the possibility of individuals collecting damages related to sex, religious, or disability related discrimination. Organizations had developed a policy of adjusting scores on employment tests so a certain percentage of protected class would be hired. This amendment to Title VII specifically prohibits quotas, which are diversity goals to increase the number of protected class in a work force (Gomez-Mejia, Balkin & Cardy, 2012).

Age Discrimination in Employment Act of 1967: This act protects employees and job applicants 40 years and older from discrimination as it applies to hiring, firing, promotion, layoffs, training, assignments, and benefits. Older employees file lawsuits for age discrimination in job termination. It applies to employers with 20 or more employees and is enforced by the EEOC.

During difficult economic times, older employees file complaints with the EEOC because of their termination. In November 2010, Hawaii Professional Homecare Services was sued by the EEOC because the owner fired a 54-year-old employee, referring to her as a 'bag of old bones' and she sounded old over the phone. The owner did not want her representing the company (U.S. EEOC, 2010).

Older Workers Benefit Protection Act of 1990: This act amended the Age Discrimination in Employment Act. Its goal was to ensure that older workers' employee benefits were protected and that organizations provide the same benefits to both younger and older workers. The act also gives employees time to decide if they would accept early retirement options and allows employees to change their mind if they have signed a waiver for their right to sue. The act is enforced by the EEOC.

Rehabilitation Act of 1973: This law applies to organizations that receive financial assistance from federal organizations, including the Department of Health and Human Services, from discriminating against individuals with disabilities from receiving employee benefits and job opportunities. These organizations and employers include many hospitals, nursing homes, mental health centers, and human service programs. Employers with 50 or more employees and federal contracts of $50,000 or greater must submit written affirmative action plans. The PPACA amends this act by requiring all healthcare manufacturers to redesign medical equipment so they can accommodate individuals with disabilities. Healthcare provider locations must also be accessible to those with disabilities. This act is enforced by the Office of Federal Contract Compliance Programs (OFCCP).

Equal Pay Act of 1963: This act, amended the Fair Labor Standards Act, enforced by the U.S. Department of Labor, mandates that all employers award pay fairly to both genders if it is determined their jobs have equal responsibilities and require the same skills. It can be difficult to assess whether two employees are performing the exact same job. One employee may have additional duties, which would affect pay. The current trend in business is pay for performance so some employees may earn more if they perform better. However, research consistently states that women earn less than men. An individual who alleges pay discrimination may file a lawsuit without informing the EEOC.

Executive Orders 11246 (1965), 11375 (1967) and 11478 (1969): The President of the United States, for federal agency directions, writes Executive Orders. These orders focus on discrimination issues and require affirmative action based on these factors. These orders focus on both federal contractors and employers with 50 or more employees.

An **affirmative action plan** is a strategy that encourages employers to increase the diversity of their workforce by hiring individuals based on race, sex, and age. These potential employees must be qualified for the job. Although an affirmative action plan encourages hiring protected class candidates, an employer cannot set quotas for this process. They can develop strategies to encourage applications by diverse candidates.

An employer who develops an affirmative action plan must perform an analysis of the demographics of the current workforce compared to the eligible pool of qualified applicants. The employer must also calculate the percentage of those protected classes in the qualified applicants. The percentages are compared to determine if there was an underrepresentation of diverse employees in the organization. If it is determined the current workforce is not diverse, then an employer develops a timetable to hire diverse employees that also includes a recruitment plan.

The **Pregnancy Discrimination Act of 1978** is an amendment to Title VII of the Civil Rights Act of 1964. This act protects female employees who are discriminated against based on pregnancy-related conditions, which constitutes illegal sex discrimination. A pregnant woman must be treated like anyone with a medical condition. For example, an organization must allow sick leave for pregnant women with morning sickness if they also allow sick leave for other nausea illnesses (Gomez-Mejia, Balking & Cardy, 2012). This act applies to employers with at least 15 employees and is enforced by EEOC.

The **Americans with Disabilities Act of 1990** (ADA) focuses on individuals who are considered disabled in the workplace. There are three sections: Section I contains employment limitations, Section II and Section III target local government organizations, hotels, restaurants, and grocery stores. This act applies to employers who have 15 employees or more and is enforced by the EEOC. According to the law, a disabled person is someone who has a physical or mental impairment that limits the ability to hear, see, speak, or walk. The act was passed to ensure that those individuals who had a disability but who could perform primary job functions were not discriminated against. According to the act, disabilities included learning, mental, epilepsy, cancer, arthritis, mental retardation, AIDS, asthma, and traumatic brain injury. From a healthcare standpoint, a nursing home cannot refuse to admit a person with

AIDS that requires a nursing service if the hospital has that type of service available (DOL, 2013). Alcohol and other drug abuses are not covered under the ADA. Individuals who are morbidly obese can be considered disabled if the obesity was related to a physical cause.

Title I of the ADA states that employment discrimination is prohibited against individuals with disabilities who can perform essential functions of a job with or without reasonable accommodation. *Essential functions* are job duties that must be performed to be a satisfactory employee. *Reasonable accommodation* refers to employers that take reasonable action to accommodate a disabled individual such as providing special computer equipment or furniture to accommodate a physical limitation. The reasonable accommodate should not cause undue financial hardship to the employer.

Individuals with disabilities have mental or physical limitations such as walking, speaking, breathing, sitting, seeing, and hearing. **Intellectual disabilities** refer to an IQ of less than 70–75, the disability occurred before 18 years of age, and issues with social skills. Intellectual disabilities must significantly limit major life activities such as walking, seeing, hearing, thinking, speaking, learning, concentrating, and working. The ADA amendments of 2008 expanded living activities to include bodily functions such as bladder, circulatory, neurological, and digestive functions.

Role of Equal Employment Opportunity Commission (EEOC)

The Equal Employment Opportunity Commission was created by Title VII, of the Civil Rights Act of 1964. They are responsible for processing complaints, issuing regulations, and collecting information from employers.

Processing Complaints

If an individual feels discriminated against, he or she files a complaint with the EEOC who, in turn, notifies the employer. The employer is responsible for safeguarding any written information regarding the complaint. The EEOC then investigates the complaint to determine if the employer did violate any laws. If a violation was found, the EEOC uses conciliation or negotiation to resolve the issue without going to court. If conciliation is not successful, litigation or going to trial is the next step. Most employers prefer to avoid litigation because it is costly and damages their reputation. Most cases are resolved by conciliation.

Issuing Regulations

The EEOC is responsible for developing regulations for any EEOC law and its amendments. They have written regulations for the ADA, ADEA, and Equal Pay Act. They also issue guidelines for different issues such as sexual harassment and affirmative action.

Information and Education

The EEOC acquires information from employers regarding their practices. Employers with 100 or more employees must file an EEO-1 report that reflects the number of women and minorities who hold positions. This report is used to assess any potential discrimination trends. The EEOC also provides written and electronic media education on discrimination to employers. They send this information to the HR departments, which disseminates the information with training classes.

These pieces of legislation focus on equal employment opportunity in the workplace. These laws ensure that protected classes, as outlined in the Civil Rights Act of 1964, are provided opportunities for equal employment without bias or discrimination. In addition to this landmark legislation, the Age in Discrimination Act, Older Worker Benefit Protection Act, and the Americans with Disabilities Act establish standards for treating individuals who are older than 40 years and those individuals who have a disability are also treated fairly in their terms of employment. Both the Age in Discrimination Act and the Americans with Disabilities Act were further strengthened by the passage of the Lilly Ledbetter Fair Pay Act regarding pay discrimination. In addition, the Pregnancy Discrimination Act and the Equal Pay Act target discrimination against women. Despite the number of antidiscrimination legislation, discrimination continues to exist in the work environment.

Occupational Safety and Health Act of 1970

This act is also important to the healthcare industry because of the high incidence of employee injury. There is a higher risk of exposure to workplace hazards such as airborne and bloodborne infectious diseases, physical injuries from lifting patients, and needle stick injuries. This law was passed to ensure that employers have a **general duty** to provide a safe and healthy work environment for their employees, which are very important for the healthcare industry because of potential exposure to bacteria, viruses, and contaminated fluids.

Employers are also required to inform employees of potential hazardous conditions and OSHA standards. Posters and other materials are posted for employees' education. The Occupational Safety and Health Administration (OSHA) is responsible for enforcing these provisions. The National Institute for Occupational Safety and Health (NIOSH) was also established as part of this act to provide research to support the standards. OSHA enforces the **Hazard Communication Standard** that requires companies to label hazardous materials. Information is contained on **Material Safety Data Sheets (MSDSs)** that are provided to employees via the Internet or on site. OSHA has also issued a standard for exposure to human immunodeficiency virus (HIV), hepatitis B virus (HBV), and other bloodborne pathogens. This standard is crucial to the healthcare industry because of increased risk of exposure by nurses and laboratory workers.

OSHA has also developed standards for **personal protective equipment (PPE)**, which require equipment for exposure to hazardous materials or working conditions. Companies must also maintain records of employee accidents. OSHA provides workers with the rights to receive training, keep a copy of their medical records, and request OSHA inspections of their workplace (Occupational Safety & Health Administration, U.S. Department of Labor, 2013b).

OSHA has also developed standards for **ergonomics**, which is the study of working conditions that affect the physical condition of employees. Studies indicate that repetitive motion can create employee injuries. A common disorder is **carpal tunnel syndrome**, which is a wrist injury common to repetitive hand motion that takes place in jobs such as grocery cashiers and computer users. Employers can provide ergonomic friendly equipment and guidelines for ergonomic actions to eliminate these types of injuries. Ergonomic equipment and actions are important to the healthcare industry because many workers often lift patients to and from beds, operating tables, and wheelchairs (Occupational Safety & Health Administration, U.S. Department of Labor, 2013a).

Immigration Reform and Control Act (1988)

The **Immigration Reform and Control Act of 1988 (IRCA)** requires employers with one or more employees to verify that all job applicants are U.S. citizens or authorized to work in the United States. Most employees are only aware of this legislation because of the I-9 form all new employees must complete. There are three categories, A, B, and C, on the form. Category A establishes identity and eligibility to work such as a passport, Permanent Resident Card, or Permanent Alien Registration Receipt Card. Category B establishes identity of the individual. Acceptable proof of identity includes driver's license and different types of identification cards with photographs. Category C focuses on eligibility of an employee to work. Documentation includes social security card or birth certificate. If an employee cannot provide this information, he or she must provide documentation in both Category B and Category C. This prohibits any company from hiring illegal aliens and penalizes employers who hire illegal aliens. However, immigrants with special skill sets or those who can satisfy a labor shortage in the United States such as nurses, will be permitted to work in the United States. This act is enforced by the U.S. Department of Labor.

OTHER EMPLOYMENT-RELATED LEGISLATION

Consumer Credit Protection Act (Title III) of 1968: This act prohibits employers from terminating an employee if the individual's earnings are subject to garnishment due to debt issues. This act also limits the weekly garnishment amount from their pay and is enforced by the Federal Deposit Insurance Corporation (FDIC).

Drug Free Workplace Act of 1988: This act requires any employers who receive federal grants or who have a federal contract of $25,000 or greater to certify that they operate a drug-free workplace. They to provide education to their employees about drug abuse. Many employers now offer drug testing. The act is enforced by the U.S. Department of Labor.

Worker Adjustment and Retraining Notification Act of 1989: Employers who have 100 employees or more must give their employees 60 days notice of layoffs and business closings. This act is enforced by the U.S. Department of Labor.

The **Employee Retirement Income Security Act of 1974 (ERISA)** regulates pension and benefit plans for employees, including medical and disability benefits. It protects employees because it forbids employers from firing an employee so that they cannot collect under their medical coverage. Employees may change the benefits provided under their plan, but employers cannot force an employee to leave so that the employer does not have to pay the employee's medical coverage.

The **Consolidate Omnibus Budget Reconciliation Act of 1986 (COBRA)**, an amendment to ERISA, was passed to protect employees who lost or changed employers so they could keep their health insurance if they paid 102% of the full premium (Anderson, Rice, & Kominski 2007). The act was passed because, at the time, people were afraid to change jobs, resulting in the concept of **job lock** (Emanuel, 2008). COBRA also includes provisions that require hospitals to provide care to everyone who presented in an emergency department, regardless of their ability to pay. Fines were accrued if it was determined that hospitals were refusing treatment (Sultz & Young, 2006). This component was very important because many individuals were refused treatment because they could not pay for the services or were uninsured.

The **Health Insurance Portability and Affordability Act of 1996 (HIPAA)** was passed to promote patient information and confidentiality in a secure environment. Fully implemented in 2003, the amount of health information released is controlled by the consumer. This is the first federal legislation that provides in-depth protection of consumer's health information. Both civil and criminal penalties, including incarceration, were included in this act. Civil penalties were capped at $100 per violation and $25,000 per year. Criminal penalties ranged from $50,000 to $250,000 with 1–10 years of incarceration (Stanwyck & Stanwyck, 2009).

HIPAA was an amendment to the ERISA and the Public Health Service Act (PHS) to increase the access to healthcare coverage when employees changed jobs. HIPAA made it illegal to obtain personal medical information for reasons other than healthcare activities, which also includes genetic information. It also guaranteed that individuals could purchase health insurance for a preexisting condition if they (1) have been covered by a previous employer program for a minimum of 18 months, (2) have exhausted any coverage through COBRA, (3) are ineligible for other health insurance programs, and (4) were uninsured for no longer than 2 months. HIPAA also prohibits employers from stating pregnancy as a preexisting condition. Employers cannot charge higher premiums to employees according to health status (Anderson, Rice, & Kominski, 2007). Other provisions include:

(1) small businesses with 2–50 employees cannot be refused insurance, (2) self-employed individuals are allowed an increased tax deduction (30–80% by 2006) for health insurance premiums, and (3) employers or insurance companies cannot drop individuals for high usage of their medical plans (Shi & Singh, 2008). This act is enforced by the Department of Health and Human Services' Office for Civil Rights and the Department of Justice.

Employee wellness programs, which can include promotion of exercise, health risk appraisals, disease management, and healthcare coaching, have become a popular employee benefit. A survey of 1,100 companies indicated that over 60% of the companies offered an employer health awareness/workplace wellness program (Moran, 2008). However, there have been legal issues surrounding the implementation of wellness programs in the workplace because they discriminate based on the health conditions of employees. HIPAA states that wellness programs that are part of a group health plan must be designed to promote health and cannot be a subterfuge discriminating against an employee based on a health condition. Many wellness programs also offer incentives for wellness program performance. The incentive program must be designed so that all employees may participate in the incentive program regardless of health conditions, which means the incentive/rewards program must be flexible to adapt to employees who want to participate but may be restricted based on a health condition (DOL, 2006).

Health Information Technology for Economic and Clinical Health Act of 2009: Effective September 23, 2009, this act amends HIPAA by requiring stricter notification protocols for breach of any patient information. These new rules apply to any associates of the health plans. It also increased HIPAA's civil and criminal penalties for violating consumer privacy regarding their health information. Civil penalties were increased to $1,500,000 per calendar year, which was a huge increase in the original penalty cap of $25,000. The criminal penalties of up to $50,000–$250,000 and 10 years of incarceration remained the same.

Releasing patient information is more complex because of the introduction of information technology to the healthcare industry. For example, patient information may be faxed as long as only necessary information is transmitted and safeguards are implemented. Physicians may also communicate via email as long as safeguards are implemented.

The **Family Medical Leave Act of 1993** (FMLA) requires employers with 50 or more employees within a 75-mile radius who work more than 25 hours per week and who have been employed more than 1 year to provide up to 12 work weeks of unpaid leave, during any 12-month period, to provide care for a family member or the employee him- or herself. This benefit can also include postchildbirth or adoption. Employers must provide healthcare benefits, although they are not required to provide wages. This benefit does not cover the organization's 10% highest paid employees. The employer is also supposed to provide the same job or a comparable position upon the return of the employee (Noe, Hollenbeck, Gerhart, & Wright, 2011).

The **National Defense Authorization Act of 2008** expanded the FMLA to include families of military service members, which means that an employee may take up to 12 weeks of leave if a child, spouse, or parent has been called to active duty in the armed forces. Additionally, if a service member is injured or ill as a result of active duty, the employee may take up to 26 weeks of leave in a single 12-month leave year (Hickman, Gilligan, & Patton, 2008).

The **Mental Health Parity Act of 1996** defines the equality or parity between lifetime and annual limits of health insurance reimbursements on both mental health and medical care. Unfortunately, the act did not require employers to offer mental health coverage, it did not impose limits on deductibles or coinsurance payments, nor did it cover substance abuse. This federal legislation spurred several states to implement their own parity legislation (Anderson, Rice, & Kominski, 2007). The Wellstone Act or the **Mental Health Parity and Addiction Equity Act of 2008** amends the Mental Health Parity Act of 1996 to include substance abuse treatment plans as part of group health plans.

The **Genetic Information Nondiscrimination Act of 2008** prohibits U.S. insurance companies and employers from discriminating based on information derived from genetic tests. Specifically, it forbids insurance companies from discriminating through reduced coverage or price increases. It also prohibits employers from making adverse employment decisions based on a person's genetic code. Employers or insurance companies cannot demand a genetic test (National Human Genome Research Institute, 2013).

The **Lilly Ledbetter Fair Pay Act of 2009** (FPA), an amendment to Title VII of the Civil Rights Act of 1964, which also applies to claims under the Age Discrimination Act of 1967 and the Americans with Disabilities Act of 1990, provides protection for unlawful employment practices related to compensation discrimination. This act was named after Lilly Ledbetter, an employee of Goodyear Tire and Rubber Company who found out near her retirement that her male colleagues were paid more than she was. The Supreme Court ruled that she should have filed a suit within 180 days of the date that Goodyear paid her less than her peers. This act allows the statute of limitations to restart every 180 days from the time the worker receives a paycheck (Drachsler, 2010).

To avoid litigation, Sedhom (2009) suggests the implementation of a program coordinated by senior management and HR to help protect employers from being accused of unfair employment practices. The following summarizes the steps of the program:

1. Establish compensation criteria;

2. Develop pay audits and document these audits for several years;

3. Document retention processes related to pay;

4. Train managers on providing objective performance evaluations; and

5. Develop and implement a rigorous statistical analysis of pay distributions.

Patient Protection and Affordable Care Act or Affordable Care Act of 2010 (ACA): This act has a major impact on the U.S. healthcare system; therefore, a separate chapter has been devoted to the act and its mandates. A brief summary of the ACA is included in this chapter because it is considered landmark legislation and should be mentioned.

The Affordable Care Act has been very controversial. There were national public protests and a huge division among the political parties regarding the components of the legislation. Several states sued the federal government because they were mandated to increase Medicaid expansion. There were objections to the universal mandate health insurance coverage for individuals. People in general agreed that the U.S. healthcare system needed some type of reform but it was difficult to develop common recommendations that had majority support. Criticism, in part, focused on the increased role of government in monitoring the healthcare system and requiring individuals to obtain health insurance.

On October 1, 2013, the federal government was shut down because there are elected politicians who do not want the Affordable Care Act to proceed further. These politicians refused to approve a bill that would continue financial operations of the U.S. government. They attempted to include defunding portions of the Affordable Care Act as part of the federal government funding bill. Government functions resumed on October 17, 2013, after the Continuing Appropriations Act of 2014, was signed by Congress. Poll results indicate that public approval ratings of Congress declined significantly during the shutdown (Newport, 2013).

The one implementation that has been generally supported is increasing the dependent coverage of health insurance from age 25 until age 26, even if the child is not living with his or her parents, is not declared a dependent on the parents' tax return, or is no longer a student. This would not apply to individuals who have employer-based coverage (U.S. Department of Labor, 2013). Another positive mandate, also implemented in July 2010, was the establishment of a Web portal, www.healthcare.gov, to increase consumer awareness about their eligibility for specific healthcare insurance.

In addition to the two reforms discussed in the previous paragraphs, the following are selected major reforms that were also implemented in 2010:

- Elimination of lifetime and annual caps on healthcare reimbursement
- Granting assistance for the uninsured with pre-existing conditions
- Creation of a temporary reinsurance program for early retirees

In the past, health insurance companies would establish an annual or lifetime cap of reimbursement for the use of healthcare insurance. These would be eliminated. Unlike the past, health insurance companies would also be prohibited from dropping individuals and children with certain conditions or not providing insurance to those individuals with pre-existing conditions. The government would provide assistance to securing health insurance for these high-risk individuals.

The following are selected major reforms that will be implemented by 2014:

- Insurance companies will be prohibited from setting insurance rates based on health status, medical condition, genetic information, or other related factors
- Effective October 1, 2013, each state must establish access to a Health Insurance Marketplace Exchange, which is a marketplace where consumers can obtain information and buy health insurance
- Most individuals must maintain minimum essential healthcare coverage or pay a fine

In the past, there were issues with health insurance companies denying coverage based on health status or other conditions. Premiums now will be based on family type, geography, tobacco use, and age. In addition, each state will establish Health Insurance Marketplace Exchanges to assist consumers with obtaining health insurance. If the state chooses not to establish a state-run operation, residents of the state will use the federal government website. The information will be provided to consumers in a standardized format so they can compare the plans. Plans and cost will vary based on level of coverage. There are exceptions based on circumstances. By 2014, most consumers will be responsible for obtaining health insurance or pay a penalty that will increase each year they do not obtain health insurance coverage (Niles, 2010).

CONCLUSION

To be an effective healthcare manager, it is important to understand basic legal principles that influence the work environment, including the legal relationship between the organization and the consumer—the healthcare provider and the patient. As both a healthcare manager and healthcare consumer, it is imperative that you are familiar with the different federal and state laws that impact the healthcare organization. It is also important that you understand the differences between civil and criminal law and the penalties that may be imposed for breaking those laws. Both federal and state laws have been enacted and policy has been implemented to protect both the healthcare provider and the healthcare consumer. New laws have been passed and older laws have been amended to reflect needed changes regarding health care to continue to protect its participants from both a patient and an employee/employer perspective.

VOCABULARY

Affirmative action plan

Age Discrimination in Employment Act of 1967

Americans with Disabilities Act of 1990

Antitrust law

Battery

Benefits Improvement and Protection Act of 2000 (BIPA)

Boycotts

Carpal tunnel syndrome

Children's Health Insurance Program (CHIP)

Civil law

Civil Rights Act of 1964, Title VII

Civil Rights Act of 1991

Clayton Act of 1914

Common law

Compensatory damages

Contractual relationship to care for a designated population

Contractual right to admission

Consolidated Omnibus Budget Reconciliation Act of 1986 (COBRA)

Consumer Credit Protection Act (Title III) of 1988

Criminal law

Defensive medicine

Department of Justice

Designated health services

Drug Free Workplace Act of 1988

Employee wellness programs

Emergency Medical Treatment and Active Labor Act (EMTALA)

Employee Retirement Income Security Act of 1974 (ERISA)

Equal Pay Act of 1963

Ergonomics

Ethics in Patient Referral Act of 1989

Executive Orders 11246 (1965), 11375 (1967) and 11478 (1969)

Express contract

False Claims Act

Family Medical Leave Act of 1993

Federal Trade Commission

Federal Trade Commission Act

General duty

Genetic Information Nondiscrimination Act of 2008

Hart-Scott-Rodino Antitrust Improvement Act of 1976

Hazard Communication Standard

Health Information Technology for Economic and Clinical Health Act of 2009

Health Insurance Portability and Accountability Act of 1996 (HIPAA)

Hill-Burton Act

HIPAA National Standards

Immigration Reform and Control Act of 1988

Implied contract

Informed consent

Intellectual disabilities

Intentional torts

Job lock

Law

Lilly Ledbetter Fair Pay Act of 2009

Material Safety Data Sheets (MSDSs)

Market division

Medical malpractice

Mental Health Parity Act of 1996

Mental Health Parity and Addiction Act of 2008

Monopolies

National Defense Authorization Act of 2008

Negligence

Noneconomic damages

Occupational Safety and Health Act of 1970

Older Workers Benefit Protection Act of 1990

Patient abandonment

Patient Bill of Rights

Patient Protection and Affordability Care Act or Affordable Care Act of 2010

Patient Self-Determination Act of 1990

Personal protective equipment (PPE)

Physician Self-Referral Laws

Punitive damages

Pregnancy Discrimination Act of 1978

Price fixing

Price information exchange

Qui tam

Reasonable patient standard

Reasonable physician standard

Rehabilitation Act of 1973

Rules and regulations

Sexual harassment

Sherman Act of 1890

Standard of care

Statutes

Tort

Tort reform

Tying

Worker Adjustment and Retraining Notification Act of 1989

REFERENCES

American Heritage Dictionary. (2000). *Medical malpractice*. Boston: Houghton Mifflin.

American Medical Association (AMA). (2013). Ending the patient-physician relationship. Retrieved from http://www.ama-assn.org//ama/pub/physician-resources/legal-topics/patient-physician-relationship-topics/ending-patient-physician-relationship.page#

Anderson, R., Rice, T., & Kominksi, G. (2007). *Changing the U.S. health care system*. San Francisco: Jossey-Bass.

Bal, B. (2009). An introduction to medical malpractice in the United States. *Clinical Orthopedics and Related Research*, *467*(2), 339–347.

Buchbinder, S., & Shanks, N. (2007). *Introduction to health care management*. Sudbury, MA: Jones and Bartlett.

Budnick, N. (2013). John Kitzhaber recommends reform for Oregon medical malpractice laws. Retrieved from http://www.oregonlive.com/health/index.ssf/2012/07/john_kitzhaber_rolls_out_his_r.html

Carroll, A., & Buchholtz, A. (2009). *Business society: Ethics and stakeholder management* (7th ed.). Mason, OH: Thomson/Southwestern.

Centers for Medicare and Medicaid Services (CMS). (2013). Emergency Medical Treatment & Labor Act (EMTALA). Retrieved from http://www.cms.hhs.gov/EMTALA

Clayton Act, 15 U.S.C. §§ 12–27 (1914). Retrieved from http://www.law.cornell.edu/uscode/text/15/12

Congressional Budget Office. (2001). H.R. 5661, Medicare, Medicaid, and SCHIP Benefits Improvement and Protection Act of 2000 (Incorporated in H.R. 4577, the Consolidated Appropriations Act): Cost estimate. Retrieved from http://www.cbo.gov/publication/13285

DefensiveMedicine. (2013). What is defensive medicine? Retrieved from http://defensivemedicine.org

Danzon, P. (1995). *Medical malpractice: Theory, evidence, and public policy*. Cambridge, MA: Harvard University Press.

Degnan, J. M., & Scoggin, S. A. (2007, July). Medical defense and health law. *IADC Committee Newsletter*, *9*.

Draschler, D. (2010). Notes on: Year one of the Lilly Ledbetter Fair Pay Act. *Labor Law Journal*, 102–106.

Emanuel, E. (2008). Health care guaranteed. New York: Public Affairs.

Federal Trade Commission (FTC). (2013). About the FTC. Retrieved from http://www.ftc.gov/ftc/about.shtm

Gomez-Mejia, L., Balkin, D., & Cardy, R. (2012). *Managing human resources*. Upper Saddle River, NJ: Pearson: 100–125.

Gosfield, A. G. (2003). The stark truth about the STARK law: Part I. *Family Practice Management, 10*(10), 27–33. Retrieved from http://www.aafp.org/fpm/2003/1100/p27.html

Hickman, J., Gilligan, M., & Patton, G. (2008). FMLA and benefit obligations: New rights under an old mandate. *Benefits Law Journal, 21*(3), 5–16.

Kaiser Family Foundation. (2011). Number of children ever enrolled in the Children's Health Insurance Program (CHIP). Retrieved from http://kff.org/other/state-indicator/annual-chip-enrollment

Kesselheim, A., & Studdert, D. (2008). Whistleblower-initiated enforcement actions against health care fraud and abuse in the United States, 1996–2005. *Annals of Internal Medicine, 149*(5), 342–349.

LaMance, K. (2012). State limits on medical malpractice awards. Retrieved from http://www.legalmatch.com/law-library/article/state-limits-on-medical-malpractice-awards

Laws. (2013). Express and implied contracts from a physician. (2013). Retrieved from http://malpractice.laws.com/professional-patient-relationship/express-implied-contracts-from-a-physician

Memmott, S., & Makwana, K. (2007). Beware the whistleblower within—Recent False Claims Act settlements remind industry that almost anyone can be a whistleblower. *Journal of Health Care Compliance, 9*, 47–65.

Miller, R. (2006). *Problems in health care law* (9th ed.). Sudbury, MA: Jones and Bartlett.

Moran, A. (2008). Wellness programs: What's permitted? *Employer Relations Law Journal, 342*(2), 111–116.

National Human Genome Research Institute. (2009). Retrieved November 10, 2009 from http://www.genome.gov/About/.

Newport, F. (2013). Congress' job approval falls to 11% amid gov't shutdown: Americans' approval of their own representative averages 44%. Retrieved from http://www.gallup.com/poll/165281/congress-job-approval-falls-amid-gov-shutdown.aspx

Niles, N. (2010). *Basics of the U.S. health care system*. Sudbury, MA: Jones and Bartlett: 247–259.

Noe, R., Hollenbeck, J., Gerhart, B., & Wright, P. (2011). *Fundamentals of human resource management* (4th ed.). Boston: McGraw Hill-Irwin.

Occupational Safety & Health Administration, U.S. Department of Labor. (2013a). Ergonomics. Retrieved from http://www.osha.gov/SLTC/ergonomics

Occupational Safety & Health Administration, U.S. Department of Labor. (2013b). Workers. Retrieved from http://www.osha.gov/workers.html

Office of Technology Assessment. (1993). Impact of legal reforms on medical malpractice cost, (OTA-BP-H-19). Washington, DC: US Government Printing Office.

Pho, K. (2012). Patient centered medical malpractice reform in New Hampshire. Retrieved from http://www.kevinmd.com/blog/2012/04/patient-centered-medical-malpractice-reform-hampshire.html

Ringholz, J. (2005). An outline of the basic requirements of EMTALA, as it relates to compliance. *Journal of Health Care Compliance*, 35–36.

Rosenbach, M., & Stone, A. (1990). Malpractice insurance costs and physician practice—1981–1986. *Health Affairs, 9*, 176–185.

Rosner, F. (2004). Informing the patient about a fatal disease: From paternalism to autonomy—The Jewish view. *Cancer Investigation, 22*(6), 949–953.

Sedhom, S. (2009). Reacting to the Lilly Ledbetter Fair Pay Act: What every employer needs to know, *Employee Relations Law Journal*, 35(3), 3–8.

Shi, L., & Singh, D. (2008). *Essentials of the U.S. health care delivery system*. Sudbury, MA: Jones and Bartlett Publishers.

Sultz, H., & Young, K. (2006). *Health care USA: Understanding its organization and delivery* (5th ed.). Sudbury, MA: Jones and Bartlett.

USLegal. (2013). Noneconomic damages law and legal definition. Retrieved from http://definitions.uslegal.com/n/non-economic-damages

U.S. Department of Health & Human Services. (2013a). Health information privacy. Retrieved from http://www.hhs.gov/ocr/privacy/hipaa/administrative

U.S. Department of Health & Human Services. (2013b). Medical treatment in Hill Burton funded healthcare facilities. Retrieved from http://www.hhs.gov/ocr/civilrights/understanding/Medical%20Treatment%20at%20Hill%20Burton%20Funded%20Medical%20Facilities/

U.S. Department of Labor. (2013). Young adults and the Affordable Care Act: Protecting young adults and eliminating burdens on families and businesses. Retrieved from http://www.dol.gov/ebsa/newsroom/fsdependentcoverage.html

U.S. Department of Labor (DOL). (2006). Nondiscrimination and wellness programs in health coverage in the group market: Rules and regulations. Retrieved from http://www.dol.gov/ebsa/Regs/fedreg/final/2006009557.htm

U.S. Equal Employment Opportunity Commission (EEOC). (2010). EEOC sues Hawaii healthcare professionals for age discrimination. Retrieved from http://www.eeoc.gov/eeoc/newsroom/release/9-28-10.cfm

NOTES

STUDENT ACTIVITY 11-1

IN YOUR OWN WORDS

Based on this chapter, please provide an explanation of the following concepts in your own words as they apply to healthcare law. DO NOT RECITE the text.

Criminal law: _____

_____

_____

Civil law: _____

_____

_____

Battery: _____

_____

_____

Defensive medicine: _____

_____

_____

Torts: _____

_____

_____

Affirmative action plan: _____

_____

_____

Qui tam: _____

_____

_____

Reasonable patient standard: _____

_____

_____

Job lock: _____

_____

_____

Reasonable physician standard: _____

_____

_____

STUDENT ACTIVITY 11-2

Complete the following case scenarios based on the information provided in the chapter. Your answer must be IN YOUR OWN WORDS.

REAL LIFE APPLICATIONS: CASE SCENARIO ONE

As a new healthcare administrator, you are in charge of orientation for four new employees regarding employment law. There is one female, one disabled, one African American, and one Muslim individual. You feel it is important to emphasize laws that were passed to protect employees from discrimination.

ACTIVITY

Select the laws you feel are the most important to the new employees. Provide a brief description of each law and their impact on the new employees.

RESPONSES

_____

_____

_____

_____

_____

_____

_____

_____

_____

_____

_____

_____

_____

CASE SCENARIO TWO

Your physician has informed you that she can no longer be your primary care provider. Her office manager called to tell you there would be a letter sent to you confirming that change. You are confused because you did not request this change.

ACTIVITY

Perform research on how a physician is required to end a relationship and develop a letter to your physician stating your findings.

RESPONSES

_____

_____

_____

_____

_____

_____

_____

_____

_____

_____

_____

_____

_____

_____

CASE SCENARIO THREE

Your cousin is involved in a lawsuit. He is the claimant of the case. You were very surprised and you asked him to give you a summary of the problem. He mentioned the words "noneconomic damages," "standard of care," and "medical malpractice." You were not sure what these words meant so you decided to do some research on them.

ACTIVITY

Research these three terms and provide specific "real world" examples of the application of these terms.

RESPONSES

_____

_____

_____

_____

_____

_____

_____

_____

_____

_____

_____

_____

_____

_____

_____

CASE SCENARIO FOUR

You just joined a company and one of the benefits was an employee wellness program. You were not sure what type of program it was and whether you would use the program.

ACTIVITY

Perform research on different types of employee wellness programs and discuss the relationship between employee wellness programs and the HIPAA law.

RESPONSES

_____

_____

_____

_____

_____

_____

_____

_____

_____

_____

_____

_____

_____

_____

STUDENT ACTIVITY 11-3

INTERNET EXERCISES

Write your answers in the space provided.

- Visit each of the websites listed here.
- Name the organization.
- Locate their mission statement on their website.
- Provide a brief overview of the activities of the organization.
- How do these organizations participate in the U.S. healthcare system?

Websites

http//:www.justice.gov

Organization Name: _____

Mission Statement:

_____

_____

_____

Overview of Activities: _____

_____

_____

Importance of organization to U.S. health care:

_____

_____

_____

http://www.americanbar.org

Organization Name: _____

Mission Statement:

_____

_____

_____

Overview of Activities: _____

_____

_____

Importance of organization to U.S. health care:

_____

_____

_____

http://www.healthlaw.org

Organization Name: _____

Mission Statement:

_____

_____

_____

Overview of Activities: _____

_____

_____

Importance of organization to U.S. health care:

_____

_____

_____

http://www.eeoc.gov

Organization Name: _____

Mission Statement:

_____

_____

_____

Overview of Activities: _____

_____

_____

Importance of organization to U.S. health care:

_____

_____

_____

http://www.medicalmalpractice.com

Organization Name: _____

Mission Statement:

_____

_____

_____

Overview of Activities: _____
_____
_____

Importance of organization to U.S. health care:

_____
_____
_____

http://www.hg.org/health-law.html

Organization Name: _____

Mission Statement:

_____
_____
_____

Overview of Activities: _____
_____
_____

Importance of organization to U.S. health care:

_____
_____
_____

STUDENT ACTIVITY 11-4

DISCUSSION QUESTIONS

The following are suggested discussion questions for this chapter.

(1) Discuss the concepts of negligence and intentional torts and give examples of these in the healthcare industry.

_____

_____

_____

_____

_____

(2) What is tort reform? Do you believe tort reform is necessary?

_____

_____

_____

_____

(3) Discuss three employment related pieces of legislation that you feel are very important and why.

_____

_____

_____

_____

(4) What is an affirmative action plan? Research on the Internet and discuss with your classmates what issues there are regarding this type of plan.

_____

_____

_____

_____

(5) What is defensive medicine? Do you think physicians really do this? Research on the Internet and locate current information on this topic to share with your classmates.

_____

_____

_____

_____

The Navigate Companion Website for this text is a great source for additional information on the U.S. health-care system. You can gain a new perspective on many of the topics presented in this chapter by visiting http://go.jblearning.com/Niles2e. You'll find additional student activities, further reading, and interactive study tools that explore:

• Understanding healthcare-related legislation as a manager and consumer
• Importance of informed consent
• Healthcare fraud
• And much more.

Chapter 12

Healthcare Ethics

LEARNING OJBECTIVES

The student will be able to:

- Discuss the concept of ethics and its application to healthcare organizations.
- Define the four basic models of healthcare provider behavior.
- Define and discuss the four ethical models of a physician–patient relationship.
- Apply the concept of stakeholder management to the healthcare industry.
- Discuss the ethical dilemmas of organ transplants.
- Describe five different types of genetic testing.

DID YOU KNOW THAT?

- The concept of *bioethics* evolved as a result of the Nazi's human experimentation in the World War II prisoner camps.
- 18 people die daily waiting for an organ transplant.
- Xenotransplantation, which is transferring organs from one species to another, was first performed in 1984 when Baby Fae, a 5-pound infant, received the heart of a baboon.
- Euthanasia is from the Greek language, meaning *good death*.

- As the cost of U.S. medical procedures has increased, **medical tourism** is becoming popular as more citizens travel overseas to have medical procedures performed because the procedures are less expensive overseas.
- Workplace bullying is common in the healthcare industry.

INTRODUCTION

Legal standards are the minimal standard of action established for individuals in a society. Ethical standards are considered one level above a legal action because individuals make a choice based on what is the "right thing to do," not what is required by law. There are many interpretations of the concept of ethics. Ethics has been interpreted as the moral foundation for standards of conduct (Taylor, 1975). The concept of **ethical standards** applies to actions that are hoped for and expected by individuals. Actions may be considered legal but not ethical. There are many definitions of ethics but, basically, **ethics** is concerned with what are right and wrong choices as perceived by society and its individuals.

The concept of ethics is tightly woven throughout the healthcare industry. It has been dated back to Hippocrates, the father of medicine, in the 4th century BC, and evolved into the Hippocratic Oath, which is the foundation for the ethical guidelines for patient treatment by physicians. In 1847, the American Medical Association (AMA) published a *Code of Medical Ethics* that provided guidelines for the physician–provider relationship, emphasizing the duty to treat a patient (AMA, 2013a). To this day, physicians' actions have followed codes of ethics that demand the "**duty to treat**" (Wynia, 2007).

Applying the concept of ethics to the healthcare industry has created two areas of ethics: medical ethics and bioethics. **Medical ethics** focuses on the decisions healthcare providers make on the patient's medical treatment. Euthanasia or physician-assisted suicide would be an example of a medical ethic. **Advance directives** are orders that patients give to providers to ensure that, if they are terminally ill and incompetent to make a decision, certain measures will not be taken to prolong that patient's life. If advance directives are not provided, the ethical decision of when to withdraw treatment may be placed on the family and provider. These issues are legally defined, although there are ethical ramifications surrounding these decisions.

This chapter will focus primarily on **bioethics**. This field of study is concerned with the ethical implications of certain biologic and medical procedures and technologies, such as cloning; **alternative reproductive methods**, such as in vitro fertilization; organ transplants; genetic engineering; and care of the terminally ill (Adelaide Center for Bioethics and Culture, 2013). Additionally, the rapid advances in medicine in these areas raised questions about the influence of technology on the field of medicine (Coleman, Bouesseau, & Reis, 2008).

It is important to understand the impact of ethics in different aspects of providing health care. Ethical dilemmas in health care are situations that test a provider's belief and what the provider should do professionally. Ethical dilemmas are often a conflict between personal and professional ethics. A **healthcare ethical dilemma** is a problem, situation, or opportunity that requires an individual, such as a healthcare provider, or an organization, such as a managed care practice, to choose an action that could be unethical. A decision-making model is presented that can help resolve ethical dilemmas in the healthcare field (Niles, 2013). This chapter will discuss ethical theories, codes of healthcare conduct, informed consent, confidentiality, special populations, research ethics, ethics in public health, end-of-life

decisions, genetic testing and profiling, and biomedical ethics, which focuses on technology use and health care.

HEALTHCARE STAKEHOLDER MANAGEMENT MODEL

A **stakeholder** is an individual or group that has an interest in an organization or activity. This term should not be confused with a "shareholder," who actually has a financial interest in an organization because they own part of the organization. The concept of **stakeholder management** focuses on the relationship between organizations and all of their constituents, including shareholders, and how management recognizes the different expectations of each group. For example, a customer stakeholder would have a large interest in an organization where they purchase a product or a service. For some organizations, the government is an important stakeholder because the government regulates the organization's activities. Managing the interests of all of the stakeholders is a challenge for management, particularly in the healthcare industry. The pressure that stakeholders may impose on a manager can impact their ethical decision-making process (Carroll & Buchholtz, 2008).

The basic stakeholder relationship in the healthcare industry is the relationship between the physician/clinician and the patient. However, Oddo (2001) has proposed that there are several other stakeholders that play a role in their relationship. Patients will have relationships that impact their interaction with the physician. The physician also has relationships with other stakeholders who have expectations of the physician. For example, the patient will have family and friends and the health insurance company or the government that is paying for the health procedure. The family and friends have expectations that the physician will cure their friend or family member. They have an emotional relationship. The health insurance company's relationship with the patient is professional. They will reimburse standardized treatment procedures.

The physician's stakeholder relationships are more complex. They may be a part of a managed care facility or have admitting privileges at a hospital so they have the relationship with that entity and the entity might have expectations of how they will treat the patient. Physicians are also impacted by health insurance companies who want them to treat the patient according to standardized diagnostic procedures. Drug companies have an interest in the physician because they want the provider to use their products. All of these stakeholders have expectations based on the simple relationship between the patient and provider. When these stakeholders place undue pressure on this relationship, the decision-making process of the provider may not always place the patient first, although, as stated previously, the provider is ethically bound to treat the patient.

BASIC CONCEPTS OF ETHICS IN THE HEALTHCARE WORKPLACE

Ethical standards are considered one level above legal standards because individuals make a choice based on what is the "right thing to do," not what is required by law. There are many interpretations of the concept of ethics. Ethics has been interpreted as the moral foundation for standards of conduct (Taylor, 1975). The concept of *ethical standards* applies to actions that are hoped for and expected by individuals. There are many definitions of ethics but, basically, ethics is concerned with what are right and wrong choices as perceived by society and its individuals. Ethical dilemmas are often a conflict between personal and professional ethics. A *healthcare ethical dilemma* is a problem, situation, or opportunity that requires an individual, such as a healthcare provider to choose an action between two obligations (Niles, 2011). The dilemma occurs when the ethical reasoning of the decision maker may conflict with the ethical reasoning of the patient and the institution. Dilemmas are often resolved because of the guidelines provided by codes of medical ethics of medical associations or healthcare institutions, ongoing training, and implementing ethical decision-making models.

HEALTHCARE CODES OF ETHICS

As a result of many public ethical crises that have occurred, particularly in the business world, many organizations have developed written **codes of ethics**, which are guidelines for industry participants' actions. Codes of ethics provide a standard for operation so that all participants understand that if they do not adhere to this code, there may be negative consequences. The healthcare industry is no different.

Physicians have been guided by many healthcare codes of ethics. The statement of ethics discussed previously in this chapter is a type of code of ethics; AMA created a code of ethics for physicians in 1847. This code was revised and adopted in 2001. Each healthcare professional has a code of conduct. The **American Nurses Association** (ANA) established a code for nurses in 1985, which was revised in 1995 and most recently in 2001 (ANA, 2013). Healthcare executives have a code of ethics that was established in 1941 that discusses the relationship with their stakeholders. **The American College of Healthcare Executives (ACHE)** represents 30,000 executives internationally who participate in the healthcare system (ACHE, 2013). They also offer ethical policy statements on relevant issues such as creating an ethical culture for employees. In addition, they offer an ethics self-assessment tool that enables employees to target potential areas of ethical weakness. Many hospitals have established a code of ethics, which may help providers when they are dealing with medical situations, such as organ donations.

Interestingly, the **Advanced Medical Technology Association** (AdvaMed), an industry association that represents medical products, has also developed a code of ethics that addresses interactions with healthcare professionals who are potential customers of their products. Their ethical issues are similar to the pharmaceutical industry because they want physicians to use their medical devices and encourage the use by providing physicians with incentives such as gifts or paying for healthcare providers' travel or medical conferences (Advanced Medical Technology Association, 2013).

HOW TO DEVELOP A CODE OF ETHICS

A code of ethics must be written clearly, because employees at all organizational levels will utilize it. If a certain employee category needs a specific code of ethics, then a written code should be specifically developed for that category. The code must be current in laws and regulations. Driscoll & Hoffman (2000) recommend the following outline for developing a code of ethics:

1. Memorable Title
2. Leadership Letter
3. Table of Contents
4. Introduction

5. Core Values of the Organization

6. Code Provisions

7. Information and Resources

The code of ethics must be a user-friendly resource for the organization. It should be updated to include current laws and regulations. The language should be specific as to what the organization should expect from its employees and training should be provided on the code of ethics so employees understand the organization's expectations.

WORKPLACE BULLYING

In 1992, Andrea Adams, a BBC journalist, coined the term **workplace bullying**, describing an ongoing harassing workplace behavior between employees, which results in negative health outcomes for the targeted employees (Adams, 1992). Workplace bullying is receiving increased attention worldwide as a negative organizational issue. It is considered a serious and chronic workplace stressor that can lead to diminished work productivity and work quality (Hoel, Faragher, & Cooper, 2004). This negative behavior is considered bullying if it is repeated over an extended period of time. It can occur between colleagues, supervisors, or supervisees, although the bully is often the supervisor. Definitions also include negative verbal or nonverbal behavior such as snide comments, verbal or physical threats, or items being thrown. Employees have also reported less aggressive behavior such as demeaning their work or gossiping about them on a continual basis. The literature has reported an increased incident of bullying reported in healthcare organizations and in academe (Ayoko, Callan, & Hartel, 2003; Vartia, 2001; Djurkovic, McCormack & Casimir, 2008).

Workplace Bullying in Healthcare

Workplace bullying has been reported as common in healthcare. Specifically, there are bullying issues between physicians and nurses. The Center for American Nurses, American Association of Critical-Care Nurses, International Council of Nurses, and National Student Nurses Association have all issued statements regarding the need for healthcare organizations to eliminate bullying in the healthcare workplace. Often, verbal abuse also occurs towards nurses by physicians, patients and their families. **Lateral**

violence also occurs in healthcare, which is defined as 'nurse to nurse' aggression, demonstrated by both verbal and nonverbal behavior (American Nurses Association, 2011).

Legal Implications of Workplace Bullying

There is no federal legislation in the United States that forbids workplace bullying. New York is the only state that has enacted legislation that forbids this type of behavior in the workplace. However, there are two federal laws that can be applied in workplace bullying: The Occupational Safety and Health Act of 1970 (OSHA) and Title VII of the Civil Rights Act of 1964. Under the OSHA Act of 1970, it states that employers must provide a safe and healthful working environment for their employees. Under Title VII of the Civil Rights Act, if a protected class employee (gender, religion, ethnicity, etc.) is bullied by another employee, the action can be illegal based on the concept of a hostile work environment, which is illegal under sexual harassment.

Recommendations to Eliminate Workplace Bullying

To date, there is no federal legislation that specifically addresses workplace bullying. In order to reduce the prevalence of workplace bullying, it is important that employers implement policies to eliminate this behavior. The following are recommendations for organizations, including health care (LaVan & Martin, 2007):

1. Adopt a policy of zero tolerance for workplace bullying and develop measures to discipline bullies in the workplace

2. Create an organizational culture that focuses on a positive work environment enabling all individuals to pursue their careers

3. Reward behaviors that encourage teamwork and collaboration among employees and their supervisors

4. Develop an educational program for all employees on what constitutes workplace bullying

Workplace bullying continues to be a pervasive organizational problem worldwide. In the United States the Workplace Bullying Institute has developed a Healthy Workplace Bill that precisely defines workplace bullying and extends protection to employees against this type of behavior. The bill has been introduced in 14 states since 2003. There is no specific federal legislation against antibullying so bullying will continue to be legal, unfortunately. It is important that workplace bullying educational programs and organizational policies be implemented to ensure that employees will be protected against this type of negative behavior. The results can be devastating from both an organizational and individual level.

In 2008, **The Joint Commission** developed a standard for workplace bullying called "intimidating and disruptive behaviors in the workplace." They issued the following statement:

> *Intimidating and disruptive behaviors can foster medical errors, contribute to poor patient satisfaction and to preventable adverse outcomes, increase the cost of care, and cause qualified clinicians, administrators, and managers to seek new positions in more professional environments. Safety and quality of patient care is dependent on teamwork, communication, and a collaborative work environment. To assure quality and to promote a culture of safety, health care organizations must address the problem of behaviors that threaten the performance of the health care team. (The Joint Commission, 2008, p. 1)*

Two leadership standards are now part of The Joint Commission's accreditation provisions:

The first requires an institution to have "a code of conduct that defines acceptable and disruptive and inappropriate behaviors." The second requires an institution "to create and implement a process for managing disruptive and inappropriate behaviors" (Yamada, 2004).

In a recent Joint Commission study, it was found that more than 50% of nurses have suffered some type of bullying with 90% observing some type of abuse. Their standard focused on the impact of these types of behavior on patient care quality. The Joint Commission requires healthcare institutions to create a code of conduct that defines appropriate behavior and has a system in place to manage inappropriate behavior such as workplace bullying. In addition to the stance of The Joint Commission, the Center for Professional Health at the Vanderbilt University Medical Center has developed a program for treating and remediating disruptive behaviors by physicians. Nurses' unions are also developing education programs on workplace bullying (Minding the Workplace, 2009).

ETHICS AND THE DOCTOR–PATIENT RELATIONSHIP

The foundation of health care is the relationship between the patient and physician. In 2004, the **American College of Physicians and Harvard Pilgrim Health Care Ethics Program** developed a statement of ethics for managed care. The following is a summary of the statements (Povar et al., 2004):

- Clinicians, healthcare plans, insurance companies, and patients should be honest in their relationship with each other.
- These parties should recognize the importance of the clinician and patient relationship and its ethical obligations.
- Clinicians should maintain accurate patient records.
- All parties should contribute to developing healthcare policies.
- The clinician's primary duty is the care of the patient.
- Clinicians have the responsibility to practice effective and efficient medicine.
- Clinicians should recognize that all individuals, regardless of their position, should have health care.
- Healthcare plans and their insurers should openly explain their policies regarding reimbursement of types of health care.
- Patients have a responsibility to understand their health insurance.
- Health plans should not ask clinicians to compromise their ethical standards of care.
- Clinicians should enter agreements with healthcare plans that support ethical standards.
- Confidentiality of patient information should be protected.
- Clinicians should disclose conflicts of interest to their patients.
- Information provided to patients should be clearly understood by the patient.

This statement was developed as a result of the continued economic and policy changes in the healthcare industry. It provided guidelines to healthcare practitioners, healthcare organizations, and the healthcare insurance industry about ethical actions in the changing healthcare environment.

PHYSICIAN–PATIENT RELATIONSHIP MODEL

It is important to further discuss the relationship between the practitioner and the patient. There are several different models that can be applied to this relationship. Veatch (1972) identified four models that apply to the doctor–patient relationship: engineering model, priestly model, contractual model, and collegial model.

The **engineering model** focuses on patients and their power to make decisions about their health care. The provider gives the patient all of the necessary information to make a decision. The provider empowers the patient with knowledge to make a decision. The **priestly model** assumes the doctor will make the best decisions for the patient's health. The patient assumes a very passive role, giving the provider great power in the decision-making process. This is a very traditional relationship that often would occur between the elderly and physicians because they were taught to revere the medical world. The **contractual model**, based on a legal foundation, assumes there is an agreement between the two parties, assuming mutual goals. It is a relationship between the two parties with equal power. The patient understands the legal ramifications of the relationship. The **collegial model** assumes trust between the patient and doctor and that decision making is an equal effort (Veatch, 1972). These models are dependent on what type of relationship a patient expects with his or her practitioner. In any case, in each model, ethics plays a role in the relationship. Although the provider may play different roles in each of these models, the underlying foundation is assuming that the doctor's actions are ethical, representing the best interest of the patient.

According to Beauchamp and Childress (2001) and Gillon (1994), the role of ethics in the healthcare industry is based on five basic values that all healthcare providers should observe:

- **Respect for autonomy:** Decision making may be different and healthcare providers must respect their patients' decisions even if they differ from their own.
- **Beneficence:** The healthcare provider should have the patient's best interests when making a decision.
- **Nonmalfeasance:** The healthcare provider will cause no harm when taking action.

- **Justice:** Healthcare providers will make fair decisions.
- **Dignity:** Patients should be treated with respect and dignity.

Each of these principles will be discussed in depth because these concepts are important to understanding the role of ethics in the healthcare industry. **Autonomy**, which is defined as self-rule, is an important concept to healthcare because it is applied to **informed consent**, which requires a provider to obtain the approval of a patient who has been provided adequate information to make a decision regarding intervention. Informed consent is a legal requirement for medical intervention. As part of the autonomy concept, it is also important that providers respect the decision of their patient even if the patient's decisions do not agree with the provider's recommendation. For example, a friend who has been diagnosed with a very advanced stage of cancer was told by her provider that she could enroll her in an experimental program that would give her 2–3 months to live. The intervention is very potent with severe side effects. My friend decided to try a homeopathic medicine to attack her disease. Her doctor was not in agreement with her choice but she respected her patient's decision. She told her that if she needed pain medication, she could come see her and she would help her. This situation is an excellent example of autonomy in medicine.

Beneficence in the healthcare industry means that the best interest of the patient should always be the first priority of the healthcare provider and healthcare organizations. Nonmalfeasance further states that healthcare providers must not take any actions to harm the patient. As discussed in the paragraph on autonomy, this concept appears to be very easy to understand; however, there may be an interpretation between the provider and the patient as to what is best for the patient. For example, Jehovah's Witnesses, a religious sect, do not believe in blood transfusions and will not give consent during an operation for a transfusion to occur, despite the procedure's ability to possibly save a life (Miller, 2006). The provider has been trained to believe in beneficence and malfeasance. However, from the provider's point of view, if they respect the wishes of the patient and family, they will be potentially harming their patient.

Justice or fairness in the healthcare industry emphasizes that patients should be treated equally and that health care should be accessible to all. Justice should be applied to the way healthcare services are distributed, which means that healthcare services are available to all individuals. Unfortunately, in the United States, the healthcare system does not provide accessibility to all of its citizens. Access to health care is often determined by the ability to pay either out of pocket or by an employer- or government-sponsored program. In countries with universal healthcare coverage, justice in the healthcare industry is more prevalent. With over 48 million uninsured in the United States, can one say that justice has not prevailed in the healthcare industry (Centers for Disease Control and Prevention, 2013)?

PHARMACEUTICAL MARKETING TO PHYSICIANS

For example, there have been many cases regarding how drug companies market their products to physicians. Over the past 2 decades, this relationship has received more scrutiny because of its appearance of unethical behavior. The drug companies provide free samples and information to physicians because the companies want the provider to use their products. Although providers deny that these "perks" influence their decisions in choosing drugs, federal legislation—the **Physician Payment Sunshine Act**—was passed in 2010 as part of the Affordable Care Act (effective August 2013) and requires manufacturers of drugs, medical devices, and other healthcare products with relationships with Medicare and Medicaid providers and CHIP programs to submit reports annually in payments and items of value. They must also report ownership interests held by physicians and their families (AMA, 2013b). In 2002 and updated in 2009, the **Pharmaceutical Research and Manufacturers of America** (PhRMA) implemented a new code of conduct governing physician–industry relationships (PhRMA, 2013). The code discourages gifts to physicians and other monetary rewards, emphasizing the relationship should focus on enhancing the quality of treatment of the patient. It emphasizes ethical marketing to the physicians. These types of codes of conducts will provide guidelines for the relationship between the provider and the companies, thereby providing more accountability for the use of certain prescriptions by providers. This type of relationship can test the ethical relationship between the provider and patient.

DECISION MODEL FOR HEALTHCARE DILEMMAS

Healthcare dilemmas require guidelines to process a solution to the dilemma. Codes of ethics and HR training can assist with a solution. Employee training can include a decision making model that will assist the individual to process the steps in resolving the situation. The PLUS ethical decision making model consists of (Ethics Resource Center, 2009):

1. Identification of the dilemma
2. Identification of the conflicting ethics of each party
3. Identification of alternatives to a solution
4. Identification of the impact of each alternative
5. Selection of the solution

Application of the Decision-Making Model

Healthcare Dilemma (discussed earlier): An oncologist has a patient with an advanced stage of melanoma (skin cancer). Prognosis: 3–6 months to live. The oncologist has developed an experimental treatment program that has severe side effects but may give the patient an additional 6 months. The patient prefers alternative remedies for medical treatment such as homeopathic solutions (natural remedies).

> **Step 1**: *Define the problem.* This is the most important part of the process. This step should define the problem and the ultimate outcome of the decision making process.
>
> Application: The problem is the differing views of treatment by both the physician and the patient. The physician does not believe in homeopathic remedies. The ultimate outcome of the decision-making process is to prolong the life of the patient, if possible.
>
> **Step 2**: *Identify the alternative(s) to the problem.* List the possible alternatives to the desired outcome. Attempt to identify at least three as a minimum, but five are preferred.
>
> > *Alternative 1*: Patient accepts experimental treatment program.
> >
> > *Alternative 2*: Patient rejects experimental treatment program.
> >
> > *Alternative 3*: Physician researches homeopathic remedies for patient.

Alternative 4: Physician refuses to research homeopathic remedies for patient.

Alternative 5: Patient seeks other medical advice from different physician.

Alternative 6: Physician refers patient to physician who is an expert in homeopathic medicine.

Step 3: *Evaluate the identified alternatives.* Discuss the positive and negative impact of each alternative.

Alternative 1: Patient accepts experimental treatment program.

Positive: Patient's cancer is eradicated or is in remission.

Negative: Treatment has no impact on cancer. Patient dies.

Alternative 2: Patient rejects experimental treatment program.

Positive: Cancer goes into remission.

Negative: Patient dies shortly.

Alternative 3: Physician researches homeopathic remedies for patient.

Positive: Physician finds a homeopathic remedy that can be used in conjunction with experimental program. Patient accepts treatment. Cancer is eradicated or goes into remission.

Negative: Physician finds no homeopathic solution that can be used in conjunction with experimental program. Patient refuses treatment. Patient dies shortly.

Alternative 4: Physician refuses to research homeopathic remedies for patient.

Positive: Patient believes in physician and agrees to try experimental program. Program is successful.

Negative: Patient cuts ties with physician. Receives no treatment and dies shortly.

Alternative 5: Patient seeks other medical advice from different physician.

Positive: Patient finds a physician who agrees with homeopathic remedies.

Patient accepts homeopathic remedies and cancer is eradicated or goes into remission.

Negative: Patient does not find a physician who would help her and dies quickly, trying to find someone.

Alternative 6: Physician refers patient to physician who is expert in homeopathic medicine.

Positive: Patient is treated with a homeopathic solution that prolongs her life.

Negative: Patient is treated with a homeopathic solution that does not prolong her life.

Step 4: *Make the decision.* In the healthcare industry, the decision must include the patient's best interest and his or her values, which can be conflicting at times. However, patients have the right to make an informed decision about their health. In this instance, alternative 6 is chosen, because the patient believes in homeopathic medicine. The physician who does not believe in natural remedies respected the patient's beliefs, which differed from hers, but she still wanted to help the patient. The physician wanted to be involved in the patient care by supporting the beliefs of her patient.

Step 5: *Implement the decision.* Once the decision is made, the physician actually finds a physician referral that would help her patient. The primary physician said she would provide any assistance with pain medication if needed.

Step 6: *Evaluate the decision.* The patient accepted the referral of the new physician and entered a homeopathic treatment program. The patient lived three more years with a high quality of life.

This decision making model is an excellent method of resolving many types of healthcare dilemmas. This model can be utilized in employee training on ethical issues in the healthcare workplace.

ETHICS AND PUBLIC HEALTH

In contrast to the bioethicist view of the relationship between physician and patient, ethical analysis has expanded to public health. There are several ethics in public health that focus on the design and implementation of measures to monitor and improve the community's health (Coleman et al., 2008). Issues in public health include: inaccessibility to health care for certain populations, response to bioterrorism, research in developing countries, health promotion and its infringement on an individual's lifestyle choices, and public health's response to emergencies. The concept of **paternalism** and public health is the concern that individual freedom will be restricted for the sake of public health activities because the government infringes on individual choices for the sake of protecting the community (Ascension Health, 2013).

The **Nuffield Council on Bioethics**, based in Great Britain, has proposed a stewardship model that outlines the principles public health policy makers should utilize globally. This model addresses the issues of paternalism in public health. The **stewardship model** states that public health officials should achieve the stated health outcomes for the population while minimizing restrictions on people's freedom of choice.

The focus of public health is to reduce the population's health risks from other people's actions such as drunk driving, smoking in public places, environmental conditions, inaccessibility to health care, and maintaining safe working environments. While promoting a healthy lifestyle, according to the Nuffield Council on Bioethics, it is also important that public health programs do not force people into programs without their consent or introduce interventions that may invade people's privacy. The Council also introduces the concept of an intervention ladder that establishes a ranking of the type of public health intervention introduced, which may minimize people's choices. As the intervention moves up the ladder, the higher the justification is required for the action (Nuffield Council on Bioethics, 2013).

Childress, Faden, and Gaare (2002) specify five justifications for public health interventions that infringe on individual choices. The criteria are: (1) effectiveness, (2) need, (3) proportionality, (4) minimal infringement, and (5) public education. **Effectiveness** is essential to demonstrate that the public health efforts were successful and, therefore, it was necessary to limit individual freedom of choice. The need for a public health intervention must be demonstrated to limit individual freedom. If the **proportionality** of the public health intervention outweighs freedom of choice, then the intervention must be warranted. If the public health

intervention satisfies effectiveness, need, and proportionality, the least restrictive intervention or **minimal infringement** on individual freedoms should be considered first. Lastly, public health must provide **public education** to explain their interventions and why the infringement on individual choices is warranted. For example, bioterrorism is now a viable threat. If it has been determined that a public health threat exists as a result of some biological weapons, then mandatory blood tests, possible quarantines, and other measures that would infringe on individual freedom of choice must be implemented (Buchanan, 2008).

Another ethical public health issue is the duty of practitioners to treat individuals during a public health crisis. If there is a natural disaster, what is the duty to treat during a time of crisis? During Hurricane Katrina, several healthcare professionals volunteered to stay behind in a local hospital. Unfortunately, several patients in the hospital died and the providers were accused of murdering their patients. As a result of this incident, many professionals are now wary of volunteering during a crisis. From their perspective, they commit to an ethical reaction and they may be rewarded with a criminal liability. There are civil liability protections that differ from state to state, such as Good Samaritan laws. Physicians practicing in free clinics are protected by federal law. Federal lawmakers should pass legislation that protects these healthcare professionals during public health emergencies (Wynia, 2007).

ETHICS AND RESEARCH

Conducting research involving human subjects requires the assessment of the risks and benefits to the human subjects, which must be explained clearly to them before the consent to participate in the research is given. The principles of ethical research are outlined in **Institutional Review Boards (IRBs)**. An IRB is a group that has been formally designated to review and monitor biomedical research involving human subjects. An IRB has the authority to approve, require modifications in (to secure approval), or disapprove research. This group review serves an important role in the protection of the rights and welfare of human research subjects (Food and Drug Administration [FDA], 2013). Any organization that performs research should develop an IRB for their organization. The ethical component of an IRB is to protect the participants of the study. The IRBs require the researchers to maximize the benefits and minimize the risks to the participant and explain these assessments clearly. It is important that the IRB does not approve a study that imposes significant risks on the subjects.

Assuming the study clears the IRB's assessment of risks and benefits, it is important the subject understands the study and its impact on them. Informed consent, as it relates to treatment, is one of the basic ethical protections for human subject research. It is designed to protect human subjects and increase autonomy. Informed consent protects human subjects because it allows the individual to consider personal issues before participating in medical research. Informed consent increases autonomy because it provides individuals with the opportunity to make a choice to exercise control over their lives (Mehlman & Berg, 2008). Research informed consent requires the disclosure of appropriate information to assist the individual in project participation. Both the Department of Health and Human Services (HHS) and FDA have outlined common rule regulations that comprise the elements of informed consent.

Common rule elements include: a written statement that includes the purpose and duration of the study, the procedures and if they are experimental, any foreseen risks and potential benefits, and any alternative procedures that may benefit the subject (FDA, 2013; Korenman, 2009). Additional requirements are needed for children, pregnant women, people with disabilities, mentally disabled people, prisoners, etc. It is clear that the IRB must provide guidelines for parents that have children who participate in research and for those subjects that may be mentally disabled who could be unduly influenced (Mehlman & Berg, 2008).

BIOETHICAL ISSUES

Designer or Donor Babies

Alternative reproductive methods are methods of conception that parents use to have children, such as in vitro fertilization, which means that the embryo is fertilized in a clinic using the sperm from the father. **Preimplantation genetic diagnosis (PGD)** can be used to test the embryo for tissue compatibility with their siblings prior to being transplanted into the mother. If one of the siblings becomes ill, the "designer baby" can save the existing sibling's life by providing bone marrow transplants. If it has been determined that the embryo is not compatible, it could be destroyed. This procedure

is considered very controversial because many people consider the embryo early human life. Secondly, are the physicians and parents "playing God" by determining whether the embryo should be saved? Does this type of control dehumanize **procreation** or creation of life? Another question is what kind of impact occurs on the child who will eventually be aware that s/he was created to save a sibling (Dayal & Zarek, 2008).

Cloning

All human beings possess **stem cells**, which are "starter" cells for the development of body tissue that have yet to be formed into specialized tissues for certain parts of the body (Sullivan, 2006). The term **cloning** applies to any procedure that creates a genetic replica of a cell or organism. There are two major types of cloning: **reproductive cloning**, which creates cloned babies, and **therapeutic** or **research cloning**, which uses the same process but the focus is replicating sources for stem cells to replaced damaged tissues. The most famous reproductive clone was Dolly, the sheep that was cloned in 1996 from an adult cell (Baylis, 2002). Several countries have banned cloning for reproductive purposes but have been more lenient in therapeutic cloning. There are several ethical issues regarding cloning. Researchers worldwide have attempted human cloning with no success. Some feel that cloning humans is unnatural and "playing God" rather than allowing procreating to progress naturally. Some people, however, have cloned their beloved pets, which has created an uproar. People are highly focused on the reproductive cloning issues rather than the potential research success of cloning that could result in effective treatment of many diseases. However, therapeutic cloning also is considered unethical because it is destroying embryos to obtain healthy stem cells for research.

Research has focused on stem cells that could replace damaged body tissues from spinal injuries or cure diseases such as Parkinson's disease. These stem cells could be derived from surplus human embryos that are stored at in vitro fertilization clinics and were not used for fertility procedures. The ethical issue, similar to the designer baby issues, is that, in order to use the stem cells, they would be destroying human embryos for research purposes because embryos are considered human life by many people. The issue in both cases also is what should happen to the excess embryos that are stored in clinics? Studies have indicated there may be an estimated 400,000 embryos stored in U.S. clinics that may eventually be destroyed (The Coalition of Americans for Research Ethics, 2013). Could these embryos be used to develop therapies and cures for disease?

Genetic Testing

Genetic testing is carried out on populations based on age, gender, or other risk factors to determine if they are at risk for a serious genetic disease or if they have a carrier gene that they may pass on to their children. Genetic tests may be analyzed from bodily tissue, including blood, cells from your mouth, saliva, hair, skin, tumors, or fluid surrounding the fetus during pregnancy (National Human Genome Research Institute [NHGRI], 2013). The specimen is analyzed by a laboratory. There are several different types of tests:

- **Diagnostic testing** is used to identify the disease when a person is exhibiting symptoms.

- **Predictive and asymptomatic** (no symptoms) tests are used to identify any gene changes that may increase the likelihood of a person developing a disease.

- **Carrier testing** is used to identify individuals who carry a gene that is linked to a disease. The individual may exhibit no symptoms but may pass the gene to offspring who may develop the disease or carry the gene themselves.

- **Prenatal testing** is offered to identify fetuses with potential diseases or conditions.

- Newborn screening is performed during the first 1–2 days of life to determine if the child has a disease that could impact its development.

- **Pharmacogenomic testing** is performed to assess how medicines react to an individual's genetic makeup.

- **Research genetic testing** focuses on how genes impact disease development.

The **Human Genome Project**, a long-term government-funded project completed in 2003, identified all of the 20,000–25,000 genes found in human DNA. They catalogued these genes, which has made it easier to quickly determine the genes an individual possesses. As a result of genetics research, several genes have been identified as markers of prediction of disease in families such as breast cancer, colon cancer, cystic fibrosis, and Down syndrome in fetuses (Oak Ridge National Laboratory [ORNL], 2013).

Although this information gained from genetic testing is important to individuals and their families, there are several ethical issues regarding genetic testing. If employers were aware of this information, would they use it to discriminate against employees? Would parents decide against having a child because of a result of a genetic test? How accurate are the genetic tests? There are no regulations regarding genetic tests so individuals and families may make decisions based on faulty laboratory tests. It is important that genetic testing is provided in conjunction with genetic counseling to ensure that individuals understand the results. Recently, private companies have developed home kits for genetic testing. This type of information without discussion with a genetic counselor or physician may have repercussions because an individual may make decisions based on lack of comprehension.

Euthanasia: Treating the Terminally Ill

End-of-life issues of a patient can be an ethical challenge. Healthcare providers may find this difficult to understand because they have been trained to save lives. The term **euthanasia** is the term most often associated with end-of-life issues. This Greek word meaning *good death* may seem unethical because you are allowing an individual to die. Letting a patient die may be morally justifiable if it has been determined that any medical intervention is completely futile. There are two major types of euthanasia: voluntary and nonvoluntary. **Voluntary euthanasia** is assisting a patient with ending his or her life at the patient's request. **Nonvoluntary euthanasia** means ending the life of an incompetent patient usually at the request of a family member. The two most famous nonvoluntary euthanasia cases are Karen Quinlan and Terri Shiavo. In 1975, the New Jersey Supreme Court granted Ms. Quinlan's father the right to remove his daughter's respirator, which resulted in her death 10 years later. She had remained in a coma or persistent vegetative state for 10 years. Because she was not able to make the decision herself, the judge granted the father the right to limit any medical interventions to continue her life. Terri Shiavo suffered a heart attack in 1990 and remained in a coma on a feeding tube until 2005, when the Florida Supreme Court allowed the husband of Terri Schiavo to remove her feeding tube despite her parent's protests (University of Miami Ethics Programs, 2013).

There is confusion regarding the difference between euthanasia and physician-assisted suicide. **Physician-assisted suicide** refers to the physician providing the means for death, most often with a prescription. The patient, not the physician, will ultimately administer the lethal medication. Euthanasia generally means that the physician would act directly, for instance by giving a lethal injection, to end the patient's life.

Although euthanasia is illegal in all states except Oregon, Washington (2008), and Vermont (2013) (physician-assisted suicide), it is important to examine end-of-life issues because many of us will face them ourselves or with a loved one. The **Oregon Death with Dignity Act** (DWDA) was passed in 1994 and became effective in 1998. Since they started maintaining data in 1998, each year there are more physician-assisted suicides. January 2013 statistics indicate that prescriptions for lethal medications were written for 115 people during 2012 under the provisions of the DWDA, compared to 114 during 2011. At the time of this report, there were 77 known DWDA deaths during 2012. This corresponds to 23.5 DWDA deaths per 10,000 total deaths (Death with Dignity Act, 1994). The Washington mandate, effective 2009, was modeled after the Oregon law. In both states, the patient needs to be deemed terminal by two physicians. If physicians have doubts about a patient's mental state, a mental health professional will be consulted. The patient must make an oral and witnessed written request and another request 15 days later. The physicians must inform the patient about hospice and palliative care options (O'Reilly, 2009). Similar to the Oregon results, more terminal patients each year request lethal prescriptions. In 2009, there were 63 deaths; 2010, 85 deaths; 2011, there were 101 deaths; and in 2012, data indicates that 121 individuals requested lethal prescriptions from physicians. Of the 121 patients, 83 used the prescription. A survey of terminal patients showed they requested the prescriptions because they felt they were becoming a burden on their families, they were losing their independence, and losing the ability to enjoy life (Washington State Department of Health, 2012).

This has been a controversial piece of legislation that has generated more commentary throughout the country and worldwide. Healthcare providers who support euthanasia feel that (1) it is an opportunity to relieve the pain a patient is experiencing at the end of his or her life; (2) it is an example of autonomy in life by allowing a person to choose when he or she is dying; and (3) it allows an opportunity to be released from a life that no longer has quality. Healthcare providers who believe that euthanasia is unethical feel that (1) it devalues the concept of life, (2) it may merely be an opportunity to contain medical costs for both the families and health insurance companies and, most importantly, (3) a provider should not be directly involved in killing a patient (Sullivan, 2005). The opponents of euthanasia also feel that a physician cannot, with medical certainty, tell patients that they will die within 6 months. The patient's emotional state and response to medication may alter that prognosis.

Dr. Jack Kevorkian and Dr. Phillip Nitschke

It is important to mention two physicians who have strongly supported euthanasia throughout the years. U.S. physician Dr. Jack Kevorkian, or Dr. Death as he was called, had provided assisted suicide services to at least 45 ill patients. In 1989, he developed a suicide machine that allowed patients to administer a lethal injection of medication to themselves. In 1997, the U.S. Supreme Court ruled that individuals who want to kill themselves, but are physically unable to do so, have no constitutional right to end their lives. Dr. Kevorkian was sentenced to 10–25 years in prison that same year. He was paroled in 2007 because he was in failing health and died in 2011 (Notable Names Database, 2013).

Australian physician Dr. Phillip Nitschke travels internationally presenting "how to commit suicide" clinics. Several years ago, he created a concoction from household ingredients that he calls the "Peaceful Pill." He believes that if there is a right to life, there is also a right to die and that individuals should have the right to choose to end life. He does not restrict this right to just the terminally ill. He also believes that the depressed, the elderly, and the grieving should have the right to end their lives (Exit International, 2013).

Transplantation

Transplantation is the general procedure of implanting a functional organ from one person to another. This procedure can include blood transfusions or complicated procedures such as heart and lung transplants and bone marrow transplants. Organ transplants are becoming a more common approach to the treatment of diseased organs, making organ donations important to saving lives. Many patients have a significant chance for long-term survival because of impressive gains in the field (Burrows, 2004; Woloschak, 2003). Organs can be harvested from a living or dead person. As a result, the waiting list for organs has increased from 35,000 to 85,000 while the number of organ donors has remained stagnant (Berman, 2005). There are two major ethical and legal issues associated with organ transplants between humans, including (1) the decision-making process for who receives the organ and (2) financial remuneration from selling organs, which has resulted in a black market for buying organs. It is important to note that since 1984, as a result of the passage of the National Organ Transplant Act, it is illegal in the United States to buy and sell organs, which has resulted in 6,500 Americans dying annually because of lack of available organs. By 1990, many countries and the World Health Organization have issued similar bans. The Ethics Committee of the Transplantation Society issued a policy statement further supporting the ban on illegally buying and selling organs (Friedman & Friedman, 2006).

Who Should Receive the Organ?

According to the **United Network for Organ Sharing (UNOS)**, there are 76,026 active organ waiting list candidates, with 4,534 donors available—a nearly 2 to 1 ratio (UNOS, 2013). There are ethical questions when making the decision as to who receives an organ. In the United States, there is an organ waiting list. Should the sickest recipient waiting on the organ list receive the organ or should the patient who may live longer receive the organ? Under the current UNOS, patients awaiting a transplant are assigned a priority based on medical need. If a patient is waiting for a heart transplant, the patient who is on life support or is in intensive care has first priority. Kidneys are allocated based on a point system maintained by UNOS. Liver transplants also include guidelines on alcohol abuse, which often destroys livers. UNOS guidelines require 6 months of sobriety prior to a transplant. Should the alcoholic receive a liver transplant at all? Some organ transplant centers will not provide any liver transplants to any alcoholics (Giuliano, 1997).

A recent trend over the last decade is transplanting organs in the elderly. The number of people over the age of 65 has tripled between 1996 and 2005. The ethical dilemma for a surgeon is whether to transplant an organ in an older patient rather than trying to save the life of a younger patient. Studies have indicated that survival rates for elderly lung recipients are acceptable—a 73.6% 3-year survival rate compared to 74.2% for younger patients (Davis, 2008). However, does the surgeon opt to shorten the life of a younger patient in order to give an additional 3 years of life to an elderly patient who already has lived a full life?

Consent for Organ Donations

As stated in the previous paragraph, organ donations may also occur when a person dies. Depending on the state of residence, individuals may enroll in a program that gives permission for organ harvest when they die, alleviating the pressure on families of having to make that decision to harvest the organs. However, in some states, permission is required by the family, which places pressure on them. Some families feel it is unethical to donate their family member's body for science because of religious or personal philosophical reasons.

The Health Services and Research Administration collects organ donor data. According to historical data, in 1988 there were only nearly 6,000 donors, of which 4,000 were deceased donors. There has been a continued increase in donors over the decades. In 2013, there were 4,530 donors of which 2,640 were deceased. Despite these numbers, there continues to be long waiting lists for organs with 18 people dying daily waiting for a transplant (Organ Procurement and Transplantation Network, 2013).

In other parts of the world, countries use **presumed consent**, which means that if a parent does not actively oppose the transplantation, the procedure automatically occurs. In the United States, the consent must be actively received from the family first. As a result of presumed consent, those countries receive significantly more donations (Burrows, 2004). Is it an ethical policy to assume the family will consent to organ donations? Oftentimes, a family is frozen with grief and cannot make a coherent decision.

Organ Transplants from Family Member

Often, organ transplants may occur between two family members because it has been determined that the compatibility is very high, which would result in less risk for an organ to be rejected. An ethical issue with this situation is the pressure a family member feels from other family members to agree to give one of their organs to another member. Most parents would gladly donate organs to their sick offspring. What about siblings who don't like each other? Should they feel compelled to give an organ? Are they being pressured by other family members to go into surgery? The donors are also at risk. Any time surgery is performed there is a risk to the individual. Should physicians provide a "medical excuse" to the potential family donor as a way to rationalize their decision not to give their organ to a family member? The family member should not be coerced or forced to have the surgery.

Financial Payoff for Organ Donations

Living donor organ transplantation is the only field in medicine in which two individuals are ultimately involved—the person donating the organ and the person receiving the organ. Because of the success of organ transplantation, more treatments are focusing on this alternative. As stated previously, the statistics indicate that the need for organ donations is far outstripping the number of donors. In the United States, 18 states offer a tax incentive to donate organs or marrow. These states are Arkansas, Georgia, Idaho, Iowa, Louisiana, Maryland, Massachusetts, Minnesota, Mississippi, New Mexico, New York, North Dakota, Ohio, Oklahoma, South Carolina, Utah, Virginia, and Wisconsin. Louisiana residents who donate are allowed to take a tax credit as much as $10,000 on their state income taxes for travel, lodging, and lost wages related to the donation process (American Transplant Foundation, 2013).

Also, as a result of the increasing need for organs, a **black market**, which is an illegal form of commerce, has developed for the buying and selling of organs. **Organs Watch**, established in 1999 at the University of California at Berkeley, has monitored organ transplants in 12 countries worldwide. They have witnessed Israeli patients who travel to Turkey to receive kidneys sold by Romanians and European and North American patients receiving kidneys purchased from Manila whose operations were set up by an independent liver broker, Liver4You. There have been few prosecutions; however, in 2013, in Kosovo, five people were convicted of operating an organ trafficking ring around the world. The physician involved received 8 years in jail (Bilefsky, 2013). The procurement of body parts from poor people may be considered illegal in most countries in the world and certainly unethical, but nothing has been done because many of the organ recipients need these organs to live and those individuals that sell the organs are making an informed choice (Scheper-Hughes, 2003).

As a result of the inequity of healthcare costs between the United States and other countries, the concept of *medical tourism* or "medical value travel" has evolved. U.S. organ transplants can cost $100,000, but are considerably less expensive overseas. IndUShealth and Global Health Administrators, Inc. have collaborated with insurance companies to arrange for U.S. residents to obtain medical treatment in India. United Group Programs offers living and deceased organ donor transplants from foreign countries such as Thailand (Bramstedt & Xu, 2007). Medical tourism has become so popular that the first medical tourism association was formed. The Medical Tourism Association, also referred to as the Medical Travel Association (MTA), is the first membership-based international nonprofit trade association for the medical tourism and global healthcare industry comprised of international hospitals, healthcare providers, medical travel facilitators, insurance companies, and other affiliated companies and members with the common goal of promoting quality healthcare worldwide (Medical Tourism Association, 2013). Although these programs are cost-effective, concerns about follow-up care or complications may determine the effectiveness of these medical value plans. Are these programs ethical? Are insurance companies focusing on cost rather than safety of the patient? Is the patient fully aware of the risk of these types of options?

Xenotransplantation

Another type of transplantation is **xenotransplantation**, which is the transfer of organs from one species to another. This has evolved as a result of the shortage of human organs available for donation. The first xenotransplantation was the transfer of a baboon heart into a 5-pound infant in 1984. Baby Fae survived 3 weeks before the baboon heart was rejected (Ascension Health, 2013). Since that time, several other xenotransplants have occurred using pig livers and hearts. Pigs are the preferred choice for xenotransplantation. There have been few successful xenotransplants because of the high risk of rejection.

Although xenotransplantation is promising, the ethical dilemma is that we are killing animals for these procedures, which are considered experimental. Is there a difference between killing animals for food and killing them for organ transplants? Although we may be ultimately saving lives, for some individuals, xenotransplantation is not ethical. Another issue is the contraction of animal disease to humans. If xenotransplantation is to be successful, it is important that the animals be screened for any diseases humans may contract such as rabies and viruses. The Food and Drug Administration is responsible for regulating xenotransplantation activities.

CONCLUSION

There are several ethical issues discussed in this chapter involving the healthcare industry and its stakeholders. There are two components of ethics in health care: medical ethics, which focus on the treatment of the patient, and bioethics, which focus on technology and how it is utilized in health care. The most important stakeholder in health care is the patient. The most important relationship with this stakeholder is their healthcare provider. Their relationship is impacted by the other stakeholders in the industry, including the government who regulates healthcare provider activities, the insurance companies who interact with both provider and patient, and healthcare facilities, such as hospitals or managed care facilities, where the physician has a relationship. All of these stakeholders can influence how a healthcare provider interacts with the patient because they have an interest in the outcome. For that reason, many organizations that represent these stakeholders have developed codes of ethics so individuals are provided guidance for ethical behavior. Codes of ethics for the physicians and other healthcare providers, nurses, pharmaceutical companies, and medical equipment companies were discussed that emphasize how these stakeholders should interact with both the healthcare providers and patients. These codes of conduct also apply to the relationship between employees in a healthcare facility. The issue of workplace bullying has been a continued problem for many years. The Joint Commission issued a statement and guidelines for workplace behavior in the healthcare industry. The Joint Commission indicated that this type of behavior can be destructive, resulting in medical errors.

Another major area of ethics is the treatment of patients who are dying. Euthanasia, including physician-assisted suicide, illegal in all states but Oregon, Washington, and most recently, Vermont, has been a controversial patient issue for years. There are supporters of euthanasia because they feel it is the individual's right to choose when they want to end their life and they should have assistance from a physician, if needed. Opponents feel it is unethical because it is the responsibility of a physician to save a life, or not to take a life. This issue is tied into advance directives that a patient gives to the provider requesting that certain treatments be administered or not. If the patient is incompetent, advanced directives provide guidance on how the provider should treat the patient at the end of his or her life.

Another area of ethical discussion is organ transplantation. There are not enough organ donors in the United States, thereby creating a long waiting list. With limited supply, the ethical dilemma of organ transplants is how to determine who should receive an organ. For example, the famous New York Yankee baseball player, Mickey Mantle, a long-time alcoholic, received a liver transplant. He needed a liver transplant as a result of his alcoholism. There was a public outcry because people felt that he received the liver because he was famous. Although the doctors explained that was not the case, people were upset because they felt that his addiction caused the liver failure. Why should he receive a new liver after he damaged his first one? As a result of designer or donor babies, children must be included in the transplant discussion. Should parents have another child specifically to save their other child's life? Children designated as donor babies may have emotional issues because they will eventually be aware that they were created specifically for their sibling's transplant needs.

When Dolly the sheep was cloned in 1995, she created an international furor. There are diametrically opposed views on cloning. Opponents feel that cloning takes the natural procreation process and turns it into a scientific experiment. Supporters feel that the scientific community has provided an opportunity to recreate a specimen, at will, with the desired genes.

And, finally, it is necessary to address the ethical foundation of our healthcare system. With over 48 million uninsured citizens in the United States, is it unethical that there is no universal healthcare system? The United States is the only industrialized nation, with the exception of South Africa, that has no universal healthcare coverage. Other nations have stated that health care is a right, not a privilege. Is it unethical for the United States to have a system that does not provide for all citizens? The recent legal battles over the implementation of the individual mandate to purchase health insurance indicates the various beliefs of access to healthcare insurance to most citizens. This text cannot provide answers to ethical situations because ethics are viewed differently by each individual. This chapter can only provide questions for readers so they can assess their ethical viewpoint as it relates to the healthcare industry.

VOCABULARY

Advance directives

Advanced Medical Technology Association

Alternative reproductive methods

American College of Healthcare Executives (ACHE)

American College of Physicians and Harvard Pilgrim Health Care Ethics Program

American Nurses Association

Autonomy

Beneficence

Bioethics

Black market

Carrier testing

Cloning

Code of ethics

Collegial model

Common rule

Contractual model

Diagnostic testing

Dignity

Duty to treat

Effectiveness

Engineering model

Ethical standards

Ethics

Euthanasia

Genetic testing

Healthcare ethical dilemma

Human Genome Project

Informed consent

Institutional Review Boards (IRBs)

Justice

Lateral violence

Medical ethics

Medical tourism

Minimal infringement

Nonmalfeasance

Nonvoluntary euthanasia

Nuffield Council on Bioethics

Oregon Death with Dignity Act

Organs Watch

Paternalism

Preimplantation genetic diagnosis (PGD)

Pharmaceutical Research and Manufacturers of America

Pharmacogenic testing

Physician-assisted suicide

Physician Payment Sunshine Act

Predictive and a symptomatic testing

Prenatal testing

Presumed consent

Priestly model

Procreation

Proportionality

Public education

Reproductive cloning

Research cloning

Research genetic testing

Respect for autonomy

Stakeholder

Stakeholder management

Stem cells

Stewardship model

The Joint Commission

Therapeutic cloning

Transplantation

United Network for Organ Sharing (UNOS)

Voluntary euthanasia

Workplace bullying

Xenotransplantation

REFERENCES

Adams, A. (1992). *Bullying at work*. London: Virago Press: 1–20.

Adelaide Center for Bioethics and Culture. (2013). Healthcare, Retrieved from http://www.bioethics.org.au/Resources/Resource%20Topics/Healthcare.html

Advanced Medical Technology Association (AMTA). (2013). Code of ethics. Retrieved from http://advamed.org/issues/code-of-ethics

American College of Healthcare Executives (ACHE). (2013). About ACHE. Retrieved from http://www.ache.org/aboutache.cfm

American Medical Association (AMA). (2013a). Medical ethics. Retrieved from http://www.ama-assn.org/ama/pub/physician-resources/medical-ethics.shtml

American Medical Association (AMA). (2013b). Toolkit for physician financial transparency reports (Sunshine Act). Retrieved from https://www.ama-assn.org/ama/pub/advocacy/topics/sunshine-act-and-physician-financial-transparency-reports.page

American Nurses Association (ANA). (2011). Lateral violence and bullying in nursing. Retrieved from http://nursingworld.org/Mobile/Nursing-Factsheets/lateral-violence-and-bullying-in-nursing.html

American Nurses Association (ANA). (2013). Ethics. Retrieved from http://www.nursingworld.org/MainMenuCategories/EthicsStandards.aspx

American Transplant Foundation. (2013). Tax incentives and organ donation. Retrieved from http://www.americantransplantfoundation.org/2012/11/tax-incentives-and-organ-donation/

Ascension Health. (2013). Cases. Retrieved from http://www.ascensionhealth.org/ethics/public/cases/case4.asp

Ayoko, O., Callan, V., & Hartel, C. (2003). Workplace conflict, bullying and counterproductive behaviors. *International Journal of Organizational Analysis, 11*, 283–301.

Baylis, F. (2002). Human cloning: Three mistakes and an alternative. *Journal of Medicine and Philosophy, 27*(3), 319–337.

Beauchamp, T., & Childress, J. (2001). *Principles of biomedical ethics* (5th ed.). Oxford: Oxford University Press.

Berman, R. (2005). Lethal legislation. *Robert Kennedy School Review, 6*, 13–18.

Bilefsky, D. (2013, April 29). Five convicted in Kosovo organ trafficking. *New York Times*. Retrieved from http://www.nytimes.com/2013/04/30/world/europe/in-kosovo-5-are-convicted-in-organ-trafficking.html?_r=0

Bramstedt, K., & Xu, J. (2007). Checklist: Passport, plane ticket, organ transplant. *American Journal of Transplantation, 7*, 1698–1701.

Buchanan, D. (2008). Autonomy, paternalism and justice: Ethical priorities in public health. *American Journal of Public Health, 98*, 15–21.

Burkett, L. (2007). Medical tourism. Concerns, benefits, and the American legal perspective. *The Journal of Legal Medicine, 28*, 223–245.

Burrows, L. (2004). Selling organs for transplantation. *The Mount Sinai Journal of Medicine, 71*(4), 251–254.

Campbell, E. (2007). Doctors and drug companies—Scrutinizing influential relationships. *New England Journal of Medicine, 357*, 18, 1796–1796.

Carroll, A., & Buchholtz, A. (2008). *Business society: Ethics and stakeholder management* (7th ed.). Mason, OH: Thomson/Southwestern.

Centers for Disease Control and Prevention (CDC). (2013). Health insurance coverage. Retrieved from http://www.cdc.gov/nchs/fastats/hinsure.htm

Childress, J., Faden, R., & Gaare, R. (2002). Public health ethics: Mapping the terrain. *Journal of Law Medical Ethics*, *30*, 170–178.

The Coalition of Americans for Research Ethics. (2013). Do no harm. Retrieved from http://www.stemcellresearch.org

Coleman, C., Bouesseau, M., & Reis, A. (2008). The contribution of ethics to public health. *Bullletin of the World Health Organization*, *86*(8), 578–589.

Davis, R. (2008). More elderly patients are having transplantation surgery. Retrieved from http://www.usatoday.com/news/health/2008-02-04-transplant_N.htm

Dayal, M., & Zarek, S. (2008). Preimplantation genetic diagnosis. Retrieved from http://emedicine.medscape.com/article/273415-overview

Death with Dignity Act, O.R.S. 127.800-995 (1994). Retrieved from http://public.health.oregon.gov/ProviderPartnerResources/EvaluationResearch/DeathwithDignityAct/Pages/index.aspx

Djurkovic, N., McCormack, D., & Casimir, G. (2008). Workplace bullying and intention to leave: The modernizing effect of perceived organizational support. *Human Resource Management Journal*, *18*(4), 405–420.

Ethics Resource Center. (2009). The PLUS decision making model. Retrieved from http://www.ethics.org/resource/plus-decision-making-model

Exit International. (2013). Voluntary euthanasia and assisted suicide information by Exit International. Retrieved from http://www.exitinternational.net

Food and Drug Administration (FDA). (2013). Information sheet guidance for institutional review boards, clinical investigators, and sponsors. Retrieved from http://www.fda.gov/oc/ohrt/irbs/facts .html#IRBOrg

Friedman, E., & Friedman, A. (2006). Payment for donor kidneys: Pros and cons. *International Society of Nephrology*, January, 960–962.

Gillon, R. (1994). Principles of medical ethics. *British Medical Journal*, *309*, 184.

Giuliano, K. (1997). Organ transplants: Tackling the tough ethical questions. *Nursing*, *27*, 34–40.

Hoel, H., Faragher, B., & Cooper, C. (2004). Bullying is detrimental to health but all bullying behaviors are not necessarily equally damaging. *British Journal of Guidance & Counseling*, *32*(3), 367–387.

Keashly, L. (2001). Interpersonal and systemic aspects of emotional abuse at work: The target's perspective. *Violence and Victims,* 16, 233–268.

Korenman, S. G. (2009). Teaching the responsible conduct of research in humans. Retrieved from http://ori.hhs.gov/education/products/ucla/chapter2/page04b.htm

LaVan, H., & Martin, W. (2007). Bullying in the U.S. workplace: Normative and process-oriented ethical approaches. *Journal of Business Ethics*, *83,* 147–165.

Medical Tourism Association (MTA). (2013). About the MTA. Retrieved from http://www.medicaltourismassociation.com/en/about-the-MTA.html

Mehlman, M., & Berg, J. (2008). Human subjects' protections in biomedical enhancement research: Assessing risk and benefit and obtaining informed consent. *Journal of Law, Medicine & Ethics*, *36*(3), 546–559.

Miller, R. (2006). *Problems in health care law* (9th ed.). Sudbury, MA: Jones and Bartlett.

Minding the Workplace. (2009). Workplace bullying in healthcare I: The Joint Commission standards. Retrieved from http://newworkplace.wordpress.com/2009/12/15/workplace-bullying-in-healthcare-i-the-joint-commission-standards/

Morgan, S., Harrison, T., Long, S., Afiffi, W., Stephenson, M., & Reichert, T. (2005). Family discussions about organ donations: How the media influences opinions about organ donations. *Clinical Transplant, 19*, 674–682.

National Human Genome Research Institute. (2013). Regulation of genetic tests. Retrieved from http://www.genome.gov/10002335

Niles, N. (2011). *Basics of the U.S. health care system*. Sudbury, MA: Jones and Bartlett.

Niles, N. (2013). *Basic concepts of health care human resource management*. Sudbury, MA: Jones and Bartlett: 50

Notable Names Database. (2013). Jack Kevorkian. Retrieved from http://www.nndb.com/people/272/000023203/

Nuffield Council on Bioethics Report. (2013). Public health: Ethical issues guide to the report. Retrieved from http://www.nuffieldbioethics.org/fileLibrary/pdf/Public_Health_-_short_guide.pdf

Oak Ridge National Laboratory (ORNL). (2013). Human Genome Project information. Retrieved from http://www.ornl.gov/sci/techresources/Human_Genome/home.shtml

Oddo, A. (2001). Health care ethics: A patient-centered decision model. *Journal of Business Ethics, 29*, 126.

O'Reilly, K. B. (2009). Five people die under new Washington physician-assisted suicide law. Retrieved from http://www.amednews.com/article/20090706/profession/307069977/7

Organ Procurement and Transplantation Network, Health Resources and Services Administration, U.S. Department of Health & Human Services. (2013). Donors recovered in U.S. by donor type. Retrieved from http://optn.transplant.hrsa.gov/latestData/viewDataReports.asp

Peng, T. (2008). Opening the books. Retrieved from http://www.newsweek.com/id/160894?from=rss?nav=slate

Pharmaceutical Research and Manufacturers of America (PhRMA). (2013). About PhRMA. Retrieved from http://www.phrma.org/about

Povar, C., Blumen, H., Daniel, J., Daub, S., Evans, L., Holm, R., . . . Campbell, A. (2004). Ethics in practice: Managed care and the changing health care environment. *American College of Physicians, 4*(2), 131–136.

Scheper-Hughes, N. (2003). Keeping an eye on the global traffic in human organs. *Lancet, 361*, 1645–1648.

Sullivan, D. (2005). Euthanasia versus letting die: Christian decision-making in terminal patients. *Ethics and Medicine, 21*(2), 109–118.

Sullivan, D. (2006). Stem cells 101—An audio/MP3 version. Retrieved from http://www.bioethics.com/?page_id=533

Sultz, H., & Young, K. (2006). *Health care USA: Understanding its organization and delivery* (5th ed.). Sudbury, MA: Jones and Bartlett.

University of Miami Ethics Programs. (2013). Schiavo timeline, part 1. Retrieved from http://www.miami.edu/index.php/ethics/projects/schiavo/schiavo_timeline/

Taylor, P. (1975). *Principles of ethics: An introduction to ethics* (2nd ed.). Encino, CA: Dickinson.

The Joint Commission. (2008, July 9). Behaviors that undermine a culture of safety. *Sentinal Event Alert, 40*. Retrieved from http://www.jointcommission.org/assets/1/18/SEA_40.PDF

United Network for Organ Sharing (UNOS). (2013). Homepage. Retrieved from http://www.unos.org

Vartia, M. (2001). Consequences of workplace bullying with respect to the well-being of its targets and the observers or bullying . *Scandinavian Journal of Work Environment and Health, 27*, 63–59.

Veatch, R. (1972). Medical ethics: Professional or universal. *Harvard Theological Review, 65*, 531–559.

Washington State Department of Health. (2012). Washington State Department of Health 2012 Death with Dignity Act Report: Executive summary. Retrieved from http://www.doh.wa.gov/portals/1/Documents/Pubs /422-109-DeathWithDignityAct2012.pdf

Wazana, A. (2000). Physicians and the pharmaceutical industry: Is a gift ever just a gift? *Journal of American Medical Association*, *283*, 373–380.

Woloschak, G. (2003). Transplantation: Biomedical and ethical concerns raised by the cloning stem cell debate. *Zygon*, *8*, 599–704.

Wynia, M. (2007). Ethics and public health emergencies: Encouraging responsibility. *The American Journal of Bioethics*, *7*, 1–4.

Xue, J., Ma, J., & Louis, T. (2001). Forecast of the number of patients with end-stage renal disease in the United States to the year 2010. *Journal of American Sociological Nephrology*, *12*, 2753–2758.

Yamada, D. C. (2004). Crafting a legislative response to workplace bullying. *Employee Rights and Employment Policy Journal, 8*, 475. Retrieved from http://ssrn.com/abstract=1303725

NOTES

STUDENT ACTIVITY 12-1

IN YOUR OWN WORDS

Based on this chapter, please provide an explanation of the following concepts in your own words. DO NOT RECITE the text.

Paternalism: _____
_____
_____

Medical tourism: _____
_____
_____

Therapeutic cloning: _____
_____
_____

Stem cell: _____
_____
_____

Transplantation: _____
_____
_____

Xenotransplantation: _____
_____
_____

Presumed consent: _____
_____
_____

Autonomy: _____
_____
_____

Stewardship model: _____
_____
_____

Institutional Review Boards: _____
_____
_____

STUDENT ACTIVITY 12-2

REAL LIFE APPLICATIONS: CASE SCENARIO ONE

A friend from high school moved into your neighborhood, who is pregnant with her third child. She told you that her eldest child was very ill and required a bone marrow transplant. There were no matching donors on the national list. She and her husband decided to have a baby that could be used to save her other child. She asked what you thought of her actions. Before making any statements that could hurt your friend, you decide to do some research on the topic.

ACTIVITY

(1) Explain this type of procedure and what the procedure entails, (2) identify any ethical issues associated with this type of procedure, and (3) provide an opinion on this procedure—would you do it or not and why?

RESPONSES

_____

_____

_____

_____

_____

_____

_____

_____

_____

_____

_____

_____

_____

CASE SCENARIO TWO

You need a back operation but cannot afford your cost share of the operation. You have heard that other countries may offer less expensive medical procedures. You decide to investigate this option.

ACTIVITY

Perform an Internet search and use textbook information on medical tourism. Locate two countries that offer lower cost surgeries. Write a report and submit to the class.

RESPONSES

_____

_____

_____

_____

_____

_____

_____

_____

_____

_____

_____

_____

_____

_____

CASE SCENARIO THREE

One of your best friends is on the waiting list for a new liver. According to current research, there is a huge waiting list for organ donations. Several states have offered tax incentives to encourage organ donation. You are unsure of how to encourage her to be optimistic.

ACTIVITY

You decide to do research on tax incentives in the different states and other options to encourage organ donation.

RESPONSES

_____

_____

_____

_____

_____

_____

_____

_____

_____

_____

_____

_____

_____

CASE SCENARIO FOUR

You and your friend were discussing euthanasia and whether it was an ethical procedure. Your friend does not believe in it but you feel it is an option depending on the circumstance. You think of your great grandmother who is terminally ill but is in pain and is on life support.

ACTIVITY

Using the textbook and the Internet, research both the pros and cons of euthanasia.

RESPONSES

_____

_____

_____

_____

_____

_____

_____

_____

_____

_____

_____

_____

_____

STUDENT ACTIVITY 12-3

INTERNET EXERCISES

Write your answers in the space provided.

- Visit each of the websites listed here.
- Name the organization.
- Locate their mission statement on their website.
- Provide a brief overview of the activities of the organization.
- How do these organizations participate in the U.S. healthcare system?

Websites

http://www.nursingworld.org

Organization Name: _____

Mission Statement:

_____

_____

_____

Overview of Activities: _____

_____

_____

Importance of organization to U.S. health care:

_____

_____

_____

http://www.thehastingscenter.org

Organization Name: _____

Mission Statement:

_____

_____

_____

Overview of Activities: _____

_____

_____

Importance of organization to U.S. health care:

_____

_____

_____

Organization Name: _____

Mission Statement:

_____

_____

_____

Overview of Activities: _____

_____

_____

Importance of organization to U.S. health care:

_____

_____

_____

Organization Name: _____

Mission Statement:

_____

_____

_____

Overview of Activities: _____

_____

_____

Importance of organization to U.S. health care:

_____

_____

_____

Organization Name: _____

Mission Statement:

_____

_____

_____

Overview of Activities: _____

_____

_____

Importance of organization to U.S. health care:

_____

_____

_____

http://stemcells.nih.gov

Organization Name: _____

Mission Statement:

_____

_____

_____

Overview of Activities: _____

_____

_____

Importance of organization to U.S. health care:

_____

_____

_____

STUDENT ACTIVITY 12-4

DISCUSSION QUESTIONS

The following are suggested discussion questions for this chapter.

(1) If you were going to develop a code of ethics for this class, what behavior components should be included?

_____

_____

_____

_____

_____

(2) Do you believe in cloning? Do you think humans should be cloned? Defend your answer.

_____

_____

_____

_____

_____

(3) What is your definition of ethics? What do you think are some unethical situations in the healthcare industry?

_____

_____

_____

_____

_____

(4) What is workplace bullying? Have you witnessed this behavior in the workplace? Do you consider this behavior unethical? Defend your answer.

_____

_____

_____

_____

(5) What is voluntary euthanasia? Do you believe there should be national legislation to make it legal in all states? Defend your answer.

_____

_____

_____

_____

The Navigate Companion Website for this text is a great source for additional information on the U.S. healthcare system. You can gain a new perspective on many of the topics presented in this chapter by visiting http://go.jblearning.com/Niles2e. You'll find additional student activities, further reading, and interactive study tools that explore:

• Understanding healthcare ethics
• Workplace bullying in health care
• Ethical decision making in health care
• And much more.

Chapter 13

Mental Health Issues

LEARNING OBJECTIVES

The student will be able to:

- List the six types of mental health professionals and their roles in mental health care.

- List and define at least 10 mental health disorders as defined by the American Psychiatric Association's *Diagnostic and Statistical Manual of Mental Disorders*.

- Discuss at least five liability issues surrounding mental health professionals.

- Define mental health behavioral companies and discuss their relationship to mental health care.

- Discuss mental health issues in high-risk populations.

- Define and discuss why posttraumatic stress disorder (PTSD) occurs.

- Evaluate the importance of the National Institute for Mental Health and the American Psychological Association (APA) to mental health care.

DID YOU KNOW THAT?

- Surveys indicate that one in four Americans suffer from a mental disorder in any one year.

- Half of all lifetime mental health illnesses begin by age 14; three-quarters occur by age 24.

- The annual economic, indirect cost of mental illness is estimated to be $79 billion.

- Over 50% of students with a mental disorder age 14 and older drop out of high school—the highest dropout rate of any disability group.

- Mental health ranks second to heart disease as a limitation on health and productivity.

INTRODUCTION

According to the World Health Organization, mental wellness or mental health is an integral and essential component of health. It is a state of well-being in which an individual can cope with normal stressors, can work productively, and is able to make a contribution to his or her community. Mental health behavioral disorders can be caused by biological, psychological, and personality factors. By 2020, behavioral health disorders will surpass all physiological diseases as a major cause of disability worldwide (World Health Organization, 2010). Mental disorders are the leading cause of disability in the United States. Mental illnesses can impact individuals of any age, race, religion, or income. In 2011, an estimated 10 million adults ages 18 years and older had a serious mental illness. Two million youths ages 12–17 years had a major depressive episode during a year (SAMHSA, 2011). Although mental health is a disease that requires medical care, its characteristics set it apart from traditional medical care. U.S. Surgeon

General David Satcher released a landmark report in 1999 on mental health illness, *Mental Health: A Report of the Surgeon General*. The Surgeon General's report on mental health defines **mental disorders** as conditions that alter thinking processes, moods, or behavior that result in dysfunction or stress. It can be psychological or biological in nature. The most common conditions include **phobias**, which are excessive fear of objects or activities; substance abuse; and affective disorders, which are emotional states such as depression. Severe mental illness would include schizophrenia, major depression, and psychosis. Obsessive–compulsive disorders (OCD), mental retardation, Alzheimer's disease, and dementia are also considered mentally disabled conditions. According to the report, mental health ranks second to heart disease as a limitation on health and productivity (U.S. Public Health Service, 1999). People who have mental disorders often exhibit feelings of anxiety, or may have hallucinations or feelings of sadness or fear that can limit normal functioning in their daily life. Because the cause or etiology of mental health disorders are less defined and less understood compared to traditional medical problems, interventions are less developed than other areas of medicine (Anderson, Rice, & Kominski, 2007). This chapter will provide a discussion on the following topics: the history of the U.S. mental healthcare system, a background of healthcare professionals, mental healthcare law, insurance coverage for mental health, barriers to mental health care, the populations at risk for mental disorders, the types of mental health disorders as classified by the American Psychiatric Association's *Diagnostic and Statistical Manual of Mental Disorders (DSM),* liability issues associated with mental health care, an analysis of the mental healthcare system, and guidelines and recommendations to improve U.S. mental health care.

HISTORY OF U.S. MENTAL HEALTH CARE

Over the past 3 centuries, the mental health system has consisted of a patchwork of services that has become very fragmented (Regier et al., 1993). Initially, mentally ill individuals were relegated to care by their families. State governments built **insane asylums**, later known as hospitals. In the mid-18th century, the state of Pennsylvania opened a hospital in Philadelphia where the mentally ill were housed in the basement. During this period, Virginia was the first state to build an asylum in its capital city of Williamsburg. If the mentally ill were not cared for by their families or sent to an asylum, they were found in jails or almshouse. It was not until the 19th century that the mentally ill were treated with sensitivity. This **moral treatment** approach was used in Europe earlier with success. Mental health patients in hospitals were treated while participating in work and educational activities. The first mental health reformers in the United States were Dorothea Dix and Horace Mann, who crusaded for this moral movement by convincing the public that some mentally ill patients can be treated in a controlled environment outside the confines of an asylum. Asylums should be focused on housing those mentally ill with chronic conditions that were untreatable. During this period, more states built more asylums, which became overcrowded. It is important to note that the local governments were responsible for funding the care of the asylum residents, which resulted in deteriorating conditions and exposure of the patients to inhumane treatment. State care acts were passed that mandated state funding for treatment between 1894 and World War I. Asylums were renamed mental hospitals. Psychiatric units were also opened in general hospitals to promote mental health as part of general health care (Regier et al., 1993).

After World War I, many war veterans returned home with mental disorders, or what is now known as PTSD (posttraumatic stress disorder), because of their war experiences. It was not until the 1930s that prescriptions became available. However, other controversial treatments were used, such as **electrotherapy**. Brain surgery or lobotomies became a method to treat the mentally ill. World War II further focused the government on mental health issues and the National Institute of Mental Health was created. Government funding was awarded for mental health training and research. The Department of Veterans Affairs (VA) established psychiatric hospitals and clinics. During this period, most health care focused on inpatient services. The VA also developed mental health disorder categories in order to better treat their war veterans. By the mid-1950s, over 500,000 mental health patients were being treated in government mental health hospitals. In 1952, the **American Psychiatric Association** published their first *DSM*, which was coordinated with the World Health Organization's (WHO) International Classification of Disease (American Psychiatric Association, 2012a) to encourage acceptance of mental health disorders.

Finally, the first psychoactive medication was developed that allowed outpatient treatment of mentally disabled patients. In 1955, the **U.S. Commission on Mental Health** was established. They investigated the quality of mental hospitals and allocated funding for outpatient facilities. As more **psychotropic medications** were developed, Congress provided more funding allocations for community-based services. Medicaid, Medicare, Supplemental Security Income (SSI), Social Security, and Disability insurance became accessible for mental health care (Grob, 1983, 1994; Sultz & Young, 2006).

During the 1960s and 1970s, community mental health centers were developed and supported by the federal government. Most of the funding focused on the less severe mentally ill who could live normally with outpatient services. In the late 1970s, President Carter appointed a Presidential Committee on Mental Health, which had limited success; however, Medicaid payments for outpatient mental health services were increased. By 1990, most mental health services were offered as outpatient services. Research in the 1990s indicated that the reason people did not seek assistance for mental health disorders is their shame and embarrassment. The Mental Health Parity Act was passed in 1996 to ensure there was adequate coverage for mental health illnesses and that annual lifetime reimbursement limits on mental health services were similar to other medical benefits.

In 2002, President George W. Bush established the **New Freedom Commission on Mental Health** that was charged with implementing an analytical study on the U.S. mental health service system and developing recommendations to improve the public mental health system that could be implemented at the federal, state, and local levels. This was the first study performed since 1978 when President Jimmy Carter's Mental Health Commission's report was published. In 2003, the Commission issued a final report that contained nearly 20 recommendations that focused primarily on mental illness recovery, including a comprehensive approach to mental health care, such as the screening of mental illness for children and other high-risk populations (APA, 2003).

The **Mental Health Parity and Addiction Equity Act of 2008** further supported mental health care by requiring insurance plans to offer mental health benefits and cost sharing similar to those of traditional medical benefits. Over the past 15 years, increased funding has increased the quality of mental health services. As with the 1996 act, there were loopholes that reduced the effectiveness of the 2008 act. The current administration has recognized the importance of funding mental health initiatives, including teacher training programs for mental health awareness (Mohney, 2013). The current administration has finally issued the final rule on guidance to implement the regulations regarding the 2008 act. The final rule requires transparency of health plans on how they interpret medical coverage for mental health problems. The final rule should strengthen the impact of the 2008 act. The final rule applies to health insurance plans that becomes effective on July 1, 2014 (Moran, 2013).

BACKGROUND OF MENTAL HEALTH SERVICES

Mental Health Professionals

Mental health problems impact not only the individual but family members and friends as well. As a result of the vast impact of mental health disabilities, behavioral services are provided by psychiatrists, psychologists, social workers, nurses, counselors, and therapists (Shi & Singh, 2008). Social workers will receive training in counseling, normally a master's degree, and can provide support for an individual with a mental health disability. Family and vocational counselors may also be involved in the treatment plan as well as recreational therapists. Mental health can be such a complex condition that impacts different aspects of the life of a mentally ill person that often many different mental health professionals are there for support and treatment. Most of these mental health professionals provide outpatient or ambulatory care for the mentally ill. Inpatient care may be offered in the psychiatric units of a hospital, mental hospitals, or substance abuse facilities (Pointer, Williams, Isaacs, & Knickman, 2007).

Psychiatrists are specialty physicians who can prescribe medication and admit patients to hospitals. **Psychologists**, who also participate in the treatment of mental health, cannot prescribe drugs but provide different types of therapy. Social workers focus on mental health counseling. Nurses may also specialize in psychiatric care. There may be additional counselors and therapists who participate in the treatment of the mentally disabled.

However, there are liability issues that mental health professionals may face. A recent study (Woody, 2008) indicated that there were seven reasons mental health professionals are at high risk for liability and complaints:

- When mental health professionals provide services to both children and their families they are at risk for more complaints from their patients regarding care. Families may be wary when a mental health professional provides services to their children.

- Because of the increased government regulations of the licensing of practitioners, professionals no longer have a say in establishing standards for care.

- The litigious U.S. society has included the mental health profession in their complaints.

- Patients have become more distrustful of their providers and are not always willing to adhere to treatment guidelines. If they are not cured, they blame the provider.

- Managed care has imposed restrictions on the number of sessions that have increased the liability of providers.

- Because of the high cost of health care, more patients are abandoning their healthcare treatment, which has reduced revenues. As a result, practitioners have developed practices to cut costs, which may result in more errors.

- Mental health practitioners are ignoring their professional liability issues and do not hire professionals to resolve their problems. As a result, many practitioners are ill prepared to defend their actions and are found liable.

Mental Health Commitment Law

Commitment laws are laws that enable family members, law enforcement, or healthcare professionals to commit a person to a facility or a treatment program. **Voluntary commitment** occurs when people commit themselves willingly to receive care. If a person voluntarily commits for treatment, that person can leave of his or her own free will. **Involuntary commitment** occurs when people are being forced to receive treatment or are committed to a facility against their wishes. A hearing must be held to prove the person is dangerous to him- or herself or others or is suffering from a mental disorder. If they are committed, they are not free to leave (Pointer et al., 2007). An involuntary commitment may occur as an outpatient mental health treatment plan. This type of involuntary commitment is normally a court-ordered program for mental health services.

Managed Care Behavioral Organizations

Mental health services are provided by distinct components of the healthcare system. There are specialty healthcare providers, as explained previously, such

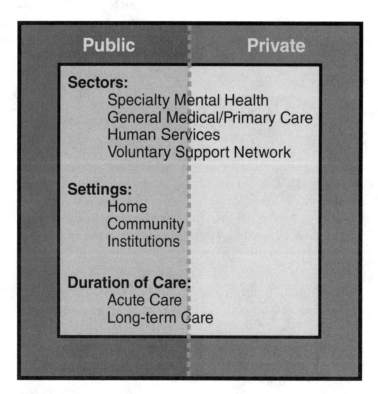

Figure 13-1 The De Facto Mental Health Service System
Source: U.S. Public Health Service. (1999). Mental health: A report of the Surgeon General. Retrieved from http://mentalhealth.samhsa.gov/features/surgeongeneralreport/chapter2/sec7.asp

as psychiatrists and psychologists. However, the primary care provider (e.g., family physicians, internists, etc.) is often the initial contact for the mentally ill and may often serve as the provider for their problems. An important component of their care is the social service sector, such as social service workers and counselors, who provide assistance to both the individual and the family. Finally, there is a growing sector of nonprofit groups and organizations for the mentally ill that provide education and support, including the **National Alliance on Mental Illness (NAMI)** and **Mental Health America**. These components are known as the **de facto mental health service system** (**Figure 13-1**) (U.S. Public Health Service, 1999).

PRIVATE AND PUBLIC FUNDING FOR MENTAL HEALTH

Private insurance coverage for mental health conditions and substance abuse or behavioral care is less generous than the coverage for traditional medical care. Many small companies do not offer mental health coverage. Employers routinely impose higher employee copayments and may limit outpatient visit reimbursement. The **Mental Health Parity Act of 1996**, enacted in 1998, provided the mental health field with more equity for health insurance coverage to ensure mental health services were being reimbursed on an equal level of traditional medical care. The Mental Health Parity and Addiction Equity Act of 2008 requires group health insurance plans (those with more than 50 insured employees) that offer coverage for mental illness and substance use disorders to provide those benefits in a no more restrictive way than all other medical and surgical procedures covered by the plan. It does not require group health plans to cover mental health (MH) and substance use disorder (SUD) benefits, but when plans do cover these benefits, MH and SUD benefits must be covered at levels that are no lower and with treatment limitations that are no more restrictive than would be the case for the other medical and surgical benefits offered by the plan (SAMHSA, 2013b). Many mental health advocates were dismayed by the weakness of this legislation, so in November 2013, a final rule was issued on the 2008 act that includes the following consumer protections:

- "Ensuring that parity applies to intermediate levels of care received in residential treatment or intensive outpatient settings;

- Clarifying the scope of the transparency required by health plans, including the disclosure rights of plan participants, to ensure compliance with the law;

- Clarifying that parity applies to all plan standards, including geographic limits, facility-type limits, and network adequacy; and

- Eliminating the provision that allowed insurance companies to make an exception to parity requirements for certain benefits on the basis of 'clinically appropriate standards of care,' which clinical experts advised was not necessary and which is confusing and open to potential abuse" (Cassells, 2013).

Medicare and Medicaid are a large source of mental health funding, particularly for those individuals with serious mental disabilities who often cannot work. Medicaid is the single largest payer for state-financed mental health care (Shi & Singh, 2008). Medicare does impose a 50% copayment rate for outpatient services other than initial diagnoses and drug management. The normal copayment rate is 20% for traditional medical care (Anderson, Rice, & Kominski, 2007). However, as a result of cost concerns over mental health care, managed care organizations contracted with external vendors that focused on mental health care. These external vendors became known as **managed behavioral healthcare organizations**.

There is still a stigma that is attached to being mentally disabled. Individuals may be embarrassed to admit they may have a mental health problem and ignore it or they do not understand what is happening to them. Families can be embarrassed by a member that is mentally disabled. A patient's primary care provider may also be uncomfortable dealing with a patient that may have a mental health disorder.

Who Are the Mentally Ill?

The Diagnostic and Statistical Manual of Mental Disorders (DSM) is a guide published by the American Psychiatric Association that explains the signs and symptoms that mark more than 300 types of mental health conditions. Traditionally, mental health providers use the *DSM* to diagnose everything from anorexia to voyeurism and, if necessary, determine appropriate treatment. Health insurance companies also use the *DSM* to determine coverage and benefits and to reimburse mental health providers (Mayo Clinic, 2013). The *DSM* has been in publication since 1952 and periodically publishes an updated manual. The most recent update was in 2013.

However, the **National Institute of Mental Health**, the world's largest funding agency of mental health research, has refused to endorse the 2013 *DSM* and will no longer fund mental health research based on the *DSM* mental health categories. The NIMH states that the *DSM* has not categorized mental health disorders based on objective science but more from inconsistent information gathered from clusters of symptoms that are then categorized as a mental health disorder. The NIMH is developing a new classification system of mental health disorders based on science and genetics. The *DSM* has been used by mental health professionals to assist them with their diagnoses. It will be interesting to see if there will be less reliance on the *DSM* (Lane, 2013; American Psychiatric Association, 2012b).

SPECIAL POPULATIONS

Children and Adolescents

According to the **National Institute of Mental Health** (NIMH), 9% of teens (13–18 years) suffer from an anxiety disorder with only 18% receiving mental health care. They can be diagnosed with the following: attention deficit hyperactivity disorders (ADHD), posttraumatic stress disorder, panic disorder, bipolar disorder, autism, depressive disorders, borderline personality disorder, eating disorders, social phobia, and schizophrenia. In some instances, these disorders can follow them throughout their lives. It is particularly difficult to assess teen mental disorders because of their stage in life. Many teens are worried about peer pressure, family issues, schoolwork and activities, and making decisions about going to college or not. It is important that there is open communication with both children and teens either with their parents, counselors, or friends to ensure that, if there is a mental disorder, it will be addressed. Suicide is a major concern among children and adolescents, being the fifth leading cause of death among ages 5–14 years (Agency for Healthcare Research and Quality, 2002; NIMH, 2013a)

Treatment for Children and Adolescents

According to the APA, it is important that parents recognize problems in their children so that they can be treated appropriately. The most common mental disorders are depression, ADHD, and conduct disorders.

Although there is limited research on mental disorders in children, it is estimated that 1 in 10 children may suffer from persistent feelings of sadness, which can lead to depression. In some instances, children may not be able to verbalize their emotions, so it is important to notice any behavioral changes such as poor school performance, loss of interest in hobbies, angry outbursts, anxiety, alcohol or drug abuse, and irrational behavior (SAMHSA, 2013a). The following is a list of medications that are being used for the treatment of children. This is a summary of the recommendations made by NIMH (NIMH, 2013a).

Antidepressant and Anti-anxiety Medicine

These types of medications are prescribed almost as frequently as stimulant medications among children and adolescents. They are used for depression, a disorder recognized only in the last 20 years as a problem for children, and for anxiety disorders, including OCD.

Antipsychotic Medications

These medications are used to treat children with schizophrenia, bipolar disorder (manic-depressive illness), autism, Tourette's syndrome, and severe conduct disorders. Some of the older **antipsychotic medications** have specific indications and dose guidelines for children. Some of the newer medications, which have fewer side effects, are also being used effectively for children.

Mood Stabilizing Medications

These medications are used to treat bipolar disorder. However, because there is very limited data on the safety and efficacy of most mood stabilizers in youth, treatment of children and adolescents is based mainly on experience with adults.

Elderly and Mental Health

As the U.S. population ages and continues to live longer, mental health disorders will become more prevalent in the elderly. As we age, we will experience loss of family members and friends, which is a major trigger of depression and possibly suicide. Unfortunately, many elderly are not treated for mental illness for several reasons. Often the elderly are being treated for other traditional illnesses, so the focus is treating those illnesses. Also, as we age, society assumes that we lose our memory and some of our faculties as part of the normal aging process, which is not an inevitable fact, so primary care providers and family members do not attribute these symptoms to dementia or Alzheimer's disease, both mental disorders. It is also more difficult to see a specialist because of lack of transportation. The elderly are focused on seeing their primary care provider for their main ailments, so both the patient and the provider may ignore the symptoms. Also, the primary care provider may not be comfortable addressing mental health issues. If the primary care provider refers the elderly patient to a psychologist, a recent APA survey indicated that fewer than 30% of psychologists have had graduate coursework in **geropsychology**, which deals with mental health issues in the elderly, and that 70% would be interested in attending programs in geropsychology. The APA has provided guidelines, called **Guideline 20**, for psychologists for older adults (American Psychological Association, 2014). Finally, the family of an elderly person may not want to acknowledge the problems because they may be afraid of hurting their feelings. Alzheimer's disease and other dementias are difficult for a family member to acknowledge, knowing the end result of these diseases. It is important that the primary care provider, the family, and the patient work together to assess the elderly patient's mental status. Research estimates that over 60% of elderly patients do not receive treatment for mental health disorders (Kessler et al., 2006).

COMMON TYPES OF MENTAL DISORDERS IN THE ELDERLY

Depression and Dementia

Depression may strike more than 10% of the elderly population. It can imitate dementia because its victims withdraw, cannot focus, and appear confused at times. **Dementias**, which have symptoms of memory loss and confusion, are often considered a part of growing old—but they are not an inevitable part of the aging process. Only 15% of the elderly population suffers from dementia. Of that percentage, over 60% suffer from Alzheimer's disease, for which there is no cure as of this writing. Approximately 40% of dementias can be caused by conditions such as high blood pressure or a stroke or other diseases such as Parkinson's and Huntington's, which are disorders that, in their advanced stages, can cause dementia (American Psychiatric Association, 2013).

Alzheimer's Disease

This disease causes the death of brain cells that control memory. The longer the person has **Alzheimer's disease**, the greater the memory loss as more cells die. One million people 65 years or older have severe Alzheimer's disease with approximately 2 million in the moderate stages of the disease (American Psychiatric Association, 2013).

Pseudo (False) Dementias

Pseudo dementias may develop as a result of medications, drug interactions, and poor diet, or heart and gland diseases. These dementias may occur accidentally because of these conditions. Many elderly have multiple prescriptions so it is important to note any potential interactions that could result in dementia. Also, if the elderly person does not eat well and has poor nutrition, this habit could also cause dementia as well. It is important that family members or providers monitor the dietary habits of the elderly patient. Fortunately, because of the causes, most of these pseudo dementias are reversible if treated (American Psychiatric Association, 2013).

MENTAL HEALTH AND CULTURE, RACE, AND ETHNICITY

Mental health disorders occur across race and culture; however, according to NIMH, diverse communities are often underserved. The following is mental health information related to African Americans, Latinos, American Indians, Alaska Natives, and Asian Americans.

African Americans

African Americans are hesitant to access mental health care due to prior misdiagnoses, inadequate treatment, and cultural misunderstandings. Although the percentage is increasing, there is a small percentage of psychologists, psychiatrists, and social workers who are African American. African Americans rely on religious and social communities for social support, so rather than visit a specialist, they may rely on spiritual guidance. Unfortunately, there is a higher percentage of African Americans in the foster home system, homeless population, and prison. Those environments have a higher level of mental health disorders than other environments.

Latino Community

The Latino population has been identified as a high-risk group for depression, anxiety, and substance abuse. Like the African American population, Latinos may seek treatment from the clergy rather than specialists. There is a small percentage of Latinos who are mental health professionals, so the comfort level is lower between the patient and provider. This is also tied to language barriers. Like the African Americans, they are overrepresented in the prison and juvenile justice system (NAMI, n.d.).

Asian Americans

The Asian American population is composed of 50 cultures with different languages and religious traditions. Asian Americans have the highest life expectancy of any ethnic group in the United States. Mental health disorders are lower among Asians than whites. They are much less likely to report mental health disorders to friends or medical professionals because they feel it is shameful and consider it a personal weakness. The suicide rates of elderly and young Asian American women are higher than women of other ethnicities. They will seek help for mental health disorders from alternative medicine providers; however, because they delay treatment for so long due to embarrassment, their problems are more severe. Like the Hispanic population, there may also be issues with language (APA, 2006).

American Indian and Alaskan Natives

Recent statistics indicate that American Indians and Alaskan Native youths use alcohol by 14 years old. They use marijuana and prescription drugs at twice the rate of the national average. Many of these youths believe their parents are permissive with this type of behavior, which encourages them. However, the federal Indian Health Service (IHS) has established a public health marketing campaign targeted to youths to resist drug and alcohol use. The IHS currently funds 11 centers nationwide that address mental health and substance abuse disorders by providing holistic health care, which is accepted by this culture.

The IHS also uses **telebehavioral health**, which is a method of service delivery that broadens the availability to, quality of, and access to care across all behavioral health program areas. Using video conferencing technology, telebehavioral health services allow "real time" visits with a behavioral health specialist in another location who can assist in the evaluation, diagnosis, management, and treatment of health problems (IHS, 2013).

It is important to recognize the differences in cultural beliefs and adapt the system to recognize these value systems. Language barriers may also be a reason why minority cultures do not access the system. Hiring mental health counselors and providers that are from the same culture would be a first step in encouraging more culturally diverse individuals to use the system.

Women and Mental Health

Depression affects women significantly more than men—nearly twice as often as men. They tend to experience it earlier, longer, and more severely. Women many experience depression as a result of biologic and social reasons. **Premenstrual dysphoric disorder**, a severe disorder that relates depression and anxiety to menstruation, impacts between 3% and 5% of women. Women may also feel depressed as a result of infertility, miscarriage, and menopause. Married women suffer depression more than married men. The more children a woman has, the more likely she may suffer from depression. Women who have been victims of sexual abuse or domestic violence may also suffer from depression.

As the baby boomer generation ages, there will be unique psychological needs for older women (Smith, 2007). By the year 2030, 20% of the population will be 65 years or older. Per decade above 65 years of age, the proportion of women increases. Older women comprise the large majority of nursing home residents. Unfortunately, women in nursing homes do not often receive mental health care. Throughout their lives, women have been traditional caregivers. Women may provide up to 13 hours of care a day for more than 20 years for both physical and emotional illnesses (Bradley, 2003). As a result of this role, many elderly women experience more depression and anxiety. Unfortunately, research indicates that healthcare providers do not provide appropriate mental health care to a large majority of older females (Qualls, Segal, Norman, Niederehe, & Gallagher-Thomson, 2002).

The Homeless and Mental Health

Approximately 3.5 million people in the United States experience homelessness each year. Over 33% of the homeless are families with children, which is the fastest growing segment. While economic factors are the main reason for homelessness, other behavioral factors such as alcoholism and mental illness can also be factors. Approximately 25% of the homeless population has mental health issues such as personality disorders.

The health status of the homeless is overall poor because of lack of housing. They are exposed to more disease and do not have adequate access to health care, thus their health status deteriorates over time. Mental health and substance abuse problems are common in the homeless population. As a result of their lack of stability, it is difficult to provide adequate mental health care and general health care (National Alliance to End Homelessness, 2013).

MENTAL HEALTH ISSUES AND DISASTERS, TRAUMA, AND LOSS

Disasters can impact communities and their citizens. Natural disasters can be natural, such as hurricanes, earthquakes, floods, and tornadoes, or manmade events such as the September 11, 2001 terrorist attacks or the wars in Iraq and Afghanistan. Many losses occur after these events, such as the loss of family and loved ones, pets, neighbors, colleagues, and the community infrastructure such as schools, churches, and homes. These disasters may be short or long term. These events may impact individuals emotionally. They may experience fear and anxiety because of the uncertainty in their lives. According to the **International Society for Traumatic Stress Studies (ISTSS)**, individuals may experience feelings of shock, disbelief, grief, anger, guilt, helplessness, and emotional numbness. They may have difficulty with cognitive thinking and may experience physical reactions such as fatigue and illness (ISTSS, 2001). They may also have difficulty interacting with others. As with any mental health condition, it is important to reach out for assistance before the condition controls an individual's life.

Mental Health Impact of Terrorist Attacks and Natural Disasters

September 11, 2001

Terrorist attacks are different than natural disasters such as hurricanes, earthquakes, avalanches, or tornados because these attacks are deliberately aimed at harming populations. An evaluation of the federal emergency mental health program indicated that over

1 million New Yorkers received one or more face-to-face counseling or public education services as a result of the September 11 terrorist attacks (Neria et al., 2007). Interestingly, the emotional impact of the terrorist attacks was felt nationwide. The federal emergency preparedness model of the **Federal Emergency Management Agency** (FEMA) and the **Substance Abuse and Mental Health Services Administration (SAMHSA)**, is helpful to victims with short-term mental health issues as a result of different types of disasters (Felton, 2004). The **American Psychological Association Task Force on Promoting Resilience in Response to Terrorism** has produced fact sheets that are intended to provide information to psychologists assisting those target populations impacted by terrorist events (APA, 2013). However, those inflicted with long-term mental health issues as a result of these types of events are often not treated. The assumption is that the traditional healthcare system will treat those long-term mentally ill. However, as discussed previously, individuals who have long-term mental health issues feel stigmatized about seeking mental health services. Those individuals who have experienced traumatic events often feel uncomfortable because they feel that they should have recovered from the events without help.

Hurricane Katrina

Hurricane Katrina devastated nearly 90,000 square miles that were declared a natural disaster area. At least 1 million individuals, including 370,000 school-aged children, were displaced. Many were evacuated throughout 46 states (Cook, 2006). Parents were very anxious because their homes were destroyed and had to start a new life elsewhere, which was not their choice. The Centers for Disease Control and Prevention (CDC) surveyed Hurricane Katrina survivors in October 2005 and found that 50% needed mental health services and 33% needed an intervention, with only 2% actually receiving assistance (Weisler, Barbee, & Townsend, 2006). Mental health providers reported grief, anxiety, and fear. This experience was magnified for survivors who had a previous history of trauma and who suffered from mental health disorders. Long-term mental health care is needed for the survivors of Hurricane Katrina. It is critical that mental health issues be included in the health care of those impacted by events such as terrorist and natural disasters. Mental health issues do not only impact the survivors but also the providers of care to those survivors.

MENTAL HEALTH AND VETERANS

With nearly 155 hospitals serving nearly 8 million war veterans and current servicemen, the VA operates the largest healthcare system and is the largest single employer of psychologists in the country. In 1989, the **National Center for Posttraumatic Stress Disorder** was created within the VA to address the needs of the military-related PTSD (National Center for PTSD, 2013). Current statistics indicate that the suicide rate for male veterans 18–29 years of age rose 26% from 2005 to 2007 with record rates in 2009. Of the 1.7 million veterans returning from Afghanistan and Iraq, 20% suffer from **posttraumatic stress disorder** or major depression. Mental health issues are the leading cause of hospitalizations for active duty military. According to recent research, military suicides are the result of untreated mental illnesses (American Psychiatric Association, 2014). Many veterans seek help outside the VA healthcare system. Their reasons for not seeking help were because of the fear of being stigmatized for seeking these types of service. The Army, which has a longtime policy of requiring the commanding officer to be notified if a soldier voluntarily seeks counseling, is seeking to suspend this rule (McFarling et al., 2011). This fear of stigmatization is similar in the general population. There are new military healthcare models to ensure that mental health services are being offered confidentially to allay these fears.

MANAGED BEHAVIORAL HEALTH CARE

Managed behavioral healthcare organizations (MBHOs), also known as behavioral healthcare carve outs, are specialized managed care organizations that focus on mental health services. According to the NCQA, an MBHO can be part of a health plan, an independent organization, or be supported by healthcare providers.

MBHOs dominate private mental health coverage. Research has indicated that MBHOs have reduced mental health treatment costs (Zuvekas, Rupp, & Norquist, 2008). The National Committee for Quality Assurance's **Managed Behavioral Healthcare Organization Accreditation Program** provides consumers, employers and others with information about the quality of the nation's managed behavioral healthcare organizations. National Committee for Quality Assurance (NCQA) accreditation includes a rigorous review against standards for improving behavioral healthcare access and services and the process of credentialing practitioners. Currently, there are 300 MBHOs that serve 120 million U.S. citizens. The NCQA program is designed to:

- Develop accountability measures for quality of care
- Provide employers and consumers with MBHO information
- Develop quality improvement MBHO programs
- Encourage coordination of behavioral care with medical care treatment (NCQA, 2013)

NATIONAL INSTITUTE FOR MENTAL HEALTH STRATEGIC PLAN

As the lead federal government agency on mental health, NIMH developed a long-term or strategic plan for mental health care in the United States. Revised in 2013, they identified four core areas of focus, which include:

Strategic Objective 1: Promote Discovery in the Brain and Behavioral Sciences to Fuel Research on the Causes of Mental Disorders

We will support basic, translational, and clinical research to gain a more complete understanding of the genetic, neurobiological, behavioral, environmental, and experiential factors that contribute to mental disorders.

Strategic Objective 2: Chart Mental Illness Trajectories to Determine When, Where, and How to Intervene

We will chart the course of mental disorders over the lifespan in order to understand ideal times and methods for intervention to preempt or treat mental disorders and hasten recovery.

Strategic Objective 3: Develop New and Better Interventions That Incorporate the Diverse Needs and Circumstances of People with Mental Illnesses

We will improve existing approaches and devise new ones for the prevention, treatment, and cure of mental illness, allowing those who may suffer from these disorders to live full and productive lives.

Strategic Objective 4: Strengthen the Public Health Impact of NIMH-Supported Research

Through research, evaluation, and collaboration, we will further develop the dissemination capacity of the Institute to help close the gap between the development of new, research-tested interventions and their widespread use by those most in need (NIMH, 2013b).

THE VIRGINIA TECH MASSACRE: A CASE STUDY OF THE MENTAL HEALTH SYSTEM

On April 16, 2007, a senior Virginia Tech student, Seung Hui Cho—who had been diagnosed with and treated for severe anxiety disorders in middle school until his junior year of high school, had been accused of stalking two female students at Virginia Tech, had been declared mentally ill by a Virginia special justice, and was asked to seek counseling by at least one Virginia Tech professor—killed 32 people, students and professors. It was the worst school massacre in U.S. history.

The Virginia Tech Review Panel was charged by Virginia Governor Kaine to review the mental health history of Cho. According to the Panel's findings, even as a young boy, Cho was extremely shy and often refused to speak. He was uncomfortable in his school surroundings and was often bullied. As a result of testing, he did receive counseling throughout middle and high school until he was 18 years of age. He had responded well to the counseling and did not want to continue the counseling so his parents allowed him to stop. When he decided to go to Virginia Tech, the school did not know of his mental health issues because of personal privacy issues. The **Family Educational Rights and Privacy Act of 1974 (FERPA)** and the Americans with Disabilities Act (ADA) generally allow for special education records to be transferred to a higher education facility. However, the law prohibits a university from making an inquiry pre-admission about an applicant's disability status. After a student's admission, they may make inquiries on a confidential basis. Cho could have made his disability known to the University but chose not to. Unfortunately, Virginia law allowed Cho to purchase a handgun without detection by the National Instant Criminal Background Check System (NCIS) (Virginia Tech Review Panel, 2007). This tragedy led to the first major federal gun control measure in more than a decade, which strengthened the NCIS, eliminating the legal loophole that allowed Cho to purchase a handgun (Cochran, 2008).

ALTERNATIVE APPROACHES TO MENTAL HEALTH CARE

Alternative approaches to mental health care emphasize the relationships between the body, mind, and spirituality (SAMHSA, 2009). Established in 1992, the National Center for Complementary and Alternative Medicine at the National Institutes of Health evaluates different types of alternative therapies and treatments and whether to integrate them into traditional medicine culture. The following techniques are outlined in a fact sheet from the National Mental Health Information Center. The following is a discussion of the different types of treatment:

- **Self-help organizations**: Many mentally ill individuals often seek comfort in self-help organizations. They find solace with others who have experienced similar conditions. Many of them are nonprofit and are free of charge. They also provide education and support to the caregivers for those individuals who are mentally ill. Often, these organizations are anonymous because of the stigma attached to mental disorders.

- **Nutrition**: Some research has demonstrated that certain types of diets may assist with certain mental disorders. Eliminating wheat and milk products may alleviate the severity of symptoms of children with autism.

- **Pastoral counseling**: Mental health counselors have recognized that incorporating spiritual guidance with traditional medical care may alleviate mental disorder symptoms.

- **Animal-assisted therapies**: Animals are often used to increase socialization skills and encourage communication among the mentally ill. Integrating animals into individuals' lives may alleviate some symptoms of the mental ill.

- **Art therapy**: Art activities such as drawing, painting, and sculpting may help people express their emotions and may help treat disorders such as depression. There are certificates in art therapy for this purpose.

- **Dance therapy**: Moving a body to music may help with those individuals recovering from physical abuse because the movement may help develop a sense of ease with their bodies.

- **Music therapy**: Research supports that music elevates a person's emotional moods. It has been used to treat depression, stress, and grief.

Culturally Based Healing Arts

Oriental and Native American medicine believe that wellness is a state of balance between the physical, spiritual, and emotional needs of an individual and that illness results from an imbalance (Center for Mental Health Services, 2009). Their remedies focus on natural medicine, nutrition, exercise, and prayers to regain the balance.

Acupuncture is the Chinese practice of the insertion of needles in specific points of the body to balance the system. Acupuncture has been used to treat stress and anxiety, depression, ADHD in children, and physical ailments. Acupuncture is often used in conjunction with chiropractic medicine.

Ayurveda medicine incorporates diet, meditation, herbal medicine, and nutrition to treat depression and to release stress.

Yoga is an Indian system that uses breathing techniques, stretching, and meditation to balance the body. Yoga is offered at many athletic clubs and gyms and has become a popular mainstream form of exercise. It has been used for depression and anxiety.

Native American practices include ceremonial dances and baptismal rituals as part of Indian health. These dances and rituals are used to treat depression, stress, and substance abuse.

Relaxation and Stress Reduction Techniques

Biofeedback is a technique that focuses on learning to control heart rate and body temperature. This technique may be used in conjunction with medication to treat depression and schizophrenia. Biofeedback may be used to control issues with stress and hyperventilation.

Visualization is when a patient creates a mental image of wellness and recovery. This may be used by traditional healthcare providers to treat substance abuse, panic disorders, and stress.

Massage therapy manipulates the body and its muscles and is used to release tension. It has been used to treat depression and stress.

Technology-Based Applications

Technology aided development of electronic tools that can be used from home and increase access to isolated geographic areas can increase access to mentally ill individuals with minimal access to health care.

Telemedicine is when providers and patients are connected using the Internet for communication for consultation. Those who are mentally ill living in rural areas, for example, have an opportunity to have access to providers.

Telephone counseling is an important part of mental health care. As stated previously, because of the stigma attached to receiving mental health services, individuals prefer to talk to a counselor on the telephone because they do not have to face anyone and do not have to tell anyone where they are going if they have an appointment in an office. Counselors receive training for telephone counseling. Like telemedicine, telephone counseling provides an opportunity for outreach for individuals who live in isolated locations.

The Internet, including email services (**electronic communication**), has provided an opportunity to increase an individual's exposure to knowledge regarding his or her condition. Consumer groups and medical websites can be accessed anonymously.

Radio psychiatry has been used in the United States for over 30 years. Radio psychologists and psychiatrists provide advice, information, and referrals to consumers. Both the APA and the American Psychiatric Association have issued guidelines for radio show programs that focus on mental health.

CONCLUSION

Mental health issues impact millions of U.S. citizens. Mental health disabilities limit the life expectancy of individuals by 25 years. Treatment of mental health disorders have been traditionally underfunded because of the attitude of the traditional healthcare system, confusion by health insurance companies, and fear by individuals who are mentally ill that they will be discriminated against because of their conditions. In 1999, Surgeon General David Satcher's report on mental health brought awareness to the issues with the U.S. mental healthcare system. The Mental Health Parity Act of 1996 was an attempt to establish a fair system of treatment between mental health disorders and traditional healthcare conditions by mandating annual and lifetime limits to be equal between mental health care and traditional health care. President Bush's Freedom Commission on Mental Health focused on an analysis of the mental health system and recommendations to improve mental health care.

The Mental Health Parity and Addiction Equity Act (2008) and its 2013 final rules further support mental health care by requiring insurance plans to offer similar benefits to traditional medical benefits and to make cost sharing similar to other medical benefits. Over the past 15 years, increased funding has increased the quality of mental health services. The current administration has recognized the importance of funding mental health initiatives, including teacher training programs for mental health awareness (Mohney, 2013).

Despite the progress in mental health care, there continues to be issues with the U.S. mental health care system.

Recent tragedies such as the Sandy Hook Elementary School, the Aurora, Colorado movie theater, and the Navy Yard massacres were executed by mentally ill individuals. Several questions must be answered in order to understand how mental health care can be administered to individuals who need it the most. Was there adequate access to mental health care for these individuals? Were these individuals properly diagnosed? Did their families recognize their problems? Did they refuse care? The U.S. mental healthcare system continues to be analyzed to ensure that these types of tragedies cease.

VOCABULARY

Acupuncture

Alternative approaches to mental health care

Alzheimer's disease

American Psychiatric Association

American Psychological Association

Animal-assisted therapies

Antipsychotic medications

Art therapy

Ayurveda

Biofeedback

Dance therapy

De facto mental health service system

Dementia

Diagnostic and Statistical Manual of Mental Disorders (DSM)

Electronic communication

Electrotherapy

Family Educational Rights and Privacy Act of 1974 (FERPA)

Federal Emergency Management Agency

Geropsychology

Guideline 20

Hurricane Katrina

Insane asylums

International Society for Traumatic Stress Studies (ISTSS)

Involuntary commitment

Managed behavioral health care organization accreditation program

Managed behavioral healthcare organizations

Massage therapy

Mental disorders

Mental Health America

Mental Health Parity Act of 1996

Mental Health Parity and Addiction Equity Act of 2008

Mood stabilizing medications

Moral treatment

Music therapy

National Alliance on Mental Alliance (NAMI)

National Center for Posttraumatic Stress Disorder

National Institute of Mental Health

Native American practice

New Freedom Commission on Mental Health

Nutrition

Pastoral counseling

Phobias

Posttraumatic stress disorder

Premenstrual dysphoric disorder

Pseudo dementias

Psychiatrists

Psychologists

Psychotropic medications

Radio psychiatry

Self-help organizations

Substance Abuse and Mental Health Services Administration (SAMHSA)

Task Force on Promoting Resilience in Response to Terrorism

Telebehavioral health

Telemedicine

Telephone counseling

U.S. Commission on Mental Health

Visualization

Voluntary commitment

Yoga

REFERENCES

Agency for Healthcare Research and Quality (AHRQ). (2002). Specialized training helps ER nurses better manage children at risk for suicide. Retrieved from http://archive.ahrq.gov/research/feb02/0202RA8.htm

American Psychiatric Association. (2012a). DSM: History of the manual. Retrieved from http://www.psychiatry.org/practice/dsm/dsm-history-of-the-manual

American Psychiatric Association. (2012b). Recent updates to proposed revisions for *DSM-5*. Retrieved from http://www.dsm5.org/Pages/RecentUpdates.aspx

American Psychiatric Association. (2013). Seniors. Retrieved from http://www.psychiatry.org/mental-health/people/seniors

American Psychiatric Association. (2014). Military. http://www.psychiatry.org/mental-health/people/military

American Psychological Association (APA). (2003, July). Office of Public Affairs. American Psychological Association applauds final report of President's New Freedom Commission on Mental Health. *American Psychological Association Press Release*. Retrieved from http://www.apa.org/releases/mentalhealth_rpt.html

American Psychological Association (APA). (2006). Asian-American mental health. Retrieved from http://www.apa.org/monitor/feb06/health.aspx

American Psychological Association (APA). (2013a). Fostering resilience in response to terrorism: For psychologists working with older adults. Retrieved from http://www.apa.org/pi/aging/resources/older-adults.pdf

American Psychological Association (APA). (2014). Guidelines for Psychological Practice with Older Adults. Retrieved from http://www.apa.org/practice/guidelines/older-adults.aspx

Anderson, R., Rice, T., & Kominski, G. (2007). *Changing the U.S. Healthcare System* (439–479). San Francisco, CA: Jossey-Bass.

Bradley, P. (2003). Family caregiver assessment: Essential for effective home health care. *Journal of Gerontological Nursing, 29*, 29–36.

Cassells, C. (2013). Feds Issue Final Rule for Mental Health Parity Legislation. Retrieved from http://www.medscape.com/viewarticle/814063?src=wnl_edit_newsal

Center for Mental Health Services. (2009). Alternative approaches to mental health care. Retrieved January 24, 2009, from http://mentalhealth.samhsa.gov/publications/allpubs/ken98-0044/default.asp

Cochran, J. (2008, January 12). New gun control law is killer's legacy. Retrieved from http://abcnews.go.com/Politics/story?id=4126152

Cook, G. (2006). Schooling Katrina's kids. *American School Board Journal, 193,* 18–26.

Everett, A., Mahler, J., Biblin, J., Ganguli, R., & Mauer, B. (2008). Improving the health of mental health consumers. *International Journal of Mental Health, 37*(2), 8–48.

Felton, C. (2004). Lessons learned since September 11 2001 concerning the mental health impact of terrorism, appropriate response strategies and future preparedness. *Psychiatry, 67*(2), 147–153.

Grob, G. (1983). *Mental illness and American society: 1875–1940.* Princeton, NJ: Princeton University Press.

Grob, G. (1994). *The mad among us: A history of the care of America's mentally ill.* New York: Free Press.

Indian Health Service (IHS). (2013). Behavioral health. Retrieved from http://www.ihs.gov/communityhealth/behavioralhealth

International Society for Traumatic Stress Studies (ISTSS). (2001). Mass disasters, trauma, and loss. Retrieved from http://www.istss.org/AM/Template.cfm?Section=PublicEducationPamphlets&Template=/CM/ContentDisplay.cfm&ContentID=1464

Kessler, R. C., Chiu, W. T., Colpe, L., Demler, O., Merikangas, K. R., Walters, E. E., & Wang, P. S. (2006). The prevalence and correlates of serious mental illness (SMI) in the National Comorbidity Survey Replication (NCSR). In Manderscheid, R. W., & Berry, J. T. (Eds.). *Mental health, United States, 2004* (DHHS Publication No. SMA-06-4195). Rockville, MD: Substance Abuse and Mental Health Services Administration.

Lane, C. (2013). The NIMH withdraws support for *DSM-5.* Retrieved from http://www.psychologytoday.com/blog/side-effects/201305/the-nimh-withdraws-support-dsm-5

Luongo, T. (2008). The Mental Health Parity and Addiction Equity Act of 2008: Equal footing for those suffering from mental health and addition disorders. Retrieved from http://www.hrtutor.com/en/news_rss/articles/2008/1202MentalHealthParityandAddictionEquityActof2008.aspx

Mayo Clinic. (2013). Mental health: What's normal and what is not. Retrieved from http://www.mayoclinic.com/health/mental-health/MH00042

McFarling, L., D'Angelo, M., Drain, M., Gibbs, D., & Olmstead, K., (2011). Stigma as a barrier to substance abuse and mental health treatment. *Military Psychology, 23,* 1–5.

Mohney, G. (2013). Obama budget includes $235 million for mental health care. Retrieved from http://abcnews.go.com/Health/obama-budget-includes-235-million-mental-health-initiatives/story?id=18922699

Moran, M. (2013). Final rule clarifies regulations for parity law. Retrieved from http://psychnews.psychiatryonline.org/newsarticle.aspx?articleid=1787387&RelatedNewsArticles=true

National Alliance on Mental Illness (NAMI). (n.d.). Latino community mental health fact sheet. Retrieved from http://www.nami.org/Content/NavigationMenu/Find_Support/Multicultural_Support/Annual_Minority_Mental_Healthcare_Symposia/Latino_MH06.pdf

National Alliance to End Homelessness. (2013). Snapshot of homelessness. Retrieved from http://www.endhomelessness.org/pages/snapshot_of_homelessness

National Center for Posttraumatic Stress Disorder. (2013). About us. Retrieved from http://www.ptsd.va.gov/about/mission/history_of_the_national_center_for_ptsd.asp

National Committee for Quality Assurance (NCQA). (2013). Accreditation programs. Retrieved from http://www.ncqa.org/Programs/Accreditation.aspx

National Institute of Mental Health (NIMH). (2013a). Child and adolescent mental health. Retrieved from http://www.nimh.nih.gov/health/topics/childandadolescentmentalhealth/index.shtml

National Institute of Mental Health (NIMH). (2013b). The National Institute of Mental Health strategic plan. Retrieved from http://www.nimh.nih.gov/about/strategic-planning-reports/index.shtml

Neria, Y., Gross, R., Litz, B., Maguen, S., Insel, B., Seirmarco, G., . . . Marshall, R. D. (2007). Prevalence and psychological correlates of complicated grief among bereaved adults 2.5–3.5 years after September 11 attacks. *Journal of Traumatic Stress*, 20(3), 251–262.

Pointer, D., Williams, S., Isaacs, S., & Knickman, J. (2007). *Introduction to U.S. health care*. Hoboken, NJ: Wiley Publishing.

Qualls, S., Segal, D., Norman, D., Niederehe, G., & Gallagher-Thomson, D. (2002). Psychologists in practice with older adults: Current patterns, sources of training, and need for continuing education. *Professional Psychology: Research and Practice*, 33, 435–442.

Regier, D., Narrow, W., Rae, D., Manderscheid, R., Locke, B., & Goodwin, F. (1993). The de facto US mental and addictive disorders service system. Epidemiologic catchment area prospective 1-year prevalence rates of disorders and services. *Archives of General Psychiatry*, 50, 85–94.

Shi, L., & Singh, D. (2008). *Essentials of the U.S. health care delivery system*. Sudbury, MA: Jones and Bartlett.

Smith, H. (2007). Psychological service needs of older women. *Psychological Services*, 4, 277–286.

Substance Abuse and Mental Health Services Administration (SAMHSA). (2009). Alternative approaches to mental health care. Retrieved from http://mentalhealth.samhsa.gov/publications/allpubs/ken980044/default.asp

Substance Abuse and Mental Health Services Administration (SAMHSA). (2011). Leading change: A plan for SAMHSA's roles and actions: 2011–2014. Retrieved from http://store.samhsa.gov/shin/content//SMA11-4629/02 -ExecutiveSummary.pdf

Substance Abuse and Mental Health Services Administration (SAMHSA). (2013a). Children and Adolescents with Mental, Emotional and Behavioral Disorders. Retrieved from http://mentalhealth.samhsa.gov/publications /allpubs/CA0006/default.asp

Substance Abuse and Mental Health Services Administration (SAMHSA). (2013b). The Mental Health Parity and Addiction Equity Act of 2008. Retrieved from http://www.samhsa.gov/healthreform/parity

Sultz, H., & Young, K. (2006). *Health care USA: Understanding its organization and delivery* (5th ed.). Sudbury, MA: Jones and Bartlett.

U.S. Public Health Service. (1999). Mental health: A report of the Surgeon General. Retrieved from http://mentalhealth .samhsa.gov/features/surgeongeneralreport/chapter2/sec7.asp

Virginia Tech Review Panel. (2007). *Mass shootings at Virginia Tech: Report of the Review Panel presented to Governor Kaine, Commonwealth of Virginia*. Retrieved from http://www.governor.virginia.gov/TempContent/techPanel Report.cfm

Weisler, R., Barbee, J., & Townsend, M. (2006). Mental health and recovery in the Gulf Coast after Hurricanes Katrina and Rita. *Journal of the American Medical Association*, 296, 585–588.

World Health Organization (WHO). (2010, September). Mental health: Strengthening our response. Retrieved from http://www.who.int/mediacentre/factsheets/fs220/en/index.html

Woody, R. (2008). Obtaining legal counsel for child and family mental health practice. *The American Journal of Family Therapy*, 36, 323–331.

Zuvekas, S., Rupp, A., & Norquist, G. (2008). The impacts of mental health parity and managed care in one large employer group: A reexamination. *Health Affairs*, 24, 1668–1671.

NOTES

STUDENT ACTIVITY 13-1

IN YOUR OWN WORDS

Based on this chapter, please provide a definition of the following vocabulary words in your own words. DO NOT RECITE the text definition.

Posttraumatic stress disorder: _____
_____
_____

Mental disorders: _____
_____
_____

Moral treatment: _____
_____

Involuntary commitment: _____
_____
_____

Telebehavioral health: _____
_____
_____

Visualization: _____

Psychiatrists: _____

New Freedom Commission on Mental Health: _____
_____
_____

Family Educational Rights and Privacy Act: _____
_____
_____

Ayurveda: _____
_____
_____

STUDENT ACTIVITY 13-2

Complete the following case scenarios based on the information provided in the chapter. Your answer must be IN YOUR OWN WORDS.

REAL LIFE APPLICATIONS: CASE SCENARIO ONE

You have been concerned about your grandmother recently. Yesterday, she left the stove on when she went out to the grocery store. Your grandfather has been chronically ill for years and she is his main caregiver. She regularly visits her primary care provider who has told her that it is nothing more than old age. You decide to research mental health issues among the elderly and have found very interesting statistics, particularly for women.

ACTIVITY

(1) Provide three statistics about mental health issues in the elderly population; (2) discuss two reasons why mental health issues are not addressed with the elderly.

RESPONSES

_____

_____

_____

_____

_____

_____

_____

_____

_____

_____

_____

_____

_____

_____

CASE SCENARIO TWO

You are thinking about going to school to become a mental health professional. However, you have heard that mental health professionals face liability issues and complaints—but you are unsure why.

ACTIVITY

Perform research using this text and the Internet to find five reasons why mental health professionals are at high risk for complaints.

RESPONSES

_____

_____

_____

_____

_____

_____

_____

_____

_____

_____

_____

_____

_____

CASE SCENARIO THREE

The American Psychiatric Association has developed a guide for diagnosing mental health disorders. This guide has been used for years by many mental health professionals. Recently, the APA has been criticized heavily regarding the guide.

ACTIVITY

You are curious as to why this guide has been challenged for its quality. You perform research to determine what the issue is with this landmark publication.

RESPONSES

_____

_____

_____

_____

_____

_____

_____

_____

_____

_____

_____

_____

_____

CASE SCENARIO FOUR

You are concerned about your grandmother who recently lost her spouse, your grandfather. You feel she is depressed. You want to take her to her primary care provider for a checkup.

ACTIVITY

Prior to taking her to her doctor, you want to familiarize yourself with mental health issues in the elderly. You do some research to find out what mental health issues are common in the elderly population.

RESPONSES

_____
_____
_____
_____
_____
_____
_____
_____
_____
_____
_____
_____
_____
_____

STUDENT ACTIVITY 13-3

INTERNET EXERCISES

Write your answers in the space provided.

- Visit each of the websites listed here.
- Name the organization.
- Locate their mission statement on their website.
- Provide a brief overview of the activities of the organization.
- How do these organizations participate in the U.S. healthcare system?

Websites

http://www.apa.org

Organization Name: _____

Mission Statement:

_____

_____

_____

Overview of Activities: _____

_____

_____

Importance of organization to U.S. health care:

_____

_____

_____

http://www.samhsa.gov

Organization Name: _____

Mission Statement:

_____

_____

_____

Overview of Activities: _____

_____

_____

Importance of organization to U.S. health care:

_____

_____

_____

Organization Name: _____

Mission Statement:

_____

_____

_____

Overview of Activities: _____

_____

_____

Importance of organization to U.S. health care:

_____

_____

_____

Organization Name: _____

Mission Statement:

_____

_____

_____

Overview of Activities: _____

_____

_____

Importance of organization to U.S. health care:

_____

_____

_____

Organization Name: _____

Mission Statement:

_____

_____

_____

Overview of Activities: _____

_____

_____

Importance of organization to U.S. health care:

_____

_____

_____

http:// www.nami.org

Organization Name: _____

Mission Statement:

_____

_____

_____

Overview of Activities: _____

_____

_____

Importance of organization to U.S. health care:

_____

_____

_____

STUDENT ACTIVITY 13-4

DISCUSSION QUESTIONS

The following are suggested discussion questions for this chapter.

(1) What is the *DSM*? Why is it important to mental health care?

_____

_____

_____

_____

(2) Do you believe that mental health care is important to veterans and military?

_____

_____

_____

_____

(3) What are some issues regarding the treatment of African American patients who experience mental health issues?

_____

_____

_____

_____

(4) Do you believe in holistic healing? Support your answer.

_____

_____

_____

_____

(5) Do you think the Indian Health Service is important? Discuss its activities.

_____

_____

_____

_____

The Navigate Companion Website for this text is a great source for additional information on the U.S. healthcare system. You can gain a new perspective on many of the topics presented in this chapter by visiting http://go.jblearning.com/Niles2e. You'll find additional student activities, further reading, and interactive study tools that explore:

- Mental health issues in special populations such as the elderly and children
- Importance of mental health law
- How disasters and trauma can impact our mental health
- And much more.

Chapter 14

Analysis of the U.S. Healthcare System

LEARNING OBJECTIVES

The student will be able to:

- Discuss the advantages and disadvantages of e-prescribing.
- Describe the universal healthcare systems of Massachusetts and San Francisco, California.
- Describe the major components of the healthcare delivery systems of Japan, France, and Switzerland.
- Discuss three current healthcare trends.
- Assess the pros and cons of a pay-for-performance (P4P) healthcare system.
- Evaluate the differences between the types of universal health coverage programs.

DID YOU KNOW THAT?

- More than 7,000 medication-related deaths occur each year as a result of incompatible drug interactions and drug allergies. These deaths are caused by illegible handwritten prescriptions and because the healthcare provider is unaware of patient allergies.
- In April 2006, the state of Massachusetts passed legislation to implement a type of universal healthcare coverage for its residents.

- Robotic hands used in surgery are so sensitive that they can easily peel a grape or thread a needle.
- Both Walgreens and CVS have drugstore clinics that are run by nurse practitioners or physician assistants who provide routine care.
- The Department of Labor's Bureau of Labor Statistics indicates that the fastest growing jobs in the next decade will be in the healthcare industry.
- Back pain is the most common reason why healthcare consumers use alternative medicine approaches.

INTRODUCTION

The U.S. healthcare system has long been recognized for providing state-of-the-art health care. It has also been recognized as the most expensive healthcare system in the world and the price tag is expected to increase. Despite offering two large public programs—Medicare and Medicaid for the elderly, indigent, and disabled—current statistics indicate that over 48 million individuals are uninsured.

This chapter will provide an international comparison between the U.S. healthcare system and the healthcare systems of other countries and discuss whether universal healthcare coverage should be implemented in the United States. This chapter will also discuss U.S. healthcare trends that may positively impact the healthcare system, including the increased use of technology in prescribing medicine and providing health care, complementary and alternative medicine use, new nursing home models, accountable care organizations, and a discussion of the universal healthcare coverage programs in Massachusetts and San Francisco, California. The Affordable Care Act (ACA) will also be discussed because of its major impact on the U.S. healthcare system.

HIGHLIGHTS OF THE U.S. HEALTHCARE SYSTEM

The U.S. healthcare system is a complicated system that is composed of both public and private resources (**Figure 14-1**). Health care is available to those individuals who have health insurance or are entitled to health care through a public program or who can afford to pay out of pocket for their care. Think of the healthcare system as concentric circles that surround the most important circle—the healthcare consumers and healthcare providers. Immediately surrounding

this relationship is the circle that contains healthcare insurance companies and government programs such as Medicaid and Medicare, state and local public health departments, federal government healthcare organizations such as the Centers for Disease Control and Prevention (CDC), healthcare facilities, allied health professionals, pharmaceutical companies, and laboratories that all provide services to consumers to ensure that they receive quality health care and support providers to ensure that they are able to provide quality health care. The next circle consists of peripheral stakeholders that do not immediately impact that main relationship but are still important to the industry: professional associations such as the American Medical Association, accreditation associations such as The Joint Commission, research organizations, and medical and training facilities.

The one commonality with the world's healthcare systems is that they all have consumers or users of their systems. Systems were developed to provide a service to their citizens. The U.S. healthcare system, unlike other systems in the world, does not provide healthcare access to all of its citizens. Healthcare expenditures comprise approximately 17.6% of the gross domestic product (GDP). Healthcare costs are very expensive and most

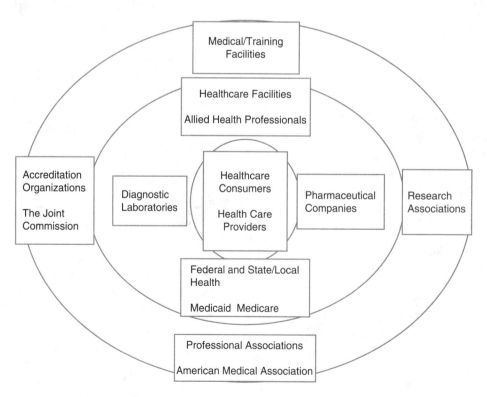

Figure 14-1 Healthcare Industry Stakeholders

citizens would be unable to afford it if they had to pay for it themselves. Individuals rely on health insurance to pay a large portion of their healthcare costs. Health insurance is predominantly offered by employers. According to a 2011 CDC survey, there were over 48 million people uninsured in the United States, with approximately 29 million who were underinsured, which means their health insurance did not adequately cover their medical expenses. (It will be interesting to assess the impact of the Affordable Care Act on this statistic because a major focus is individual insurance coverage nationwide. The ACA projects there will be a decrease of nearly 70% in these statistics when the ACA is fully implemented) (Affordable Health Care for America, 2010).

AFFORDABLE CARE ACT IMPACT

The Patient Protection and Affordable Care Act of 2010 or Affordable Care Act and its amendment have focused on primary care as the foundation for the U.S. healthcare system (Goodson, 2010). The legislation has focused on 10 areas to improve the U.S. healthcare system: quality, affordable and efficient healthcare, public health and primary prevention of disease, healthcare workforce increases, community health, and increasing revenue provisions to pay for the reform. However, once the bill was signed, several states filed lawsuits. Several of these lawsuits argue that the Act violates the Constitution because of the mandate of individual healthcare insurance coverage as well as infringes on state rights with the expansion of Medicaid (Arts, 2010). The 2012 U.S. Supreme Court decision that supported the constitutionality of the individual mandates should decrease the number of lawsuits. In October 2013, there were major problems with the operations of the federal government website (www.healthcare. gov) that housed the Health Insurance marketplace. On October 1, the first day of the individual health insurance coverage mandate, consumers were unable to enroll in health insurance plans nationally, although over 2 million have enrolled using the federal website as of January 1, 2014 and hope to enroll 7 million by the deadline of March 31, 2014. State run health insurance marketplaces have also experienced the same types of technological issues creating frustration as well. This major computer issue has created a firestorm of criticism. Despite these lawsuits and operational problems, this legislation has clearly provided opportunities to increase consumer empowerment in the healthcare system by providing temporary insurance to those

individuals with pre-existing conditions until they can purchase their own insurance, eliminating lifetime and annual caps on health insurance payouts, improving the healthcare workforce, and providing databases so consumers can check the quality of their healthcare. The Affordable Care Act enables healthcare consumers to select a health insurance plan based on the amount of cost sharing the consumer wants to pay. There are three types of plans: gold, silver and bronze. Gold plans have the lowest cost sharing but is the most expensive. The silver plan has moderate cost sharing and is not as expensive as the gold plan and the bronze plan has high cost sharing but the premiums are the lowest. This type of structure enables the consumer to select a plan that fits their budget. The ACA's focus is to increase the role of public health and primary care in the U.S. healthcare system while increasing accessibility to the system by providing affordable healthcare opportunities. The next stage in the ACA assessment is to determine how effective the new health insurance plans are, which became effective January 1, 2014.

GOVERNMENT'S ROLE

The government plays an important role in the quality of the U.S. healthcare system. The federal government provides funding for state and local government programs and sets policy for many aspects of the U.S. healthcare system. The federal government is also responsible for the implementation of Medicare, the entitlement program for the elderly. Federal healthcare regulations are implemented and enforced at the state and local levels. Funding is primarily distributed from the federal government to the state government, which consequently allocates funding to its local health departments. Local health departments provide the majority of services for their constituents and are collaborating with local organizations such as schools and physicians to increase their ability to provide education and prevention services.

PUBLIC HEALTH

Public health is challenged by its very success because consumers now take public health measures for granted. There are several successful vaccines that have targeted all childhood diseases, tobacco use has decreased significantly, accident prevention has increased, there are safer workplaces because of the Occupational Safety and Health Administration (OSHA), the fluoridation of water has been established, and there has been a decrease in mortality from heart attacks (Novick & Morrow, 2008). The National Association of County and City Health Officials (NACCHO) and the Association of State and Territorial Health Officials (ASTHO) are important support organizations for both state and local governments by providing policy expertise, technical advice, and lobbying at the federal level for appropriate funding and regulations. When some major event occurs like a natural or manmade disaster, people immediately think that public health will automatically control these problems. The public may not realize how much effort, dedication, and research takes place to protect the public. President Obama has recognized the importance of public health with the passage of the Affordable Care Act, which focuses on increasing access to and quality of the U.S. healthcare system. The ACA also focuses on primary prevention activities, which are the foundation of public health.

As a healthcare consumer, it is important to recognize the role that public health plays in our health care. If you are sick, you go to your physician for medical advice, which may mean providing you with a prescription. However, oftentimes you may not go see your physician because you do not have health insurance or you do not feel that sick or you would like to change one of your lifestyle behaviors. Public health surrounds consumers with educational opportunities to change a health condition or behavior. You can visit the Centers for Disease Control and Prevention website (www.cdc.gov) for information about different diseases and health conditions. You can also visit your local health department.

HOSPITAL AND OUTPATIENT SERVICES

Many hospitals have experienced financial problems. As a result of the increased competition of outpatient services (which are often more cost-effective, efficient, and consumer friendly) and reduced reimbursement from Medicare and Medicaid, many hospitals have developed strategies to increase their financial stability. Due to pressure to develop cost containment measures, hospitals are forming huge hospital systems and building large physician workforces. In order to compete with the Affordable Care Act's mandated state healthcare exchanges where consumers can purchase health insurance, health insurance companies are developing relationships with hospitals and creating joint marketing plans and sharing patient data (Mathews, 2011).

Over the years, outpatient services have become the major competitors of hospitals. Advanced technology has enabled more ambulatory surgeries and testing, which has resulted in the development of many specialty centers for radiology and imaging, chemotherapy treatment, and kidney dialysis. These services were often performed in a hospital. What is even more interesting is that physicians or physician groups own some of the centers. They are receiving revenue that used to be hospital revenue. Hospitals have recognized that fact and have embraced outpatient services as part of their patient care. Hospitals have to continue to focus on revenue generation by operating more outpatient service opportunities. They own 25% of urgent care centers in the United States; 21% have ownership interest in ambulatory surgery centers and 3% of hospitals have sole ownership (ASCA, 2013).

HEALTHCARE PERSONNEL

The healthcare industry is the fastest growing industry in the U.S. economy, employing a workforce of 18 million healthcare workers. Considering the aging of the U.S. population and the impact of the Affordable Care Act, it is expected that the healthcare industry will continue to experience strong job growth (Centers for Disease Control and Prevention, 2013). When we think of healthcare providers, we automatically think of physicians and nurses. However, the healthcare industry is comprised of many different health services professionals. The healthcare industry includes dentists, optometrists, psychologists, chiropractors, podiatrists, non-physician practitioners (NPPs), administrators, and allied health professionals. A new type of healthcare professional is the care coordinator, the fastest growing occupation, integrates nursing, social work and disability counseling for the elderly with chronic conditions who need additional assistance. It is important to identify allied health professionals because they provide a range of essential healthcare services that complement the services provided by physicians and nurses. This category of health professionals is an integral component of providing quality health.

Health care can occur in varied settings. Physicians have traditionally operated in their own practices but they also work in hospitals, mental health facilities, managed care organizations, or community health centers. They may also hold government positions or teach at a university. They could be employed by an insurance company. Health professionals, in general, may work at many different organizations, both for profit and nonprofit. Although the healthcare industry is one of the largest employers in the United States, there continues to be shortages of physicians in geographic areas of the country. Rural areas continue to suffer physician shortages, which limits consumer access to health care. There have been different incentive programs to encourage physicians to relocate to rural areas, but shortages still exist. In most states, only physicians, dentists, and a few other practitioners may serve patients directly without the authorization of another licensed independent health professional. Those categories authorized include chiropractic, optometry, psychotherapy, and podiatry. Some states authorize midwifery and physical therapy (Jonas, 2003). There also continues to be a shortage of registered nurses nationwide. The American Association of Colleges of Nursing (AACN) is publicizing this issue with policy makers (AACN, 2013).

HEALTHCARE EXPENDITURES

The percentage of the U.S. gross domestic product (GDP) devoted to healthcare expenditures has increased over the past several decades. In 2010, the United States spent $2.6 trillion on healthcare spending or 17.6% of the gross domestic product, which is the highest in the world. In 2011, U.S. Census data indicates there were over 48 million uninsured U.S. citizens, which is a decrease from 50 million in 2010. The Centers for Medicare and Medicaid Services (CMS) predicts annual healthcare costs will be $4.64 trillion by 2020, which represents nearly 20% of the U.S. gross domestic product (CMS, 2013). The increase in healthcare spending can be attributed to three causes: (1) When prices increase in an economy overall, the cost of medical care will increase and, even when prices are adjusted for inflation, medical prices have increased; (2) as life expectancy increases in the United States, more individuals will require more medical care for chronic diseases, which means there will be more healthcare expenses; and (3) as healthcare technology and research provide for more sophisticated and more expensive procedures, there will be an increase in healthcare expenses (Pointer, Williams, Isaacs, & Knickman, 2007).

As healthcare expenditures continue to increase, the major focus of the healthcare industry is cost control,

in both the public and private sectors. For years, healthcare costs were unchecked. The concept of retrospective reimbursement methods (when a provider submitted a bill for healthcare services to a health insurance company and was automatically reimbursed) gave healthcare insurers no incentive to control costs in health care. This type of reimbursement method contributed to expensive health care for both the healthcare insurance companies and the individual who was paying out of pocket for services. As a result, the establishment of a prospective reimbursement system for Medicare (reimbursement is based on care criteria for certain conditions, regardless of providers' costs) became an incentive for providers to manage how they were providing services. The Center for Medicare and Medicaid Innovation is providing grants to healthcare organizations to explore different payment models based on performance.

The managed care model for healthcare delivery was developed for the primary purpose of containing healthcare costs. By administering both the healthcare services and the reimbursement of these services, and therefore eliminating a third-party health insurer, the industry felt that this model would be very cost-effective. The consumer's (or patient's) and the physician's concerns were the same—worry about providing quality care while focusing predominantly on cost. The consumer was also worried about loss of freedom of choice of primary care provider. The physician was worried about loss of income.

As managed care evolved, managed care organizations (MCOs) were developed, which allowed more choice for both the consumer and the physician. Eventually, there were models such as preferred provider organizations (PPOs) and point-of-service (POS) plans that allowed consumers to more freely choose their provider; however, there was a financial disincentive to use a provider outside the network of the MCO. Providers were also able to see non-MCO patients, which increased their income, but they also received a financial deterrent because any MCO patient was given health care at a discounted rate.

INFORMATION TECHNOLOGY

The healthcare industry has lagged behind utilizing information technology (IT) as a form of communicating important data across healthcare systems nationally.

Despite that fact, there have been specific applications developed for HIT, such as e-prescribing, telemedicine, e-health, and specific applied technology such as the PatientPoint, MelaFind optical scanner, the Phreesia Pad, Sapien heart valve, robotic checkups, Electronic Aspirin, Accuson P10, and the Piccolo xpress, which were discussed elsewhere in this text. Healthcare organizations have recognized the importance of IT and have hired chief information officers (CIOs) and chief technology officers (CTOs) to manage their data. However, healthcare consumers need to embrace an electronic patient record. This will enable patients to be treated effectively and efficiently nationally. The patient health record can be integrated into the electronic health records that are being utilized nationwide. Having the ability to access a patient's health information could assist in reducing medical errors. As a consumer, utilizing a tool like HealthVault could provide an opportunity to consolidate all medical information electronically, so if there are any medical problems, the information will be readily available.

HEALTHCARE LAW

To be an effective healthcare manager, it is important to understand basic legal principles that influence the work environment including the legal relationship between the organization and the consumer—the healthcare provider and the patient. As both a healthcare manager and healthcare consumer, it is imperative that you are familiar with the different federal and state laws that impact the healthcare organization. It is also important that you understand the differences between civil and criminal law and the penalties that may be imposed for breaking those laws. Both federal and state laws have been enacted and policy has been implemented to protect both the healthcare provider and the healthcare consumer. New laws have been passed and older laws have been amended to reflect needed changes regarding health care to continue to protect its participants from both a patient and an employee/employer perspective.

U.S. citizens continue to experience some of the poorest health outcomes in the industrialized world. It is the responsibility of the government and policymakers, clinicians, and researchers to become involved in the progress of developing a systematic healthcare transformation in order to improve the health outcomes in this country. The goal of the *Healthy People* reports is to improve the quality of life and to eliminate health disparities among different segments of the population. These goals must be supported by lawmakers to ensure that at least a minimum standard is established and that health justice is achieved (Department of Health and Human Services [HHS], 2000). The Affordable Care Act and its mandates have attempted to rectify these problems.

HEALTHCARE ETHICS

Legal standards are the minimal standard of action established for individuals in a society. Ethical standards are considered one level above a legal action because individuals make a choice based on what is the "right thing to do," not what is required by law. There are many interpretations of the concept of ethics. Ethics has been interpreted as the moral foundation for standards of conduct (Taylor, 1975). The concept of ethical standards applies to actions that are hoped for and expected by individuals. Actions may be considered legal but not ethical. There are many definitions of ethics but, essentially, ethics is concerned with what are right and wrong choices as perceived by society and its individuals.

There are also several ethical issues involving the healthcare industry and its stakeholders. There are two components of ethics in health care: medical ethics, which focus on the treatment of the patient, and bioethics, which focus on technology and how it is utilized in health care. The most important stakeholder in health care is the patient. The most important relationship with this stakeholder is with his or her healthcare provider. Their relationship is impacted by the other stakeholders in the industry, including the government, who regulates healthcare provider activities; the insurance companies, who interact with both provider and patient; and healthcare facilities, such as hospitals or managed care facilities, where the physician has a relationship. All of these stakeholders can influence how a healthcare provider interacts with the patient because they have an interest in the outcome. For that reason, many organizations that represent these stakeholders have developed codes of ethics so individuals are provided guidance for ethical behavior. Codes of ethics for the physicians and other healthcare providers, nurses, pharmaceutical companies, and medical equipment companies were discussed previously and emphasize how these stakeholders should interact with both the healthcare providers and patients. These codes of conduct also apply to the relationship between employees in a healthcare facility. The issue of workplace bullying has been a continuous problem for many years. The Joint Commission issued a statement and guidelines for workplace behavior in the healthcare industry. The Joint Commission indicated that this type of behavior can be destructive, resulting in medical errors.

MENTAL HEALTH

Mental health issues impact millions of U.S. citizens. Mental health disabilities limit the life expectancy of individuals by 25 years. Treatment of mental health disorders has been traditionally underfunded because of the attitude of the traditional healthcare system, confusion by health insurance companies, and fear of discrimination by individuals who are mentally ill. In 1999, Surgeon General David Satcher's report on mental health brought awareness to the issues with the U.S. mental healthcare system. The Mental Health Parity Act of 1996 was an attempt to establish a fair system of treatment between mental health disorders and traditional healthcare conditions by mandating annual and lifetime limits to be equal between mental health care and traditional health care. President George W. Bush's Freedom Commission on Mental Health focused on an analysis of the mental health system and recommendations to improve mental health care.

The Mental Health Parity and Addiction Equity Act (2008) further supported mental health care by requiring insurance plans to offer similar benefits to traditional medical benefits and cost sharing to be similar to other medical benefits. However, mental health experts and legislators felt the Act was overall weak and recently passed a final rule that would strengthen the Act, increasing parity of mental health insurance coverage with traditional health insurance coverage. The Obama administration has recognized the importance of funding mental health initiatives, including teacher training programs for mental health awareness (Mohney, 2013).

TRENDS IN HEALTH CARE

Complementary and alternative medicine (CAM) is a group of diverse medical care practices that are not considered part of traditional medicine. "Complementary" generally refers to using a nonmainstream approach together with conventional medicine. "Alternative" refers to using a nonmainstream approach in place of conventional medicine. **Integrative medicine** means a combination of alternative and complementary medicine with a mainstream approach.

Examples of CAM include acupuncture, chiropractic manipulation, diet therapies, meditation, natural products (e.g., flaxseed and fish oil), yoga, and massage. In 2012, approximately 40% of adults used CAM. CAM use is more predominant in females and those individuals with higher education and income. The National Center for Health's recent statistics indicate that back pain was the most common reason people used CAM (National Center for Complementary and Alternative Medicine, 2013). U.S. consumers spend an average of $34 billion on CAM. It is anticipated that more CAM therapies, particularly alternative medicine therapies, will be used by those individuals that are uninsured and underinsured.

Nursing Home Trends

In 2001, the Robert Wood Johnson Foundation funded a pilot project developed by Dr. Bill Thomas, the **Green House Project**, which is a unique type of nursing home that focuses on creating a residence that not only provides services but is also a home to the residents, not an institution where they receive care. It alters the size of the facility, the physical environment, and delivery of services (Fine, 2009).

The home is managed by a team of workers who share the care of the residents, including the cooking and housekeeping. The daily staff members are certified nursing assistants (CNAs). All mandated professional personnel, such as physicians, nurses, social workers, and dieticians, form visiting clinical support teams that assess the **elders** and supervise their care (Kane, Lum, Cutler, Degenholtz, & Yu, 2007).

The residents can eat their meals when they choose. The word "patient" is not used; all residents are called "elders." The Green House is designed for 6–10 elders. Each resident has a private room and private bathroom. The elder rooms have lots of sunlight and are located near the kitchen and dining areas. There are patios and gardens for elders and staff to enjoy. Although these new types of nursing homes look like a residential home, they adhere to all long-term housing requirements. They look like other homes in their designated neighborhood (Fine, 2009).

Residents can also have their own pets, which are not allowed in traditional nursing homes. According to a recent study performed by the University of Minnesota, the residents of the Green House are able to perform their activities of daily living longer and are less depressed than residents of traditional nursing homes and are able to be self-sufficient longer than residents from traditional nursing homes. The staff also enjoy working at the Green House, resulting in less staff turnover (Kane et al., 2007).

The first Green House was constructed in Tupelo, Mississippi. There are now 18 homes nationwide. Dr. Thomas has partnered with the Robert Wood Johnson Foundation (RWJF) and NCB Capital Impact, which is a not-for-profit organization that provides financial assistance to underserved communities. The NCB Capital Impact has a loan program that provides financial assistance of up to $125,000 to support engineering, architectural, and other expenses for a selected Green House site. The borrower must contribute 25% of the loan amount (NCB Capital Impact, 2013).

Since 2002, the Foundation has awarded $12 million, primarily to NCB Capital Impact, to develop, test, and evaluate the Green House model. In 2011, the Foundation decided to expand its support, with the goal of helping the Green House model achieve greater reach and impact. With NCB Capital Impact, RWJF announced a 10-year, $10 million low-interest credit line to finance the building of Green House homes. Specifically, this investment reduces the cost of financing Green House projects to serve low-income elders. RWJF support is helping to spread the Green House model across the United States. Today, hundreds of Green House homes are open or under development in many states (Robert Wood Johnson Foundation, 2013).

Accountable Care Organizations: Value Based Purchasing

The Affordable Care Act of 2010 established the **Hospital Value-Based Purchasing Program**. It is a Centers for Medicare & Medicaid Services (CMS) initiative that rewards acute-care hospitals with incentive payments for the quality of care they provide to people with Medicare, not just the quantity of procedures performed. Hospitals are rewarded based on how closely they follow best clinical practices and how well hospitals enhance patients' experiences of care. When hospitals follow proven best practices, patients receive higher quality care and see better outcomes. Hospital value-based purchasing is just one initiative CMS is undertaking to improve the quality of care Medicare beneficiaries receive.

Innovative Finance Models

According to the CMS website, **Accountable Care Organizations** (ACOs) are groups of providers and hospitals who volunteer to give coordinated care to Medicare patients. The goal of ACOs is to ensure that patients, especially with chronic conditions, receive timely care while avoiding duplication of services and preventing medical errors. Medicare has developed three major programs for providers to become ACOs:

- **Medicare Shared Savings Program**—a program that helps Medicare fee-for-service program providers become an ACO.
- **Advance Payment ACO Model**—a supplementary incentive program for smaller practices: physician-based and rural providers in the Shared Savings Program. They receive monthly payments to use for coordinated care. There are currently 35 who participate in the program.
- **Pioneer ACO Model**—a program designed for early adopters of coordinated care. Any monetary savings are shared with Medicare (CMS, 2013).

There are 32 ACOs enrolled in the Pioneer ACO model. According to recent results, only 13 of the ACOs improved patient quality of healthcare services, patient satisfaction, and saved money. Two of the ACOs owe Medicare $4 million because they spent more on their patients than the traditional Medicare fee-for-service rates. (Bleach, 2013). As of July 2013, seven ACOs have opted to leave the Pioneer Model and enter the Medicare Shared Savings Program and two will be leaving the Medicare ACO program entirely. The 13 that saved money while improving quality of care saved $87.6 million in 2012, saving about $33 million for Medicare (Zigmond, 2013).

Pay-for-performance (P4P) or value-based purchasing (VBP) are terms that describe healthcare payment systems that reward healthcare providers, including hospitals, physicians, and other providers for their efficiency, which is defined as providing higher quality care for less cost. From a healthcare consumer's perspective, these stakeholders should hold healthcare providers accountable for both the cost and high quality of their care. Since most health care in the United States has been historically provided by employers, in VBP, employers should select healthcare plans based on demonstrated performance of quality and cost-effective health care (Agency for Healthcare Research and Quality [AHRQ], 2013). For the past decade, the Centers for Medicare & Medicaid Services (CMS) has been collaborating with the National Quality Forum, The Joint Commission, the National Committee for Quality Assurance, AHRQ, and the American Medical Association to implement initiatives to assess P4P systems nationwide.

For example, California's **Integrated Healthcare Association's** (IHA) P4P program, started in 2003, has operated as the largest nongovernmental program nationally. The program targets 225 medical groups representing 35,000 physicians that contracted with the 8 largest health maintenance organizations (HMOs) and P4Ps in the state, which have 10 million enrollees. The IHA scored physician care based on the healthcare effectiveness data, information measures, and paid performance-based payments. These report cards are available to patients so they can review the performance of the health plans. The results are posted on the California Office of the Patient Advocate website (State of California, 2013). The concept of P4P is a valid concept for health care. Its goals of quality and access are similar to the goals of the Affordable Care Act. There are nearly 200 P4Ps worldwide that indicate improvements in clinical quality performances, although fewer improvements in patient satisfaction. These programs also encourage physicians to adopt clinical decision support systems (Integrated Healthcare Association, 2013).

Electronic Prescribing

E-prescribing developed as a result of the Medicare Prescription Drug, Improvement and Modernization Act. Part D, which authorized a drug prescription program for enrollees, also supported a voluntary electronic prescription program for providers. It also called for the adoption of technical standards to develop a system that would support e-prescribing. This electronic system would enable physicians to check the ingredients of the drugs, which would enable an increased use of generic drugs because they could automatically compare the drug ingredients to brand name prescription drugs (Friedman, Schueth, & Bell, 2009). E-prescribing is not only more efficient, it enhances patient safety. More than 7,000 medication-related deaths occur each year as a result of incompatible drug interactions and drug allergies. These deaths are because of illegible handwritten prescriptions and because the healthcare provider is unaware of patient allergies.

E-prescriptions are immediately notified about patient-specific drug allergies and potential drug interactions (Brunetti & Jay, 2009). According to the 2012 National Progress Report on E-Prescribing and Safe-RX Rankings, 93% of internists, 85% of cardiovascular specialists, and 84% of family practice providers have adopted e-prescribing. Nearly 70% of physicians' offices prescribe and nearly 90% of prescribers also use an electronic health record. Over 90% of pharmacies can accept electronic prescriptions (Surescripts, 2012).

Section 132 of the **Medicare Improvements for Patients and Providers Act of 2008 (MIPPA)** authorized incentives to encourage physicians to e-prescribe. In January 2009, Medicare and some private healthcare plans began paying a bonus to physicians who e-prescribe to their Medicare patients. Medicare will also penalize physicians who do not e-prescribe by 2012 by reducing their reimbursement rates by 1%, 1.5% for 2013, and 2% for 2014 and all subsequent years. (Electronic Prescribing Incentive Program, 2013). IT companies are providing free software to physicians to encourage them to electronically prescribe.

Telemedicine

Telemedicine refers to the use of information technology to enable healthcare providers to communicate with rural care providers regarding patient care or to communicate directly with patients regarding treatment. The basic form of telemedicine is a telephone consultation. Telemedicine is most frequently used in pathology and radiology because images can be transmitted to a distant location where a specialist will read the results. Telemedicine is becoming more common because it increases healthcare access to remote locations such as rural areas. It also is a cost-effective mode of treatment. It is also possible that employers and health plans recognize the potential to improve access to medical care while reducing medical costs (Gingrich, Boxer, & Brooks, 2008). For example, eEmergency, established in 2009, provides immediate electronic access of emergency certified physicians and nurses to rural providers to help them with diagnosis of patients with critical conditions. Since its inception in 2009, eEmergency has served more than 15,000 patients at 70 locations. Rural clinicians and administrators agreed that eEmergency services have demonstrated significant impact on the quality of clinical services provided in rural areas (Telemedicine case studies, 2013). This type of consumer-centric approach may become more popular.

Radio Frequency Identification

Radio frequency identification (RFID) chips transmit data to receivers. Each of these chips is uniquely identified by a signal indicating where it is located. RFID has been used in the business industry for inventory management by placing a chip on each of the pieces of inventory. Walmart was one of the first retailers to use RFID technology to manage their massive inventory. Recently, RFID technology is being used in many aspects of the operations of the healthcare industry. RFID can be used for the following:

- Tracking pharmaceuticals as they are shipped from the manufacturer to the customer
- Tracking pharmaceutical inventory in a healthcare facility
- Tracking wait time in emergency rooms
- Tracking the use of what is being used in surgeries
- Tracking costly medical equipment to ensure easy access
- Identifying providers in hospitals to ensure efficiency in care
- Identifying laboratory specimens to reduce medical errors
- Tracking patients, including infants, while they are hospitalized
- Tracking hazardous materials that pose a public health threat
- Tracking hand washing use to ensure employee compliance (RFID Solutions, 2013)

Robotic Surgery

Robots were first introduced as a surgical tool in 1987. **Robotic surgery** is a type of minimally invasive surgery (MIS) that it is less invasive than traditional surgery—there are smaller incisions, which reduce the risk of infection, shorten hospital stays, and reduce recuperation times. Surgeons manipulate robotic arms to perform surgeries normally performed by human hands. Surgeons have to be trained in robotic surgery and use a machine that will reduce the possibility of errors caused by tremors in the surgeons' hands.

As robotic surgery became more popular, the National Aeronautic and Space Administration (NASA) developed the concept of **telesurgery** or **medical robotics and computer assisted surgery (MRCAS)**, which combines virtual reality, robots, and medicine. The U.S. Army also became involved in robotic surgery because they

were interested in bringing surgery to the soldiers who were fighting and needed surgery immediately. They hoped robotic surgery would reduce war mortality rates. It is important to note that there are also other tools that can be used for MIS. Studies have indicated that some procedures such as an appendectomy show very little difference if performed by the traditional method or the robotic method. However, robotic surgeries performed on the prostate have shown significant positive outcomes (Guidarelli, 2006; Loisance, 2007).

The robotic system that has dominated the current market is the **da Vinci Surgical System**, which was developed by Intuitive Surgical of Sunnyvale, California. It is used in areas of cardiac, urologic, gynecologic, and general surgery. This tool was used for 1,500 cases in the year 2000, but use increased to 20,000 cases in 2004 and 48,000 procedures in 2006. Recent data indicates this equipment was used in 350,000 cases (Langreth, 2013). The initial investment for a da Vinci system is $1.5 million, with an annual upkeep of $100,000 (Intuitive Surgical, Inc., 2013). Despite the initial cost, experts feel that the actual procedure is cost-effective because recuperation time is far less for the patients. The continued issue with telesurgery is patient injuries as a result of the use of robotic equipment. There has been continued issues with the DaVinci tool. The FDA, who regulates medical devices, in 2013, received 3,700 reports of injuries, deaths, and malfunctions from robotic surgery. Industry experts believe these adverse events are being underreported (Langreth, 2013). As with any technological advances, the costs should decrease and the tool will become more advanced and more efficient, but the safety issues must be addressed.

Drugstore Clinics

Rite Aid, Walgreen's, and CVS, three national chain pharmacies, have established **drugstore clinics**. CVS, the leader in this innovative type of health care, now has 640 **Minute Clinics** nationwide. They have decided to expand their treatment options to include conditions handled normally by a physician. Their goal is not to replace primary care providers but to increase access to health care. Walgreens, which has nearly 400 **Take Care Clinics** nationwide, will follow the CVS policy. Many of the patients who use drugstore clinics do not have a primary care provider (Modern Healthcare, 2013). According to the **Convenient Care Association** (CCA), since the walk-in clinics opened in 2000, an estimated 5 million people have been treated. According to the

CCA, there are 1,400 clinics in 35 states. Like urgent care clinics, they are open late, on weekends, and you do not need an appointment. This type of access may encourage more individuals to seek health care (Witsil, 2013).

Care Managers

Care managers, or care coordinators, are individuals who combine nursing, social services and disability assistance to individuals primarily who are eligible for both Medicare and Medicaid or dual eligibles, suffer from chronic conditions and often cannot handle managing their own chronic conditions. The goal of a care coordinator is to avoid the patient's placement into a nursing home. Dual eligible patients utilize 35% of Medicare and Medicaid spending so this type of assistance with patient life issues may reduce government spending. According to the CMS, eight states have signed agreements with the CMS to develop care coordination plans (Dickson, 2013).

Care coordinators are the fastest growing occupation in the healthcare industry and are primarily registered nurses.

The Villages Health System

The Villages is one of the largest over-55 golf cart communities in the United States. They have developed a partnership with the University of South Florida to create a **patient-centered**, community-based and primary care driven healthcare system. A primary care network is being developed in which all residents have access to a **medical home** or care center that will be located within 10 minutes by golf cart. There will be 6–10 facilities with 5–9 physicians in each care center that will serve as a gatekeeper for the patient's care. Although many patients are Medicare eligible, the physicians will be salaried and not focused on the quantity of patients they receive for their Medicare reimbursement but on the development of a relationship with their patients. Each facility will serve a designated geographic area of patients. They will collaborate with their patients on their care by educating them on healthy behaviors. If they need a specialist, they will help the patient with the referral. They will have extended hours and emergency operations. They will implement the electronic health record system to enable patient data sharing among the centers. They will also have health coaches on staff that will work with patients on developing a healthy lifestyle. At this point, there is one care center in operation. All of these centers will be accredited by the NCQA (The Villages Health, 2013).

INTERNATIONAL HEALTHCARE SYSTEMS

For years, there has been a movement toward healthcare reform in the United States because many feel that because the United States is so powerful and wealthy, compared to the rest of the world, we should not have nearly 50 million uninsured citizens. However, universal healthcare coverage may not be the answer. It, too, has problems.

There is continued controversy over the expense of the U.S. healthcare system. If we spend so much of our gross domestic product on health care, why are there geographic disparities on who receives it? This may result in lower health indicators in the United States, such as life expectancy and infant mortality rates, compared to the rest of the world. Although the United States can provide state-of-the-art health care, we are reminded of the Institute of Medicine report that estimates 44,000–90,000 annual deaths are a result of medical errors (Kohn, Corrigan, & Donaldson, 1999). As with any large system, there are system errors that were just outlined. The United States is not the only country with a healthcare system that has problems.

UNIVERSAL HEALTHCARE CONCEPTS

Countries with national healthcare programs provide universal access to health care to all citizens. They have a **single-payer system**, which means the government pays for the healthcare services. There are three models for structuring a universal or national healthcare system: national health insurance, national health system, and socialized health insurance system. **National health insurance**, as in Canada, is funded by the government through general taxes, although the delivery of care is by private providers. In a **national health system**, as in Great Britain, taxes support the system but the government also manages the infrastructure for healthcare delivery. In a **socialized health insurance system**, as in Germany, the government mandates financial contributions by both the employer and employee with private providers delivering health care. Sickness funds, which are not-for-profit insurance companies, collect the contributions and pay the healthcare providers (Shi & Singh, 2008). The U.S. healthcare system is employer–employee based and government funded. The U.S. system provides 100% coverage of people older than 65 years of age with the Medicare program, and 82% coverage for people younger than 65 years of age through employer-based insurance, Medicaid, Indian Health Services, Veterans' Administration (TRICARE), and the federal government employee program. Infant mortality rates and life expectancy rates are common healthcare indicator comparisons among countries. Based on Organization for Economic Cooperation and Development data, Japan, Switzerland, and Sweden, which had the best infant mortality and life expectancy rates, were selected for discussion. These analyses will demonstrate that although these countries offer a type of universal healthcare coverage, they also have problems.

Japan

Japan's social security system is divided into four components: social insurance, social welfare, public assistance, and public health. The core social insurance is mandatory and provides a designated monetary amount or benefits to citizens for disease, injury, childbirth, death, old age, disability, and loss of job. A universal healthcare insurance system provides appropriate healthcare anywhere at any time. Citizens have to be covered by any of the following medical insurances: (1) employees health insurance, (2) national health insurance for self-employed or unemployed for those 75 years or older. Health care for the elderly was established in 2008 but there have been complaints about the high premiums and care so it may be abolished.

As part of their health insurance system, the insured pay a premium to the health insurance companies, and in case of a care visit pay a copayment to the healthcare institutions. Healthcare institutions receive reimbursement from health insurance companies. Healthcare expenditures are paid on a fee-for-service basis.

Employees and their dependents under age 75 years are required to enroll in the coverage offered either by their employers (if employed by large companies) or the Japan Health Insurance Association (if employed by small- or medium-sized companies). All enrollees have to pay coinsurance of 30% for services and goods covered, except for children (20%) and people age 70 years and over with low incomes (10%). In 2010, out-of-pocket payments for cost sharing accounted for 16% of total health expenditures (Japanese Nursing Association, 2013).

The remaining population under age 75 (unemployed, self-employed, retired, and others) is covered by municipal-run "Citizens Health Insurance" plans. Those age 75 years and over are covered by health insurance plans operated by insurers established in each prefecture

(H-Old). There are penalties if citizens do not enroll. Most citizens purchase supplementary private health insurance. The devastating earthquake, tsunami, and nuclear emergency that occurred in the last several years has created a health crisis while also destroying a significant part of the healthcare infrastructure, particularly in the Tohoku region. Restoring these services to the affected areas has been a national priority.

Similarly to Germany's socialized health insurance system, Japan's healthcare system centers on mandatory employment-based insurance. Health spending is 9.5% of their gross domestic product. Japan has universal coverage that is comprehensive, including dental and prescription drug coverage. Average annual spending per person is $3,035, which breaks down as $1,927 from government funds, $71 from private insurance, and $360 out-of-pocket by consumers. With the graying of their population, approximately 90% of Japan's healthcare costs are the result of the elderly's utilization of the healthcare system. It is anticipated that Japan will triple government spending on health care in the next 20 years (NPR News, 2008; OECD, 2012a). Like the United States, Japan is very focused on the integration of technology in health care; however, they are not as advanced in the use of technology. Released in 2010, the New Strategy in Information and Communications Technology (IT), outlines four goals regarding the health sector: (1) to develop patient electronic medical records that can be accessed by all providers; (2) to develop health information technology and telehealth platforms that help link patients with doctors and nurses in underserved areas; (3) to create a platform that can monitor pharmaceutical prescriptions and adverse events in real time in order to improve patient safety and monitoring; and (4) to create a claims database of all conditions and interventions to facilitate assessment of community needs and development of interventions (Michael J. Bass Group, 2013). In spite of a number of initiatives over the past decade, electronic health records have not been widely used.

France

France's healthcare system has many characteristics of a socialized health insurance program similar to Germany and Japan. Many healthcare experts feel that France's system should be used as a benchmark when retooling the U.S. healthcare system. In 2011, health spending was 11.6% of their gross domestic product, which is tied with Germany as the third most expensive in the world. They have universal coverage for approximately 99% of French citizens. France has several health insurance funds heavily regulated by the government. The largest fund, the General National Insurance Scheme, covers approximately 80% of French residents. There are two secondary funds for the self employed and agricultural workers. In 2011, average annual spending per person was $4,118 (OECD, 2012b).

Payroll taxes provide the largest source of funding. The employed have 20% of their gross salary deducted to fund healthcare funding. Nearly 90% of citizens have a supplemental insurance policy from private for-profit insurers that they purchase from their employer. Often, the employer pays for the supplemental policy (OECD, 2012b).

Private health insurers are central to the French system because of the supplemental insurance policies that most citizens purchase. More than 118 insurance companies offer some form of health insurance coverage. The national system pays 100% of costs for 30 chronic conditions including cancer and diabetes (OECD, 2012b). Unlike the United States, the government makes it very difficult for insurance companies to deny any coverage because of preexisting conditions. Citizens who are very ill receive increased care and coverage, which is unlike the U.S. system where individuals may go financially bankrupt because of their cost sharing during a chronic disease.

All physicians in France participate in the nation's public health insurance (like Medicaid). The average American physician earns more than five times the average U.S. wage while the average French physician makes only about two times the earnings of the average French wage. However, in France, medical schools, although extremely competitive to enter, are tuition free. Therefore, French physicians enter their careers with minimal debt. Unlike U.S. physicians who pay high malpractice premiums, they pay much lower malpractice insurance premiums because their society is much less likely to sue a physician. French physicians have less administrative expenses because the government has created a standardized efficient system for physician billing and patient reimbursement using electronic funds. It is interesting to note that the French government allows physicians to charge more than the government's reimbursement schedule, although physicians employed by hospitals are not allowed to set their own fees. Most physicians do not overcharge because of the intense competition in their field (Dutton, 2007). The government has also attempted to limit the use of prescription drugs by focusing on less expensive, generic type drugs. Because physicians prescribe a tremendous amount of drugs on an annual basis, the French government recently developed a list of drugs that would not be reimbursed by the government. However, a recent study indicated that 90% of asthmatics did not receive the appropriate medication. Citizens may purchase drugs not on the reimbursable list for which they will have to pay (OECD, 2012b).

France's healthcare system is experiencing a billion dollar deficit that is largely responsible for France's overall budget deficit. The French government is examining a healthcare system based on taxes, fees, and income levels. Consumers have had no restrictions on physician selection; they may visit several physicians before they find a physician they prefer. This type of **medical nomadism** drives up healthcare costs. In response to this issue, in 2005, the government established a **coordinated care pathway**, which is similar to the U.S. managed care system (Tanner, 2008). Individuals are recommended to choose a preferred doctor and follow the doctor's pathway for their care. At this point, this is not a mandate; this is a choice for the citizens. The French had the highest level of satisfaction with their healthcare system worldwide (Tanner, 2008).

In a 2013 *Bloomberg Business Week* article, the healthcare system is having tremendous financial problems, although it appears to be working. Their life expectancy is higher than the United States, their infant mortality rates were half of the United States, and their heart disease and obesity rates are lower than the United States. The government feels the system may only last 5–6 more years and feels healthcare reform is desperately needed. The government is now requiring physicians to reduce the number of drugs they prescribe and to substitute generics, which will save approximately $700 million annually. They are also fining pharmacists who sell too many brand name drugs. Critics say the French government must examine the entire system to cut costs in order for the system to survive (Torsoli, 2013).

Switzerland

Switzerland's healthcare system is considered one of the best in the world, and like the United States, the system must be carefully analyzed due to the increase of chronic disease rates in the country. It is unique because all residents are required to purchase health insurance, so, in a sense, it is a country with universal healthcare coverage. Approximately 99.5% of Swiss have health insurance. Health spending is 11.7% of their gross domestic product. They are tied with France as third most expensive of the OECD countries. They have universal coverage with individuals buying insurance directly from private insurance providers. The Swiss system is similar to the "managed competition" healthcare plan proposed by the Clintons in the early 1990s (Shafrin, 2008). Swiss law requires all citizens to purchase a health insurance package. Insurers cannot reject an applicant based on his or her health status. Healthier consumers pay higher premiums to subsidize the costs for the less healthy. Nonsmokers pay less costly premiums than smokers. Insurers compete on price.

Unlike the other countries discussed in this chapter, few Swiss employers provide insurance or contribute to insurance so individuals bear the full cost of insurance plans. They pay twice the amount of out-of-pocket expenses than the United States. Average annual spending per person is $5,270 (OECD, 2012a).

The government subsidizes the indigent. Their healthcare insurance industry is private but regulated by the government. Their citizens pay more for health insurance in Europe than other countries. The government controls prescription drug prices, of which consumers pay 10% (Rovner, 2008). Like the United States and Japan, Switzerland has focused on health technology. Unlike the United States, Switzerland has strong regulations for nonphysician healthcare professionals such as nurse practitioners, which results in more expensive provider care. The government also sets rates for all providers and hospitals. Insurance companies may not make a profit on a basic insurance plan, which is very comprehensive, but can make a profit on supplemental insurance policies that cover dental, alternative medicine, or private or semiprivate hospital rooms. Consumers, however, can adjust their premium up or down by choosing a larger or smaller annual deductible, or by joining an HMO-type plan. Switzerland ranks second only to the United States in the ability of patients to choose their provider (Rovner, 2008; Shafrin, 2008; Tanner, 2008).

LOCAL GOVERNMENT HEALTHCARE REFORM

Massachusetts Universal Healthcare Program

In April 2006, the state of Massachusetts passed legislation to implement a type of universal healthcare coverage for its residents. The legislation mandated that all adult residents obtain health insurance coverage by July 1, 2007. At the time, 90% of residents had health care; the mandate would result in 98% of residents having health insurance. The cost would be based on the income of the individual. For those residents who did not register, a financial penalty of up to 50% of the health insurance plan cost would be assessed. By July 1, 2007, employers with 11 or more employees were required to provide health insurance coverage or pay a fair share contribution of $295 annually per employee. Employers were also required to offer a Section 125 Cafeteria Plan that permits employees to purchase health care using pretax funds. A specially designed health coverage option was available for residents 19–36 years of age (Brown, 2013).

As part of the healthcare reform, the state established a clearinghouse system, the **Commonwealth Health Insurance Connector**, which facilitated the buying, selling, and administration of affordable, quality, private insurance coverage for employers with 50 or fewer employees. A major component of this reform was the provision of government-funded subsidies to low income individuals to assist with the purchase of health insurance. Plans offered through the Commonwealth Care have no deductibles and are offered by Medicaid managed care organizations (Commonwealth Health Insurance Connector, 2013).

Any resident could purchase coverage through the clearinghouse or nonresidents could purchase insurance if their employer designated the nonresident as part of their group plan. Insurance purchased through this clearinghouse could be transferred within the state, during periods of unemployment, part-time employment, or self-employment (Haisimaier & Owcharenko, 2006). As a result of this program, an estimated 440,000 individuals have health insurance coverage. However, a major problem resulting from this new program is a lack of primary care physicians. Many uninsured that now have insurance require the services of a primary care physician. There are now huge waiting lists to obtain appointments for an initial visit. This problem is reflective of the geographic maldistribution of primary care physicians in the United States—there are more specialists than there are primary care physicians. The state has passed incentive legislation, such as loan forgiveness for their medical training, to encourage primary physicians to practice in Massachusetts (Brown, 2008). Despite this issue, this program is being examined by other states as a way to provide more health insurance coverage for those who are underinsured.

As a result of the program, the state of Massachusetts has the highest rate of healthcare coverage in the nation. Of the previously 439,000 uninsured residents, 83% obtained insurance through publicly funded programs. Residents had eight plans to choose from. Like the Affordable Care Act, those individuals who could afford a health insurance plan but did not enroll received a fine. The fine in Massachusetts ranged from $19 a month to $105 per month, depending on income. As a result of this mandate, Massachusetts spends $9,278 per person annually, which is one of the highest in the country.

Hospitals are seeing fewer uninsured patients, and visits to the emergency rooms for primary health care are down by approximately 33%. A benefit of this program is a healthier population. The current governor has been able to reject healthcare premium rate increases as well (Hirschkorn, 2012).

Healthy San Francisco Program

In February 2006, then San Francisco Mayor Gavin Newsom created a Universal Healthcare Council to develop a plan to provide access to health care for San Francisco's uninsured adults. This collaborative effort, comprised of representatives from the health care, business, labor, philanthropy, and research communities, met for 4 months. The Council reviewed demographic and actuarial data, and heard from community advocates and employers to identify and quantify the needs of the uninsured. As a result of these meetings, in April 2007, the city's **Healthy San Francisco (HSF) Program** was established and it made comprehensive health care available to the 73,000 uninsured San Francisco residents between 18 and 65 years of age. The San Francisco Department of Public Health (DPH) is responsible for the overall planning, development, implementation, and ongoing administration of Healthy San Francisco. Those eligible are required to obtain care at the San Francisco Medical Home Network, which consists of public health clinics, community clinics, and private providers.

Employers with 100 employees or more are also required to spend $1.76 per work hour per employee on health benefits. Employees with 20–99 employees are required to spend $1.17 per hour. It is not an insurance program, but a restructuring of the county's program for the uninsured (Department of Public Health, San Francisco, 2013). This type of managed care program

provides inpatient and outpatient care, prescription coverage, lab services, and treatments for mental health and substance abuse. Any resident is eligible to apply for the program regardless of income status, pre-existing conditions, or immigration status. Those eligible must choose a primary care provider home among the 14 clinics and they are provided with an identification card and a handbook explaining the services. Small fees are charged based on income. Recent data indicated that 70% of enrollees have incomes 100% at or below the federal poverty levels. As of May 2009, there are 41,000 enrollees in the program (Katz, 2008). Patient satisfaction surveys indicate the enrollees are very pleased with the HSF and would encourage others that are eligible to take advantage of the program (Kaiser Family Foundation, 2009).

Both the Massachusetts and San Francisco programs focus on the uninsured in their geographic areas and attempt to provide affordable and quality medical care to all individuals, regardless of income.

LESSONS TO BE LEARNED FROM OTHER HEALTHCARE SYSTEMS

Japan, France, and Switzerland have different types of universal health insurance programs, but their systems all have flaws. Although Japan ranks at or near the top in the OECD country rankings for infant mortality rates and life expectancy, there are issues with their system. Like the United States, employer insurance provides a large percentage of their health care. Like the United States, the elderly use the healthcare system more than any other demographic and, as a result of this, Japan's healthcare spending is expected to triple over the next several years. In the United States, Medicare spending continues to be an issue; however, the Affordable Care Act has developed financing models for Medicare providers that may rectify this major problem.

France, which has been applauded for a quality healthcare system, also has financial problems. Similar to the United States, employers pay a portion of an employee's health insurance premium. However, unlike the United States, employers are mandated to pay a percentage of the employee's salary to a national health insurance program, not to a private health insurance plan. In France, the taxes on tobacco, alcohol, and pharmaceutical company revenues are used for health care. Similar to the United States, private health insurance companies participate in their healthcare industry because 90% of citizens purchase supplemental insurance. However, unlike the United States, the sicker a citizen/resident becomes, the more coverage he or she receives from the government. There is a mandate in the ACA that prohibits health insurance companies from denying coverage based on catastrophic illness. That mandate is a positive step in improving health care for those who are seriously ill. There are 30 chronic conditions for which the French government will pay the coverage, such as cancer and diabetes. In the United States, some citizens become bankrupt if they have chronic conditions because they cannot pay for the out-of-pocket expenses. France's healthcare providers all participate in public health insurance, which is similar to Medicare and Medicaid. Unlike the United States, physicians voluntarily enroll in the program. The French providers earn much less than U.S. providers but medical school tuition is free.

As with the U.S. system, France is experiencing a huge budget deficit for health care. Their government is now examining the possibility of developing a new system that is based on increased taxes, fees, and the income of individuals. There is a continual outcry regarding raising individuals' personal taxes for a universal healthcare program in the United States. Like the United States, France is developing a managed care–type program that will encourage citizens to select a provider who will become the gatekeeper for their care. Managed care contained costs in the United States during the 1990s and has become commonplace in the U.S. healthcare system.

Switzerland has an expensive healthcare system. The program is similar to the new healthcare system in Massachusetts because they both require all of their residents to purchase healthcare insurance. Like Japan, Swiss insurers cannot reject any applicant based on their health status. They also cannot make any profit on the basic insurance package but can make a profit on the supplemental insurance packages that most citizens buy. The government supports the indigent like the United States does with its Medicaid program.

The Affordable Care Act has targeted insurance companies by requiring them to spend at least 80% of premium revenues on providing quality care. The Affordable Care Act has also imposed a flat annual fee on the pharmaceutical companies, makers of medical

devices, and health insurance providers, based on market share. There is also a 10% tax on indoor tanning bed facilities. Those monies will be used to support the public portion of the U.S. healthcare system.

CONCLUSION

The U.S. healthcare system continues to evolve. Technology will continue to have a huge impact on health care. Consumers have more information to make healthcare decisions because of information technology. Healthcare providers have more opportunities to utilize technology in their delivery such as robotic surgery, e-prescribing, and clinical decision support systems that will assist them with diagnoses. The Green House Project is an exciting initiative that may transform how long-term care will be implemented. As our population becomes grayer, more citizens will want to live as independently as possible for a longer period of time and the Green House Project is an excellent template for achieving this goal. All of these initiatives are exciting for the healthcare consumer. The implementation of an EHR, which will enable providers to share information about a patient's health history, will provide the consumer with the opportunity to obtain more cost-effective and efficient health care. The Veterans Administration hospitals use the EHR system. Duke University Health System also uses an EHR system across North Carolina (Ritzenthaler, 2009). There are hospitals, physician practices, and other healthcare organizations that utilize EHR systems across the country. Even though implementing the system nationally will be extremely expensive—costs have been estimated in the billions—it will eventually be a cost-saving measure for the United States. The Affordable Care Act has provided many incentives to improve the quality of and access to the U.S. healthcare system. The Centers for Medicaid and Medicare Innovation has over 40 demonstration projects that focus on different types of financing models that are based on the performance of healthcare providers.

The discussion on the different country healthcare systems analyses indicate that all countries have problems with their healthcare systems. Establishing a universal healthcare system in the United States may not be the answer. There are aspects of each of these programs that could be integrated in the U.S. system. There were surprisingly many similarities. The major differences were the control the government placed on pharmaceutical prices and the health insurers. They limited their profitability in order to increase healthcare access to their citizens. The main difference between these three countries and the United States are the citizens' willingness to pay more so all citizens can receive health care. That collectivistic attitude is not prevailing here in the United States; that would be difficult to change. However, the mandates for both business and individuals to purchase health insurance coverage through the establishment of state health insurance marketplaces should improve the overall health of the United States.

VOCABULARY

Accountable Care Organizations

Advance Payment ACO Model

Care manager

Commonwealth Health Insurance Connector

Convenient Care Association

Coordinated care pathway

da Vinci Surgical System

Drugstore clinics

Elders

Electronic prescribing (e-prescribing)

Green House Project

Healthy San Francisco Program

Hospital Value-Based Purchasing Program

Integrated Healthcare Association

Integrative medicine

Medical homes

Medical nomadism

Medical robotics and computer assisted surgery (MRCAS)

Medical Shared Savings Program

Medicare Improvements for Patients and Providers Act of 2008 (MIPPA)

Minute Clinics

National health insurance

National health system

Patient-centered

Pay-for-performance (P4P) or value-based purchasing (VBP)

Pioneer ACO Model

Radio frequency identification

Robotic surgery

Single-payer system

Socialized health insurance system

Take Care Clinic

Telemedicine

Telesurgery

REFERENCES

Affordable health care for America. (2010). Retrieved from http://www.speaker.gov/newsroom/legislation?id=0361

Agency for Healthcare Research and Quality (AHRQ). (2013). Theory and reality of value-based purchasing: Lessons from the pioneers. Retrieved from http://www.ahrq.gov/qual/meyerrpt.htm

Ambulatory Surgery Center Association (ASCA). (2013). Retrieved from http://ascassociation.org/faqs/faqaboutascs/#1

American Association of Colleges of Nursing (AACN). (2013). Nursing shortage. Retrieved from http://www.aacn.nche.edu/media-relations/fact-sheets/nursing-shortage

Arts, K. (2010). Legal challenges to health reform: An alliance for health reform toolkit. Retrieved from http://www.allhealth.org/publications/Uninsured/Legal_Challenges_to_New_Health_Reform_Law_97.pdf

Bleasch, G. (2013). All Pioneer ACOs improved quality; only third lowered costs. Retrieved from http://www.modernhealthcare.com/article/20130716/NEWS/307169958/all-pioneer-acos-improved-quality-only-third-lowered-costs

Brown, K. (2008). Mass health care reform reveals doctor shortages. Retrieved from http://www.npr.org/templates/story/story.php?storyId=97620520

Brunetti, L., & Jay, R. (2009). Using technology for more effective pharmacy benefit management. *Benefits & Compensation Digest, 46,* 16–21.

Centers for Disease Control and Prevention (CDC). (2013). Workplace safety and health topics: Healthcare workers. Retrieved from http://www.cdc.gov/niosh/topics/healthcare

Centers for Medicare & Medicaid Services (CMS). (2013). Medicare program—General information. Retrieved from http://www.cms.gov/Medicare/Medicare-General-Information/MedicareGenInfo/index.html

Commonwealth Health Insurance Connector Authority. (2013). Retrieved from http://www.mahealthconnector.org

Department of Health and Human Services (DHHS). (2000). *Healthy People 2010.* Retrieved from http://www.healthypeople.gov/Publications

Department of Public Health, San Francisco. (2013). Key facts and reports. Retrieved from http://healthysanfrancisco.org/about-healthy-san-francisco/key-facts-report

Dickson, V., (2013). Partners in health. Retrieved from http://www.modernhealthcare.com/article/20131221/MAGAZINE/312219933/?cslet=UnhOY2lLZjhMZkNkK2lneHNiZlNOSTRldWUzaXMyZlBNYnJCalE9PQ%3D%3D

Dutton, P. V. (2007). France's model healthcare system. Retrieved from http://www.boston.com/news/globe/editorial_opinion/oped/articles/2007/08/11/frances_model_healthcare_system

Fine, S. (2009, May 31). Where to live as we age. *Parade Magazine,* 8–9.

Friedman, M., Schueth, A., & Bell, D. (2009). Interoperable electronic prescribing in the U.S.: A progress report. *Health Affairs, 28*(2), 393–403.

Gingrich, N., Boxer, R., & Brooks, B. (2008). Telephone medical consults answer the call for accessible, affordable and convenient health care. Retrieved from http://www.healthtransformation.net/galleries/defaultfile/teladoc.pdf

Goodson, J. (2010). Patient Protection and Affordable Care Act: Promise and peril for primary care. Retrieved from http://www.annals.org/content/early/2010/04/15/0003-4819-152-11-201006010-00249.full

Guidarelli, M. (2006). Robotic surgery. *The Next Generation: An Introduction to Medicine, 2.* Retrieved from http://www.nextgenmd.org/vol2–5/robotic_surgery.html

Haisimaier, E., & Owcharenko, N. (2006). The Massachusetts approach: A new way to restructure state health insurance markets and public programs. *Health Affairs, 25*(6), 1580–1590.

Hirschkorn, P. (2012, June 25). Massachusetts' health care plan: 6 years later. Retrieved from http://www.cbsnews.com/2102-18563_162-57459563.html

Integrated Healthcare Association. (2013). Pay for performance overview. Retrieved from http://www.iha.org/performance_measurement.html

Intuitive Surgical, Inc. (2009). da Vinci surgery. Retrieved from http://www.davincisurgery.com

Japanese Nursing Association. (2013). Nursing in Japan. Retrieved from http://www.nurse.or.jp/jna/english/nursing/medical.html

Kaiser Family Foundation. (2009, August). Survey of Healthy San Francisco Participants. Retrieved from http://www.healthysanfranciso.org/files/PDF/HSF_Satisfaction_Survey_Kaiser.pdf

Kane, R., Lum, T., Cutler, L., Degenholtz, H., & Yu, T. (2007). Resident outcomes in small house nursing homes: A longitudinal evaluation of the initial Green House program. *Journal of Geriatrics Society*, *55*(6), 832–839.

Katz, M. (2008). Golden Gate to health care for all? San Francisco's new universal access program. *New England Journal of Medicine*, *258*(4), 327–329.

Kohn, L. T., Corrigan, J. M., & Donaldson, M. S. (1999). *To err is human: Building a safer health system*. Washington, DC: National Academy Press.

Langreth, R. (2013). Unreported robot surgery injuries presents problems for FDA. Retrieved from http://www.bloomberg.com/news/2013-12-30/unreported-robot-surgery-injuries-open-questions-for-fda.html

Loisance, A. (2007). Robotic surgery and telesurgery: Basic principles and description of a novel concept. *Journal de Chirugie*, *3*(3), 211–214.

Mathews, A. W. (2011, December 12). The future of U.S. health care. Retrieved from http://online.wsj.com/article/SB10001424052970204319004577084553869990554.html

Michael J. Bass Group. (2013). Patent valuation report update. Retrieved from http://michaelbass.com/PDF/Patent_Valuation.pdf

Modern Healthcare. (2013, April 4). Walgreen clinics expand care into chronic illness. Retrieved from http://www.modernhealthcare.com/article/20130404/INFO/304049978

Mohney, G. (2013, April 10). Obama budget includes $235 million for mental health care. Retrieved from http://abcnews.go.com/Health/obama-budget-includes-235-million-mental-health-initiatives/story?id=18922699

National Center for Complementary and Alternative Medicine (NCCAM). (2013). About NCCAM. Retrieved from http://nccam.nih.gov/about

NCB Capital Impact. (2013). Retrieved from http://www.ncbcapitalimpact.org/default.aspx?id=146&terms=Green+House

Novick, L., & Morrow, C. (2008). A framework for public health administration and practice. In L. Novick & C. Morrow (Eds.), *Public health administration: Principles for population-based management* (pp. 35–68). Sudbury, MA: Jones and Bartlett.

Organisation for Economic Cooperation and Development (OECD). (2012a). Retrieved from http://stats.oecd.org/Index.aspx?DataSetCode=CSP2009

Organisation for Economic Cooperation and Development (OECD). (2012b). France healthcare statistics. Retrieved from http://www.oecd.org/france

Pointer, D., Williams, S., Isaacs, S., & Knickman, J. (2007). *Introduction to U.S. health care*. Hoboken, NJ: Wiley Publishing.

State of California, Office of the Patient Advocate. (2013). PPO quality ratings summary. Retrieved from http://reportcard.opa.ca.gov/rc2013/pporating.aspx

Ritzenthaler, B. A. (2009). Healthcare and President Obama's address: Electronic health records are a key element to healthcare reform. Retrieved from http://generalmedicine.suite101.com/article.crm/healthcare_and_president_obamas_address

Robert Wood Johnson Foundation. (2013). Green House Research Collaborative. Retrieved from http://www.rwjf.org/en/research-publications/research-features/green-house-research-collaborative.html

Rovner, J. (2008). In Switzerland, a health care model for America? Retrieved from http://www.npr.org/templates/story/story.php?storyId=92106731

Shafrin, J. (2008). Health care around the world: Switzerland. Retrieved from http://healthcareeconomist .com/2008/04/23/healthcarearoundtheworldswitzerland/

Shi, L., & Singh, D. (2008). *Delivering health care in America*. Sudbury, MA: Jones and Bartlett.

Surescripts. (2012). National Progress Report on EPrescribing and Safe-RX Rankings. Retrieved from http://www .surescripts.com/about-e-prescribing/progress-reports/national-progress-reports#downloads

Tanner, M. (2008). The grass is not always greener—A look at national health care systems around the world. Cato Institute. *Policy analysis*, *613*, 1–48.

Taylor, P. (1975). *Principles of ethics: An introduction to ethics* (2nd ed.). Encino, CA: Dickinson.

The Villages Health. (2013). About us. Retrieved from http://www.thevillageshealth.com/aboutus.php

Torsoli, A. (2013, January 3). France's health-care system is going broke. Retrieved from http://www.businessweek .com/articles/2013-01-03/frances-health-care-system-is-going-broke

Witsil, F. (2013, March 28). Drugstore clinics: A rapidly growing option for sick people. Retrieved from http://www.freep.com/article/20130328/BUSINESS06/303280154/Drugstore-clinics-A-rapidly-growing-option -for-sick-people

Zigmond, J. (2013). CMS names ACOs leaving Pioneer program. Retrieved from http://www.modernhealthcare .com/article/20130716/NEWS/307169945/cms-names-acos-leaving-pioneer-program

NOTES

STUDENT ACTIVITY 14-1

IN YOUR OWN WORDS

Based on this chapter, please provide a description of the following concepts in your own words. DO NOT RECITE the text description.

Commonwealth Health Insurance Connector: _____

_____

_____

Coordinated care pathway: _____

_____

_____

Green House Project: _____

_____

_____

Healthy San Francisco Program: _____

_____

_____

Medical nomadism: _____

_____

_____

National health insurance: _____

_____

_____

National health system: _____

_____

_____

Pay-for-performance (P4P): _____

_____

_____

Single-payer system: _____

_____

_____

Robotic surgery: _____

_____

_____

STUDENT ACTIVITY 14-2

Complete the following case scenarios based on the information provided in the chapter. Your answer must be IN YOUR OWN WORDS.

REAL LIFE APPLICATIONS: CASE SCENARIO ONE

You need to do a research paper for your international healthcare class. Select one of the countries discussed in the chapter and assess two strengths of one of these systems.

ACTIVITY

Apply these two strengths to the U.S. healthcare system. Write a two page report on how you would integrate these characteristics into U.S. healthcare.

RESPONSES

_____

_____

_____

_____

_____

_____

_____

_____

_____

_____

_____

_____

_____

_____

CASE SCENARIO TWO

You have a friend that you believe is suffering from some mental health issues. You are concerned about him but do not know what to do.

ACTIVITY

Do an Internet search and review the different legislative acts that pertain to mental health. Research mental health statistics in the United States. Write up a report that discusses these acts and the data you found regarding mental health in the United States.

RESPONSES

_____

_____

_____

_____

_____

_____

_____

_____

_____

_____

_____

_____

_____

_____

CASE SCENARIO THREE

Your family believes in a holistic approach to medicine. They have bad backs and they refuse to take prescription drugs. They believe that complementary and alternative medicine (CAM) is the best approach. You are not sure.

ACTIVITY

Research the field of CAM. Identify three ways that CAM is used to treat a medical problem.

RESPONSES

_____

_____

_____

_____

_____

_____

_____

_____

_____

_____

_____

_____

_____

_____

_____

CASE SCENARIO FOUR

Your parents have asked you to assist in placing your grandparents into a skilled nursing facility. They are very concerned about the care they will receive. You have heard of a new model of nursing home that may be appropriate for your grandparents.

ACTIVITY

Write up a report on the Green House Project and explain the differences between a traditional skilled nursing facility and the Green House Project.

RESPONSES

_____

_____

_____

_____

_____

_____

_____

_____

_____

_____

_____

_____

_____

_____

STUDENT ACTIVITY 14-3

INTERNET EXERCISES

Write your answers in the space provided.

- Visit each of the websites listed here.
- Name the organization.
- Locate their mission statement or statement of purpose on their website.
- Provide a brief overview of the activities of the organization.
- How do these organizations participate in the U.S. healthcare system?

Websites

http://www.healthline.com

Organization Name: _____

Mission Statement:

_____

_____

_____

Overview of Activities: _____

_____

_____

Importance of organization to U.S. health care:

_____

_____

_____

http://www.drugstorenews.com

Organization Name: _____

Mission Statement:

_____

_____

Overview of Activities: _____

_____

Importance of organization to U.S. health care:

_____

_____

_____

Organization Name: _____

Mission Statement:

_____

_____

_____

Overview of Activities: _____

_____

_____

Importance of organization to U.S. health care:

_____

_____

_____

http://www.ncbcapitalimpact.org

Organization Name: _____

Mission Statement:

_____

_____

_____

Overview of Activities: _____

_____

_____

Importance of organization to U.S. health care:

_____

_____

_____

http://www.iom.edu

Organization Name: _____

Mission Statement:

_____

_____

_____

Overview of Activities: _____

_____

_____

Importance of organization to U.S. health care:

_____

_____

_____

http://www.kff.org

Organization Name: _____

Mission Statement:

_____

_____

_____

Overview of Activities: _____

_____

_____

Importance of organization to U.S. health care:

_____

_____

_____

STUDENT ACTIVITY 14-4

DISCUSSION QUESTIONS

The following are suggested discussion questions for this chapter.

(1) What are accountable care organizations? What value can they provide to the healthcare industry?

_____

_____

_____

_____

_____

(2) Research a code of ethics of a healthcare organization and report back to the discussion board about your analysis of the code.

_____

_____

_____

_____

_____

(3) What is eprescribing? Do you think it will help reduce the number of mistakes that have occurred from hand-written prescriptions?

_____

_____

_____

_____

_____

(4) What is telemedicine? Would you feel comfortable receiving medical care electronically?

_____

_____

_____

_____

_____

(5) What is RFID? Provide three examples of RFID use in the healthcare industry.

_____

_____

_____

_____

_____

The Navigate Companion Website for this text is a great source for additional information on the U.S. healthcare system. You can gain a new perspective on many of the topics presented in this chapter by visiting http://go.jblearning.com/Niles2e. You'll find additional student activities, further reading, and interactive study tools that explore:

- New trends in health care
- Impact of the Affordable Care Act on healthcare consumers
- Comparing the United States to international healthcare systems
- And much more.

Index